MW01489188

THE

LETTERS OF JUNIUS.

STAT NOMINIS UMBRA.

WITH

NOTES AND ILLUSTRATIONS,

HISTORICAL, POLITICAL, BIOGRAPHICAL, AND CRITICAL;

BY ROBERT HERON, Esq.

IN TWO VOLUMES.

VOL. II.

BALTIMORE:

PUBLISHED BY M. AND J. CONRAD & Co.
NO. 138, MARKET-STREET.

PRINTED BY ROBERT CARR, PHILADELPHIA.

1804.

Printing Statement:

Due to the very old age and scarcity of this book,
many of the pages may be hard to read due to the
blurring of the original text, possible missing pages,
missing text and other issues beyond our control.

Because this is such an important and rare work, we
believe it is best to reproduce this book regardless of
its original condition.

Thank you for your understanding.

CONTENTS.

VOL. II.

CONTENTS.

LETTERS OF JUNIUS, &c.

LETTER XXX.

TO THE PRINTER OF THE PUBLIC ADVERTISER.

WHEN a people despise the weakness of their government, or suspect its intentions of hostility to the general welfare ; the slightest irregularity, in the exercise of its authority, whether by the principal ministers, or even by the meanest subordinate officers, is sufficient to rouse their angry clamours, or almost to make them rise against it in arms. The people of England, and especially of the metropolis, being encouraged by a strong minority in parliament, had almost since the beginning of the present reign, looked with a sort of braving contempt upon the executive exercise of the sovereign power. Various irregularities, inconsiderately committed by the ministers, had alarmed them with the dread of an intention to suppress their liberties, which made them regard a watchfulness to harass the government, as the first of patriot virtues.

Thus actuated, they looked almost with the jealousy of madness, on every instance of the interposition of military aid, to support the magistrates in the maintenance of public order. They complained, that the government industriously sought occasions for employing the soldiers against their fellow-subjects. In Juries, they shewed a disposition to condemn soldiers, as if guilty of wanton murder, in every instance of accidental death by the use of their arms against rioters. Still more, when, as in the case related in the following Letter, the soldiers actually dared to violate the just respect due to the authority of the civil magistracy, was the strongest indignation of the people naturally provoked against them.

It might seem to require extraordinary alacrity of suspicion against the ministers, to induce one to impute as a crime to them, the unauthorised act of a few individuals of the guards. But, their approbation of the conduct of the soldiers, upon occasions when riots had been suppressed with bloodshed, was supposed to have encouraged the soldiers to dare almost any act of wanton audacity against the civil power. Hence, though not directly and immediately guilty of the rescue of General Gansel, the ministers were, however, regarded as being primarily the authors of that, and of whatever other like irregularity the soldiery should proceed to commit.

The circumstances of the transaction, are detailed with sufficient minuteness in the following Letter.

Mrs. G. A. Bellamy, in her Memoirs.....A book exceedingly well written, but very incorrect in facts....Relates of the father of General Gansel, that he had, in his youth, made a vow, never to have more than one sort of animal food on his table, at one meal; that he, ever after, religiously observed his vow; and that, when she paid him a visit at his house in the country, he entertained her at supper, on her arrival, with three boiled chickens, three broiled ones, and three roasted ones.

Though JUNIUS, and the party of which he was the popular orator, certainly made too much clamour concerning the rescue of General Gansel; yet, in taking notice of the case, and in procuring the redress of the irregularity, they appear to have discharged a patriotic duty, of which the neglect might have proved even fatally mischievous.

JUNIUS, in this Letter, shews his power of narrative to be not inferior to his skill in reasoning, and his ability in the arts of persuasive eloquence.

17. *October*, 1769.

SIR,

IT is not wonderful, that the great cause in which this country is engaged, should have roused and engrossed the whole attention of the people. I rather admire the generous spirit with which they feel and assert their interest in this important question, than blame them for their indifference about any other. When the constitution is openly invaded, when the first original right of the people, from which all laws derive their authority, is directly attacked, inferior grievances naturally lose their force, and are suffered to pass by without punishment or observation. The present ministry are as singularly marked by their fortune, as by their crimes. Instead of atoning for their former conduct by any wise or popular measure, they have found, in the enormity of one fact, a cover and

They have found, in the enormity of one fact, &c.] JUNIUS thus strives to persuade his readers, that the people were *so* completely occupied with their resentment, on account of the decision in the case of the Middlesex election, and with their endeavours to procure redress of the injury inflicted by that decision upon the constitution, *as* to disregard those inferior violations of their rights, which the ministry were every day perpetrating. He insinuates, too, that so wicked were the ministers, as to pay no other regard to the general concern of the nation, respecting the wrong done to the electors of Middlesex, save that of committing other wrongs with increased assiduity, as these might now escape unheeded. The train of this exordium, is well adapted to fix attention on the facts which are to follow, and to enhance their apparent importance.

defence for a series of measures, which must have been fatal to any other administration. I fear we are too remiss in observing the whole of their proceedings. Struck with the principal figure, we do not sufficiently mark in what manner the canvas is filled up. Yet surely it is not a less crime, nor less fatal in its consequences, to encourage a flagrant breach of the law by a military force, than to make use of the forms of parliament to destroy the constitution....The ministry seem determined to give us a choice of difficulties ; and, if possible, to perplex us with the multitude of their offences. The expedient is worthy of the Duke of Grafton. But, though he has preserved a gradation and variety in his measures, we should remember that the principle is uniform. Dictated by the same spirit, they deserve the same attention. The following fact, though of the most alarming nature, has not yet been clearly stated to the public ; nor have the consequences of it been sufficiently understood.... Had I taken it up at an earlier period, I should have been accused of an uncandid, malignant precipitation, as if I watched for an unfair advantage against the ministry, and would not allow them a reasonable time to do their duty. They now stand without excuse. Instead of employing the leisure

---

Had I taken it up at an earlier period, &c.] JUNIUS probably waited, till he should see whether the facts which he is about to relate, might be successfully employed with the public, to excite a new clamour against the ministers, and to embarrass them.

they have had, in a strict examination of the offence, and punishing the offenders, they seem to have considered *that* indulgence as a security to them that, with a little time and management, the whole affair might be buried in silence, and utterly forgotten.

* A MAJOR-GENERAL of the army is arrested by the sheriffs officers for a considerable debt. He persuades them to conduct him to the Tilt-Yard in St. James's Park, under some pretence of business which it imported him to settle before he was confined. He applies to a serjeant, not immediately on duty, to assist with some of his companions in favouring his escape....He attempts it....A bustle ensues....The bailiffs claim their prisoner. † An officer of the guards, not then on duty, takes part in the affair, applies to the ‡ lieutenant, commanding the Tilt-Yard guard, and urges him to turn out his guard to relieve a general officer. The lieutenant declines interfering in person; but stands at a distance, and suffers the business to be done. The officer takes upon himself to order out the guard. In a moment they are in arms, quit the guard, march, rescue the general, and drive away the sheriffs officers; who, in vain, represent their right to their prisoner, and the nature of the arrest. The soldiers first conduct the general into the guard-

---

* Major-General Gansel.   † Lieutenant Dodd.
‡ Lieutenant Garth.

room, then escort him to a place of safety with bayonets fixed, and in all the forms of military triumph. I will not enlarge upon the various circumstances which attended this atrocious proceeding. The personal injury received by the officers of the law in the execution of their duty, may perhaps be atoned for by some private compensation. I consider nothing but the wound which has been given·to the law itself, to which no remedy has been applied, no satisfaction made. Neither is it my design to dwell upon the misconduct of the parties concerned, any farther than is necessary to shew the behaviour of the ministry in its true light. I would make every compassionate allowance for the infatuation of the prisoner, the false and criminal discretion of one officer, and the madness of another. I would leave the ignorant soldiers entirely out of the question. They are certainly the least guilty, though they are the only persons who have yet suffered, even in the appearance of punishment*. The fact itself, however atrocious, is not the principal point to be considered. It might

---

I consider nothing but the wound, &c.] No similar incident could have more highly deserved such animadversion. An interference of the soldiers against the civil power executing the law ....at the very seat of the Court....of the King's Guard....not of private soldiers alone, but also of officers....was, in truth, after the praise which had been bestowed on the soldiers, for their readiness to act against the unarmed people, a very heinous and dangerous crime against constitutional liberty.

* A few of them were confined.

have happened under a more regular government, and with guards better disciplined than ours. The main question is, in what manner have the ministry acted on this extraordinary occasion? A general officer calls upon the King's own guard, then actually on duty, to rescue him from the laws of his country: yet, at this moment, he is in a situation no worse than if he had not committed an offence equally enormous in a civil and military view.... A lieutenant upon duty designedly quits his guard, and suffers it to be drawn out by another officer, for a purpose which he well knew (as we may collect from an appearance of caution, which only makes his behaviour the more criminal) to be in the highest degree illegal. Has this gentleman been called to a court-martial, to answer for his conduct? No. Has it been censured? No. Has it been in any shape enquired into? No....Another lieutenant, not upon duty, nor even in his regimentals, is daring enough to order out the King's Guard, over which he had properly no command, and engages them in a violation of the laws of his country, perhaps the most singular and extravagant that ever was attempted....What punishment has *he* suffered? Literally, none. Supposing he should be prose-

---

Has it been censured? No. Has it, &c.] Here is a fine example of the successful use of the figure of *interrogation*. It deserves to be particularly studied, by the reader who would learn eloquence from JUNIUS.

What punishment has he suffered? Literally, none.] The fact was, as JUNIUS states it. The ministry, and the commanding

cuted at common law for the rescue, will that circumstance, from which the ministry can derive no
merit, excuse or justify their suffering so flagrant a
breach of military discipline to pass by unpunished,
and unnoticed? Are they aware of the outrage
offered to their sovereign, when his own proper
guard is ordered out to stop, by main force, the
execution of his laws? What are we to conclude
from so scandalous a neglect of their duty, but that
they have other views, which can only be answered by securing the attachment of the guards? The
minister would hardly be so cautious of offending
them, if he did not mean, in due time, to call for
their assistance.

With respect to the parties themselves, let it
be observed, that these gentlemen are neither young
officers, nor very young men. Had they belonged
to the unfledged race of ensigns, who infest our
streets, and dishonour our public places, it might
perhaps be sufficient to send them back to that

---

officer under whose immediate orders Lieutenant Dodd was, had
evidently failed in their duty. In this case, then, the interposition
of JUNIUS cannot be said to have been too eager and malignant.

Unfledged race of Ensigns, &c.] If we consider, that early
education in any profession, is almost indispensably necessary to
the attainment of excellence in it, we cannot but confess the rea-
sonableness of allowing young gentlemen to enter the army as soon
as they are at all able to carry arms and learn the discipline. It
is enough if mere infancy be excluded. Here, then, JUNIUS rather repeats a topic of popular clamour, than points out any real
abuse.

discipline, from which their parents, judging lightly from the maturity of their vices, had removed them too soon. In this case, I am sorry to see, not so much the folly of youth, as the spirit of the corps, and the connivance of government. I do not question that there are many brave and worthy officers in the regiments of guards. But, considering them as a corps, I fear it will be found, that they are neither good soldiers, nor good subjects. Far be it from me to insinuate the most distant reflection upon the army. On the contrary, I honour and esteem the profession; and, if these gentlemen were better soldiers, I am sure they would be better subjects. It is not that there is any internal vice or defect in the profession itself, as regulated in this country, but that it is the spirit of this particular corps to despise their profession, and that while they vainly assume the lead of the army, they make it matter of impertinent comparison and triumph

---

Considering them as a corps, &c.] The guards, as being that part of the army which was the most under the observation of the inhabitants of the metropolis, was the most odious to them. Hence the severity of satire, with which JUNIUS, here and in other places in these Letters, speaks of them. Both good sense, and no contemptible knowledge of military affairs, undeniably appear in the observations on the army, which are here introduced. But, if any serious doubt could be ever entertained, as if the guards were a soldiery fit only for the parade of peace; the gallantry and importance of their services during the present war, must have for ever removed it. We have not forgotten, with what generous ardour they attended the Duke of York to Holland; nor, how bravely they fought; nor, how much they suffered, amid the battles and disasters of that expedition.

over the bravest troops in the world (I mean, our
marching regiments) that *they* indeed stand upon
higher ground, and are privileged to neglect the
laborious forms of military discipline and duty.
Without dwelling longer upon a most invidious
subject, I shall leave it to military men, who have
seen a service more active than the parade, to determine whether or no I speak truth.

How far this dangerous spirit has been encouraged by government, and to what pernicious purposes it may be applied hereafter, well deserves our
most serious consideration. I know, indeed, that
when this affair happened, an affectation of alarm
ran through the ministry. Something must be done
to save appearances. The case was too flagrant to
be passed by absolutely without notice. But how
have they acted? Instead of ordering the officers
concerned, (and who, strictly speaking, are alone
guilty) to be put under arrest, and brought to trial,
they would have it understood, that they did their
duty completely, in confining a serjeant and four
private soldiers, until they should be demanded by
the civil power; so that, while the officers who or-

---

*Did their duty completely, in confining a serjeant and four
private soldiers, &c.* This was, indeed, to trifle with their duty,
and with the opinion of the people. The ministers who could
act thus, well deserved the sharpest censure of JUNIUS. There
was a violation both of the peace, and of military discipline, in
the conduct of the officers and soldiers who had been concerned
in the rescue. The officers were more guilty than the soldiers.

dered or permitted the thing to be done, escape without censure, the poor men who obeyed those orders, who in a military view are no way responsible for what they did, and who for that reason have been discharged by the civil magistrates, are the only objects whom the ministry have thought proper to expose to punishment. They did not venture to bring even these men to a court-martial, because they knew their evidence would be fatal to some persons whom they were determined to protect.. Otherwise, I doubt not, the lives of these unhappy, friendless soldiers, would long since have been sacrificed without scruple, to the security of their guilty officers.

I have been accused of endeavouring to inflame the passions of the people....Let me now appeal to their understanding. If there be any tool of administration daring enough to deny these facts, or shameless enough to defend the conduct of the ministry, let him come forward. I care not under what title he appears. He shall find me ready to maintain the truth of my narrative, and the justice of my observations upon it, at the hazard of my utmost credit with the public.

Under the most arbitrary governments, the common administration of justice is suffered to take its course. The subject, though robbed of his share in the legislature, is still protected by the laws. The political freedom of the English constitution was

once the pride and honour of an Englishman. The
civil equality of the laws preserved the property,
and defended the safety of the subject. Are these
glorious privileges the birth-right of the people, or
are we only tenants at the will of the ministry ?....
But that I know there is a spirit of resistance in the
hearts of my countrymen ; that they value life, not
by its conveniences, but by the independance and
dignity of their condition ; I should, at this moment,
appeal only to their discretion. I should persuade
them to banish from their minds all memory of what
we were ; I should tell them this is not a time to
remember that we were Englishmen ; and give it as
my last advice, to make some early agreement with
the minister, that since it has pleased him to rob us
of those political rights which once distinguished
the inhabitants of a country where honour was happiness, he would leave us at least the humble, obe-
dient security of citizens, and graciously condescend to protect us in our submission.

JUNIUS.

But that I know there is a spirit of resistance, &c.] This is
one of the boldest and most truly eloquent passages in the whole
of these Letters. It involves argument with lofty and vehement
sentiment. It cannot be read without emotion. To hear it spoken
with due majesty and force of elocution, were enough to rouse a
nation to arms.

LETTER XXXI.

TO THE PRINTER OF THE PUBLIC ADVERTISER,

———

THE advocates for administration learned to imitate the accusatory and the defensive artifices of JUNIUS. *They exclaimed against the outrageous malignity of his imputing to ministry, as a public crime, a private transaction which they could not foresee nor prevent. They appealed to the humanity of the public, whether it were not barbarous to endeavour to add to the pecuniary distresses of General Gansel, both the displeasure of government and the indignation of the public? They asked, what joy could it give to the friends of liberty, if Captain Dodd and Captain Garth should be reduced to want and overwhelmed with ignominy, by being deprived of their commissions and dismissed from the army? They strove to inflame the resentment of all the officers of the guards, on account of the bitter abuse which had been thrown out by* JUNIUS *against those troops. They declared, that it was left to the civil power to vindicate its own authority by legal process against both the officers and the soldiers by whom the rescue had been effected. They loudly proclaimed it to be unworthy of the generous spirit of British justice, to punish any person twice.....by both civil and military authority....for the same offence. They exclaimed, that the government must surely be excellent, under which no more serious subject of complaint could be found, than the accidental rescue of a prisoner from the sheriff's officers by a few disorderly soldiers. Nor were these pretences without effect. Many were disposed to pity the sufferers: and many to excuse the lenity with which their crime was treated by government.*

JUNIUS *found it, therefore, necessary to support and enforce, by another Letter, that which he had before advanced on this subject. To accomplish this the more effectually, he thought proper to write in the character of* PHILO JUNIUS. *He begins with vindicating* JUNIUS *with modesty and art from the charge of malignity, and with solemnly affirming the truth of the facts which he had stated. Having thus far undeniably succeeded; he finds it easy to expose the unseasonableness of that claim of compassion, which had been set up in favour of General Gansel and his riotous deliverers. The charge of wanton malice against the ministers, he easily answers, by shewing, that he had blamed them, not for failing to prevent, but for not punishing, the military irregularities of which he complained. Even the praise of the guards is turned against themselves, by the observation, that the more excellent the military character of the guards, so much the more were they dishonoured by that disorderly conduct of their officers and soldiers, which they shewed, in this instance, a forwardness to justify. He, then, again warns the public against suffering their compassion for Gansel, to betray them to the sacrifice of their common liberties; and concludes with insinuating the necessity of a parliamentary enquiry, to ascertain the truth of the facts, and procure effectual redress of the grievance.*

This Letter is written with plainness, but with admirable propriety of style.

---

14. *November*, 1769.

SIR,

THE variety of remarks which have been made upon the last Letter of JUNIUS, and my own opinion of the writer, who, whatever may be his faults, is certainly not a weak man, have induced me to examine, with some attention, the subject of that Letter. I could not persuade myself that, while he had plenty of important materials, he would have taken up a light or trifling occasion to

---

He would have taken up a light or trifling occasion, &c.] Here is an incorrectness of phrase. We cannot, in English, say, with propriety, *take up an occasion.* We *seize, avail ourselves of, do*

attack the ministry; much less could I conceive, that it was his intention to ruin the officers concerned in the rescue of General Gansel, or to injure the general himself. These are little objects, and can no way contribute to the great purposes he seems to have in view by addressing himself to the public.....Without considering the ornamental style he has adopted, I determined to look farther into the matter, before I decided upon the merits of his Letter. The first step I took, was to enquire into the truth of the facts; for, if these were either false or misrepresented, the most artful exertion of his understanding, in reasoning upon them, would only be a disgrace to him.....Now, Sir, I have found every circumstance stated by J U N I U S to be literally true. General Gansel persuaded the bailiffs to conduct him to the parade, and certainly solicited a corporal and other soldiers, to assist him in making his escape. Captain Dodd did certainly apply to Captain Garth for the assistance of his guard.... Captain Garth declined appearing himself, but stood aloof, while the other took upon him to order

---

not let slip, an occasion. But, propriety of speech allows us not to say, that we *take it up*.] An occasion is supposed to be as it were, a golden portion of something which is passing before us. We may *seize* it, to make it the ground work for some part of the structure of our fortunes. We do not *take it up*, to crown our heads with it.

The first step I took, was, &c.] How skilful! To pretend that he had doubted the truth of the facts, and had, only after painful enquiry, been convinced of their certainty! Double force is thus added to the previous testimony of J U N I U S.

out the King's guard, and by main force rescued
the General. It is also strictly true, that the General was escorted by a file of musqueteers to a place
of security....These are facts, Mr. Woodfall, which
I promise you no gentleman in the guards will
deny. If all or any of them are false, why are
they not contradicted by the parties themselves?
However secure against military censure, they have
yet a character to lose; and surely, if they are innocent, it is not beneath them to pay some attention
to the opinion of the public.

The force of JUNIUS's Observations upon these
facts, cannot be better marked than by stating and
refuting the objections which have been made to
them. One writer says, " Admitting the officers
" have offended, they are punishable at common
" law; and will you have a British subject punish-
" ed twice for the same offence?"....I answer, that
they have committed two offences, both very enormous, and violated two laws. The rescue is one
offence, the flagrant breach of discipline another;
and, hitherto, it does not appear that they have
been punished, or even censured, for either. Another gentleman lays much stress upon the calamity
of the case; and, instead of disproving facts, appeals

However secure against military censure, &c.] This is a reflection of bitter irony against the discipline of the guards.

Lays much stress, &c.] On most occasions, there would be
vulgarity in the use of this phrase. Here, however, it seems to
be forcibly expressive, and not too mean.

at once to the compassion of the public. This
idea, as well as the insinuation that *depriving the
parties of their commissions would be an injury to
their creditors,* can only refer to General Gansel.
The other officers are in no distress; therefore, have
no claim to compassion: nor does it appear, that
their creditors, if they have any, are more likely
to be satisfied by their continuing in the guards.
But this sort of plea will not hold in any shape.
Compassion to an offender, who has grossly violated
the laws, is in effect a cruelty to the peaceable subject who has observed them; and, even admitting
the force of any alleviating circumstances, it is
nevertheless true, that in this instance the royal
compassion has interposed too soon. The legal
and proper mercy of a King of England may re-
mit the punishment, but ought not to stop the
trial.

Besides these particular objections, there has
been a cry raised against JUNIUS, for his malice
and injustice, in attacking the ministry upon an
event which they could neither hinder nor foresee.
This, I must affirm, is a false representation of his
argument. He lays no stress upon the event itself,
as a ground of accusation against the ministry, but
dwells entirely upon their subsequent conduct. He
does not say that they are answerable for the offence; but, for the scandalous neglect of their
duty, in suffering an offence, so flagrant, to pass by
without notice or enquiry. Supposing them ever

so regardless of what they owe to the public, and as indifferent about the opinion as they are about the interests of their country, what answer, as offi- cers of the crown, will they give to JUNIUS, when he asks them, *Are they aware of the outrage offered to their Sovereign, when his own proper guard is ordered out to stop, by main force, the execution of his laws?*.....And when we see a ministry giving such a strange, unaccountable protection, to the officers of the guards, is it unfair to suspect, that they have some secret and unwarrantable motives for their conduct? If they feel themselves injured by such a suspicion, why do they not immediately clear themselves from it by doing their duty? For the honour of the guards, I cannot help expressing another suspicion, that if the commanding officer had not received a secret injunction to the con- trary, he would, in the ordinary course of his busi- ness, have applied for a court-martial to try the two subalterns; the one for quitting his guard....the other for taking upon him the command of the guard, and employing it in the manner he did. I do not mean to enter into, or defend, the severity with which JUNIUS treats the guards. On the contrary, I will suppose for a moment that they deserve a very different character. If this be true, in what light will they consider the conduct of

---

Strange, unaccountable protection, &c.] This is an unjustifia- ble vulgarity of phraseology, borrowed from the license of com- mon conversation.

the two subalterns, but as a general reproach and disgrace to the whole corps? And will they not wish to see them censured in a military way, if it were only for the credit and discipline of the regiment.

Upon the whole, Sir, the ministry seem to me to have taken a very improper advantage of the good-nature of the public; whose humanity, they found, considered nothing in this affair but the distress of General Gansel. They would persuade us, that it was only a common rescue by a few disorderly soldiers, and not the formal, deliberate act, of the King's guard headed by an officer; and the public has fallen into the deception. I think, therefore, we are obliged to JUNIUS for the care he has taken to enquire into the facts, and for the just commentary with which he has given them to the world....For my own part, I am as unwilling as any man to load the unfortunate; but, really, Sir, the precedent with respect to the guards, is of a most important nature, and alarming enough (considering the consequences with which it may be attended) to deserve a parliamentary enquiry: when the guards are daring enough, not only to

The formal, deliberate act, of the King's guard, &c.] This is an exaggeration. The rescue of Gansel was certainly as far from being a deliberate act, as from being merely the riotous interposition of a few disorderly soldiers.

When the guards are daring enough, &c.] This concluding sentence is in the best manner of JUNIUS; involving forcible

violate their own discipline, but publicly, and with the most atrocious violence, to stop the execution of the laws, and when such extraordinary offences pass with impunity, believe me, Sir, the precedent strikes deep.

PHILO JUNIUS.

argument with vehement sentiment, addressed in a manner the most skilful, to accomplish his purpose with his reader, and breathing that rising animation, which is requisite at the close of a discourse, to inflame the mind of the reader or hearer, in favour of what you may have advanced.

LETTER XXXII.

TO THE PRINTER OF THE PUBLIC ADVERTISER.

---

*JUNIUS had not disdained to reply to one Letter with the signa-
ture of* Modestus, *that was addressed to him in the* Gazetteer.
*He was called to reply to another Letter with the same signa-
ture, which insinuated, that ministry had not neglected their duty
in regard to the rescuers of General Gansel; but that* JUNIUS
*and his friends were too impatient, and complained of evil-inten-
tioned negligence in government, before it could have time to execute that justice, which was so clamorously demanded. It had
also warmly reprobated the malevolence of* JUNIUS, *and had represented his eager interposition in this and other similar cases,
as the effect rather of innate mischievousness of disposition, than
of pure and genuine public spirit.*

JUNIUS, *in this Letter, makes a brief reply; expresses himself ready
to be satisfied with the due punishment of the guilty officers ; menaces farther revenge on the Duke of Grafton, if the offenders
should be suffered to escape ; asserts, in a high tone, the public
importance of the affair in question ; and declares his resolution,
not to be frightened by any unjust imputations from his ground.
Government would not persist in a contention with public opinion,
respecting so small a matter.* JUNIUS *finally prevailed.*

---

15. *November*, 1769.

SIR,

I ADMIT the claim of a gentleman, who
publishes in the Gazetteer under the name of *Modestus*. He has some right to expect an answer

from me; though, I think, not so much from the merit or importance of his objections, as from my own voluntary engagement. I had a reason for not taking notice of him sooner; which, as he is a candid person, I believe he will think sufficient. In my first Letter, I took for granted, from the time which had elapsed, that there was no intention to censure nor even to try, the persons concerned in the rescue of General Gansel; but *Modestus* having since either affirmed, or strongly insinuated that the offenders might still be brought to a legal trial, any attempt to prejudge the cause, or to prejudice the minds of a jury, or a court-martial, would be highly improper.

A man more hostile to the ministry than I am, would not so often remind them of their duty. If the Duke of Grafton will not perform the duty of his station, why is he minister?....I will not descend to a scurrilous altercation with any man: but this is a subject too important to be passed over with silent indifference. If the gentlemen, whose conduct is in question, are not brought to a trial, the Duke of Grafton shall hear from me again.

The motives on which I am supposed to have taken up this cause, are of little importance, com-

---

If the gentlemen, &c.] It is evident, that the growing favour of the public seduced the author of these Letters to conceive an overweening opinion of his own consequence. It were to be wished, that he had spared these and some other braggard threats.

pared with the facts themselves, and the observations I have made upon them. Without a vain profession of integrity, which in these times might
justly be suspected, I shall shew myself in effect a
friend to the interests of my countrymen ; and leave
it to them to determine, whether I am moved by a
personal malevolence to three private gentlemen, or
merely by a hope of perplexing the ministry, or
whether I am animated by a just and honourable
purpose of obtaining a satisfaction to the laws of
this country, equal, if possible, to the violation they
have suffered.

JUNIUS.

LETTER XXXIII.

TO HIS GRACE THE DUKE OF GRAFTON.

———

The present administration was not to be dissolved, while the Duke of Grafton stood unmoved at the head of the Treasury. JUNIUS, *therefore, still returns to the charge against that minister personally. He seized, in the present instance, a fair occasion for harassing him. Treachery to his friendship, dishonour from his wife, perfidious baseness to his mistress, weak versatility of political principles, a violation of the rights of election, and the abandoning of the laws to be slighted at pleasure by the excesses of the soldiery, were so many signs of topics of disgrace, which the eloquence of this writer had already charged, with great plausibility, against the Duke. To these, he in this Letter adds the charge of corruption in office, committed at the very time when the Duke was opening a prosecution against a man whom he accused of having attempted to corrupt him.*

Mr. Samuel Vaughan, a merchant in London, wished to obtain for his family, the reversion of the office of Clerk to the Supreme Court, *in the Island of Jamaica. He was informed, that this office, though not lawfully to be sold, might however,* by *proper* management, *be purchased from the First Lord of the Treasury. He therefore made affidavit before the Lord Mayor, that he would pay the sum of five thousand pounds, for the benefit of whoever should procure to him that office, for the lives of his three sons, or of any other three persons whom he should choose to name. Making this affidavit, he first attempted to procure the appointment from the Duke of Grafton, for the proferred money, by the intermediation of a Mr. Newcome, of Hackney, whom he understood to possess the Duke's confidence. Newcome refused to become the agent of such a negotiation. Vaughan then asked the office, and proffered the money, in a Letter to the Duke himself. The Duke directed a prosecution to be commenced against*

Vaughan, in the court of King's Bench, on account of this attempt upon the integrity of a minister. It was argued, unsuccessfully, in defence of Vaughan, by his counsel, that offices in the Colonies were legally saleable, especially Patent-Offices, such as that which Mr. Vaughan had proposed to purchase. But, the prosecution was suddenly discontinued; and Mr. Vaughan escaped. He was connected with the city-patriots; and had even taken an active part in their most bustling transactions. On this account, he was, of course, the less likely to obtain a good bargain at court. But, for the same reason, he had so much the more of the favour of his patriot friends. They refused, at first, to believe him guilty; and had at last, the bold effrontery to assert, that his guilt, with all its undeniable circumstances, was unimpeachable innocence. This was the case in which the Duke of Grafton was said to have affected the praise of an official purity that did not truly belong to him.

Another patent-place, in the collection of the customs at Exeter, was sold about the same time to a Mr. Hine, for the sum of three thousand and five hundred pounds; which was paid to General Burgoyne, as a secret re-imbursement of his expences in a very disgraceful election-contest at Preston. The circumstances of this transaction became known to the adversaries of the ministry. They were loudly proclaimed and reprobated by JUNIUS, *particularly in the two following Letters. The Duke of Grafton was held to be as criminal in the sale, as if the money had been converted to his own personal use. The prosecution of Vaughan was supposed to have been discontinued, in order to quiet the clamour relative to Hine. Vaughan was under prosecution, at the time when the following Letter was published.*

———

29. *November*, 1769.

MY LORD,

THOUGH my opinion of your Grace's integrity was but little affected by the coyness with which you received Mr. Vaughan's proposals, I confess I give you some credit for your discretion. You had a fair opportunity of displaying a certain delicacy, of which you had been suspected; and you were in the right to make use of it. By laying in a moderate stock of reputation, you undoubtedly meant to provide for the future necessities of your character, that with an honourable resistance upon record, you might safely indulge your genius, and yield to a favourite inclination with security. But you have discovered your purposes too soon; and, instead of the modest reserve of virtue, have shewn us the termagant chastity of a prude, who gratifies her passions with distinction, and prosecutes one lover for a rape, while she solicits the lewd embraces of another.

Your cheek turns pale; for a guilty conscience tells you, you are undone......Come forward, thou virtuous minister, and tell the world by what interest Mr. Hine has been recommended to so extraordinary a mark of his Majesty's favour; what was the price of the patent he has bought, and to

---

Have shewn us the termagant chastity of a prude, &c.] A comparison more entertainingly illustrative of the imputation which JUNIUS meant to alledge, could not easily have been found. But, there is good reason for thinking, that the Duke of Grafton was a minister above corruption. The fact in regard to Hine and Burgoyne, ought probably to be regarded as an instance of his acquiescence in favour of another, in what he would have for himself indignantly despised.

what honourable purpose the purchase money has been applied? Nothing less than many thousands could pay Colonel Burgoyne's expences at Preston. Do you dare to prosecute such a creature as Vaughan, while you are basely setting up the Royal Patronage to auction? Do you dare to complain of an attack upon your own honour, while you are selling the favours of the crown, to raise a fund for corrupting the morals of the people? And, do you think it possible such enormities should escape without impeachment? It is, indeed, highly your interest to maintain the present House of Commons. Having sold the nation to you in gross, they will undoubtedly protect you in the detail; for, while they patronize your crimes, they feel for their own.

JUNIUS.

Do you dare to prosecute such a creature as Vaughan, &c.] The eloquence of this closing paragraph is awfully energetic. Perhaps the whole is not exceeded by any one of those before it. Even its brevity is well adapted to render its impression more forcible. A rhetorician, who should strive to imitate this eloquence, would probably labour in vain. It is the correspondence between the matter and the manner; it is the suitableness of the address to the purpose intended; it is because the exterior forms are filled with the whole soul of eloquence; that we so irresistibly feel, in perusing this Letter, the Orator's power. Junius's invective wears, sometimes, an air of rude ferocity; but not in this instance.

LETTER XXXIV.

TO HIS GRACE THE DUKE OF GRAFTON.

IN this Letter, JUNIUS repeats the charge he had brought against the Duke of Grafton in that which is immediately preceding; relates the particulars of the fact more in detail ; urges a multitude of aggravating circumstances ; and boldly calls upon the Duke for explanation or denial. The character of General Burgoyne, falls incidentally in his way; and he neglects not such a fair occasion to treat it with malignant asperity.

———

12. *December*, 1769.

MY LORD,

I FIND, with some surprize, that you are not supported as you deserve. Your most determined advocates have scruples about them, which you are unacquainted with ; and, though there be nothing too hazardous for your grace to engage in, there are some things too infamous for the vilest prostitute of a news-paper to defend *. In what other manner shall we account for the profound, submissive silence, which you and your friends have ob-

* From the publication of the preceding to this date, not one word was said in defence of the infamous Duke of Grafton. But vice and impudence soon recovered themselves, and the sale of the royal favour was openly avowed and defended. We acknowledge the piety of St. James's ; but what is become of *his* morality ?

The profound, submissive silence, &c.] An answer which should match the eloquence, or confound the boldness of JUNIUS, was not to be made. A silence was, therefore, not unwisely preferred, which might be interpreted to be that of virtuous contempt, just as well as that of conscious guilt.

served upon a charge, which called immediately for the clearest refutation, and would have justified the severest measures of resentment ? I did not attempt to blast your character by an indirect ambiguous insinuation; but candidly stated to you a plain fact, which struck directly at the integrity of a privy counsellor, of a first commissioner of the treasury, and of a leading minister, who is supposed to enjoy the first share in his Majesty's confidence *. In every one of these capacities, I employed the most moderate terms to charge you with treachery to your Sovereign, and breach of trust in your office. I accused you of having sold a patent place in the collection of the customs at Exeter, to one Mr. Hine ; who, unable or unwilling to deposit the whole purchase-money himself, raised part of it by contribution, and has now a certain Doctor Brooke quartered upon the salary for one hundred pounds a year......No sale by the candle was ever conducted with greater formality......I affirm, that the price at which the place was knocked down(and which, I have good reason to think, was not less than three thousand five hundred pounds) was, with your connivance and consent, paid to Colonel Burgoyne, to reward him, I presume, for the decency of his deportment at Preston ; or to reimburse him, perhaps, for the fine of one thousand pounds, which for that very deportment the court of King's Bench thought proper to set upon him......It is not often that the

* And by the same means preserves it to this hour.

chief justice and the prime minister are so strangely at variance in their opinions of men and things.

I thank God, there is not in human nature a degree of impudence daring enough to deny the charge I have fixed upon you. Your courteous secretary *, your confidential architect†, are silent as the grave. Even Mr. Rigby's countenance fails him. He violates his second nature, and blushes whenever he speaks of you........Perhaps the noble colonel himself will relieve you. No man is more

I thank God, there is not in human nature, &c.] It must be owned that it was not easy to make contemptuous silence appear the most satisfactory mode of dealing, with one who had acquired such a sovereignty as JUNIUS over public opinion. But the outrageous violence of this Letter ought surely to have excited the indignation of the patriots, in favour of a government whose powers were thus insulted. What must have been the spirit of the people, when Juries would not find such a publication as this to be a libel?

* Tommy Bradshaw.

† Mr. Taylor. He and George Ross, (the Scotch agent and worthy confidante of Lord Mansfield) managed the business.

Perhaps the noble colonel himself will relieve you.] General Burgoyne, though not free from the follies, not to speak of the vices, of a man of rank and fashion, nor pure from the usual corruptions of political life, was in different respects a man of high and honourable eminence. Of respectable descent, he entered, at an early age, into the military service. He had risen to the rank of a colonel, with great reputation, when he was....in the war of 1756, after the hostility of the Spaniards had been added against Britain to that of the French....placed, in the command of a part of the British forces in Portugal, in a situation in which he had opportunity to distinguish himself. He did distinguish himself by

tender of his reputation. He is not only nice, but perfectly sore, in every thing that touches his honour. If any man, for example, were to accuse him of taking his stand at a gaming-table, and

a better display of true military talents, than was exhibited by any other British officer that had, in that war, a separate command in Europe. Discipline, general plans, care for the health, nourishment, and spirits of his troops, the most admirable dexterity of stratagem, incomparable alertness and activity, with the most generous valour, and a vigilance that defied surprise, were eminently displayed by him in the defence of the Portuguese territories. After the peace, his services were rewarded as JUNIUS relates. He returned to live at home with that splendour of character which had been justly earned by his services ; and which, when added to taste, wit, intelligence, and masterly proficiency in all the wonted fashionable accomplishments, could not but make him a leader in the amusements of the great and the gay. He was an adept in gaming ; and I shall not venture, hastily, to deny that which JUNIUS tells, concerning the use he made of his skill to play the fashionable games. He possessed parliamentary talents ; and it was even requisite to his advancement in the army, that he should have a seat in parliament. Hence the struggle, and the corruption, in which he unsuccessfully expended not less than ten thousand pounds, to obtain the representation of the burgh of Preston, in the parliament which met in 1768. He possessed talents for elegant literature ; and he successfully distinguished these....in that happy and fantastic trifle, the *Maid of the Oaks*, which *Horace Walpole* has peevishly branded with the charge of egregious dullness,....and in the HEIRESS, one of the finest comedies which have been represented on the English stage. When the American war broke out, General Burgoyne was appointed to a command in it, under Sir William Howe. His service was able, but finally unfortunate. He surrendered an army prisoners, upon terms of capitulation which were afterwards but ill observed by the victors. He returned home, a prisoner, upon his word of honour ; was ungraciously received by the ministers ; was refused admission to his Sovereign's pre-

watching, with the soberest attention, for a fair opportunity of engaging a drunken young nobleman at piquet, he would undoubtedly consider it as an infamous aspersion upon his character, and resent it like a man of honour....Acquitting him, therefore, of drawing a regular and splendid subsistence from any unworthy practices, either in his own house or elsewhere, let me ask your Grace, for what military merits you have been pleased to reward him with military government? He had a regiment of dragoons, which one would imagine was at least an equivalent for any services he ever performed. Besides, he is but a young officer, considering his preferment; and, except in his activity at Preston, not very conspicuous in his profession. But, it seems, the sale of a civil employment was not sufficient; and military governments, which were intended for the support of worn out veterans, must be thrown into the scale, to defray the extensive bribery of a contested election. Are these the steps you take to secure to your Sovereign the attachment of his army? With what countenance dare you appear in the royal presence, branded as you are with the infamy of a notorious breach

sence; threw himself into the arms of Opposition; aided their efforts by his complaints and information; took up his pen to vindicate his military character; and succeeded in shewing, at least, that for what had happened, he was not solely, nor chiefly, to blame. He died some years afterwards; not indeed dishonoured, but without that splendour of fortune, or of military character, which his earlier services in Portugal had seemed to promise.

of trust? With what countenance can you take your seat at the treasury-board or in council, when you feel that every circulating whisper is at your expence alone, and stabs you to the heart? Have you a single friend in parliament so shameless, so thoroughly abandoned, as to undertake your defence? You know, my Lord, that there is not a man in either house, whose character, however flagitious, would not be ruined by mixing his reputation with yours; and does not your heart inform you, that you are degraded below the condition of a man, when you are obliged to hear these insults with submission, and even to thank me for my moderation?

We are told by the highest judicial authority, that Mr. Vaughan's offer to purchase the reversion of a patent in Jamaica, (which he was otherwise sufficiently entitled to) amounted to a high misdemeanour. Be it so: and, if he deserves it, let him be punished. But the learned judge might have had a fairer opportunity of displaying the powers of his eloquence. Having delivered himself with so much energy upon the criminal nature and dangerous consequences, of any attempt to cor-

You know, my Lord, that there is not a man, &c.] It were hard to say, whether genuine eloquence, or virulent abuse, predominate in this paragraph. It is, for both, perhaps, incomparable in the works of any other English writer.

rupt a man in your Grace's station, what would he have said to the minister himself, to that very privy counsellor, to that first commissioner of the treasury, who does not wait for, but impatiently solicits the touch of corruption : who employs the meanest of his creatures in these honourable services ; and, forgetting the genius and fidelity of his secretary, descends to apply to his house-builder for assistance?

This affair, my Lord, will do infinite credit to government, if, to clear your character, you should think proper to bring it into the House of Lords, or into the Court of King's Bench.......But, my Lord, you dare not do either.

JUNIUS.

———

A little before the publication of this and the preceding Letter, the chaste Duke of Grafton had commenced a prosecution against Mr. Samuel Vaughan, for endeavouring to corrupt his integrity by an offer of five thousand pounds for a patent place in Jamaica. A rule to shew cause, why an information should not be exhibited against Vaughan for certain misdemeanours, being granted by the

———

What would he have said, &c.] It was delightful to the author of these Letters, thus to find occasion to employ Lord Mansfield's authority and doctrine, in invective against that very administration which his Lordship was anxious to support.

To bring it into the House of Lords, &c.] What unparalleled insolence! JUNIUS knew his facts to be true; and he challenges the Duke of Grafton to prosecute him, either for *scandalum magnatum* or for a *libel.*

the court of King's Bench, the matter was solemnly argued on
the 27th of November, 1769; and, by the unanimous opinion of
the four judges, the rule was made absolute. The pleading and
speeches were accurately taken in short-hand and published.
The whole of Lord Mansfield's speech, and particularly the following extracts from it, deserve the reader's attention........" A
" practice of the kind complained of here, is certainly dishonour-
" able and scandalous.....If a man, standing under the relation of
" an officer under the King, or of a person in whom the King
" puts confidence, or of a minister, takes money for the use of
" that confidence the King puts in him, he basely betrays the
" King....he basely betrays his trust.....If the King sold the office,
" it would be acting contrary to the trust the constitution hath
" reposed in him. The constitution does not intend the crown
" should sell those offices, to raise a revenue out of them.....Is it
" possible to hesitate, whether this would not be criminal in the
" Duke of Grafton;....contrary to his duty as a minister;....con-
" trary to his duty as a subject?......His advice should be free,
" according to his judgment.....It is the duty of his office;.....he
" has sworn to it.".....Notwithstanding all this, the chaste Duke
of Grafton certainly sold a patent place to Mr. Hine for three
thousand five hundred pounds; and, for so doing, is now Lord
Privy Seal to the chaste George, with whose piety we are perpetually deafened. If the House of Commons had done their duty,
and impeached the black Duke for this most infamous breach of
trust, how woefully must poor honest Mansfield have been
puzzled! His embarrassment would have afforded the most ridiculous scene that ever was exhibited. To save the worthy judge
from this perplexity, and the no less worthy Duke from impeachment, the prosecution against *Vaughan* was immediately dropped,
upon my discovery and publication of the Duke's treachery. The
suffering this charge to pass without any enquiry, fixes shameless
prostitution upon the face of the House of Commons, more
strongly than even the Middlesex election.....Yet the licentious-
ness of the press is complained of!

LETTER XXXV.

TO THE PRINTER OF THE PUBLIC ADVERTISER.

———

THIS is the celebrated Letter to the King, for the publication of which, Woodfall, the printer, was prosecuted by the Attorney General.

It was published on the eve of an occasion, upon which the Whigs hoped at last, to force themselves in a body, into administration, on their own terms. The Grenvilles, the Earl of Chatham, the Marquis of Rockingham, with their respective adherents, were now united; and professed to believe, that their purposes, whether of patriotism, avarice, or ambition, could be accomplished, only by unswerving fidelity to their present union. The opening of the next session of parliament was near. They supposed that the business of government could not be done in that session, unless the King should implicitly resign the whole ministerial powers into their hands. They were preparing, by every means, to secure, beyond the possibility of disappointment, the grand object of their expectations. Not unconscious of the strength of public opinion, they used every artifice to make it raise a voice continually louder and more furious in their favour. JUNIUS privy to their secrets, though they might not be conscious of his, was willing to promote, in an exertion bolder and of greater effort than any he had hitherto made, that success of his party, of which he was perhaps to share the spoils. He, with this view, raised the aim of his invective above the Duke of Grafton, or Duke of Bedford, and dared to try whether he might not make Majesty itself shrink from his attack.

In the following Letter, written with this purpose, he, after a prefatory address to the printer, proceeds to inform the King, that he had been held in ignorance of the true interests of his government, and of the real wishes and dispositions of his people. He contrasts the high popularity of his Sovereign at his accession to the throne, *with those clamorous discontents which were now excited by almost every exertion of his authority. He accuses the private friendships of his Sovereign, as restoring the unconstitutional reign of* Favouritism ; *and he virulently inveighs against the Scots, as unworthy of meeting from their Prince equal encouragement, even when they should appear to have equal merits, with his English subjects. He complains, that the King, by adopting the passions and the prejudices of his favourites, while he lent himself to their selfish interests, had been betrayed to conclude an ignominious peace, after a glorious war, and to deprive himself of the services of those who, of all his subjects, possessed the most eminent ministerial talents. He imputes to his Sovereign the meanness of having prosecuted Mr. Wilkes with a spirit of personal resentment ; and affirms, that Wilkes cannot fail to triumph, in the end, even over the unforgiving anger of his King. He asserts, that, in the decision of the Middlesex election, the principles of the constitution had been deeply violated ; and that, if the King would not dissolve the parliament, who were the authors of that decision, he must unavoidably set himself in direct hostility against the great body of his people. He warmly affirms, that a King of England, if not popular among his subjects, cannot but be weak and miserable. He complains, that the Irish were oppressed, insulted, and irritated almost to rebellion. He affirms that, notwithstanding their remoteness from the scene where government appeared the most unjust and the most contemptible, even the American Colonists had, at last, learned to look upon their King as their foe. He renews, with added spite, his invectives against the Scots ; and asserts, that they would again betray a Sovereign who should confide in them, as a Scottish army had betrayed Charles the First. He tells him, that the guards were the most worthless part of the army ; and that the rest of the army despised their effeminacy and pride, and were not much disposed to imitate their blind loyalty. After this oratorical detail, he earnestly informs the monarch, that, unless he would throw himself into the arms of the Whig faction, he must instantly be at war with his people, and without a single resource from which he might derive a hope to prevail over their liberties*

or their just revenge ; exhorts him to slight the counsels of his
ministers, and ask the advice of his whole Privy Council ; bids
him dissolve his parliament, address his people in the language of
conscious error and penitence, and dismiss from his heart the hope
of being permitted ever to have a private friend.

This Letter exhibits a courteous loftiness in its tone of address ; and
preserves, even in the bitterness of invective, somewhat of that
language of respect, which is alone fit to be used in offering coun-
sel to Kings. It is comprehensive in its survey of characters,
events, political measures, and party-interests. It manages the
address with great skill, as being to a good prince who loved his
people, and sincerely desired to obtain, by good government, their
love. It blends sublimity and vehemence, with smartness and
pathos. Yet, in the whole, I cannot but judge it inferior to what,
after the former Letters, so great an occasion might have been
expected to call forth from the mind of JUNIUS.

---

19. *December*, 1769.

WHEN the complaints of a brave and powerful
people are observed to increase in proportion to
the wrongs they have suffered; when, instead of
sinking into submission, they are roused to resistance; the time will soon arrive, at which every
inferior consideration must yield to the security
of the Sovereign, and to the general safety of the
state. There is a moment of difficulty and dan-

There is a moment of difficulty and danger, &c.] JUNIUS
means, that the combination of the Pitt and Grenville party, with
the Rockingham and Newcastle Whigs, and the perseverance of
the city of London and the other addressers, in their former
efforts in favour of Mr. Wilkes, had actually brought a crisis, in

ger, at which flattery and falsehood can no longer
deceive, and simplicity itself can no longer be
misled. Let us suppose it arrived. Let us suppose a gracious, well-intentioned Prince, made
sensible at last of the great duty he owes to his
people, and of his own disgraceful situation: that
he looks round him for assistance; and asks for no
advice, but how to gratify the wishes, and secure
the happiness of his subjects. In these circumstances, it may be matter of curious SPECULA-
TION to consider, if an honest man were permitted to approach a King, in what term she would
address himself to his Sovereign. Let it be imagined, no matter how improbable, that the first
prejudice against his character is removed; that
the ceremonious difficulties of an audience are
surmounted; that he feels himself animated by
the purest and most honourable affections to his
King and country; and, that the great person
whom he addresses has spirit enough to bid him
speak freely, and understanding enough to listen

---

which the monarch must either go to war with his people, or
throw himself into the arms of the Whigs, and abandon those
principles of government which he had hitherto followed.

Matter of curious speculation, &c.] The author thus assumes
the air of speaking, as if it were merely in a case of fiction. He
wished that, as to any prosecution which should be meditated
against the printer, his Letter might appear to be written in a
feigned case, and addressed to a fancied King; but that, as to
every other effect, it might be understood by the nation and the
court, to be addressed to the reigning King, and to relate to the
British government.

to him with attention. Unacquainted with the vain impertinence of forms, he would deliver his sentiments with dignity and firmness, but not without respect.

He would deliver his sentiments, &c.] The introductory part of this Letter here ends. The reader will do well to look back upon it with attention; and to remark, how skilfully the author brings into one point of view, the reasons for addressing his sovereign in this remarkable manner; how artfully he endeavours to assume, just to the requisite degree, the air of here speaking but as if it were in jest; how happily he reconciles an appearance of delicate respect for his sovereign, with the act of accosting him in the language of reproof and unbidden advice!

SIR,

IT is the misfortune of your life, and originally the cause of every reproach and distress which has attended your government, that you should never have been acquainted with the language of truth, until you heard it in the complaints

---

That you should never have been acquainted with the language of truth, &c.] It was now the general cry of the parties which had been excluded from substantial power ever since the commencement of the present reign....that their King had been educated a stranger to those principles which ought to regulate the conduct of an English monarch; that he still blindly obeyed the wishes of his mother, and of the Earl of Bute; and that he was even now hindered from knowing the real sentiments of his people, and supposed himself to be promoting their welfare at a time when his ministers were trampling under foot the fundamental principles of the constitution.

They pretended that, to be a truly good and able prince, he ought to have been educated in a partial predilection for those Whigs of whom their faction was at present composed; in a dislike for the Tories; in an abhorrence of the Scots; in an utter incapacity to entertain any opinion concerning the affairs of government which was not dictated by the person whom the Whigs should give him for his minister. They did not wish him to judge and decide for himself, but to allow them alone to judge and decide for him.

But the progress of his majesty's reign has sufficiently vindicated both the wisdom of those principles of conduct towards the political parties among his subjects which he early adopted; and the strength of his own talents, which Junius and others contemptuously alledged that his education had marred.

Doddington's Diary presents several not uninteresting anecdotes concerning the court of Frederick Prince of Wales; and, afterwards, of the court of the Princess Dowager, from the time

of your people. It is not, however, too late to correct the error of your education. We are still inclined to make an indulgent allowance for the pernicious lessons you received in your youth, and

of her husband's death, to that of the death of George the Second. In these, the Princess appears in a very favourable light; usurping no authority over her husband's political affairs, during his life; after his death, shewing encouragement to his servants and friends, without maintaining a party in opposition to the measures of his father's government. She had to act a very delicate and difficult part. The Pelhams were jealous of what passed at Leicester-House; the Princess Amelia regarded the Princess of Wales with strong suspicion and dislike; the Duke of Cumberland also had his party, who were sufficiently willing to hold him at variance with his sister-in-law. Yet, the Princess gave as little offence as possible to every one; and, even where she saw malignity, was not provoked to angry indiscretion. Doddington, an old man of fair character and eminent talents, was more kindly treated by her, than he had been by her husband; was often asked for his advice; and never saw it slightingly received. She was assiduous in the education of her own children. She readily submitted to that choice of governors and tutors for the Prince, her son, which the king and his ministers chose to make. None but persons of at least decent abilities, and of fair character, were encouraged to frequent her court. Whigs were as much favoured by her as Tories. The Tories had, indeed, possessed greater favour with her husband, than they were permitted to retain with her. The Earl of Bute had been among the servants of the late Prince of Wales. He was a man of unblemished character in private life, elegant in his manners, a judge in the liberal arts, not unskilled in the sciences. He knew how to recommend himself to the young Prince; and was not then hated by any party. Contracting a friendship with Bute, the Prince was withheld from friendships which might have hurried him into wild dissipation. Mr. Pitt was not a little indebted to the court at Leicester-House, for that parliamentary unanimity which gave so much energy and splendour to the short career of his administration. The Newcastle Whigs had, before, made themselves odious to the whole nation,

to form the most sanguine hopes from the natural benevolence of your disposition*. We are far from thinking you capable of a direct, deliberate purpose, to invade those original rights of your

by their corruption, arrogance, and ill fortune. Mr. Pitt, being without any great parliamentary interest, insufferably overbearing, at last even to the most unbounded confidence a favourite with George the Second....the favourite, no less, both of fortune and of the people....was, on all these accounts, so extremely disagreeable to all that was great, both at court and in parliament, that at the accession of our present sovereign there was nothing more earnestly desired by the leaders of all the great parties, than Pitt's dismissal from power. Mr. Legge, whose political virtue was so highly praised, had descended as much as any person into the duplicity of political intrigue.

There was, therefore, no dishonest plan for keeping the King in perpetual pupilage, formed between his mother and the Earl of Bute. Neither had George the Second, nor the Princess Dowager of Wales, committed the education of the young Prince to the Jacobites and Tories. His education was not neglected, but managed with admirable success and care. Not the young King, but their incapacity and unpopularity, drove the Newcastle party from power. Not the King, but his own arrogance, and the opposition and dislike of the Newcastle party and others, dismissed Mr. Pitt from the administration. The union of parties, and the breaking down of the great Whig party, was originally the measure of Pitt, and arose from the natural progress of things. So unjust are the imputations with which this Letter of JUNIUS commences.

* The plan of tutelage and future dominion over the heir apparent, laid many years ago at Carleton-House, between the princess Dowager and her favourite the Earl of Bute, was as gross and palpable, as that which was concerted between Anne of Austria and Cardinal Mazarin, to govern Lewis the Fourteenth, and in effect to prolong his minority until the end of their lives. That Prince had strong natural parts, and used frequently to blush for his own ignorance and want of education, which had been wilfully

subjects, on which all their civil and political liberties depend. Had it been possible for us to entertain a suspicion so dishonourable to your character,
we should long since have adopted a style of remonstrance very distant from the humility of complaint. The doctrine inculcated by our laws, *That
the King can do no wron*g, is admitted without reluctance. We separate the amiable, good-natured

neglected by his mother and her minion. A little experience, however, soon shewed him how shamefully he had been treated, and
for what infamous purposes he had been kept in ignorance. Our
great Edward, too, at an early period, had sense enough to understand the nature of the connection between his abandoned mother
and the detested Mortimer. But, since that time, human nature,
we may observe, is greatly altered for the better. Dowagers may
be chaste, and minions may be honest. When it was proposed to
settle the present King's household as Prince of Wales, it is well
known that the Earl of Bute was forced into it, in direct contradiction to the late King's inclination. *That* was the salient point,
from which all the mischiefs and disgraces of the present reign
took life and motion. From that moment, Lord Bute never suffered the Prince of Wales to be an instant out of his sight....We need
not look farther.

We separate the amiable, &c.] Without approving the manner
in which JUNIUS alludes to the private virtues of his Sovereign,
one may take occasion here to observe, that there never was a
more conspicuous and striking instance of the advantage of possessing a good character, for both virtue and discretion, than that
of George the Third. How else should he have triumphed over
the unpopularity which it was so industriously striven to excite
against the first twelve years of his reign? How else should he
have retained the fond attachment of his people, amid the disasters of the American war? Is it not the force of character that
has preserved him so much more in favour with the nation than
his eldest son; notwithstanding that fickleness of the people,
which so commonly prefers youth to age, the hope of the future,

Prince, from the folly and treachery of his servants; and the private virtues of the man, from the vices of his government. Were it not for this just distinction, I know not whether your Majesty's condition, or that of the English nation, would deserve most to be lamented. I would prepare your mind for a favourable reception of truth, by removing every painful, offensive idea, of personal reproach. Your subjects, Sir, wish for nothing but that, as *they* are reasonable and affectionate enough to separate your person from your government, so *you*, in your turn, should distinguish between the conduct which becomes the permanent dignity of a King, and that which serves only to promote the temporary interest and miserable ambition of a minister.

You ascended the throne with a declared, and, I doubt not, a sincere resolution, of giving universal satisfaction to your subjects. You found them pleased with the novelty of a young Prince, whose

to the fair possession of the present day? What else has enabled him to triumph over the shock of democracy, and over all the trials of the present war? The excellence of our Sovereign's character, both as a King and as a man, has in truth been to him infinitely more useful, than any advantage that his fortune has bestowed. To every private man who chooses to cultivate honestly this most important of all possible acquisitions, it will prove, in his station, equally beneficial. Alas! how rarely youth understands the value of character, till it is for ever lost!

And that which serves only to promote, &c.) The King was addressed in this manner, precisely because he would not make himself the mere tool of any minister!

countenance promised even more than his words; and loyal to you, not only from principle, but passion. It was not a cold profession of allegiance to the first magistrate; but a partial, animated attachment, to a favourite Prince, the native of their country. They did not wait to examine your conduct, nor to be determined by experience; but gave you a generous credit for the future blessings of your reign, and paid you in advance the dearest tribute of their affections. Such, Sir, was once the disposition of a people, who now surround your throne with reproaches and complaints. Do justice to yourself. Banish from your mind those unworthy opinions, with which some interested persons have laboured to possess you. Distrust the men, who tell you that the English are naturally light and inconstant;......that they complain without a cause. Withdraw your confidence equally from all parties; from ministers, favourites, and relations: and let there be one moment in your life, in which you have consulted your own understanding.

When you affectedly renounced the name of Englishman, believe me, Sir, you were persuaded

From ministers, favourites, and relations, &c.] That is to say, become at once a stranger to all with whom you have hitherto particularly conversed; believe them to be, all, without exception, knaves and fools; throw yourself, not gradually, but at once, into the hands of persons of whom you have little or no knowledge; and do all this, because we endeavour to frighten you into it, by our clamour. .

When you affectedly renounce, &c.] Nothing but the general prevalence of this prejudice could have hindered the intellect of

to pay a very ill-judged compliment to one part of your subjects, at the expence of another. While the natives of Scotland are not in actual rebellion, they are undoubtedly entitled to protection; nor do I mean to condemn the policy of giving some encouragement to the novelty of their affections for the House of Hanover. I am ready to hope for every thing from their new-born zeal, and from the future steadiness of their allegiance. But, hitherto, they have no claim to your favour. To honour them with a determined predilection and confidence, in exclusion of your English subjects, who placed your family, and in spite of treachery and rebellion have supported it, upon the throne is a

JUNIUS from discerning its absurdity. There were, comparatively, but very few Scotsmen in official employment. Lord Chatham made it his chief boast, that he had been the first to make the Scottish Highlanders engage heartily in the military service of the House of Hanover.

Who placed your family on the throne, &c.] Let it be remembered, that the Scots were, even more than the English, the authors of the revolution in 1688; that Bishop Burnet, a Scotsman, first proposed the calling of the House of Hanover to the British succession; that the English Jacobites were as ill-disposed as the Scots, in the year 1715, much more numerous, but far less faithful and resolute; that it was the Duke of Argyle who first broke the strength of that rebellion; that it was the Earl of Stair, who, by his skilful conduct at the court of the Regent Duke of Orleans, disappointed the rebels of 1715, of all aid from France; that Stair commanded in the only splendidly successful battle that was fought by a British army against a foreign enemy, from the peace of Utrecht to the war of 1765; that the service of the Highlanders in America, in the war of 1756, had been confessed to transcend all praise!

mistake too gross, even for the unsuspecting gene-rosity of youth. In this error, we see a capital violation of the most obvious rules of policy and prudence. We trace it, however to an original bias in your education, and are ready to allow for your inexperience.

To the same early influence we attribute it, that you have descended to take a share, not only in the narrow views and interests of particular persons, but in the fatal malignity of their passions. At your accession to the throne, the whole system of government was altered; not from wisdom or deliberation, but because it had been adopted by your predecessor. A little personal motive of pique and resentment was sufficient to remove the ablest

To remove the ablest servants of the crown, &c.] Mr. Legge, Chancellor of the Exchequer, was dismissed, as JUNIUS in his Note relates. But, the Earl of Bute, even after Mr. Legge's refusal to desist from a contest with Sir Simeon Stuart, for the representation of Hampshire, and after Mr. Legge's success in the canvass obliged Sir Simeon to forego his pretensions, still endeavoured to concert some friendly compromise with Mr. Legge, for the time to come, which should leave it possible for Legge and Bute afterwards to co-operate amicably in administration. Mr. Legge shunned all compromise : and, when Lord Bute insinuated threats of the resentment of his Master, then Prince of Wales, set them fairly at defiance. After this, it might have been nobly generous, and greatly prudent, to forget the contest and the injury, at a time when Lord Bute had acquired the power of revenge. But Bute was a man of only fair morals; sentiments, like those of the people about him, moderately just and beneficent; a sagacity which, though not despicable, attained not to the comprehen-

servants of the Crown*; but it is not in this country, Sir, that such men can be dishonoured by the

sive intelligence, nor the bold intuition, of genius. He was not
capable of acting a part greatly above the level of ordinary minds.
He did what any other man, but a simpleton, a hero, or a sage,
would have done; and, when the accession of his friend and master to the throne gave him power, procured Legge to be turned
out of office.

There was another reason for Legge's dismissal. All whom
Bute could consult, whether Whigs or Tories, agreed in one common desire to see the pride of Pitt and the Grenvilles humbled,
and to see them driven from office before they should be able to
fortify themselves in it too strongly to be removed. But they could
not be abruptly dismissed; and were, therefore, to be first gradually
weakened. Legge was the limb, which their party would, with
the least shrinking, suffer to be lopped off. He had previously
shewn himself to be not absolutely incapable of betraying them,
nor did he possess the whole confidence of Mr. Pitt.

Now, is it possible, after considering these facts, to affirm that
the King was greatly blameable for the dismissal of Legge? He
had reason to esteem the character and conduct of Lord Bute.
Very many were ready to support Bute's opinions before he came
into office. The war was thought to be ruinous, though glorious;
and Pitt was not disposed to bring it to an end. These were sufficient reasons to justify the young monarch in adopting Lord Bute
for his ministry. Making him minister, it was requisite to do for
him what must have been done for any other man; to give him
such a choice of his co-adjutors, as might be necessary to render
his official authority effective. Had there been, in the dismissal
of Legge, any thing notoriously vindictive, capricious, or imprudent; this might have been sufficient to alarm the King against
his favourite. But since, in that act, Bute did nothing but what
would have been done by any other man, save one of extraordinary magnanimity and wisdom, or of excessive weakness, in his
situation, how should the King have, in this instance, refused his
approbation? There is no reason that the King had, against
Legge, any private resentment of his own.

* One of the first acts of the present reign was to dismiss Mr.
Legge, because he had, some years before, refused to yield his

frowns of a King. They were dismissed, but could not be disgraced. Without entering into a minuter discussion of the merits of the peace, we may observe, in the imprudent hurry with which the first overtures from France were accepted, in the conduct of the negotiation and terms of the treaty, the strongest marks of that precipitate spirit of concession with which a certain part of your subjects have been at all times ready to purchase a peace with the natural enemies of this country. On *your* part, we are satisfied that every thing was honourable and sincere ; and, if England was sold to France, we doubt not that your Majesty was equally betrayed. The conditions of the peace were matter of grief and surprise to your subjects, but not the immediate cause of their present discontent.

Hitherto, Sir, you had been sacrificed to the prejudices and passions of others. With what firmness will you bear the mention of your own ?

A Man, not very honourably distinguished in the world, commences a formal attack upon your favourite ; considering nothing, but how he might

interest in Hampshire to a Scotchman recommended by Lord Bute. This was the reason publickly assigned by his lordship.

The conditions of the peace, &c.] Of that peace, I shall never attempt the defence. Compare its terms, and the advantages under which it was negotiated, with the terms of the peace of

best expose his person and principles to detestation, and the national character of his countrymen to contempt. The natives of that country, Sir, are as much distinguished by a peculiar character, as by your Majesty's favour. Like another chosen people, they have been conducted into the land of plenty, where they find themselves effectually marked, and divided from mankind. There is hardly a period at which the most irregular character may not be redeemed. The mistakes of one sex find a retreat in patriotism ; those of the other, in devotion. Mr. Wilkes brought with him into politics, the same liberal sentiments by which his private conduct had been directed ; and seemed to think that, as there are few excesses in which an English gentleman may not be permitted to indulge, the same latitude was allowed him in the choice of his political principles, and in the spirit of maintaining them......I mean to state, not entirely to defend, his conduct. In the earnestness of his zeal, he suffered some unwarrantable insinuations to escape him. He said more than moderate men would justify ; but not enough to entitle him to the honour of your Majesty's personal resentment. The rays of royal indignation, collected upon him, served only to illuminate, and could not consume. Animated by the favour of the people on one side,

Utrecht, and the opposition and embarrassments with which St. John had to struggle in accomplishing *it* ; and you shall then be fully sensible of all the losses and dishonour of the peace of 1763.

and heated by persecution on the other, his views
and sentiments changed with his situation. Hardly
serious at first, he is now an enthusiast. The
coldest bodies warm with opposition, the hardest
sparkle in collision. There is a holy mistaken zeal
in politics as well as religion. By persuading
others, we convince ourselves. The passions are
engaged, and create a maternal affection in the
mind, which forces us to love the cause for which
we suffer...Is this a contention worthy of a King?
Are you not sensible how much the meanness of
the cause gives an air of ridicule to the serious difficulties into which you have been betrayed? The
destruction of one man has been now, for many
years, the sole object of your government; and, if
there can be any thing still more disgraceful, we
have seen, for such an object, the utmost influence
of the executive power, and every ministerial artifice, exerted without success. Nor can you ever
succeed, unless *he* should be imprudent enough to
forfeit the protection of those laws to which you
owe your crown, or unless your ministers should
persuade you to make it a question of force alone,
and try the whole strength of government in opposition to the people. The lessons *he* has received

---

The lessons he has received, &c.] The case of Wilkes, the
subject of this and of the following paragraph, has already engaged our attention, and will again return under our more particular review. For the present, let it suffice to observe, that even
in any former period of the British history, papers so seditious as
those of the North Briton would have provoked prosecution ; that

from experience, will probably guard him from such excess of folly; and, in your Majesty's virtues, we find an unquestionable assurance, that no illegal violence will be attempted.

Far from suspecting you of so horrible a design, we would attribute the continued violation of the laws, and even this last enormous attack upon the vital principles of the constitution, to an ill advised, unworthy, personal resentment. From one false step you have been betrayed into another; and, as the cause was unworthy of you, your ministers were determined that the prudence of the execution should correspond with the wisdom and dignity of the design. They have reduced you to the necessity of choosing out of a variety of difficulties;....to a situation so unhappy, that you can neither do wrong without ruin, nor right without affliction. These worthy servants have undoubtedly given you many singular proofs of their abilities. Not contented

they were more remarkable for vulgar outrage than for any other quality; that there was nothing tyrannical nor unjust in the attempted prosecution, but the rash use of a general warrant; that such warrants, though certainly unconstitutional, had been before used even by the most popular ministers, and upon occasions sufficiently trivial; that, to have hastily pardoned Wilkes, would have been, in some sort, to offer prizes for sedition; that, for the errors of his ministers, in the continued contest with Wilkes, the King was not to be blamed; that, since opposition used every artifice-to magnify the case of Wilkes, as a matter of infinite importance, administration could not, without weakness, overlook it.

with making Mr. Wilkes a man of importance, they have judiciously transferred the question, from the rights and interests of one man, to the most important rights and interests of the people; and forced your subjects, from wishing well to the cause of an individual, to unite with him in their own. Let them proceed as they have begun, and your Majesty need not doubt that the catastrophe will do a dishonour to the conduct of the piece.

The circumstances to which you are reduced, will not admit of a compromise with the English nation. Undecisive, qualifying measures, will disgrace your government still more than open violence; and, without satisfying the people, will excite their contempt. They have too much understanding and spirit to accept of an indirect satisfaction for a direct injury. Nothing less than a repeal, as formal as the resolution itself, can heal the wound that has been given to the constitution, nor will any thing less be accepted. I can readily believe, that there is an influence sufficient to call their pernicious vote. The House of Commons undoubtedly consider their duty to the Crown as paramount to all other obligations. To *us* they are only indebted for an accidental existence, and have justly transferred their gratitude from their parents to their benefactors....from those who gave them birth, to the minister from whose benevolence they derive the comforts and pleasures of their political life....who has taken the tenderest care of their infancy, and relieves their necessities without offending their delicacy. But, if it were possible for their integrity to be degraded to a condition so vile and abject, that, compared with it, the present estimation they stand in is a state of honour and respect, consider, Sir, in what manner you will afterwards proceed. Can you conceive that the people of this country will long submit to be governed by so flexible a House of Commons? It is. not in the nature of human society, that any form of government, in such circumstances, can long be preserved. In ours, the general contempt of the people is as fatal as their detestation. Such, I am persuaded, would be the necessary effect of any base concession made by the

Can you conceive that the people of this country, &c.] As the measures of the crown were still supported by a majority in the House of Commons, the enemies of the prevalent system of administration found it extremely necessary to call the opinion of the people to their aid, against both the ministry and the majority in parliament. They believed that the decision in the case of the Middlesex election had given such offence to the electors in general, throughout the kingdom, that, if an immediate dissolution of Parliament might be obtained, the subsequent election would return a majority of representatives hostile to the authors of that decision, and to the principles upon which it had been made. Hence their zeal to magnify the authority of the people; their malignant assiduity to vilify the House of Commons; their endeavours to persuade the King, that rebellion must ensue, unless he would yield to their wishes. The decision on the case of the Middlesex election was certainly unconstitutional. Various irregularities had been committed in the prosecution of Wilkes. There was often capricious weakness, and sometimes, perhaps, injustice, in the other conduct of the administration. But, the general system of government was good. Nor could any thing have proved more unfortunate to this country, than if the King's firmness had been subdued, and he had suddenly been frightened to abandon that system.

present House of Commons ; and, as a qualifying measure would not be accepted, it remains for you to decide, whether you will, at any hazard, support a set of men who have reduced you to this unhappy dilemma, or whether you will gratify the united wishes of the whole people of England by dissolv‑ ing the parliament.

Taking it for granted, as I do very sincerely, that you have personally no design against the con‑ stitution, nor any view inconsistent with the good of your subjects, I think you cannot hesitate long upon the choice which it equally concerns your in‑ terest and your honour to adopt. On one side, you hazard the affections of all your English subjects ; you relinquish every hope of repose to yourself, and you endanger the establishment of your family for ever. All this you venture for no object whatso‑ ever, or for such an object as it would be an affront to you to name. Men of sense will examine your conduct with suspicion ; while those who are inca‑ pable of comprehending to what degree they are

All this you venture for no object whatsoever, &c.] The reader cannot but perceive, that there is in this period an air of the care‑ lessness and inaccuracy of conversation. But it affords, also, other subject for remark. If the matter in contest were so exceedingly trivial, how should it provoke a rebellion? Were the true friends to English liberty, men who would take up arms against their prince for a quarrel of a straw? It gives, indeed, to my apprehension, some‑ thing of an air of ridicule to the complaints and invectives of JUNIUS, when he strives to persuade the nation, that they were ready to rush into civil war, on account of Wilkes and the Middlesex election.

injured, afflict you with clamours equally insolent and unmeaning. Supposing it possible that no fatal struggle should ensue, you determine at once to be unhappy, without the hope of a compensation either from interest or ambition. If an English King be hated or despised, he *must* be unhappy; and this, perhaps, is the only political truth which he ought to be convinced of without experiment. But, if the English people should no longer confine their resentment to a submissive representation of their wrongs; if, following the glorious example of their ancestors, they should no longer appeal to the creature of the constitution, but to that high Being who gave them the rights of humanity, whose gifts it were sacrilege to surrender, let me ask you, Sir, upon what part of your subjects would you rely for assistance?

The people of Ireland have been uniformly plundered and oppressed. In return, they give you

---

Ireland.] The Irish are a very ancient people. Till the æra of their conversion to Christianity, they lived in a state of extreme rudeness. Christianity contributed somewhat, though not much, to humanize their manners. The invasion of the Norwegians and Danes, in the eighth and ninth centuries, served partly to desolate their isle, and in part to make them usefully acquainted with new arts and manners. They were Christians, but not submissive to all the forms of the Romish communion: and an English monarch was, therefore, authorised to convert, by conquering, them. From the reign of Henry the Second, the conquest of Ireland was vigorously pursued by the English, till the Irish tribes were reduced to general submission. Robert Bruce of Scotland, and his brother Edward, attempted, but without success, to deliver Ireland from the English yoke. For a long time subsequent, the obedience of the Irish to

every day fresh marks of their resentment. They despise the miserable governor you have sent them*, because he is the creature of Lord Bute; nor is it from any natural confusion in their ideas, that they

their English masters was extremely uncertain. The rebellion, and the wars which ensued, in the reign of Queen Elizabeth, did not subside into a calm, till the new settlement of the Irish government under James the First. The dissensions between the Catholic and the Protestant religions, combined with the mutual hatred between the English colonists and the ancient Irish, to renew the wonted disturbances in the reign of Charles the First; these were vigorously suppressed by the Earl of Strafford. Under the pretence of fidelity to Charles the First, the Irish, in the civil wars, broke into the wildest dissolution of all order. Ireland was again conquered by the arms of Cromwell. A new settlement of its affairs and government took place, after the Restoration, agreeably to the counsels of the Earl of Clarendon. In the reign of James the Second, the Catholics were so much more favoured than the Protestants, that the former earnestly devoted themselves to the interests of their Sovereign, and the latter were almost ready to rise in rebellion against him. The attachment of the Catholics to the unfortunate James, exposed them to the miseries of another conquest. The settlement of Irish affairs, after the Revolution, raised the Protestants to an oppressive superiority over the Catholics. Of the Catholics, some consequently embraced the Protestant religion; others sought preferment in the service of Catholic princes on the continent; the rest remained in contemptible, though impatient, subjection at home. Even of the Protestants, the political condition was despicable. They were subject, not only to the crown, but to the legislature of Britain; and the hope of equal union was denied them. In spite of every disadvantage, the Irish Protestants gradually became, to a formidable degree, opulent and powerful; and, in spite of every cause of mutual dissatisfaction, the Catholics and Protestants of Ireland gradually learned to combine their strength against England. The English government was thus forced, by slow

* Viscount Townshend, sent over on the plan of being resident Governor. The history of his ridiculous administration shall not be lost to the public.

are so ready to confound the original of a King
with the disgraceful representation of him.

The distance of the Colonies would make it impossible for them to take an active concern in your

degrees, to lay its hand still lighter and lighter upon them. The
fidelity of the Irish to the House of Hanover, at the crisis of 1745,
contributed to make them still more the objects of the favour of government. No new hardships had been inflicted, since the commencement of the century. As the fears of popery and rebellion
became still lighter ; the condition of the Irish Catholics was continually meliorated. Yet, in the progress of the present reign, some
discontents had been excited among the Irish Protestants. Lord
Townshend was involved in some public disputes with the parliament ; and in a private difference with Lord Bellamont, which
terminated afterwards in a harmless duel. It was during the administration of Lord Townshend, that the law for octennial elections
was passed in Ireland ; and jealousies and disagreements unavoidably arose between the English ministers and the Irish political
leaders, on account of that measure. The Irish were even embold-
ened to make some shew of imitating the conduct of the English
demagogues, But the authority of government prevailed ; and, till
the unfortunate close of the American war, Ireland continued in its
wonted subjection. The emancipation of the Irish legislature was
then accomplished. That measure has since appeared to have
been.......as to the connexion necessary between England and Ireland, too much ;....as to redress of the grievances of the Catholics,
far too little. After much contention and mischief, an IMPERIAL
and LEGISLATIVE UNION of Ireland with England, has been, at
last accomplished, which may probably prove the most splendidly
useful transaction of the present reign.

The distance of the colonies, &c.] It should seem, as if, in writing
this paragraph, JUNIUS felt himself at a loss, whether to be of the
opinion of Mr. Grenville, or that of Lord Chatham, in respect to
the treatment of the Americans. He avoids the declaration of his
sentiments : but seems, from his comparison of the Americans to
the Scottish Presbyterians, to have inclined to the creed of George
Grenville.

affairs, if they were as well affected to your government as they once pretended to be to your person.
They were ready enough to distinguish between
you and your ministers. They complained of an
act of the legislature, but traced the origin of it no
higher than to the servants of the crown: They
pleased themselves with the hope that their Sovereign, if not favourable to their cause, at least was
impartial. The decisive personal part you took
against them, has effectually banished that first distinction from their minds*. They consider you as
united with your servants against America; and
know how to distinguish the Sovereign and a venal
parliament on one side, from the real sentiments of
the English people on the other. Looking forward
to Independence, they might possibly receive you
for their King; but, if ever you retire to America,
be assured they will give you such a covenant to
digest, as the Presbytery of Scotland would have
been ashamed to offer to Charles the Second. They
left their native land in search of freedom, and found
it in a desert. Divided as they are into a thousand
forms of policy and religion, there is one point in
which they all agree:.....they equally detest the pa-

---

* In the King's speech of 8. November 1768, it was declared,
" That the spirit of faction had broken out afresh in some of the
" colonies ; and, in one of them, proceeded to acts of violence and
" resistance to the execution of the laws ;.....that Boston was in a
" state of disobedience to all law and government, and had pro-
" ceeded to measures subversive of the constitution, and attended
" with circumstances that manifested a disposition to throw off their
" dependance on Great-Britain."

geantry of a King, and the supercilious hypocrisy
of a Bishop.

It is not, then, from the alienated affections of
Ireland or America, that you can reasonably look for
assistance; still less from the people of England,
who are actually contending for their rights, and in
this great question are parties against you. You
are not, however, destitute of every appearance of
support: You have all the Jacobites, Nonjurors,
Roman Catholics, and Tories, of this country; and
all Scotland, without exception. Considering from
what family you are descended, the choice of your
friends has been singularly directed; and truly, Sir,
if you had not lost the Whig interest of England, I
should admire your dexterity in turning the hearts
of your enemies. Is it possible for you to place
any confidence in men who, before they are faithful to you, must renounce every opinion, and betray
every principle, both in church and state, which
they inherit from their ancestors, and are confirmed
in by their education? whose numbers are so inconsiderable, that they have long since been obliged
to give up the principles and language which distinguish them as a party, and to fight under the
banners of their enemies? Their zeal begins with
hypocrisy, and must conclude in treachery. At first
they deceive; at last they betray.

As to the Scotch, I must suppose your heart and
understanding so biassed from your earliest infancy,

in their favour, that nothing less than *your own* misfortunes can undeceive you. You will not accept
of the uniform experience of your ancestors, and,
when once a man is determined to believe, the very
absurdity of the doctrine confirms him in his faith.
A bigotted understanding can draw a proof of attachment to the House of Hanover, from a notorious
zeal for the House of Stuart, and find an earnest of
future loyalty in former rebellions. Appearances
are, however, in their favour: so strongly, indeed,
that one would think they had forgotten that you
are their lawful King, and had mistaken you for a
Pretender to the Crown. Let it be admitted, then,
that the Scotch are as sincere in their present professions, as if you were, in reality, not an Englishman, but a Briton of the North. You would not
be the first Prince, of their native country, against
whom they have rebelled, nor the first whom they
have basely betrayed. Have you forgotten, Sir, or
has your favourite concealed from you that part of
our history, when the unhappy Charles (and he too
had private virtues) fled from the open, avowed indignation, of his English subjects, and surrendered
himself at discretion to the good faith of his own
countrymen? Without looking for support in their
affections as subjects, he applied only to their
honour as gentlemen, for protection. They received
him as they would your Majesty, with bows, and
smiles, and falsehood, and kept him until they had
settled their bargain with the English parliament;
then basely sold their native King to the vengeance

of his enemies. This, Sir, was not the act of a few traitors, but the deliberate treachery of a Scotch parliament, representing the nation. A wise Prince might draw from it two lessons of equal utility to himself. On one side, he might learn to dread the undisguised resentment of a generous people, who dare openly assert their rights, and who, in a just cause, are ready to meet their Sovereign in the field. On the other side, he would be taught to apprehend something far more formidable;......a fawning treachery, against which no prudence can guard, no courage can defend. The insidious smile upon the cheek, would warn him of the canker in the heart.

From the uses to which one part of the army has been too frequently applied, you have some reason to expect that there are no services they would refuse. Here, too, we trace the partiality of your understanding. You take the sense of the army from the conduct of the guards, with the same justice with which you collect the sense of the people from the representations of the ministry. Your marching regiments, Sir, will not make the guards their example, either as soldiers or subjects. They feel, and resent, as they ought to do, that invariable, undistinguishing favour, with which the guards are treated*; while those gallant troops, by whom

---

* The number of commissioned officers in the guards are to the marching regiments, as *one* to eleven;....the number of regiments given to the guards, compared with those given to the line, is about three to one, at a moderate computation : consequently, the parti-

every hazardous, every laborious service is performed, are left to perish in garrisons abroad, or pine in
quarters at home, neglected and forgotten. If they
had no sense of the great original duty they owe
their country, their resentment would operate like
patriotism, and leave your cause to be defended
by those to whom you have lavished the rewards
and honours of their profession. The Prætorian
Bands, enervated and debauched as they were, had
still strength enough to awe the Roman populace;
but when the distant legions took the alarm, they
marched to Rome, and gave away the empire.

On this side, then, which ever way you turn
your eyes, you see nothing but perplexity and distress. You may determine to support the very
ministry who have reduced your affairs to this deplorable situation : you may shelter yourself under
the forms of a parliament, and set your people at
defiance. But be assured, Sir, that such a resolution
would be as imprudent as it would be odious. If

ality in favour of the guards is as thirty-three to one....So much for
the officers....The private men have four-pence a day to subsist on ;
and five hundred lashes, if they desert. Under this punishment,
they frequently expire. With these encouragements, it is supposed
they may be depended upon, whenever a certain person thinks it
necessary to butcher his *fellow-subjects.*

The Praetorian bands, &c.] This is one among many passages,
which shew, that the writer of these Letters was fresh from the
perusal of Tacitus. The period of the Roman History to which
he alludes, is that which ensued when Vitellius, and the army from
Germany, defeated the Prætorian guards, that ravished the imperial power from Otho.

it did not immediately shake your establishment, it would rob you of your peace of mind for ever.

On the other, how different is the prospect! How easy, how safe and honourable, is the path be-fore you! The English nation declare they are grossly injured by their representatives, and solicit your Majesty to exert your lawful prerogative, and give them an opportunity of recalling a trust which they find has been scandalously abused. You are not to be told, that the power of the House of Com-mons is not original, but delegated to them for the welfare of the people from whom they received it. A question of right arises between the constituent and the representative body. By what authority shall it be decided? Will your Majesty interfere in a question in which you have properly no immedi-ate concern? It would be a step equally odious and unnecessary. Shall the Lords be called upon to determine the rights and privileges of the Com-mons? They cannot do it, without a flagrant breach of the constitution. Or, will you refer it to the judges? They have often told your ancestors, that the law of parliament is above them. What party then remains, but to leave it to the people to determine for themselves? They alone are injured; and, since there is no superior power to which the cause can be referred, they alone ought to deter-mine.

I do not mean to perplex you with a tedious ar-gument upon a subject already so discussed that inspiration could hardly throw a new light upon it. There are, however, two points of view, in which it particularly imports your Majesty to consider the late proceedings of the House of Commons. By depriving a subject of his birth-right, they have attributed to their own vote an authority equal to an act of the whole legislature ; and, though perhaps not with the same motives, have strictly followed the example of the Long Parliament, which first declared the regal office useless, and soon after, with as little ceremony, dissolved the House of Lords. The same pretended power which robs an English subject of his birth-right, may rob an English King of his crown. In another view, the resolution of the House of Commons, apparently not so dangerous to your Majesty, is still more alarming to your people. Not contented with divesting one man of his right, they have arbitrarily conveyed that right to another. They have set aside a return as illegal, without daring to censure those officers who were particularly apprized of Mr. Wilkes's incapacity, not only by the declaration of the House, but expressly by the writ directed to them, and who nevertheless returned him as duly elected. They have rejected the majority of votes, the only criterion by |which our laws judge of the sense of the people; they have transferred the right of election

---

Without daring to censure those officers, &c.] It was indeed absurd, to suppose the Electors obliged to know and act upon a principle which it was owned that the returning officers were not obliged to know nor act upon.

from the collective to the representative body; and by these acts, taken separately or together, they have essentially altered the original constitution of the House of Commons. Versed, as your Majesty undoubtedly is, in the English history, it cannot easily escape you, how much it is your interest, as well as your duty, to prevent one of the three estates from encroaching upon the province of the other two, or assuming the authority of them all. When once they have departed from the great constitutional line by which all their proceedings should be directed, who will answer for their future moderation? Or what assurance will they give you, that, when they have trampled upon their equals, they will submit to a superior? Your Majesty may learn, hereafter, how nearly the slave and tyrant are allied.

Some of your council, more candid than the rest, admit the abandoned profligacy of the present House of Commons, but oppose their dissolution, upon an opinion, I confess, not very unwarrantable, that their successors would be equally at the disposal of the treasury. I cannot persuade myself that the nation will have profited so little by experience. But, if that opinion were well founded, you might then gratify our wishes at an easy rate, and appease the present clamour against your government, without

---

To prevent one of the three estates, &c.] This is a sound observation; not new and peculiar, yet sufficiently worthy of the sagacity of JUNIUS.

offering any material injury to the favourite cause of corruption.

You have still an honourable part to act. The affections of your subjects may still be recovered. But before you subdue *their* hearts, you must gain a noble victory over your own. Discard those little, personal resentments, which have too long directed your public conduct. Pardon this man the remainder of his punishment ; and, if resentment still prevails, make it, what it should have been long since, an act, not of mercy, but of contempt. He will soon fall back into his natural station....a silent senator, and hardly supporting the weekly eloquence of a newspaper. The gentle breath of peace would leave him on the surface, neglected and unremoved. It is only the tempest that lifts him from his place.

Without consulting your minister, call together your whole council. Let it appear to the public, that you can determine and act for yourself. Come forward to your people. Lay aside the wretched

Pardon this man the remainder, &c.] No bad advice.....what seems to have been, in fact, followed.

Come forward to your people.] This paragraph, with that which immediately precedes, and those which follow to the end of the Letter, are written in a fine strain of eloquence. They seem to breathe a sincere and tender concern for the true interests of him to whom they are addressed ; they are produced in a tone, as if the writer felt that his eloquence, sagacity, and integrity, gave him a right to speak with authority even to Majesty itself; they exhort,

formalities of a King, and speak to your subjects
with the spirit of a man, and in the language of a
gentleman. Tell them you have been fatally deceived. The acknowledgment will be no disgrace,
but rather an honour, to your understanding. Tell
them you are determined to remove every cause of
complaint against your government ; that you will
give your confidence to no man who does not possess the confidence of your subjects ; and leave it to
themselves to determine, by their conduct at a future election, whether or no it be, in reality, the general sense of the nation, that their rights have been
arbitrarily invaded by the present House of Commons, and the constitution betrayed. They will
then do justice to their representatives and to themselves.

These sentiments, Sir, and the style they are
conveyed in, may be offensive, perhaps, because
they are new to you. Accustomed to the language of
courtiers, you measure their affections by the vehemence of their expressions ; and, when they only
praise you indirectly, you admire their sincerity.
But this is not a time to trifle with your fortune.
They deceive you, Sir, who tell you that you have
many friends whose affections are founded upon a

they alarm, they soothe, and they menace ; they employ precisely
that mode of address, which seems the fittest to confound obstinacy,
or to unnerve resolution, and to reduce the person whom it assails
to that self-abasement and uncertainty, in which he shall be willing
to resign himself even to the triumph of a foe.

principle of personal attachment. The first foundation of friendship is not the power of conferring
benefits, but the equality with which they are received, and *may* be returned. The fortune which
made you a King, forbade you to have a friend. It
is a law of nature, which cannot be violated with
impunity. The mistaken Prince, who looks for
friendship, will find a favourite, and in that favourite
the ruin of his affairs.

The people of England are loyal to the house of
Hanover, not from a vain preference of one family
to another, but from a conviction that the establish-

The fortune which made you a King, &c.] Kings certainly will
not find friends in those who desire to make a traffic of their favours.
Yet there is no reason why Kings should not, as well as other men,
occasionally find that moderate and imperfect friendship, which is
all that the present condition of humanity requires. Friendship
takes place in its highest purity and sincerity, in cases in which
there is not such a difference of character and condition as may prevent a competition of interests between the friends. Such is the attachment between man and woman, when sexual appetite has little
or no share in it. Such is the friendship between ingenuous youth,
and mild old age. Such friendship, too, may take place between a
good King, and men of virtue in his court. The sentiments of virtuous loyalty on the one hand, and of a sort of paternal benignity on
the other, may even give a truth and delicacy to such a friendship,
which the friendships of equals cannot so certainly possess. Besides, careless familiarity is frequently the bane of friendship ; and
from the friendship between a subject and his Sovereign, such familiarity is the most likely to be excluded.

At least, to tell Princes that their fate denies them the common
advantages of humanity, is to teach them to shut their hearts
against sympathy in human woe, and against those benign affections
which can alone give Tituses or Trajans to the people over whom
they reign.

ment of that family was necessary to the support of their civil and religious liberties. This, Sir, is a principle of allegiance equally solid and rational; ....fit for Englishmen to adopt, and well worthy of your Majesty's encouragement. We cannot long be deluded by nominal distinctions. The name of Stuart, of itself, is only contemptible;....armed with the Sovereign authority, their principles are formidable. The Prince, who imitates their conduct, should be warned by their example; and, while he plumes himself upon the security of his title to the crown, should remember that, as it was acquired by one revolution, it may be lost by another.

JUNIUS.

We cannot long be deluded by nominal distinctions,] JUNIUS is unhappy in this observation. It was precisely because the distinctions between Whig and Tory were no longer more than nominal, in the respects of fidelity to the constitution, and loyalty to the House of Hanover, that the King had adopted the system of government against which JUNIUS inveighs.

LETTER XXXVI.

TO HIS GRACE THE DUKE OF GRAFTON.

———

THE Whigs had tried their strength. At first, the ministry stood their ground. Parliament was assembled. Although many insolent petitions for a redress of grievances had been recently presented to the King, he deigned not even to allude to their purport, when in the opening of the session he addressed his parliament from the throne. In the debate, which arose when an address in answer to the speech was moved in the House of Lords, the Earl of Chatham began the attack upon the ministers and their supporters. The affairs of America, the complaints of the people, the iniquity of the decision upon the Middlesex election, were the principal topics of which he spoke. Though his harangues were loose and declamatory, though they breathed even somewhat of a democratical spirit, though he was opposed by the vigorous and artful talents of Lord Mansfield; yet, the authority of his character, the majesty of his elocution, and the knowledge that all the Whigs were now ready to echo his voice, gave extraordinary force to what he uttered. It was supposed, that the ministry could not long withstand the opposition, at the head of which he now stood. The Duke of Beaufort, the Earl of Coventry, the Marquis of Granby, the Duke of Manchester, the Earl of Huntingdon, Mr. Dunning, solicitor-general, chusing rather to make their peace in good time with the opposition, than to share the disgrace of that which they supposed to be befalling ministry, resigned their offices. Lord Camden, the chancellor, being suspected of betraying to Lord Chatham the secrets of the cabinet, was indignantly required to deliver up the seals. Even the Speaker of the House of Commons, on the pretence of ill health, but perhaps not uninfluenced by the circumstances of the doubtful contest which he saw proceeding, resigned that employment. The Honourable Charles Yorke, who had not hitherto distinguished himself by any violent fidelity to Whig principles, accepted the seals as chancellor: but, reflecting on the choice he had made, he was

either so much ashamed of the part he had taken, or so much dis-
satisfied with his bargain, that he ended his own life with a pistol.....
a conduct unexampled in the case of ministerial promotion, since
the time when the only son of Sir William Temple drowned himself
in the Thames. At last, on the 28th of January, 1770, even the
Duke of Grafton himself, resigned the office of First Lord of the
Treasury; retiring to the less active and responsible appointment
of Keeper of the Privy Seal. Even all this moved not the court
from its purpose. The Whigs were not called to office; the former
system of measures was not abandoned; and, when the Sovereign's
firmness was thus decisively evinced, persons were easily found to fill
the vacant offices. While all was still in uncertain agitation, JUNIUS
renewed his attack on the Duke; probably believing that his former
Letters had been not without considerable influence in moving his
Grace to retire from the head of the Treasury; and that he who
had retired in terror from the place of the most conspicuous respon-
sibility, might be driven, by renewed invective, from all ministerial
employment.

In this Letter, JUNIUS exults over what he accounted the weakness
of the retiring minister; endeavours to convince him that, even by
retreat, he might not escape from vengeance and ignominy; and
uses, against him, that malignant hand which stabs the deeper, be-
cause the wound is known to be felt with exquisite anguish. Lord
North had succeeded the Duke of Grafton as First Lord of the
Treasury: and JUNIUS, therefore, turns, at the close of his Letter,
from harassing the Duke, to try the force of contemptuous ridi-
cule against his successor.

This Letter seems a more masterly composition than that which im-
mediately precedes it.

———

MY LORD, 14. *February*, 1770.

IF I were personally your enemy, I might
pity and forgive you. You have every claim to
compassion, that can arise from misery and distress.
The condition you are reduced to, would disarm a

private enemy of his resentment, and leave no consolation to the most vindictive spirit, but that such an object as you are, would disgrace the dignity of revenge. But, in the relation you have borne to this country, you have no title to indulgence; and if I had followed the dictates of my own opinion, I never should have allowed you the respite of a moment. In your public character, you have injured every subject of the empire; and though an individual is not authorised to forgive the injuries done to society, he is called upon to assert his separate share in the public resentment. I submitted, however, to the judgment of men more moderate, perhaps more candid, than myself. For my own part, I do not pretend to understand those prudent forms of decorum, those gentle rules of discretion, which some men endeavour to unite with the conduct of the greatest and most hazardous affairs. Engaged in the defence of an honourable cause, I would take a decisive part....I should scorn to provide for a future retreat, or to keep terms with a man who preserves no measures with the public. Neither the abject submission of

---

Leave no consolation to the most vindictive spirit, &c.] Here is an inaccuracy of expression, such as JUNIUS is sometimes betrayed into, by the attempt at excessive refinement of thought, and elaborateness of phrase. He says, in the preceding periods, that the Duke's condition would disarm personal resentment, *by the pity* which it could not but move. But, in this period, that private resentment is said to be subject to be thus disarmed, *not by pity*, but by the impossibility of reaching an object so very low. The contradiction is striking.

deserting his post in the hour of danger, nor even the *sacred shield of cowardice, should protect him. I would pursue him through life, and try the last exertion of my abilities to preserve the perishable infamy of his name, and make it immortal.

What then, my Lord, is this the event of all the sacrifices you have made to Lord Bute's patronage, and to your own unfortunate ambition? Was it for this you abandoned your earliest friendships....the warmest connexions of your youth, and all those honourable engagements by which you once solicited, and might have acquired, the esteem of your country? Have you secured no recompence for such a waste of honour? Unhappy man! What party will receive the common deserter of all parties? Without a client to flatter, without a friend to console you, and with only one companion from the honest house of Bloomsbury, you must now retire into a dreadful solitude. At the most active period of life, you must quit the busy scene, and conceal yourself from the world, if you would hope to save the wretched remains of a ruined reputation. The vices operate like age....bring on disease before its time; and, in the prime of youth, leave the character broken and exhausted.

* ......*Sacro tremuere timore.* Every coward pretends to be planet-struck.

What then, my Lord, &c.] Had the severity of this passage been deserved, it were impossible not to admire its transcendent eloquence. No language, ancient nor modern, can afford a specimen of impressive eloquence superior to this.

Yet your conduct has been mysterious, as well
as contemptible. Where is now that firmness, or
obstinacy, so long boasted of by your friends, and
acknowledged by your enemies? We were taught
to expect, that you would not leave the ruin of this
country to be compleated by other hands, but were
determined either to gain a decisive victory over
the constitution, or to perish bravely at least behind the last dyke of the prerogative. You knew
the danger, and might have been provided for it....
You took sufficient time to prepare for a meeting with your parliament, to confirm the mercenary
fidelity of your dependants, and to suggest to your
Sovereign, a language suited to his dignity at least,
if not to his benevolence and wisdom. Yet, while
the whole kingdom was agitated with anxious expectation upon one great point, you meanly evaded
the question; and, instead of the explicit firmness
and decision of a King, gave us nothing but the
misery of a ruined * grazier, and the whining

You knew the danger, &c.] The Duke is said to have retired
from the Treasury, on account of a disagreement in opinion with
the majority of the cabinet, concerning a leading measure; not
from fear of JUNIUS, nor of Lord Chatham. Yet, the attacks to
which the ministry were exposed, tended to set them more at variance among themselves, and to make them more uncertain in their
counsels.

The grand crime of the Duke now was, in the eyes of the Whigs,
that he did not abandon the King entirely, and again range himself
under the banner of Lord Chatham.

* There was something wonderfully pathetic in the mention of
the horned cattle.

Misery of a ruined grazier, &c.] A contagious mortality of the
cattle had prevailed in the preceding year, on the Continent. The

piety of a Methodist. We had reason to expect, that notice would have been taken of the petitions which the King had received from the English nation; and although I can conceive some personal motives for not yielding to them, I can find none, in common prudence or decency,· for treating them with contempt. Be assured, my Lord, the English people will not tamely submit to this unworthy treatment......they had a right to be heard; and their petitions, if not granted, deserved to be considered. Whatever be the real views and doctrine of a court, the Sovereign should be taught to preserve some forms of attention to his subjects; and, if he will not redress their grievances, not to make them a topic of jest and mockery among lords and ladies of the bed-chamber. Injuries may be atoned for, and forgiven; but insults admit of no compensation. They degrade the mind in its own esteem, and force it to recover its level by revenge. This

infection made its way into this island. The Privy Council, to stop its progress, ordered, by a proclamation, that all cattle which could be suspected of having caught it, should be instantly slain, and the carcasses buried. And, to enforce the proclamation, re-imbursement, at a certain rate a head for the cattle slain, was offered to those who should give timely obedience to it. The danger was great; the alarm general; the measure of prevention salutary. The King mentioned it in his speech, at the opening of the next session of parliament; both for these reasons, and because the order of the Privy Council, was one which, without the express directions of parliament, nothing but an extraordinary exigence of circumstances could justify. The first paragraph of the King's speech to both Houses of Parliament, was employed upon the distemper among the *horned cattle.* Nor can we deny, that a wag or a satirist might indeed find in it matter for ridicule.

neglect of the petitions was however a part of your original plan of government; nor will any consequences it has produced account for your deserting your Sovereign, in the midst of that distress in which you and your * new friends had involved him. One would think, my Lord, you might have taken this spirited resolution before you had dissolved the last of those early connexions, which once, even in your own opinion, did honour to your youth;...before you had obliged Lord Granby to quit a service he was attached to;....before you had discarded one chancellor, and killed another.... To what an abject condition have you laboured to

* The Bedford party.

Obliged Lord Granby, &c.] Lord Granby probably acted in resigning, that part which, according to the opinions he had been persuaded to adopt, honour and conscience dictated to him. But, the resigners in general resigned, only that they might come in again with the Earl of Chatham and the Marquis of Rockingham.

Discarded one Chancellor.] Lord Camden.

Killed another.] Mr. Yorke. Whatever might be the cause of the rash act that was said to have ended Mr. Yorke's life; he did not, in accepting the seals, shew any political versatility that he had not before evinced. His Whiggism had never been obstinate. On this occasion, indeed, he deserted the Duke of Newcastle, and all his father's ancient friends, by accepting the office of Chancellor. Perhaps he might, on reflection, feel a remorse for deserting his friends, which would not have been excited by the desertion of his principles. He was a sound lawyer, an eloquent pleader, a polite scholar. The Athenian Letters, the production chiefly of himself and his brother, Lord Hardwicke, contain some fine specimens of his taste and skill in classical literature.

He was much beloved in private life.

He was said to have accepted the seals reluctantly, and only at the pressing solicitation of the King himself.

reduce the best of princes, when the unhappy man, who yields at last to such personal instance and solicitation as never can be fairly employed against a subject, feels himself degraded by his compliance, and is unable to survive the disgraceful honours which his gracious Sovereign had compelled him to accept. He was a man of spirit, for he had a quick sense of shame, and death has redeemed his character. I know your Grace too well, to appeal to your feelings upon this event; but there is another heart, not yet, I hope, quite callous to the touch of humanity, to which it ought to be a dreadful lesson for ever*.

Now, my Lord, let us consider the situation to which you have conducted, and in which you have thought it adviseable to abandon, your royal master. Whenever the people have complained, and nothing better could be said in defence of the measures of government, it has been the fashion to answer us, though not very fairly, with an appeal to the private virtues of your Sovereign. " Has he not, " to relieve the people, surrendered a considera- " ble part of his revenue?.....Has he not made the " judges independent, by fixing them in their " places for life?"....My Lord, we acknowledge the gracious principle which gave birth to these concessions; and have nothing to regret but that it has

---

* The most secret particulars of this detestable transaction, shall in due time be given to the public. The people shall know what kind of man they have to deal with.

never been adhered to. At the end of seven years, we are loaded with a debt of above five hundred thousand pounds upon the civil list, and we now see the Chancellor of Great Britain tyrannically forced out of his office, not for want of abilities not for want of integrity, or of attention to his duty, but for delivering his honest opinion in parliament, upon the greatest constitutional question that has arisen since the revolution....We care not to whose private virtues you appeal.....the theory of such a government is falsehood and mockery;... the practice is oppression. You have laboured then (though I confess to no purpose) to rob your master of the only plausible answer that ever was given in defence of his government.....of the opinion which the people had conceived of his personal

Loaded with a debt, &c.] There had been no excessive profusion in the expenditure upon the civil list. But, in fixing the allowance of that list, it had been endeavoured to make the sum as moderate as possible: and due provision had not been made for those uncertain occasions of expence, which cannot be particularly foreseen, yet never fail to arise.

The Chancellor of Great Britain tyrannically forced, &c.] This complaint is unjust. It were absurdly weak to retain ministers in office, when they will no longer support the measures which have been agreed upon in the cabinet.

Opinion which the people had conceived, &c.] This passage is one, among many others in these Letters, proving that the Opposition found the fair character of their Sovereign among his people to be the most formidable of all the obstacles which stood in the way of their ambition. It gave a force to the expression of his intentions, which nothing else could have added to them : and it commanded the confidence of the people in the general system of his government, at a time when, but for this, the minds of many might have been wholly alienated from it.

honour and integrity.....The Duke of Bedford was more moderate than your Grace. He only forced his master to violate a solemn promise made to an individual*. But you, my Lord, have successfully extended your advice to every political, every moral engagement, that could bind either the magistrate or the man. The condition of a King is often miserable, but it required your Grace's abilities to make it contemptible.....You will say, perhaps, that the faithful servants, in whose hands you have left him, are able to retrieve his honour, and to support his government. You have publickly declared, even since your resignation, that you approved of their measures, and admired their conduct....particularly that of the Earl of Sandwich. What a pity it is that, with all this appearance, you should think it necessary to separate yourself from such amiable companions! You forget, my Lord, that while you

---

* Mr. Stuart Mackenzie.

Earl of Sandwich.] This nobleman was of the Bedford party; a man of talents, and notoriously profligate. Wilkes's famous pamphlet, *An Essay on Woman*, was complained of to the House of Lords, by Lord Sandwich and Dr. Warburton: and much obloquy was excited against the former, for putting himself forward as an accuser of blasphemy and obscenity, while he was, himself, not a little addicted to these vices of speech. He was at the head of the Admiralty, during the difficult period of the American war: and it is well known, that the naval service was never more gloriously maintained, than throughout that perilous, and in many respects disastrous time. A continued neglect of character, on his own part, however, hindered the public from doing justice to the talents and virtues which he certainly possessed.

You forget, my Lord, &c.] The Duke of Grafton might disagree with the other Members of the Cabinet Council, in regard to

are lavish in the praise of men whom you desert, you are publickly opposing your conduct to your opinions, and depriving yourself of the only plausible pretence you had for leaving your Sovereign overwhelmed with distress: I call it plausible; for, in truth, there is no reason whatsoever, less than the frowns of your master, that could justify a man of spirit for abandoning his post at a moment so critical and important. It is in vain to evade the question; if you will not speak out, the public have a right to judge from appearances. We are authorised to conclude, that you either differed from your colleagues, whose measures you still affect to defend, or that you thought the administration of the King's affairs no longer tenable......You are at liberty to choose between the hypocrite and the coward. Your best friends are in doubt which way they shall incline. Your country unites the characters, and gives you credit for them both. For my own part, I see nothing inconsistent in your conduct. You began with betraying the people....you conclude with betraying the King.

In your treatment of particular persons, you have preserved the uniformity of your character.

some particular measure, without disapproving the general system: or, he might feel himself unequal to the ministerial difficulties of the time: or, he might have a virtuous fear of exposing himself longer to all that obloquy and odium, which the measures of the administration continued to draw upon him.

Even Mr. Bradshaw declares that no man was ever so ill used as himself. As to the provision * you have made for his family, he was entitled to it by the house he lives in. The successor of one Chancellor might well pretend to be the rival of another. It is the breach of private friendship which touches Mr. Bradshaw; and, to say the truth, when a man of his rank and abilities had taken so active a part in your affairs, he ought not to have been let down at last with a miserable pension of fifteen hundred pounds a year. Colonel Luttrell, Mr. Onslow, and Governor Burgoyne, were equally engaged with you, and have rather more reason to complain than Mr. Bradshaw. These are men, my Lord, whose friendship you should have

---

Even Mr. Bradshaw, &c.] JUNIUS's note, and his text, are here at variance. The one says, that Bradshaw's pension was too little; the other represents it to have been too much. It was, in truth, enough for his services, but too little for his wants.

* A pension of 1500l. per annum, insured upon the 4 1-half per cents, (he was too cunning to trust it to Irish security) for the lives of himself and all his sons. This gentleman, who a very few years ago was clerk to a contractor for forage, and afterwards exalted to a petty post in the war-office, thought it necessary, (as soon as he was appointed Secretary to the Treasury) to take that great house in Lincoln's-Inn Fields, in which the Earl of Northington had resided while he was Lord High Chancellor of Great Britain. As to the pension, Lord North very solemnly assured the House of Commons, that no pension was ever so well deserved as Mr Bradshaw's ....N. B. Lord Camden and Sir Jeffery Amherst, are not near so well provided for; and Sir Edward Hawke, who saved the state, retires with two thousand pounds a year on the Irish establishment, from which he in fact receives less than Mr. Bradshaw's pension.

adhered to, on the same principle on which you deserted Lord Rockingham, Lord Chatham, Lord Camden, and the Duke of Portland. We can easily account for your violating your engagements with men of honour ; but why should you betray your natural connexions ? Why separate yourself from Lord Sandwich. Lord Gower, and Mr. Rigby, or leave the three worthy gentlemen above-mentioned to shift for themselves ? With all the fashionable indulgence of the times, this country does not abound in characters like theirs ; and you may find it a difficult matter to recruit the black catalogue of your friends.

The recollection of the royal patent you sold to Mr. Hine, obliges me to say a word in defence of a man whom you have taken the most dishonour-able means to injure. I do not refer to the sham prosecution which you affected to carry on against him. On that ground, I doubt not, he is prepared to meet you with ten-fold recrimination, and set you at defiance. The injury you had done him af-

Mr. Hine, &c.] In respect to Hine's place, the truth is....that General Burgoyne was actually nominated Comptroller of Chester ; but left the duty, and the annual income from it, to persons who paid him, at once, a round sum for the whole.

The injury you had done him, &c.] This attempt to justify Vaughan is vain. He himself applied to the Duke, in a way that shewed him to be conscious of the illegality of that which he pro-posed. The life interest of some particular patentee, might, in-deed have been sold *under a decree of the Court of Chancery ;* but the office itself had never been directly and avowedly sold by the crown.

fects his moral character. You knew that the offer to purchase the reversion of a place, which has heretofore been sold under a decree of the Court of Chancery, however imprudent in his situation, would no way tend to cover him with that sort of guilt which you wished to fix upon him in the eyes of the world. You laboured, then, by every species of false suggestion, and even by publishing counterfeit letters, to have it understood, that he had proposed terms of accommodation to you, and had offered to abandon his principles, his party, and his friends. You consulted your own breast for a character of consummate treachery, and gave it to the public for that of Mr. Vaughan. I think myself obliged to do this justice to an injured man, because I was deceived by the appearances thrown out by your Grace, and have frequently spoken of his conduct with indignation. If he really be, what I think him, honest though mistaken, he will be happy in recovering his reputation, though at the expence of his understanding. Here, I see, the matter is likely to rest. Your Grace is afraid to carry on the prosecution. Mr. Hine keeps quiet possession of his purchase ; and Governor Burgoyne relieved from the apprehension of refunding the money, sits down, for the remainder of his life, INFAMOUS AND CONTENTED.

I believe, my Lord, I may now take my leave of you for ever. You are no longer that resolute minister who had spirit to support the most violent

measures; who compensated for the want of good
and great qualities, by a brave determination (which
some people admired and relied on) to maintain
himself without them. The reputation of obstinacy and perseverance might have supplied the
place of all the absent virtues. You have now
added the last negative to your character, and
meanly confessed that you are destitute of the common spirit of a man. Retire then, my Lord, and
hide your blushes from the world; for, with such a
load of shame, even BLACK may change its colour.
A mind such as yours, in the solitary hours of domestic enjoyment, may still find topics of consolation. You may find it in the memory of violated
friendship; in the afflictions of an accomplished
prince, whom you have disgraced and deserted;
and in the agitations of a great country, driven by
your counsels to the brink of destruction.

The palm of ministerial firmness is now transferred to Lord North. He tells us so himself, with
the plenitude of the *ore rotundo* *; and I am ready

Lord North.] Lord North was, from early youth, esteemed one
of the most amiable and promising young noblemen in England.
He was proposed by the Princess Dowager, for a place about the
King, before his accession to the throne. The utmost intreaties of
the same lady, were necessary to persuade his Lordship to accept
the office of Chancellor of the Exchequer, after the death of
Charles Townshend. He was modest, candid, yielding, upright,
of vigorous and lively yet not overbearing talents. Few ministers
have ever been so much personally beloved as he, even by their
political opponents.

* This eloquent person has got as far as the *discipline* of Demos-

enough to believe that, while he can keep his place, he will not easily be persuaded to resign it. Your Grace was the firm minister of yesterday; Lord North is the firm minister of to-day. To-morrow, perhaps, his Majesty, in his wisdom, may give us a rival for you both. You are too well acquainted with the temper of your late allies, to think it possible that Lord North should be permitted to govern this country. If we may believe common fame, they have shewn him their superiority already. His Majesty is, indeed, too gracious to insult his subjects, by choosing his first minister from among the domestics of the Duke of Bedford. That would have been too gross an outrage to the three kingdoms. Their purpose, however, is equally answered by pushing forward this unhappy figure, and forcing it to bear the odium of measures, which they, in reality direct. Without immediately appearing to govern, they possess the power, and distribute the emoluments of government, as they think proper. They still adhere to the spirit of that calculation, which made Mr. Luttrell representative of Middlesex. Far from regretting your retreat, they assure us very gravely, that it increases the real strength of the ministry.

thenes. He constantly speaks with pebbles in his mouth, to improve his articulation.

Their purpose, &c.] It is true, that the party of the Duke of Bedford now predominated in the administration.

It increases the real strength, &c.] There might now be greater unanimity in the cabinet.

According to this way of reasoning, they will probably grow stronger, and more flourishing, every hour they exist; for I think there is hardly a day passes, in which some one or other of his Majesty's servants does not leave them to improve by the loss of his assistance. But, alas! their countenances speak a different language. When the Members drop off, the main body cannot be insensible of its approaching dissolution. Even the violence of their proceedings is a signal of despair. Like broken tenants, who have had warning to quit the premises, they curse their landlord, destroy the fixtures, throw every thing into confusion, and care not what mischief they do to the estate.

JUNIUS.

When the members drop off, &c.] These prophetic periods are admirably eloquent. But the prophecy was disappointed.

LETTER XXXVII.

TO THE PRINTER OF THE PUBLIC ADVERTISER.

*THE combination of the Whigs ; the bold harangues of Chatham,
breathing more of wild democracy, and of the pride of high character and acknowledged talents, than of reason or true eloquence ;
even the dissentions and mutual suspicions among the ministers ;
and all the clamours and addresses of the people, though sustained,
exasperated, and enforced, by the eloquence of* JUNIUS, *failed of
compelling the King to abandon those principles of government, to
which he had adhered since the beginning of his reign. If the
people of the capital made themselves factiously busy in promoting
the views of the Opposition ; on the other hand, the* country gentlemen *in parliament, whose independency of fortune set them
above any base subserviency to ministers, and who were not by
any connexions involved in the cabals of faction, indignant of
the seditious abuse with which they saw the powers of government insulted, overlooked for the time its errors, and earnestly supported its authority.*

*With a rage which was exasperated by the sense of its impotence, the
agitators of the metropolis were excited to an insolent exercise of
the right of petitioning, such as rivalled the boldest audacity of the
Londoners in the beginning of the troubles of the reign of Charles
the First. On the 14th of March* 1770, *Beckford, Lord Mayor, a
man who was the blind follower and instrument of the earl of Chatham, presented to the King, at St. James's, a remonstrating address
and petition of the Lord Mayor, Aldermen, and Livery, of the city
of London, in which the conduct of the ministry was bitterly arraigned ; and it was demanded of the King, that he should forth-
with dissolve the parliament. The authors of that remonstrance
dared to question the legality of the existence of the House of
Commons, after its decision in the case of the Middlesex Election ;
and insinuated, that the King could not, without violating his coro-
nation oath, refuse to comply with their demand. His Majesty re-*

plied with firmness : blaming, without any thing of impotent violence, the audacity and unreasonableness of the demands in the petition ; and asserting his unalterable vigilance to preserve the genuine principles of the constitution, free from all violation. There is a remarkable contrast between this petition and the Sovereign's answer. The former is filled with all the boldness of JUNIUS, without his eloquence or dignity of address. The latter is manly, dignified, and, except in one or two phrases, unites with the firmness of conscious wisdom and virtue, a calm and impressive moderation.

The cause of Opposition was not successfully served by this outrageous conduct on the part of the Livery of London. The House of Commons, having seen the legality of their own existence impeached, zealously took part with their Sovereign, against the turbulent Londoners.

In this Letter, JUNIUS regrets, with an air of deep affliction, the miseries which were threatened by what he accounted the arbitrary injustice of the government, and by that resistance which he wished it to provoke from a people whom he laboured to persuade that they were deeply injured and insulted. He pronounces an high eulogium on the seditious audacity of the Livery of London. He endeavours to persuade the rest of the nation, to take arms on their side. He attempts the justification of that daring assertion in the petition, that the legality of the existence of the House of Commons, had been destroyed by its decision respecting the Middlesex Election. He dares to reprobate the manner in which the petition of the Livery had been received at court ; and, with malignity sufficiently acute, exposes whatever was the least irreprehensible in the Sovereign's answer. With spirit and cogency of reasoning, he asserts the legality of petitions from the people for the dissolution of the parliament. In opposition to the complacent assertions in the answer to the Livery, he enumerates the errors and illegalities into which the government had fallen since the commencement of the present reign ; and affirms, that the British monarch never could be popular, whose administration was disgraced by acts of tyranny or folly, like these.

This Letter is well written. It abounds in acute distinctions of reasoning, and in bold flashes of eloquence. But, there is in it some-

what too much of vulgar abuse ; and its paragraphs seem to have been thrown out upon paper, without the preconception of any regular plan.

It seems to have been during this session of parliament, that the clamours of the Whigs began, from their continuance and their ridiculous violence, to lose all influence over the minds of the unprejudiced part of the nation. Lord Chatham, the Livery of London, and even the shrewder and more deeply artful mind of JUNIUS, by the indecency and outrage of their attacks, and by the disproportion between their complaints and the grievances of which they had to complain, actually roused the affections of a great part of the people, to the defence of the majesty of the Sovereign, and the sanctity of the legislature ; and thus contributed to the defeat of the very purpose which they themselves had in view. The event was not unlike to that which took place, when Charles the Second dissolved that parliament, by which he was so much harassed, in regard to the exclusion of the Duke of York from the hope of succession to the throne. Truth failed, for a time, of its proper effect, because it was accompanied with extravagant outrage.

SIR,   19. *March*, 1770.

I BELIEVE there is no man, however indifferent about the interests of this country, who will not readily confess that the situation to which we are now reduced, whether it has arisen from the violence of faction, or from an arbitrary system of government, justifies the most melancholy apprehensions, and calls for the exertion of whatever wisdom or vigour is left among us. The King's answer to the remonstrance of the city of London, and the measures since adopted by the ministry,

Whether it has *arisen, &c.*] JUNIUS ought to have here written *have*. The English language possesses that form of the verb, which is called the subjunctive mood; and our best grammarians have asserted the propriety of religiously employing it in its proper place.

amount to a plain declaration, that the principle on which Mr. Luttrell was seated in the House of Commons, is to be supported in all its consequences, and carried to its utmost extent. The same spirit which violated the freedom of election, now invades the declaration and bill of rights, and threatens to punish the subject for exercising a privilege,

Is to be supported in all its consequences, &c.] This did not appear. The government could not but be aware, that they were in the wrong ; for the point in contest, had been amply and decisively discussed. But they could not recede. They knew not well, what steps to take. They were saved only by the outrageous violence of their adversaries. They certainly would not have repeated the decision of the Middlesex election, though a similar occasion should have arisen. In the debate relative to the petition which is the subject of this Letter, the House of Commons suffered themselves to be braved by Beckford and the other Members for London, without daring to take any vigorous step for the vindication of their own authority.

And threatens to punish the subject, &c.] The discussion upon the petition was still prolonged. This Letter by JUNIUS was written on the 19th of March. It was not till the 23d of that month, that the House of Commons, with the concurrence of the Lords, offered an address to the sovereign, expressing deep concern for that abuse of the right of petitioning, of which the Livery of London had set an example ; and thanking their sovereign for the constitutional dignity, firmness, and rectitude, of his answer.

Severe animadversion is said to have been, at first, intended. But, upon mature deliberation, a step was preferred which in its effects would be intermediate between outrageous violence and feeble timidity.

The prudence of the government is much more to be commended in this, than in various former instances. But, any person who shall now consider that petition, will not fail to see that, in it, the Livery of London had overstepped the just bounds of petition and remonstrance, and had, in fact, committed *an act of sedition......* They did not so much ask, as clamorously command ; and they accused the proceedings of the House of Commons, in a tone, by which its *necessary* privileges were certainly infringed. Not the

hitherto undisputed, of petitioning the Crown. The grievances of the people are aggravated by insults; their complaints not merely disregarded, but check-ed by authority; and every one of those acts, against which they remonstrated, confirmed by the King's decisive approbation. At such a moment, no honest man will remain silent or inactive.... However distinguished by rank or property, in the rights of freedom we are all equal. As we are Englishmen, the least considerable man among us has an interest equal to the proudest nobleman, in the laws and constitution of his country, and is equally called upon to make a generous contribu-tion in support of them;....whether it be the heart to conceive, the understanding to direct, or the hand to execute. It is a common cause, in which we are all interested, in which we should all be en-gaged. The man who deserts it at this alarming crisis, is an enemy to his country; and, what I think of infinitely less importance, a traitor to his Sovereign. The subject who is truly loyal to the chief magistrate, will neither advise nor submit to arbitrary measures. The city of London have given an example, which, I doubt not, will be followed by the whole kingdom. The noble spirit of the

Long Parliament to Charles the First; not the Americans in the commencement of their rebellion....even though imitating the ex-ample of the citizens of London; spoke a language so violent.

Which, I doubt not, will be followed by the whole kingdom.] In spite of the endeavours of democratical agitators; in spite of the powerful eloquence of JUNIUS; it was not followed so extensively as he and his friends expected. Dr. Johnson, in his pamphlet, inti-tled, *The False Alarm*, which was, about this time, very seasona-

metropolis is the life-blood of the state, collected
at the heart: from that point it circulates, with
health and vigour, through every artery of the constitution. The time is come, when the body of the
English people must assert their own cause : conscious of their strength, and animated by a sense of
their duty, they will not surrender their birth-right
to ministers, parliaments, or kings. The city of
London have expressed their sentiments with freedom and firmness ; they have spoken truth boldly ;
and, in whatever light their remonstrance may be
represented by courtiers, I defy the most subtle
lawyer in this country to point out a single instance
in which they have exceeded the truth. Even
that assertion, which we are told is most offensive
to parliament, in the theory of the English constitution, is strictly true. If any part of the representative body be not chosen by the people, that
part vitiates and corrupts the whole. If there be
a defect in the representation of the people, that
power, which alone is equal to the making of the
laws in this country, is not complete, and the acts
of parliament under that circumstance are not the

bly published, has admirably ridiculed the arts which were in different parts of the kingdom employed, to procure those petitions
with which it was desired that the monarch should be insulted.

That part vitiates and corrupts the whole.] This doctrine cannot be adopted, in the practice of the British constitution. A House
of Commons must be considered, notwithstanding any inferior imperfections, as being legal; so long as it is acknowledged as such by
the other branches of the legislature, and not opposed, in its legislative authority, by the actual and constitutional resistance of the
whole body of the people. Should we adopt the doctrine of JUNIUS;
we must at once annul the whole system of the British statutes.

acts of a pure and entire legislature. I speak of
the theory of our constitution; and, whatever difficulties or inconveniences may attend the practice,
I am ready to maintain that, as far as the fact de-
viates from the principle, so far the practice is
vicious and corrupt. I have not heard a question
raised upon any other part of the remonstrance.
That the principle, on which the Middlesex election
was determined, is more pernicious in its effects,
than either the levying of ship-money by Charles
the First, or the suspending power assumed by his
son, will hardly be disputed by any man who understands or wishes well to the English constitution. It is not an act of open violence done by the
King, or any direct or palpable breach of the laws
attempted by his minister, that can ever endanger
the liberties of this country. Against such a King
or minister the people would immediately take the
alarm, and all the parties unite to oppose him. The
laws may be grossly violated in particular instances,
without any direct attack upon the whole system.
Facts of that kind stand alone; they are attributed
to necessity, not defended by principle. We can

That the principle, &c.] It is not to be denied, that few principles could be ultimately more dangerous, or more unconstitutional,
than.....that any member, whom the House of Commons might resolve to expel, was not re-eligible into the same parliament from
which he had been dismissed; and that the ineligibility of such a
person, must entirely annihilate whatever votes should be given in
his favour. But the *levying of ship-money*, was an arrogation to the
crown, of the whole essential power of the House of Commons. And
the irregularity controverted by JUNIUS, made but a *comparatively*
small violation of the rights of electors.

never be really in danger, until the forms of parliament are made use of to destroy the substance of our civil and political liberties;......until parliament itself betrays its trust, by contributing to establish new principles of government, and employing the very weapons committed to it by the collective body, to stab the constitution.

As for the terms of the remonstrance, I presume it will not be affirmed, by any person less polished than a gentleman-usher, that this is a season for compliments. Our gracious King indeed is abundantly civil to himself. Instead of an answer to a petition, his Majesty very graciously pronounces his own panegyric; and I confess that, as far as his personal behaviour, or the royal purity of his intentions, is concerned, the truth of those declarations which the minister has drawn up for his master, cannot decently be disputed. In every other respect, I affirm, that they are absolutely unsupported, either in argument or fact. I must add too, that supposing the speech were otherwise unexceptionable, it is not a direct answer to the petition of the city. His Majesty is pleased to say, that he is always ready to receive the requests of his subjects; yet the sheriffs were twice sent back with an excuse, and it was certainly debated in council whether or no the magistrates of the city of London should be admitted to an audience.....
Whether the remonstrance be or be not injurious to parliament, is the very question between the parliament and the people; and such a question as

cannot be decided by the assertion of a third party, however respectable. That the petitioning for a dissolution of parliament is irreconcileable with the principles of the constitution, is a new doctrine. His Majesty perhaps has not been informed, that the House of Commons themselves have, by a formal resolution, admitted it to be the right of the subject. His Majesty proceeds to assure us, that he has made the laws the rule of his conduct...... Was it in ordering or permitting his ministers to apprehend Mr. Wilkes by a general warrant?...... Was it in suffering his ministers to revive the obsolete maxim of *nullum tempus*, to rob the Duke of Portland of his property, and thereby give a decisive turn to a county election?....Was it in erecting a chamber consultation of surgeons, with authority to examine into and supersede the legal verdict of a jury? Or did his Majesty consult the laws of this country, when he permitted his secretary of state to declare that, whenever the civil magistrate

Cannot be decided by the assertion of a third party, &c.] Would JUNIUS deny, that it was as constitutional for the King to determine for himself in regard to the dissolution of the parliament, as for the City of London to demand that dissolution? The agitators in the City of London, seem to have been at that time violently inclined to play the same part, which has been since acted by the Parisians.

Was it in ordering, &c.] This and the succeeding periods of interrogation, compose the most eloquent and judicious part of this Letter. JUNIUS dwells upon the proper topics; and exhibits, together, with skilful aggravation, those acts, which were, alone, materially reprehensible, in that conduct of the government against which he inveighed.

is trifled with, a military force must be sent for, *without the delay of a moment*, and effectually employed? Or was it in the barbarous exactness with which this illegal, inhuman doctrine, was carried into execution?....If his Majesty had recollected these facts, I think he would never have said, at least with any reference to the measures of his government, that he had made the laws the rule of his conduct. To talk of preserving the affections, or relying on the support of his subjects, while he continues to act upon these principles, is indeed paying a compliment to their loyalty, which I hope they have too much spirit and understanding to deserve.

His Majesty, we are told, is not only punctual in the performance of his own duty, but careful not to assume any of those powers which the constitution has placed in other hands. Admitting this last assertion to be strictly true, it is no way to the purpose. The city of London have not desired the King to assume a power placed in other hands. If they had, I should hope to see the person, who dared to present such a petition, immediately impeached. They solicit their Sovereign to exert that constitutional authority, which the laws have vested in him, for the benefit of his subjects. They call upon him to make use of his lawful prerogative, in a case which our laws evidently supposed might happen, since they have provided for it by trusting the Sovereign with a discretionary power to dissolve the parliament. This request will, I am confident, be supported by remonstrances from all parts of the kingdom. His Majesty will find, at last, that this is the sense of his people; and that it is not his interest to support either ministry or parliament, at the hazard of a breach with the collective body of his subjects....That he is the King of a free people, is indeed his greatest glory. That he may long continue the King of a free people, is the second wish that animates my heart. The first is, THAT THE PEOPLE MAY BE FREE*.

His Majesty will find, at last, &c.] The King at last found, that his people were ready to support him against all the democratical violence of the Whigs, and the City of London; but that the illegal decision upon the Middlesex election, was in due time to be rescinded.

* When his Majesty had done reading his speech, the Lord Mayor, &c. had the honour of kissing his Majesty's hand; after which, as they were withdrawing, his Majesty instantly turned round to his courtiers, *and burst out a laughing.*

_____ *Nero fiddled, while Rome was burning.* JOHN HORNE.

⁕ LETTER XXXVIII.

TO THE PRINTER OF THE PUBLIC ADVERTISER.

—

I AM willing to believe that JUNIUS *might find it occasionally requisite, to support and defend measures which he would not have originally proposed. The hope of triumph, by the union of the two Whig parties, inspired the opposition at the beginning of the year* 1770. *By the difficulties which seemed still to thwart their success, the Earl of Chatham was provoked to break out, in parliament, into speeches, of which the spirit andt endency were wildly democratical. Even his speeches, and the strength of his party, could not prevail. The timid and the insincere, might abandon administration : but a majority of the two Houses of Parliament, and of the nation in general, were disposed to support the government of their King. The outrages of Chatham, served in truth to extenuate, and to cover, those errors of administration, which they were designed to aggravate and expose. In the impotent wrath of disappointed ambition, Chatham and the Whigs moved their creature Beckford, and the agitators of the city, to insult the sovereign with an address, in which the decency of petition and remonstrance, was strikingly violated. Had that address either frightened the Sovereign from his purpose, or driven ministry to some act, irregular, like the issuing of the general warrants against the authors, printers, and publishers, of the North Briton, or like the decision in the case of the Middlesex election ; the purpose of its advisers would have been effectually served. The King replied with dignity and firmness. The addressers and their patrons were confounded.* JUNIUS *wrote the Thirty-seventh Letter in this collection, to encourage the city ; to plead their apology with the nation : to harass the House of Commons, who were then deliberating what part it might become them to act, in asserting their own legislative authority, and in strengthening the hands of their King against the insolence of the city patriots. The House of Commons adopted a measure that was worthy of their dignity, yet not rash nor violent. The opprobrium of unconstitutional rashness, was now transferred from the government to the patriots.* JUNIUS, *in this Letter, strives again to vindicate what the city had done ; accuses his Sovereign of rash ungraciousness ; and imputes, with ridicule, the charge of pusillanimity, to the minister and the House of Commons....This Letter is powerfully and impressively written ; but wants that clearness and cogency of reasoning, which never fail to distinguish the compositions of* JUNIUS, *when he knows himself to be entirely in the right. It was, however, useful to the views of his party. The city was now meditating a new address, as a sort of answer to the address of the House of Commons. The voice of* JUNIUS *was necessary to encourage the Livery, and to recommend their conduct to support and imitation.*

SIR,   3. *April*, 1770.

IN my last Letter, I offered you my opinion of the truth and propriety of his Majesty's answer to the city of London, considering it merely as the speech of a minister, drawn up in his own defence, and delivered, as usual, by the chief magistrate. I would separate, as much as possible, the King's personal character and behaviour from the acts of the present government. I wish it to be understood, that his Majesty had, in effect, no more concern in the substance of what he said, than Sir James Hodges had in the remonstrance ;

Sir James Hodges, &c.] Sir James Hodges was, I believe, a stationer on London Bridge. He aspired to become a Common Council-man ; and succeeded. By a knack at speechifying, and a forward bustling activity, he made himself considerable among his fellows. In the days when the city-patriots deemed themselves umpires of the fate of the British government and empire, this man obtained the lucrative appointment of *Town Clerk to the City of*

and that, as Sir James, in virtue of his office, was obliged to speak the sentiments of the people, his Majesty might think himself bound, by the same official obligation, to give a graceful utterance to the sentiments of his minister. The cold formality of a well-repeated lesson, is widely distant from the animated expression of the heart.

This distinction, however, is only true with respect to the measure itself. The consequences of it reach beyond the minister, and materially affect his Majesty's honour. In their own nature, they are formidable enough to alarm a man of prudence, and disgraceful enough to afflict a man of spirit. A subject, whose sincere attachment to his Majesty's person and family is founded upon rational principles, will not, in the present conjuncture, be scrupulous of alarming, or even of afflicting, his Sovereign. I know there is another sort of loyalty, of which his Majesty has had plentiful experience. When the loyalty of Tories, Jacobites, and Scotchmen, has once taken possession of an unhappy Prince, it seldom leaves him without accomplishing his destruction. When the poison of their doc-

London. The honour of Knighthood crowned his greatness. In his character of *Town Clerk*, he signed the famous *remonstrance and petition*. JUNIUS here attempts to make the official functions of his Sovereign ridiculous, by comparing them to those of Sir James Hodges.

When the poison, &c.] The figures of this period, are splendidly elaborate ; yet neither incongruous, nor too artificial. This is an instance of ornament employed in the highest degree in which it is compatible with force or beauty, yet not exceeding that degree.

trines has tainted the natural benevolence of his disposition, when their insidious councils have corrupted the *stamina* of his government, what antidote can restore him to his political health and honour, but the firm sincerity of his English subjects ?

It has not been usual in this country, at least since the days of Charles the First, to see the Sovereign personally at variance or engaged in a direct altercation with his subjects. Acts of grace and indulgence are wisely appropriated to him, and should constantly be performed by himself. He never should appear but in an amiable light to his subjects. Even in France, as long as any ideas of a limited monarchy were thought worth preserving, it was a maxim, that no man should leave the royal presence discontented. They have lost or re-

They have lost, &c.] At this very time, the provincial parliaments, or courts of justice, in France, and still more remarkably, that of Paris, were breaking out into an opposition against the royal authority ; of which the effects were, at length, to terminate in their own destruction, and that of the power which they resisted.

. The *origin of the parliaments of France*, was nearly similar to that of the parliament of England.

France anciently consisted of a number of great Feudal Principalities, almost independent of the crown, and of one another.......
Each of the feudal chiefs of those principalities, was by the laws of feodism obliged to assemble his vassals ; that they might act as his great assize in the distribution of justice ; and that he might obtain from their consent, those extraordinary supplies, which he at any time wanted. These were the States, or Parliaments, of the different provinces of ancient France. The occasional meetings of

nounced the moderate principles of their government; and now, when their parliaments venture to remonstrate, the tyrant comes forward, and answers absolutely for himself. The spirit of their present

the States were found, gradually, to be inadequate to the purposes of the regular distribution of justice. Hence, a select number were nominated out of their body, who should permanently compose the assize, to assist the Sovereign, or his chief judicial minister, in doing justice among his vassals. Thus were the judicial parliaments formed, in all the provincial governments of old France. But the provincial parliaments were the courts of Counts or Dukes, subject, at least nominally, to the King. At Paris, was the King's own parliament, in which the Counts and Dukes could sit only as Peers, with the King's great officers of ordinary administration.... In this parliament, as in the others, it became necessary, for the sake of the regular distribution of justice, that a certain number of the members should constantly assist, as judges, and should enjoy adequate emoluments, in compensation for the functions which they discharged....After permanent committees, as it were, out of all the different parliaments, had been thus formed for the ordinary administration of justice ; the meetings of the states were as much as possible discontinued. The nobility were excused from other burthens, on account of their service in the army. The clergy, from time to time, made their own compromises with the crown. Unembarrassed by any interposition of these two bodies, the crown levied, at pleasure, whatever revenue it chose, from the people of the third estate ; treating them, not as vassals holding under charter, but as *serfs*, rising irregularly into somewhat of imperfect emancipation....The laws, for all who had an original right to the advantage of law, were understood to be permanently settled. Those new interpretations of them, which changing circumstances should demand, might, as it seemed, originate, with sufficient propriety, from the monarch alone ; provided only, that he preserved to the nobles and the clergy, their just privileges. The *edicts* of the Sovereign were however, to be inserted in the registers of the courts of justice ; and without this insertion, those edicts were not understood to receive that publication, which could alone oblige the courts to decide by them as law....It was a maxim in the French, as in the English law, *that the King could do no wrong.* Upon this maxim, the par-

constitution requires, that the King should be feared; and the principle, I believe, is tolerably supported by the fact. But, in our political system, the theory is at variance with the practice,

liaments, whenever they judged any new edict to be inconsistent with the beneficent spirit of the former laws, denied it to be actually the King's will, and refused to register it as such, till the Sovereign should personally inform them, that it was indeed so, and should command its registration....Although the parliament of Paris was, originally, the only Supreme Court of the King in all France; yet the successive annexations of all the great fiefs to the crown, brought the other parliaments to a near similarity of jurisdiction with that of Paris; made them, likewise, courts for the registration of the laws of the kingdom; and established a necessity for the formal notification of the royal edicts to those parliaments, if not by the King personally, at least by a vicegerent or lieutenant-general invested with his authority, and representing his person. Thus, with some restriction from the privileges of the nobility and the clergy, the legislative and judicial power in ancient France, remained solely with the King, and with the Parliaments, which were, in their origin, merely permanent Committees out of the Assemblies of the States.

In the progress of the French History, the States, as such, became, continually, of less weight. The nobles and the clergy, were still more completely subjugated under the power of the crown. The unprivileged people became perpetually more numerous, opulent, and impatient of oppression. The parliament, by that force, which law necessarily acquires in every civilized country, gained, constantly, new authority with the people, and new strength to withstand even the crown itself.

About the very time when JUNIUS wrote these Letters, the parliaments, supported by the growing consequence of the people, were embarrassing the French monarch with a resistance to his plans of taxation, which was very unlike to the submission of former times. The monarch threatened, banished, dissolved, but without effectual success. Louis the Sixteenth, at his accession,

for, the King should be beloved. Measures of greater severity may, indeed, in some circumstances, be necessary; but the Minister who advises, should take the execution and odium of them entirely upon himself. He not only betrays his master, but violates the spirit of the English constitution, when he exposes the chief magistrate to the personal hatred or contempt of his subjects. When we speak of the firmness of government, we mean an uniform system of measures, deliberately adopted, and resolutely maintained by the servants of the Crown, not a peevish asperity in the language or behaviour of the Sovereign. The government of a weak, irresolute Monarch, may be wise, moderate, and firm;....that of an obstinate, capricious Prince, on the contrary, may be feeble, undetermined, and relaxed. The reputation of public measures depends upon the minister, who is responsible; not upon the King, whose private opinions are not sup-

was persuaded to yield; just as the King of Great Britain would have yielded, if he had, at this juncture, put himself without conditions into the hands of the Whigs....The consequences are too well known !

The King, whose private opinions, &c.] Here, JUNIUS either does not well understand, or does not fairly explain, the constitutional principle to which he refers. The King is, by the very spirit of the constitution, expected *to be the author of every great measure of his own government ; but not to insist, that his council, or even any one of his servants, make themselves responsible to his people, for measures of which they cannot approve.* It is for the King to dictate; for his ministerial servants to say, whether they be willing to make themselves responsible to the laws for the execution of what he may command; for his council, to give their advice when it is required,

posed to have any weight against the advice of his
council; whose personal authority should, therefore, never be interposed in public affairs.....This,
I believe, is true constitutional doctrine. But, for
a moment, let us suppose it false. Let it be taken
for granted, that an occasion may arise, in which a
King of England shall be compelled to take upon
himself the ungrateful office of rejecting the petitions, and censuring the conduct of his subjects;
and let the City Remonstrance be supposed to have
created so extraordinary an occasion. On this
principle, which I presume no friend of administration will dispute, let the wisdom and spirit of the
ministry be examined. They advise the King to
hazard his dignity, by a positive declaration of his
own sentiments;....they suggest to him a language

concerning whatever measure the King desires to carry into effect.
The King can do no wrong; because he cannot compel any minister to remain in office, against his own will; and because, for whatever any minister executes, that minister is alone legally responsible to his fellow subjects. Every measure of the crown is expected
to be approved by the cabinet-council, before it be committed to
execution by any particular minister; because the duties of the
cabinet-ministers are, unavoidably, so much connected with one
another, that every one of the leading ministers would, by the
laws, be held responsible for every leading measure of government;
because it seems necessary, that all the leading ministers should be
witnesses of the conduct of one another, in their official intercourse
with Majesty; because this form has been gradually established by
long practice of the British government......Let it be no more sacri-
legiously affirmed, that the British constitution intends the Sovereign to be a mere, inert, unintelligent, pageant of state!

They suggest to him a language, &c.] The Whigs thought, that
a very daring address might alarm and overawe their Sovereign.

full of severity and reproach. What follows? When his Majesty had taken so decisive a part in support of his ministry and parliament, he had a right to expect from them a reciprocal demonstration of firmness in their own cause, and of their zeal for his honour. He had reason to expect, (and such, I doubt not, were the blustering promises of Lord North,) that the persons whom he had been advised to charge with having failed in their respect to him, with having injured parliament, and violated the principles of the constitution, should not have been permitted to escape without some severe marks of the displeasure and vengeance of parliament. As the matter stands, the minister, after placing his Sovereign in the most unfavourable light to his sub-

They could not procure such an address from either House of Parliament. In the city they accomplished their purpose. Such petitions were to be presented to the King in person : and it was usual for him to mark them with approbation, only when they deserved it. Had the King, upon this occasion, either signified approbation of the address, or even received it with a doubtful silence ; he would have appeared, either to be alarmed and overawed by city turbulence, or to be unwilling to give the necessary support to his ministers. He acted according to the wonted forms of the constitution. It was not harshness, but firmness, which he evinced. To have yielded to such democratical clamour, would have been to abandon the constitution and government to anarchy. How would Queen Elizabeth have dealt with the citizens of London, if they had dared thus to address her ?

Should not have been permitted, &c.] Junius would persuade the Livery of London, that, since they were not all hanged, or put in the pillory, they had come off with triumph. But parliament had taken the precisely right step, neither violent, nor pusillanimous.

jects, and after attempting to fix the ridicule and odium of his own precipitate measures upon the royal character, leaves him a solitary figure upon the scene, to recal, if he can, or to compensate, by future compliances, for one unhappy demonstration of ill-supported firmness, and ineffectual resentment. As a man of spirit, his Majesty cannot but be sensible, that the lofty terms in which he was persuaded to reprimand the City, when united with the silly conclusion of the business, resemble the pomp of a mock-tragedy, where the most pathetic sentiments, and even the sufferings of the hero, are calculated for derision.

Such have been the boasted firmness and consistency of a minister*, whose appearance in the House of Commons was thought essential to the King's service;.....whose presence was to influence every division:.....who had a voice to persuade, an eye to penetrate, a gesture to command. The reputation of these great qualities has been fatal to his friends. The little dignity of Mr. Ellis has been committed. The mine was sunk;.......combustibles provided; and Welbore Ellis, the Guy Faux

---

A mock-tragedy, &c.] JUNIUS, while writing these words, probably thought of Fielding's *Tom Thumb the Great.*

* This graceful minister is oddly constructed. His tongue is a little too big for his mouth, and his eyes a great deal too big for their sockets. Every part of his person sets natural proportion at defiance. At this present writing, his head is supposed to be much too heavy for his shoulders.

of the fable, waited only for the signal of command. All of a sudden, the country gentlemen discover how grossly they have been deceived :....the minister's heart fails him ; the grand plot is defeated in a moment; and poor Mr. Ellis and his motion taken into custody. From the event of Friday last, one would imagine that some fatality hung over this gentleman. Whether he makes or suppresses a motion, he is equally sure of his disgrace. But the complexion of the times will suffer no man to be vice-treasurer of Ireland with impunity*.

From the event of Friday last, &c.] The reader is, no doubt, aware, that it was the proper business of JUNIUS, writing with the views which he entertained, to represent the conduct of the House of Commons, as weak and timid, since it could not be called violent. But, whatever might be the first intentions of the ministry ; that was, certainly, the most judicious and manly measure, which they finally took.

* About this time, the courtiers talked of nothing but a bill of pains and penalties against the Lord Mayor and Sheriffs, or impeachment at the least. Little *Mannikin Ellis* told the King that, if the business were left to his management, he would engage to do wonders. It was thought very odd, that a motion of so much importance should be entrusted to the most contemptible little piece of machinery in the whole kingdom. His honest zeal, however, was disappointed. The minister took fright; and, at the very instant that little Ellis was going to open, sent him an order to sit down. All their magnanimous threats ended in a ridiculous vote of censure, and a still more ridiculous address to the King. This shameful desertion so afflicted the generous mind of George the Third, that he was obliged to live upon potatoes for three weeks, to keep off a malignant fever........Poor man ! *Quis talia fando temperet a lacrymis!*

I do not mean to express the smallest anxiety for the minister's reputation. He acts separately for himself: and the most shameful inconsistency may perhaps be no disgrace to him. But when the Sovereign, who represents the majesty of the state, appears in person, his dignity should be supported. The occasion should be important;....the plan well considered;....the execution steady and consistent. My zeal for his Majesty's real honour compels me to assert, that it has been too much the system of the present reign, to introduce him personally, either to act for, or to defend, his servants. They persuade him to do what is properly *their* business, and desert him in the midst of it *. Yet this is an inconvenience, to which he must be for ever exposed, while he adheres to a ministry divided among themselves, or unequal in credit and ability to the great task they have undertaken. Instead of reserving the interposition of the royal personage, as the last resource of government; their weakness obliges them to apply it to every ordinary occasion, and to render it cheap and common in the opinion of the people. Instead of supporting their master, they look to *him* for support; and, for the emoluments of remaining one day more in office, care not how much his sacred character is prostituted and dishonoured.

---

* After a certain person had succeeded in cajoling Mr. Yorke, he told the Duke of Grafton, with a witty smile,...." My Lord, you " may kill the next Percy yourself."......N. B. He had but that instant wiped the tears away, which overcame Mr. Yorke.

If I thought it possible for this paper to reach the closet, I would venture to appeal at once to his Majesty's judgment. I would ask him, but in the most respectful terms, " As you are a young man, " Sir, who ought to have a life of happiness in pro- " spect....as you are a husband....as you are a fa- " ther, [your filial duties, I own, have been religi- " ously performed] is it *bona fide* for your interest, " or your honour, to sacrifice your domestic tran- " quillity, and to live in a perpetual disagreement " with your people, merely to preserve such a chain " of beings as North, Barrington, Weymouth, " Gower, Ellis, Onslow, Rigby, Jerry Dyson, and " Sandwich? Their very names are a satire upon all " government, and I defy the gravest of your chap- " lains to read the catalogue without laughing."

For my own part, Sir, I have always considered addresses from parliament, as a fashionable, un- meaning formality. Usurpers, ideots, and tyrants, have been successively complimented with almost the same professions of duty and affection. But let us suppose them to mean exactly what they pro- fess. The consequences deserve to be considered. Either the Sovereign is a man of high spirit and dangerous ambition, ready to take advantage of the

---

North, &c.] Whatever may be said of the rest of these minis- terial names; worth and abilities, above mediocrity, cannot be de- nied to North; nor, to Sandwich, high ministerial talents.

treachery of his parliament, ready to accept of the surrender they make him of the public liberty;... or he is a mild, undesigning prince; who, provided they indulge him with a little state and pageantry, would of himself intend no mischief. On the first supposition, it must soon be decided by the sword, whether the constitution should be lost or preserved. On the second, a prince no way qualified for the execution of a great and hazardous enterprize, and without any determined object in view, may nevertheless be driven into such desperate measures, as may lead directly to his ruin, or disgrace himself by a shameful fluctuation between the extremes of violence at one moment, and timidity at another. The minister, perhaps, may have reason to be satisfied with the success of the present hour, and with the profits of his employment. He is the tenant of the day, and has no interest in the inheritance. The Sovereign himself is bound by other obligations; and ought to look forward to a superior, a permanent interest. His paternal tenderness should remind him, how many hostages he has given to society. The ties of nature come powerfully in aid of oaths and protestations. The father, who considers his own precarious state of health, and the possible hazard of a long minority, will wish to see the family estate free and unincumbered*. What is the dignity of the crown, though

---

Every true friend of the house of Brunswick sees with affliction, how rapidly some of the principal branches of the family have dropped off.

it were really maintained;....what is the honour of
parliament, supposing it could exist without any
foundation of integrity and justice;...or what is the
vain reputation of firmness, even if the scheme of
the government were uniform and consistent ; compared with the heart-felt affections of the people,
with the happiness and security of the royal family, or even with the grateful acclamations of the
populace ? Whatever style of contempt may be
adopted by ministers or parliaments, no man sincerely despises the voice of the English nation.
The House of Commons are only interpreters,
whose duty it is to convey the sense of the people
faithfully to the Crown. If the interpretation be
false or imperfect, the constituent powers are
called upon to deliver their own sentiments. Their
speech is rude, but intelligible;.....their gestures
fierce, but full of explanation. Perplexed by sophistries, their honest eloquence rises into action.
Their first appeal was to the integrity of their representatives;....the second, to the King's justice ;
....the last argument of the people, whenever they

If the interpretation be false, &c.] True. But the Livery of
London were not to arrogate to themselves the authority of all the
constituent powers of the state. Nor were the constituent powers
to speak otherwise than according to the forms prescribed by
law.

The last argument, &c.] It is the chief political blemish in
these Letters of JUNIUS, that he so frequently takes occasion to
remind the people, that there were perhaps some cases in which
armed resistance to the government was not forbidden them by the
laws.

have recourse to it, will carry more perhaps than persuasion to parliament, or supplication to the throne.

JUNIUS.

LETTER XXXIX.

TO THE PRINTER OF THE PUBLIC ADVERTISER.

IN parliament, in the city, in the newspapers, the contest was obstinately continued by the Whigs. The society for the support of the Bill of Rights had, in their patriot zeal, finally discharged all Mr. Wilkes's debts, to the amount of seventeen thousand pounds. The term of Wilkes's confinement had expired; and he was, on the 17th of April, set at liberty. He had been elected Alderman for the Ward of Farringdon Without; and he now took his place in the court. Lord Chatham, in the House of Peers, pursued the contention with the most earnest perseverance, almost to the last day of the session. The city-patriots, on the 23d May, again addressed their Sovereign in another remonstrating petition, somewhat less indecent than the former in its language, but in its substance equally bold and violent. And when the King, again, with his former firmness, denied their request, Beckford, with a braving audacity, accosted his Sovereign, in an insolent reply.

Yet all this was ineffectual. The necessary supplies were granted to the government. Such new laws, as its exigencies demanded, were enacted. Whatever Bills were proposed, only to thwart and harass it, were, by its influence, or by the wisdom and loyalty of a majority of the legislative body, rejected. The decision on the Middlesex election was not rescinded. The Whig faction was not yet received exclusively into ministerial power. Nor were the people throughout the kingdom, disposed to take part with the citizens of London and the Freeholders of Middlesex, so as to vilify the legislature, and to insult the throne. Those discontents were even gradually dying away, which a few imprudent and irregular acts had, once, unhappily excited. A storm was indeed about to arise from America. But its terrors were still distant: it did not yet darken the horizon: its very elements were as yet but in their first formation. In this state of things, JUNIUS wrote the following Letter. His object in it was, to prevent the people from adopting the persuasion,

*either that government were not greatly in the wrong, or that re-
dress was hopeless, and that no part remained for the complainers,
but tame acquiescence. He reviews the proceedings of parliament
during the session which had ended on the 19th of May ; blames
both the Lords and Commons, equally for what they had done, and
for what they had neglected ; arraigns the unskilfulness of the
financial measures which the new minister had adopted ; and dares
to introduce a disadvantageous comparison of the character of the
present Sovereign, with those of some of the worst and most unfortunate of his predecessors.*

*This Letter is certainly not one of the least artful or eloquent in this
collection. It affords ready topics of abuse for those who desired to
keep up, during the recess, the wonted clamour against the parliament and the government. Yet, even here, we easily see, that
JUNIUS laboured to inflame an ardour, that was, in spite of him,
continually dying away, and that he had to prompt and to vindicate measures, the detail of which he did not direct.*

———

28. May 1770.

SIR,

WHILE parliament was sitting, it would
neither have been safe, nor perhaps quite regular,
to offer any opinion to the public upon the justice
or wisdom of their proceedings. To pronounce
fairly upon their conduct, it was necessary to wait
until we should consider, in one view, the beginning, progress, and conclusion of their deliberations. The cause of the public was undertaken

While parliament was sitting, &c.] Yet, even in the last Letter, JUNIUS did offer an opinion upon the justice and wisdom of
the proceedings of parliament, even while that parliament was
sitting.

and supported by men, whose abilities and united authority, to say nothing of the advantageous ground they stood on, might well be thought suffi- cient to determine a popular question in favour of the people. Neither was the House of Commons so absolutely engaged in defence of the ministry, or even of their own resolutions, but that *they* might have paid some decent regard to the known disposition of their constituents; and, without any dishonour to their firmness, might have retracted an opinion too hastily adopted, when they saw the alarm it had created, and how strongly it was op- posed by the general sense of the nation. The ministry too would have consulted their own imme- diate interest, in making some concession satisfac- tory to the moderate part of the people. Without touching the fact, they might have consented to guard against, or give up, the dangerous principle on which it was established. In this state of things, I think it was highly improbable at the beginning of the session, that the complaints of the people, upon a matter, which, in *their* apprehension at

By men, &c.] Lord Chatham, Lord Camden, Lord Temple, Mr. Beckford, Mr. Dowdeswell, &c.

Without touching the fact, &c.] No. They could not yield, without appearing to abandon their principles, and to forego the firmness necessary to men at the head of a nation's affairs. The er- ror was in the first decision. In government, a bad measure is not easily retracted, without mischiefs worse than would attend the vindication of it. The time for virtue and caution, is when you first deliberate.

least, immediately affected the life of the constitution, would be treated with as much contempt
by their own representatives, and by the House of
Lords, as they had been by the other branch of the
legislature. Despairing of their integrity, we had
a right to expect something from their prudence,
and something from their fears. The Duke of
Grafton certainly did not foresee to what an extent the corruption of a parliament might be carried. He thought, perhaps, that there still was
some portion of shame or virtue left in the majority of the House of Commons, or that there was a
line in public prostitution, beyond which they
would scruple to proceed. Had the young man
been a little more practised in the world, or had he
ventured to measure the characters of other men by
his own, he would not have been so easily discour-
aged.

The prorogation of parliament naturally calls
upon us to review their proceedings, and to consider the condition in which they have left the
kingdom. I do not question but they have done
what is usually called the King's business, much to
his Majesty's satisfaction; we have only to lament
that, in consequence of a system introduced or re-
vived in the present reign, this kind of merit should
be very consistent with the neglect of every duty
they owe to the nation. The interval between the
opening of the last, and close of the former ses-

sion, was longer than usual. Whatever were the views of the minister in deferring the meeting of parliament, sufficient time was certainly given to every member of the House of Commons, to look back upon the steps he had taken, and the consequences they had produced. The zeal of party, the violence of personal animosities, and the heat of contention, had leisure to subside. From that period, whatever resolution they took was deliberate and prepense. In the preceding session, the dependants of the ministry had affected to believe, that the final determination of the question would have satisfied the nation, or at least put a stop to their complaints; as if the certainty of an evil could diminish the sense of it, or the nature of injustice could be altered by decision. But they found the people of England were in a temper very distant from submission; and, although it was contended that the House of Commons could not themselves reverse a resolution, which had the force and effect of a judicial sentence, there were other constitutional expedients, which would have given a security against any similar attempts for the future. The general proposition, in which the whole country had an interest, might have been

Was longer than usual.] The session of the winter 1769-70, met not till the 9th of January.

Time was certainly given, &c.] Here are a train of excellent observations concerning the views of the Whigs, and the manner in which they expected to work upon the movements of public opinion and the resolutions of the court.

reduced to a particular fact, in which Mr. Wilkes and Mr. Luttrell would alone have been concerned. The House of Lords might interpose ;....the King might dissolve the parliament ;....or, if every other resource failed, there still lay a grand constitutional writ of error in behalf of the people, from the decision of one court to the wisdom of the whole legislature. Every one of these remedies has been successively attempted. The people performed *their* part with dignity, spirit, and perseverance. For many months his Majesty heard nothing from his people but the language of complaint and resentment ;....unhappily for this country, it was the daily triumph of his courtiers, that he heard it with an indifference approaching to contempt.

The House of Commons having assumed a power unknown to the constitution, were determined not merely to support it in the single instance in question, but to maintain the doctrine in its utmost extent, and to establish the fact as a precedent in law, to be applied in whatever manner his Majesty's servants should hereafter think fit. Their proceedings upon this occasion are a strong proof, that a decision, in the first instance illegal and unjust, can

---

Unhappily for this country, &c.] The court believed that language of complaint to be artificially produced by the malignant practices of designing men. Hence was it supposed to require virtuous firmness to withstand it. Johnson, in his *Patriot* and his *False Alarm*, has eloquently expressed the notions, which, were, not unjustly, entertained of the false patriotism of the Whigs.

only be supported by a continuation of falsehood
and injustice. To support their former resolutions,
they were obliged to violate some of the best
known and established rules of the house. In one
instance, they went so far as to declare, in open defiance of truth and common sense, that it was not
the rule of the house to divide a complicated question, at the request of a member*. But, after
trampling upon the laws of the land, it was not
wonderful that they should treat the private regu-
lations of their own assembly with equal disregard.
The speaker, being young in office, began with
pretended ignorance, and ended with deciding for
the ministry. We were not surprised at the decision; but he hesitated and blushed at his own baseness, and every man was astonished †.

* This extragavant resolution appears in the votes of the house;
but, in the minutes of the committees, the instances of resolutions
contrary to law and truth, or of refusals to acknowledge law and
truth when proposed to them, are innumerable.

He hesitated and blushed, &c.] Sir Fletcher Norton, from a fierce
Whig, became a violent opponent of the Whig faction; and there
was, indeed, between the years 1760 and 1770, a political tergiver-
sation, sufficiently general and shocking to make all patriotism
seem a lie.

† When the King first made it a measure of his government to
destroy Mr. Wilkes, and when for this purpose it was necessary to
run down privilege, Sir Fletcher Norton, with his usual prostituted
effrontery, assured the House of Commons, that he should regard
one of their votes no more than a resolution of so many drunken
porters. This is the very Lawyer, whom Ben Jonson describes in
the following lines:

The interest of the public was vigorously supported in the House of Lords. Their right to defend the constitution against an encroachment of the other estates, and the necessity of exerting it at this period, was urged to them with every argument that could be supposed to influence the heart or the understanding. But it soon appeared, that they had already taken their part, and were determined to support the House of Commons, not only at the expence of truth and decency, but even by a surrender of their own most important rights....Instead of performing that duty which the constitution expected from them, in return for the dignity and independence of their station, in return for the hereditary share it has given them in the legislature,

> " Gives forked counsel; takes provoking gold,
> " On either hand, and puts it up.
> " So wise, so grave, of so perplex'd a tongue,
> " And loud withal, that would not wag, nor scarce
> " Lie still, without a fee."

In the House of Lords.] In both Houses of Parliament the Opposition, consisting of the whole Whig faction, was very numerous. Their strength in divisions of the House, was about two-fifths of the members usually present. The boldest orators were on their side. They exercised, with skill, every artifice of parliamentary management. Charles James Fox was making his first exertions, under the wing of the minister: but, Edmund Burke, under the patronage of Lord Rockingham, already dazzled the House of Commons with flashes of patriot eloquence. In the House of Peers, Lord Chatham and Lord Camden led the debate, on the side of the Opposition. Yet, I know not, but that, what with artifice, what with knowledge and eloquence, Lord Mansfield might be more than a match for both.

the majority of them made common cause with
the other house in oppressing the people, and established another doctrine as false in itself, and if
possible, more pernicious to the constitution, than
that on which the Middlesex election was determined. By resolving, " that they had no right to
" impeach a judgment of the House of Commons
" in any case whatsoever, where that house has a
" competent jurisdiction," they in effect gave up
that constitutional check and reciprocal controul of
one branch of the legislature over the other, which
is perhaps the greatest and most important object
provided for by the division of the whole legislative power into three estates : and now, let the judicial decisions of the House of Commons be ever
so extravagant, let their declarations of the law be
ever so flagrantly false, arbitrary, and oppressive
to the subject, the House of Lords have imposed a

Resolving, " *that they had no right*," &c.] This was a very ambiguous declaration. It meant no more, than " that, in all cases in
which the House of Commons had, *by the constitution*, a clear, unquestionable authority, to pronounce decisions from which there
was no legal appeal....the House of Peers possessed no right to take
abitrary cognizance of the judgment of the Commons."....This
was certainly true.

The proper question would have been...." whether, in the pecu-
liarity of the case of the Middlesex election, the House of Commons did possess, by the constitution, the right of final unappeala-
ble judgment ? "

The inferences, therefore, which JUNIUS draws, against the
House of Lords, though ingeniously conceived, and very eloquently
expressed, are utterly false.

slavish silence upon themselves....they cannot interpose....they cannot protect the subject....they cannot defend the laws of their country. A concession so extraordinary in itself, so contradictory to the principles of their own institution, cannot but alarm the most unsuspecting mind. We may well conclude, that the Lords would hardly have yielded so much to the other house, without the certainty of a compensation, which can only be made to them at the expence of the people *. The arbitrary power they have assumed, of imposing fines, and committing during pleasure, will now be exercised in its full extent. The House of Commons are too much in their debt to question or interrupt their proceedings. The Crown, too, we may be well assured, will lose nothing in this new distribution of power. After declaring, that to petition for a dissolution of parliament is irreconcileable with the principles of the constitution, his Majesty has reason to expect that some extraordinary compliment will be returned to the Royal prerogative. The three branches of the legislature seem

---

* The man who resists,and overcomes this iniquitous power, assumed by the Lords, must be supported by the whole people. We have the laws on our side, and want nothing but an intrepid leader. When such a man stands forth, let the nation look to it. It is not *his* cause, but our own.

That to petition for a dissolution of parliament, &c.] JUNIUS misrepresents the fact. This was argued, by some of the friends of government, in the debate, but was not insinuated in the address of the Lords and Commons to the Throne.

to treat their separate rights and interests as the Roman Triumvirs did their friends. They reciprocally sacrifice them to the animosities of each other, and establish a detestable union among themselves, upon the ruins of the laws and liberty of the commonwealth.

Through the whole proceedings of the House of Commons in this session, there is an apparent, a palpable consciousness of guilt. which has prevented their daring to assert their own dignity, where it has been immediately and grossly attacked. In the course of Dr. Musgrave's examination, he said every thing that can be conceived mortifying to individuals, or offensive to the house. They voted his information frivolous; but they were awed by his firmness and integrity, and sunk under it *.

Dr. Musgrave's examination, &c.] Dr. Musgrave was casually told, by some persons in Paris, that the.Princess Dowager of Wales, Lord Bute, and Mr. Henry Fox, had been bribed with French money, to give undue advantages to France, in the treaty of peace in 1763. He drank up this intelligence with greedy ears. Returning to London, he officiously communicated his information, so that government was obliged to pay some attention to it. The matter was mentioned in Parliament; and Dr. Musgrave was examined before the House of Commons: His information was truly frivolous........ Any witness giving such information, before a Court of Justice, in a private cause, would have been judged by all, to do not the slightest service to the party on whose behalf he was examined. Nothing but the credulous prejudice of the fools who were abused by the city-agitators, could have judged otherwise of it.

* The examination of this firm, honest man, is printed for *Almon*. The reader will find it a most curious and a most interesting

The terms in which the sale of a patent to Mr. Hine were communicated to the public, naturally called for a parliamentary enquiry. The integrity of the House of Commons was directly impeached ; but they had not courage to move in their own vindication, because the enquiry would have been fatal to Colonel Burgoyne and the Duke of Grafton. When Sir George Saville branded them with the name of traitors to their constituents, when the Lord Mayor, the Sheriffs, and Mr. Trecothick, expressly avowed and maintained every part of the city remonstrance, why did they tamely submit to be insulted? Why did they not immediately expel those refractory members? Conscious of the motives on which they had acted, they prudently preferred infamy to danger, and were better prepared to meet the contempt, than to rouse the indignation of the whole people. Had they expelled those five members, the consequences of the new doc-

---

tract. Doctor Musgrave, with no other support but truth, and his own firmness, resisted and overcame the whole House of Commons.

When Sir George Saville branded them, &c.] In the debate upon the subject of the city-petition, Sir George Saville, a man of ancient family, large estate, and uncorrupted virtue, was one of the most zealous friends of the Whig faction. But he was misled by his own honesty and enthusiam. He was not sufficiently aware, that *the opposition* were, *at this time*, not more *truly revolution whigs in principle*, than the administration and its supporters.

Those five members, &c.] The five members were, Sir George Saville, Mr. Beckford, Mr. Townsend, Mr. Sawbridge, and Mr. Trecothick. Their conduct in the House of Commons, upon this

trine of incapacitation would have come immediately home to every man. The truth of it would. then have been fairly tried, without any reference to Mr. Wilkes's private character, or the dignity of the house, or the obstinacy of one particular county. These topics, I know, have had their weight with men who, affecting a character of moderation, in reality consult nothing but their own immediate ease;.....who are weak enough to acquiesce under a flagrant violation of the laws, when it does not directly touch themselves, and care not what injustice is practised upon a man whose moral character they piously think themselves obliged to condemn. In any other circumstances, the House of Commons must have forfeited all credit and dignity, if, after such gross provocation, they had permitted those five gentlemen to sit any longer among them. We should then have seen and felt the operation of a precedent, which is represented to be perfectly barren and harmless. But there is a set of men in this country, whose understandings

occasion, was highly irregular. It would have become the dignity of the House, to treat them, on account of it, with sharp severity. But their error in the case of the Middlesex election, had weakened their authority, and rendered them timid. Impotent outrage is ever followed, sooner or later, by weak forbearance. Perhaps, it was not unfortunate for the constitution, that the democratical violence of the patriots was opposed to the arbitrary irregularities which were, between the years 1760 and 1770, committed in the exercise of the ministerial power.

Expulsion would, however, have been too severe a punishment for the bullying of the five members.

measure the violation of law by the magnitude of the instance, not by the important consequences which flow directly from the principle; and the minister, I presume, did not think it safe to quicken their apprehensions too soon. Had Mr. Hampden reasoned, and acted, like the moderate men of these days, instead of hazarding his whole fortune in a law-suit with the crown, he would have quietly paid the twenty shillings demanded of him;....the Stuart family would probably have continued upon the throne; and, at this moment, the imposition of ship-money would have been an acknowledged prerogative of the crown.

What then has been the business of the session, after voting the supplies, and confirming the determination of the Middlesex election? The extraordinary prorogation of the Irish parliament, and

Had Mr. Hampden reasoned, &c.] This sentence, and those which immediately precede and follow it, are admirable instances of the oratorical art of JUNIUS. The patriots of the city thought themselves every one a Hampden, when they were insulting their Sovereign, and bidding defiance to the authority of parliament. JUNIUS well knew, how to win upon their prejudices and their self-conceit.

The extraordinary prorogation of the Irish parliament, &c.] In compliance with the wishes of the people, though contrary to their own, the leaders in the Irish Legislature had lately procured a law, settling, that the parliament of Ireland should be dissolved and renewed at the end of every eight years. A dissolution of the Irish parliament immediately followed. It had been renewed by a general election. The new parliament met, on the 17th of October 1769. An augmentation of the troops; a pecuniary grant of above

the just discontents of that kingdom, have been
passed by without notice. Neither the general
situation of our Colonies, nor that particular distress

two millions sterling ; a dutiful address to the Sovereign ; and a
shew of sufficient respect to Lord Townshend, the Lord Lieutenant ; were acts by which that parliament seemed assiduously to
recommend itself to the favour of the government. But government
had proposed a money-bill that originated with the Privy Council.
The Irish parliament would pass no money-bill that did not take its
rise in the House of Commons. The Lord Lieutenant, on the 2d of
December, entered on the Journals of the House of Lords, a protest against the rejection of the Privy Council's money-bill, and
suddenly prorogued the parliament. The Irish Commons would
not permit his Lordship's protest to be entered on their Journals.
Before out of humour with government, the Irish patriots were now
in the highest degree exasperated against it. The opposition in
the English parliament gladly interfered ; and JUNIUS seized the
topic.

Neither the general situation of our Colonies, &c.] The stamp-
act, the production of George Grenville, asserted the right of the
British Legislature, to impose taxes on the American Colonies. It
was resisted, and it was repealed. The repeal seemed a dereliction of its principle, in which the British Government was not willing finally to acquiesce. The right of taxing the Americans, was
again asserted by the imposition of Custom-House duties, to be paid
in the American ports, upon glass, red lead, painters' colours, tea,
&c. Of these, the Americans again complained, as intolerably
burthensome. Except only the duty on tea, they were all remitted.
Even this, America obstinately refused to pay : for, it was the
principle of taxation, much more than any particular tax, which
displeased. The duty on tea, was, for the very same reason, not
to be remitted by the British government. Consequences the most
alarming were mutually threatened.

The Whig faction at home, zealously encouraged the American
discontents. In gratitude, the States of Carolina voted, and actually transmitted, the sum of one thousand five hundred pounds
sterling to the supporters of the Bill of Rights.

which forced the inhabitants of Boston to take up arms in their defence, have been thought worthy of a moment's consideration. 'In the repeal of those acts which were most offensive to America, the parliament have done every thing but remove the offence. They have relinquished the revenue, but judiciously taken care to preserve the contention. It is not pretended that the continuation of the tea-duty is to produce any direct benefit whatsoever to the mother country. What is it, then, but an odious, unprofitable, exertion of a speculative right, and fixing a badge of slavery upon the Americans, without service to their masters? But it has pleased

Forced the inhabitants of Boston to take up arms, &c.] It was necessary to support the government, particularly in levying the duties at the port of Boston, with a sufficient military force. The soldiers were odious to the inhabitants, who sometimes insulted, and sometimes strove to seduce, them. On March 2d, 1770, a dispute between some rope-makers, and one or two of the soldiers, was suddenly inflamed into a riot. The townsmen came in a multitude to support the rope-makers. The contention was for some days partially interrupted, without being finally composed. On the evening of the 5th, it came to a general contest between the people and the soldiers. The soldiers seeing the custom-house threatened by the people, the centinel attacked, and even the commanding officer then on duty violently struck, while he was striving to repress the mob and to restrain the ardour of his men....hastily fired....and a number of persons in the mob, were killed and wounded. The inhabitants of Boston, then, with an authoritative earnestness which might not be resisted, demanded the removal of the soldiers from the town. Captain Preston, the commanding officer, who was on duty when the soldiers fired, was afterwards tried and acquitted.

But it has pleased God, &c.] It is impossible to deny, that this period possesses all the happy and forcible severity of genuine eloquence.

God to give us a ministry, and a parliament, who are neither to be persuaded by argument, nor instructed by experience.

Lord North, I presume, will not claim an extraordinary merit from any thing he has done this year in the improvement or application of the revenue. A great operation, directed to an important object, though it should fail of success, marks the genius and elevates the character of a minister. A poor, contracted understanding, deals in little schemes, which dishonour him if they fail, and do him no credit when they succeed. Lord North had fortunately the means in his possession of reducing all the four per cents at once. The failure of his first enterprize in finance, is not half so disgraceful to his reputation as a minister, as the enterprize itself is injurious to the public. Instead of striking one decisive blow, which would have cleared the

---

Instead of striking, &c.] In the 29th year of the reign of George the Second, the sum of two millions was raised for the expenditure of government, by redeemable annuities at three pounds ten shillings per cent. and by a lottery. Of these annuities, the capital stock was, now, one million five hundred thousand pounds. They had been charged on the sinking fund. It was now in a condition to discharge them. Of this, notice was given by an order of the House of Commons, dated on the 26th of April, 1770.....
This was one of the pecuniary transactions of this session of parliament.

Lord North saw, that the debt, of which the interest was at the rate of four per cent. might be advantageously converted into three per cents ; as the four per cents were, at this time, low in the market, the three per cents comparatively high. It was, therefore, pro-

market at once, upon terms proportioned to the price of the four per cents six weeks ago, he has tampered with a pitiful portion of a commodity, which ought never to have been touched but in gross;.... he has given notice to the holders of that stock, of a design formed by government to prevail upon them to surrender it by degrees, consequently has warned them to hold up and enhance the price;.....so that the plan of reducing the four per cents must either be dropped entirely, or continued with an increasing disadvantage to the public. The minister's sagacity has served to raise the value of the thing

posed, that two millions five hundred thousand pounds of the four per cents, should be converted into three per cents, by the voluntary subscription of the proprietors of the former, between the 26th of April, and the 7th of May, 1770. In compensation for the difference between the four and three per cents, each subscriber of one hundred pound capital of the former, was to receive for the price of fourteen pounds each, two tickets in a lottery of fifty thousand shares, and five hundred thousand pounds ; the prizes to be paid on the first of March, 1771.

Lord North durst not venture on a speculation so bold, as that of converting the whole four per cents, at once, into three per cents. He probably dreaded the sudden and extraordinary fluctuations which might be thus occasioned in the price of stocks : and he might foresee, that the consequence would have been, *an excessive depreciation of the three per cents.* Even as it was, the three per cents fell in the market. Had the minister done as JUNIUS wishes that he had, their depreciation must have been, *ultimately*, much greater.

This last is the measure which JUNIUS condemns. But he was himself, evidently a man for grand and daring measures. Besides, it was necessary that he should find, in every thing, reason for disapproving the conduct of the ministers.

he means to purchase, and sink that of the three per cents which it is his purpose to.sell. In effect, he has contrived to make it the interest of the proprietor of four per cents to sell out, and buy three per cents in the market, rather than subscribe his stock upon any terms that can possibly be offered by government.

The state of the nation leads us naturally to consider the situation of the King. The prorogation of parliament has the effect of a temporary dissolution. The odium of measures adopted by the collective body sits lightly upon the separate members who composed it. They retire into summer quarters, and rest from the disgraceful labours of the campaign. But as for the sovereign, *it is not so with him.* HE has a permanent existence in this country; HE cannot withdraw himself from the complaints, the discontents, the reproaches of his subjects. They pursue him to his retirement, and invade his domestic happiness, when no address can be obtained from an obsequious parliament to encourage or console him. In other times the interest of the King and people of England was, as it ought to be, entirely the same. A new system has not only been adopted in fact, but professed upon principle. Ministers are no longer the public servants of the state, but the private domestics of the Sovereign. *One particular class of men are per-

---

* " An ignorant, mercenary, and servile crew; unanimous in
" evil, diligent in mischief, variable in principles, constant to flat-

mitted to call themselves the King's friends, as if the body of the people were the King's enemies; or as if his Majesty looked for a resource or consolation in the attachment of a few favourites, against the general contempt and detestation of his subjects. Edward, and Richard the Second, made the same distinction between the collective body of the people, and a contemptible party who surrounded the throne. The event of their mistaken conduct might have been a warning to their successors. Yet the errors of those princes were not without excuse. They had as many false friends as our present gracious Sovereign, and infinitely greater temptations to seduce them. They were neither sober, religious, nor demure. Intoxicated with pleasure, they wasted their inheritance in pursuit

---

" tery, talkers for liberty, but slaves to power ;...styling themselves
" the court party, and the prince's only friends."....*Davenant.*

One particular class of men, &c.] These were, properly, the party formed by the Earl of Bute. They believed, that their own advancement might be promoted more effectually by attaching themselves to the interests of the crown, than if they should devote themselves to any party of subjects. They were of opinion, too, that the crown at this time wanted support, more than any other branch of the constitutional powers. They had, also, personal likings, by which their political conduct was considerably influenced. I cannot see, that there was more of selfishness, or less of virtue, in their conduct, than in that of the other parties. It was advantageous to the constitution, that there existed such a party, to counterbalance the strength and violence of the Whigs, and to resist the bold usurpations of popular opinion.

of it. Their lives were like a rapid torrent, brilliant in prospect, though useless or dangerous in its course. In the dull, unanimated existence of other princes, we see nothing but a sickly stagnant water, which taints the atmosphere without fertilizing the soil....The morality of a King is not to be measured by vulgar rules. His situation is singular. There are faults which do him honour, and virtues that disgrace him. A faultless, insipid equality, in his character, is neither capable of vice nor virtue in the extreme; but it secures his submission to those persons whom he has been accustomed to respect, and makes him a dangerous instrument of *their* ambition. Secluded from the world, attached from his infancy to one set of persons, and one set of ideas, he can neither open his heart to new connexions, nor his mind to better information. A character of this sort is the soil fittest to produce that obstinate bigotry in politics and religion, which begins with a meritorious sacrifice of the understanding, and finally conducts the monarch and the martyr to the block.

At any other period, I doubt not, the scandalous disorders, which have been introduced into the government of all the dependencies in the Empire, would have roused the attention of the public.

Their lives were like a rapid torrent, &c.] This splendid paragraph is defective in nothing but truth. It bespeaks deep experimental skill in the principles of human action.

The odious abuse and prostitution of the prerogative at home....the unconstitutional employment of the military.....the arbitrary fines and commitments by the House of Lords, and Court of King's Bench; ....the mercy of a chaste and pious Prince extended cheerfully to a wilful murderer, because that murderer is the brother of a common prostitute*, would I think, at any other time, have excited universal indignation. But the daring attack upon the constitution in the Middlesex election, makes us callous and indifferent to inferior grievances. No man regards an eruption on the surface, when the noble parts are invaded, and he feels a mortification approaching to his heart. The free election of our representatives in parliament comprehends, because it is the source and security of, every right and privilege of the English nation. The ministry have

---

A wilful murderer, &c.] Matthew and Patrick Kennedy were condemned to death for the murder of John Bigby, a watchman. Their sister was a prostitute. She found means to engage some persons to ask their reprieve from the King. There was nothing of unusual atrocity in the circumstances of their crime. They were respited; and pardoned. But the widow of the person whom they had killed, laid an appeal against them; and they were reserved for a new trial. Lord Palmerston, Lord Spencer, and George Selwyn, were among those who took an especial interest in their fate. Their friends contrived to satisfy the widow; and, when the time arrived for the second trial, she did not appear against them. The sum of three hundred and fifty pounds, is said to have been paid her, as a compensation. She cried bitterly when she came to receive the money; refused to take it with her own hands; and, at last, holding up her lap, bade them shove it into it.

* Miss Kennedy.

realised the compendious ideas of Caligula. They know that the liberty, the laws, and property of an Englishman, have in truth but one neck; and that to violate the freedom of election, strikes deeply at them all.

JUNIUS.

To violate the freedom of election, &c.] This expressive sentence closes the Letter. When the purposes are considered, for which this Letter was intended; we cannot but own this to be, in art and eloquence, if not in truth and candour, one of the best of all its author's compositions.

LETTER XL.

——

TO LORD NORTH.

LET us still remember, that, in regard to the great constitutional grounds, on which the two adverse parties of the Crown and the Opposition, had taken each its separate stand, both were in the right. The Executive Power did well, to maintain its dignity with firmness, in spite of factious importunity, or mobbish outrage. It did well to preserve the Sovereign from falling to be treated, merely as an ideot-ward in the hands of the Whigs. The Opposition, on the other hand, acted a part, which, however intended, had substantially the effect of true patriotism....when they resisted the execution of general warrants ; branded with indignant reprobation an ignominious peace ; supported Wilkes, notwithstanding his private errors, against ministerial oppression ; asserted the violated rights of the Electors of Middlesex ; and eagerly watched against any undue interposition of the military force, in the ordinary exercise of the civil authority.

When the Crown inconsiderately transgressed the bounds of law, for the punishment of a seditious writer ; when it adopted the doubtful examples of bad times, as precedents worthy of imitation ; when its ministers proposed in the House of Commons unconstitutional measures, tending to make the parliament odious and contemptible to the people ; when it acted with a little timid policy, in its transactions with foreign powers....it became, deservedly obnoxious, both to the indignation and the rising contempt of the people, and the leaders of Opposition.

But, the Opposition were truly the enemies of their country, when they opposed the extinction of the principles of ancient faction. However convenient they might find the use of mobs and libels ; it was a crime against the constitution, to employ such engines. Nothing could be more unreasonable, nor more unconstitutional, than to expect, as they did, that their Prince should abandon himself to perpetual pupilage, in the hands of the great families of the Whigs.

What could be more truly unworthy, than to kindle up sedition in the City of London, and rebellion in the American Colonies ? Is it not evident, that the leaders of the Opposition were not less the slaves of blind prejudice, nor less actuated by basely selfish motives, than the servants of the crown, and the adherents of the ministry ?

Such were the good and the evil of the two opposite parties. They were usefully opposed to each other. Neither ministry nor opposition, could effectually accomplish its own views. Over government, in all its false steps, Opposition, either instantly, or at least finally, triumphed. When Opposition descended to dishonest artifices, excited sedition, or opposed measures consistent with patriotism and wisdom ; it lost its own strength in attempts so base.

In nothing in which it deserved not success, was Opposition finally successful, except in provoking the American war. But, by a natural necessity, America would undoubtedly have been detached from Britain, nearly at this very time; though neither Chatham, Fox, nor Burke, had existed to encourage American resistance.

In the matter which is the subject of the present Letter, Junius, and the Opposition, were certainly not in the wrong. However useful to ministry, the service of Mr. Luttrell; it was not a service for which good men could desire to see any one promoted. A less conspicuous promotion of such a man, might have been less offensive. But, Junius feigns to feel that alarm and indignation, which he desired to excite.

The Letter is written with admirable force, vivacity, and propriety.

---

22. *August*, 1770.

MY LORD,

MR. Luttrell's services were the chief support and ornament of the Duke of Grafton's administration. The honour of rewarding them was reserved for your Lordship. The Duke, it seems, had contracted an obligation he was ashamed to acknowledge, and unable to acquit. You, my

Lord, had no scruples. You accepted the succession with all its incumbrances, and have paid Mr.
Luttrell his legacy, at the hazard of ruining the
estate.

When this accomplished youth declared himself
the champion of government, the world was busy in
enquiring what honours or emoluments could be a
sufficient recompence to a young man of his rank
and fortune, for submitting to mark his entrance
into life with the universal contempt and detestation of his country....His noble father had not been
so precipitate....To vacate his seat in parliament;....
to intrude upon a county in which he had no interest or connexion;....to possess himself of another
man's right, and to maintain it in defiance to public
shame as well as justice; bespoke a degree of zeal,
or of depravity, which all the favour of a pious
Prince could hardly requite. I protest, my Lord,
there is in this young man's conduct, a strain of
prostitution which, for its singularity, I cannot but
admire. He has discovered a new line in the human character;....he has degraded even the name of
Luttrell, and gratified his father's most sanguine
expectations.

The Duke of Grafton, with every possible disposition to patronise this kind of merit, was content-

---

He has degraded even the name of Luttrell, &c.] What a paragraph of invective! The most pointed severity of the whole, is
contained in the words which are here quoted.

ed with pronouncing Colonel Luttrell's panegyric. The gallant spirit, the disinterested zeal of the young adventurer, were echoed through the House of Lords. His Grace repeatedly pledged himself to the house, as an evidence of the purity of his friend Mr. Luttrell's intentions;....that he had engaged without any prospect of personal benefit, and that the idea of compensation would mortally offend him*. The noble Duke could hardly be in earnest; but he had lately quitted his employment, and began to think it necessary to take some care of his reputation. A♦ that very moment the Irish negociation was probably begun.....Come forward, thou worthy representative of Lord Bute, and tell this insulted country, who advised the King to appoint Mr. Luttrell ADJUTANT-GENERAL to the army in Ireland? By what management was Colonel Cunninghame prevailed on to resign his employment, and the obsequious Gisborne, to accept of a pension for the government of Kinsale†?

---

* He now says that his great object is the rank of Colonel, and that he *will* have it.

Thou worthy representative of Lord Bute, &c.] Though Lord Bute was abroad; Opposition still delighted to represent him as swaying all the powers of government. But, his influence gradually vanished, when he ceased to be an active member of the administration. Were JUNIUS and the opposition aware, what a superiority of genius they attributed to Lord Bute, in thus making him, so remarkably, and for so long a period, the inspiring and presiding mind to so many successive administrations?

† This infamous transaction ought to be explained to the public. Colonel Gisborne was Quarter-Master-General in Ireland. Lord Townshend persuades him to resign to a Scotch officer, one Fraser,

Was it an original stipulation with the Princess of Wales? Or does he owe his preferment to your Lordship's partiality, or to the Duke of Bedford's friendship? My Lord, though it may not be possible to trace this measure to it's source, we can follow the stream, and warn the country of it's approaching destruction. The English nation must be rouzed, and put upon it's guard. Mr. Luttrell has already shewn us how far he may be trusted, whenever an open attack is to be made upon the liberties of this country. I do not doubt that there is a deliberate plan formed;....your Lordship best knows by whom:......the corruption of the legislative body on this side....a military force on the other ....and then, *Farewel to England!* It is impossible that any minister should dare to advise the King to place such a man as Luttrell in the confidential post of Adjutant-General, if there were not some secret purpose in view, which only such a man as Luttrell is fit to promote. The insult offered to the army in general, is as gross as the outrage intended to the people of England. What! Lieutenant-

---

and gives him the government of Kinsale.......... Colonel Cunninghame was Adjutant-General in Ireland. Lord Townshend offers him a pension, to induce him to resign to Luttrell. Cunninghame treats the offer with contempt. What's to be done? Poor Gisborne must move once more........He accepts of a pension of five hundred pounds a year, until a government of greater value shall become vacant. Colonel Cunninghame is made Governor of Kinsale; and Luttrell, at last, from whom the whole machinery is put in motion, becomes Adjutant-General, and in effect takes the command of the army in Ireland.

Colonel Luttrell Adjutant-General of an army of sixteen thousand men! One would think his Majesty's campaigns at Blackheath and Wimbledon might have taught him better....I cannot help wishing General Harvey joy of a colleague, who does so much honour to the employment....But my Lord, this measure is too daring to pass unnoticed, too dangerous to be received with indifference or submission. You shall not have time to new-model the Irish army. They will not submit to be garbled by Colonel Luttrell. As a mischief to the English constitution, (for he is not worth the name of enemy) they already detest him. As a boy, impudently thrust over their heads, they will receive him with indignation and contempt. As for you, my Lord, who perhaps are no more than the blind, unhappy instrument, of Lord Bute and her Royal Highness the Princess of Wales, be assured, that you shall be called upon to answer for the advice which has been given, and either discover your accomplices, or fall a sacrifice to their security.

JUNIUS.

What! Lieutenant-Colonel, &c.] This is the most solid objection. Colonel Luttrell does not appear to have then possessed sufficient military experience and ability, for the office to which he was promoted.

Her Royal Highness, &c.] The Princess Dowager of Wales, after a residence of thirty years, since her first arrival in England, had set out on a journey to the Continent, on the 8th of June. After an absence of four months, she arrived at Carleston House, on the 27th of October. The Duke of Gloucester had attended her on her journey.

LETTER XLI.

TO THE RIGHT HONOURABLE LORD MANSFIELD.

———

TIMID and cautious, from the consequences of their adventures with Wilkes, the friends and servants of government, though sorely galled by JUNIUS, *dared not to arm themselves against him, with the shield and spear of legal prosecution, till, in his* Letter to the King, *he appeared to them to have proceeded to an audacity of seditious invective, which could not fail to provoke the warmest indignation of every Englishman, in whose breast false patriotism had not utterly extinguished the sentiments of loyalty.*

Henry Sampson Woodfall, *therefore, the original publisher of that and the other Letters of* JUNIUS ; Mr. Almon, *who had sold it in a publication, intitled,* The London Museum ; Mr. Miller, *the publisher of the* London Evening Post ; *and others, who had also reprinted the same Letter to the King ; were brought at different times, to trial. Almon's trial came first on ; he was found guilty of selling the Letter, by the Jury. The sentence pronounced upon him was, to pay a fine of ten marks, and to find sureties for his good behaviour for two years ; himself to be bound in four hundred pounds, his sureties in two hundred pounds each. Woodfall was found guilty, by the Jury, of* printing and publishing only. *Miller and Baldwin were acquitted. At the trial of Robinson, one of the Jurymen starting up while the Judge was giving his charge, cried,* ...." You need not say any more, for I am determined to acquit " him. " *And, in consequence of this irregularity, the trial was put off till the next term. On these trials, the Court wished to confine the Juries to find simply the fact, without giving any opinion of its guilt or innocence. The Juries would not easily submit to be thus restrained : and they had, indeed, the Law of England on their side.*

It was, after the issue of these trials had shewn what the publishers of the Letters of JUNIUS *had to dread, that the author addressed the following, long and very eloquent one, to Lord Mansfield. In this Letter,* JUNIUS *professes to write an invective of revenge ; relates, in opprobium against Lord Mansfield, some particulars of his Lordship's early life ; condemns the general tenor of his conduct as a Judge ; accuses him of endeavouring continually to sophisticate the spirit of the Law of England, by debasing additions out of the Imperial Law of Rome ; blames him for giving evil political advice to his Sovereign ; and concludes with threatening fiercer invective, if the printers of this Letter should be harassed by prosecution.*

———

MY LORD,   14. *November*, 1770.

THE appearance of this Letter will attract the curiosity of the public, and command even your Lordship's attention. I am considerably in your debt, and shall endeavour, once for all, to balance the account. Accept of this address, my Lord, as a prologue to more important scenes, in which you will probably be called upon to act or suffer.

You will not question my veracity, when I assure you, that it has not been owing to any particular respect for your person that I have abstained from you so long. Besides the distress and danger with which the press is threatened, when your Lordship is party, and the party is to be judge, I confess I have been deterred by the difficulty of

---

A prologue to more *important scenes, &c.*] By the use of the sign of comparison *more,* JUNIUS inadvertently represents as a *scene,* that which he had just before called only *a prologue.* The expression is evidently incorrect.

the task. Our language has no term of reproach, the mind has no idea of detestation, which has not already been happily applied to you, and exhausted. ....Ample justice has been done, by abler pens than mine, to the separate merits of your life and character. Let it be *my* humble office to collect the scattered sweets, till their united virtue tortures the sense.

Permit me to begin with paying a just tribute to Scotch sincerity, wherever I find it. I own, I am not apt to confide in the professions of gentlemen of that country ; and, when they smile, I feel an involuntary emotion to guard myself against mischief. With this general opinion of an ancient nation, I always thought it much to your Lordship's honour, that, in your earlier days, you were but little infected with the prudence of your country. You had some original attachments, which you took every proper opportunity to acknowledge. The liberal spirit of youth prevailed over your native discretion. Your zeal in the cause of an un-

---

To collect the scattered, &c.] There is an ambitious and laboured refinement of thought, in the use of this figure. Yet, it is correct in its structure, and not unhappy in its application.

Your zeal in the cause of an unhappy prince, &c.] The family of Stormont, from which Lord Mansfield descended, owed its first splendor to the favour of James the First. They were long faithful to the descendants, in the male line, from that monarch. One of the brothers of his Lordship became Secretary to the Pretender. His Lordship himself, in his early youth, associated often with

happy prince was expressed with the sincerity of
wine, and some of the solemnities of religion*. This,
I conceive, is the most amiable point of view in
which your character has appeared. Like an honest man, you took that part in politics, which might
have been expected from your birth, education,
country, and connexions. There was something
generous in your attachment to the banished house
of Stuart. We lament the mistakes of a good
man, and do not begin to detest him until he affects
to renounce his principles. Why did you not adhere to that loyalty you once professed ? Why did

Jacobites. He was especially patronized, when a student in the
Temple, by a Mr. Vernon, a rich Jacobite mercer in the city. At
Vernon's table, he used to meet with other Jacobites or favourers
of Jacobitism ; and the Pretender's health was sometimes drunk
among them. In the progress of his career at the bar, Mr. Murray,
though enriched by a legacy from his friend Vernon, found it prudent to join the party of the Whigs. He did so ; and, till a particular occasion arose, his Jacobitism was forgotten. He was appointed,
together with Stone, who had been private Secretary to the Duke
of Newcastle, to an important trust in the education of our present King, when Prince of Wales. Murray and Stone were more
acceptable than some others who were about the Prince; and a
violent jealousy was excited against them. While every means was
earnestly sought by their political enemies to procure their removal,
Liddel, Lord Ravensworth, learned from an attorney in the country, that they had used to drink the Pretender's health at Vernon's
table. This was mentioned in parliament, and complained of to
ministers. It was said, that such Jacobites would undoubtedly betray the royal family to their ruin. But Ravensworth's labour was
lost. He had only his noise for his pains.

* This man was always a rank Jacobite. Lord Ravensworth
produced the most satisfactory evidence of his having frequently
drunk the Pretender's health upon his knees.

you not follow the example of your worthy brother * ? With him you might have shared in the
honour of the Pretender's confidence....with him you
might have preserved the integrity of your character ; and England, I think, might have spared you
without regret. Your friends will say, perhaps,
that although you deserted the fortune of your
liege Lord, you have adhered firmly to the principles which drove his father from the throne;....that,
without openly supporting the person, you have
done essential service to the cause ; and consoled
yourself for the loss of a favourite family, by reviv-
ing and establishing the maxims of their government. This is the way, in which a Scotchman's
understanding corrects the errors of his heart....My
Lord, I acknowledge the truth of the defence,
and can trace it through all your conduct. I see,
through your whole life, one uniform plan to enlarge the power of the crown, at the expence of

---

* Confidential Secretary to the late Pretender. This circumstance confirmed the friendship between the brothers.

Without openly supporting the person, &c.] This is a very unjust charge. The cause of Jacobitism, was the restoration of the
House of Stuart. Lord Mansfield was acquitted by all, of having
ever done any thing in his official employments, which could tend
to serve the interests of the Pretender. He rather injured the cause
of Jacobitism, by reconciling Jacobites to the family upon the
throne.

To enlarge the power of the crown, &c.] Upon a careful review
of the political and juridical life of Lord Mansfield, one cannot but
acknowledge, that a very high Tory spirit predominated throughout the whole. Not that he made any attempts which he knew to

the liberty of the subject. To this object your thoughts, words, and actions, have been constantly directed. In contempt or ignorance of the common law of England, you have made it your study to introduce into the court where you preside, maxims of jurisprudence unknown to Englishmen. The Roman code, the law of nations, and the opinion of foreign civilians, are your perpetual theme ; ....but who ever heard you mention Magna Charta, or the Bill of Rights, with approbation or respect? By such treacherous arts, the noble simplicity and free spirit of our Saxon laws were first corrupted.... The Norman conquest was not compleat, until Norman lawyers had introduced their laws, and reduced slavery to a system....This one leading prin-

be wicked and originally illegal, to enlarge the power of the Crown. But, the fundamental principles were Tory, upon which all his habits of thinking and acting had been built. Hence, even while numbered with the Whigs, and sincerely co-operating with them, his counsels and judgments still breathed the spirit of Toryism.

Treacherous arts, &c.] The accusation of treachery is unjust. In the rest of this part of the charge, JUNIUS speaks the truth with able discrimination.

. *Reduced slavery to a system.*] The common doctrine is, here, eloquently stated. But JUNIUS, and the English lawyers in general, grossly err, in regard to the true and primitive character of feodism, The feudal law, when not overborne by violence, was, of all forms of legislation, the most favourable that was ever contrived to the rights of freemen. Its chief blemish was, that it did not impose even all those restraints, which were necessary to the maintenance of civil order. The Saxon laws, during the separate existence of the principalities of the Heptarchy, were still less adequate to the support of regular government. Immediately before the accession

ciple directs your interpretation of the laws, and accounts for your treatment of juries. It is not in political questions only, (for there the courtier might be forgiven) but let the case be what it may, your understanding is equally on the rack, either to contract the power of the jury, or to mislead their judgment. For the truth of this assertion, I appeal ⟨ to the doctrine you delivered in Lord Grosvenor's cause. An action for criminal conversation being brought by a peer against a Prince of the blood, you were daring enough to tell the jury that, in fixing the damages, they were to pay no'regard to the quality or fortune of the parties ;....that it was a trial between A. and B.....that they were to consider the offence in a moral light only, and give no greater damages to a peer of the realm, than to the meanest mechanic. I shall not attempt to refute a doctrine, which, if it was meant for law, carries

of William of Normandy, the administration of the Saxon Laws was, in a very considerable degree, both oppressive and irregular. Feodism actually prevailed ; but in its worst form. Its purest form was introduced by the Normans. The oppression of the Norman monarchs, and of their courts, was in violation of the true principles of the feudal law.

The doctrine you delivered in Lord Grosvenor's cause.] On the 5th of July 1770, the cause of " Lord Grosvenor against the " Duke of Cumberland for criminal conversation with Lady Gros- " venor," was tried before Lord Mansfield, in the Court of King's Bench. The damages were laid at one hundred thousand pounds. Lord Mansfield, in his charge to the Jury, reasoned as JUNIUS relates. A verdict was given against the Duke for ten thousand pounds. The severe animadversion of JUNIUS, upon his Lordship's doctrine, was evidently just.

falsehood and absurdity upon the face of it; but if
it was meant for a declaration of your political
creed, is clear and consistent. Under an arbitrary government, all ranks and distinctions are
confounded. The honour of a nobleman is no
more considered than the reputation of a pea-
sant; for, with different liveries, they are equally
slaves.

Even in matters of private property, we see the
same bias and inclination to depart from the decisions of your predecessors, which you certainly
ought to receive as evidence of the common law.
Instead of those certain, positive rules, by which the
judgment of a court of law should invariably be
determined, you have fondly introduced your own
unsettled notions of equity and substantial justice.
Decisions given upon such principles do not alarm
the public so much as they ought, because the
consequence and tendency of each particular instance is not observed or regarded. In the mean
time, the practice gains ground; the court of
King's Bench becomes a court of equity; and the
judge instead of consulting strictly the law of the
land refers only to the wisdom of the court, and
to the purity of his own conscience. The name

The same bias and inclination, &c.] It is not to be denied, however, that in some instances the English Law was a gainer by the
disposition of Lord Mansfield, to employ Natural Equity, and the
principles of the Civil Law, somewhat too freely, in its interpretation.

of Mr. Justice Yates, will naturally revive in your mind some of those emotions of fear and detestation with which you always beheld him. That great lawyer, that honest man, saw your whole conduct in the light that I do. After years of ineffectual resistance to the pernicious principles introduced by your Lordship, and uniformly supported by your *humble friends* upon the bench, he determined to quit a court, whose proceedings and decisions he could neither assent to with honour, nor oppose with success.

* The injustice done to an individual is sometimes of service to the public. Facts are apt to alarm us more than the most dangerous principles. The sufferings and firmness of a Printer have rouzed the public attention. You knew, and felt, that your conduct would not bear a parliamentary enquiry ; and you hoped to escape it, by the meanest, the basest sacrifice, of dignity and consistency, that ever was made by a great magistrate. Where was

---

Mr. Justice Yates, &c.] Sir Joseph Yates was lately dead. The facts which JUNIUS relates, are true. Yates was an able and upright judge, but incapable of improving the spirit of the law in his interpretation of it. There was opposition of juridical principles, and of personal views, between him and Lord Mansfield. He passed to the Court of Common Pleas, on the 4th of May : his death happened on the 7th of June 1770.

* The oppression of an obscure individual, gave birth to the famous Habeas Corpus Act of 31 Car. 2. which is frequently considered as another Magna Charta of the kingdom.

Blackstone, iii. 135,

your firmness, where was that vindictive spirit of which we have seen so many examples, when a man so inconsiderable as Bingley, could force you to confess, in the face of this country, that for two years together you had illegally deprived an English subject of his liberty, and that he had triumphed over you at last? Yet I own, my Lord, that your's is not an uncommon character. Women, and men like women, are timid, vindictive, and irresolute. Their passions counteract each other; and make the same creature, at one moment hateful, at another contemptible. I fancy, my Lord, some time will elapse before you venture to commit another Englishman for refusing to answer interrogatories *.

The doctrine you have constantly delivered in cases of libel, is another powerful evidence of a settled plan to contract the legal power of juries,

Bingley, &c.] On the 28th of May 1770, after Mr. Bingley had suffered imprisonment for two years, Mr. De Grey, the Attorney General, moved, that he should be set at liberty. The Court at first refused; as Bingley still persisted in his obstinacy. But the farther representations of the Attorney General, prevailed; and Bingley was discharged from confinement.

* Bingley was committed for contempt, in not submitting to be examined. He lay in prison two years, until the Crown thought the matter might occasion some serious complaint; and therefore he was let out, in the same consumelious state he had been put in, with all his sins about him, unanointed and unannealed......There was much coquetry between the Court and the Attorney General, about who should undergo the ridicule of letting him escape....*Vide Another Letter* to ALMON, *p.* 189.

and to draw questions inseparable from fact, within the *arbitrium* of the court. Here, my Lord, you have fortune on your side. When you invade the province of the jury in matter of libel, you in effect attack the liberty of the press, and with a single stroke wound two of your greatest enemies..... In some instances you have succeeded, because jurymen are too often ignorant of their own rights, and too apt to be awed by the authority of a chief justice. In other criminal prosecutions, the malice of the design is confessedly as much the subject of consideration to a jury, as the certainty of the fact. If a different doctrine prevails in the case of libels, Why should it not extend to *all* criminal cases?....why not to capital offences? I see no reason (and I dare say you will agree with me, that there is no good one) why the life of the subject should be better protected against you, than his liberty or property. Why should you enjoy the full power of pillory, fine, and imprisonment, and not be indulged with hanging or transportation? With your Lordship's fertile genius, and merciful disposition, I can conceive such an exercise of the

---

Invade the province of jury, in matter of libel, &c.] An act of parliament declaratory of the rights of Juries in cases of libel, which Mr. Fox, with the assistance of Mr. Erskine, had the honour of bringing forward, has established the principle, " that the Jury " is in regard to libels, to judge of law, as well as fact, of intention " as well as of the exterior act." The principle which JUNIUS condemns, betrayed a strange ignorance of the original character and functions of Juries, as well as an inclination to enlarge the power of the Judge by abridging that of the Jury.

power you have, as could hardly be aggravated by that which you have not.

But, my Lord, since you have laboured, (and not unsuccessfully) to destroy the substance *of the trial*, why should you suffer the form of the *verdict* to remain? Why force twelve honest men, in palpable violation of their oaths, to pronounce their fellow subject a *guilty* man; when, almost at the same moment, you forbid their enquiring into the only circumstance which, in the eye of law and reason, constitutes guilt....the malignity or innocence of his intentions?....But I understand your Lordship....If you could succeed in making the trial by jury useless and ridiculous, you might then with greater safety introduce a bill into parliament for enlarging the jurisdiction of the court, and extending your favourite trial by interrogatories to every question in which the life or liberty of an Englishman is concerned*.

Your favourite trial by interrogatories, &c.] A happy allusion to the case of Bingley.

* The philosophical poet doth notably describe the damnable and damned proceedings of the Judge of Hell.

" Gnossius hæc Rhadamanthus habet durissima regna,
  Castigatque, auditque dolos, *subigitque fateri.*"

First he punisheth: and *then* he heareth; and, lastly, compelleth to confess; and makes and mars laws at his pleasure like as the Centurion, in the holy history, did to St. Paul; for the text saith, " Centurio apprehendi Paulum jussit, et se catenis elicari; et " *tunc* INTERROGABAT, quis fuisset, et quid secisset." But good Judges and Justices abhor these courses. *Coke*, 2 *Inst.* 55.

Your charge to the jury, in the prosecution against Almon and Woodfall, contradicts the highest legal authorities, as well as the plainest dictates of reason. In Miller's cause, and still more expressly in that of Baldwin, you have proceeded a step farther, and grossly contradicted yourself...... You may know, perhaps, though I do not mean to insult you by an appeal to your experience, that the language of truth is uniform and consistent. To depart from it safely, requires memory and discretion. In the two last trials, your charge to the jury began, as usual, with assuring them, that they had nothing to do with the law;...that they were to find the bare fact, and not concern themselves about the legal inferences drawn from it, or the degree of the defendants guilt....Thus far you were consistent with your former practice......But how will you account for the conclusion? You told the jury that, " if, after all, they would take upon themselves to determine the law, *they might do it*, but they must be very sure that they determined according to law; for it touched their consciences, and they acted at their peril.".......If I understand your first proposition, you meant to affirm, that the jury were not competent judges of the law in the criminal case of a libel;....that it did not fall within *their* jurisdiction; and that, with respect to *them*, the malice or innocence of the defendants intentions would be a question *coram non judice*.....But the second proposition clears away your own difficulties, and restores the jury to all their judicial capacities.* You make the competence of the court to depend upon the legality of the decision. In the first instance, you deny the power absolutely. In the second, you admit the power, provided it be legally exercised. Now, my Lord, without pretending to reconcile the distinctions of Westminster-Hall with the simple information of common sense, or the integrity of fair argument, I shall be understood by your Lordship, when I assert that, if a juror, or any other Court of Judicature, (for jurors are judges) have no right to entertain a cause, or question of law, it signifies nothing whether their decision be or be not according to law. Their decision is, in itself, a mere nullity; the parties are not bound to submit to it; and, if the jury run any risque of punishment, it is not for pronouncing a corrupt or illegal verdict, but for the illegality of meddling with a point on which they have no legal authority to decide*.

---

* Directly the reverse of the doctrine he constantly maintained in the House of Lords, and elsewhere, upon the decision of the Middlesex election. He invariably asserted, that the decision must be *legal*, because the court was *competent;* and never could be prevailed on to enter farther into the question.

Which they have no legal authority to decide.] The facts in this paragraph are well put; the reasonings are exceedingly ingenious and forcible. The contest between Lord Mansfield and the Juries, defeated, in a great measure, the ends of the prosecution. The Juries were inclined, at first, to *find the fact but not the guilty intention.* When they saw, that the Court would not leave it to them, to judge of the *intention;* they gave an acquittal even of the *fact.*

* These iniquitous prosecutions cost the best of Princes six thousand pounds, and ended in the total defeat and disgrace of the

I cannot quit this subject, without reminding your Lordship of the name of Mr. Benson. Without offering any legal objection, you ordered a special juryman to be set aside, in a cause where the King was prosecutor. The novelty of the fact required explanation. Will you condescend to tell the world, by what law or custom you were authorised to make a peremptory challenge of a juryman? The parties, indeed, have this power; and perhaps your Lordship, having accustomed yourself to unite the characters of judge and party, may claim it in virtue of the new capacity you have assumed, and profit by your own wrong. The time, within which you might have been punished for this daring attempt to pack a jury, is, I fear, elapsed: but no length of time shall erase the record of it.

The mischiefs you have done this country, are not confined to your interpretation of the laws. You are a minister, my Lord; and, as such, have long been consulted. Let us candidly examine what use you have made of your ministerial influence. I will not descend to little matters, but come at once to those important points on which your resolution was waited for, on which the expec-

prosecutors. In the course of one of them, Judge Aston had the unparalleled impudence to tell Mr. Morris, (a gentleman of unquestionable honour and integrity, and who was then giving his evidence on oath) *that he should pay very little regard to any affidavit he should make.*

tation of your opinion kept a great part of the nation in suspense....A constitutional question arises
upon a declaration of the law of parliament, by
which the freedom of election, and the birth-right
of the subject, were supposed to have been invaded....The King's servants are accused of violating the constitution....The nation is in a ferment...
The ablest men of all parties engage in the question, and exert their utmost abilities in the discussion of it.....What part has the honest Lord Mansfield acted? As an eminent judge of the law, his
opinion would have been respected......As a peer,
he had a right to demand an audience of his Sovereign, and inform him that his ministers were pur-
suing unconstitutional measures.......Upon other
occasions, my Lord, you have no difficulty in finding your way into the closet. The pretended neu-
trality of belonging to no party, will not save your
reputation. In questions merely political, an honest
man may stand neuter. But the laws and constitution are the general property of the subject;
not to defend, is to relinquish:....and who is there
so senseless, as to renounce his share in a common
benefit, unless he hopes to profit by a new division
of the spoil? As a Lord of Parliament, you were
repeatedly called upon to condemn or defend the
new law declared by the House of Commons. You
affected to have scruples, and every expedient was
attempted to remove them....The question was proposed and urged to you in a thousand different
shapes....Your prudence still supplied you with

evasion ; your resolution was invincible. For my own part, I am not anxious to penetrate this solemn secret. I care not to whose wisdom it is entrusted, nor how soon you carry it with you to your grave*. You have betrayed your opinion by the very care you have taken to conceal it. It is not from Lord Mansfield that we expect any reserve in declaring his real sentiments in favour of government, or in opposition to the people; nor is it difficult to account for the motions of a timid, dishonest heart, which neither has virtue enough to acknowledge truth, nor courage to contradict it..... Yet you continue to support an administration which you know is universally odious, and which, on some occasions, you yourself speak of with contempt. You would fain be thought to take no share in government, while, in reality, you are the main spring of the machine.....Here, too, we trace the *little*, prudential policy, of a Scotchman. ....Instead of acting that open, generous part, which becomes your rank and station, you meanly skulk into the closet, and give your Sovereign such advice as you have not spirit to avow or defend. You

---

* He said in the House of Lords, that he believed he should carry his opinion with him to the grave. It was afterwards reported, that he had entrusted it, in special confidence, to the ingenious Duke of Cumberland.

You have betrayed your opinion by the very care you have taken to conceal it.] What art and ingenuity of induction !

Prudential policy of a Scotchman.] What, but prudence, could contend with the blind, inveterate prepossessions of the English ?

secretly engross the power, while you decline the
title of minister; and, though you dare not be
Chancellor, you know how to secure the emoluments of the office....Are the seals to be for ever
in commission, that you may enjoy five thousand
pounds a year ?....I beg pardon, my Lord ;....your
fears have interposed at last, and forced you to resign.....The odium of continuing Speaker of the
House of Lords, upon such terms, was too formidable to be resisted. What a multitude of bad passions are forced to submit to a constitutional infir-
mity ! But though you have relinquished the salary,
you still assume the rights of a minister....Your
conduct, it seems, must be defended in parliament.....For what other purpose is your wretched
friend, that miserable serjeant, posted to the House
of Commons ? Is it in the abilities of Mr. Leigh
to defend the great Lord Mansfield ? Or, is he only
the punch of the puppet-shew, to speak as he is
prompted by the CHIEF JUGGLER behind the cur-
tain * ?

Are the seals to be for ever in commission ? &c.] Lord Camden
was suddenly dismissed. Mr. Yorke had scarcely accepted the
seals, when he terminated his existence. Sir Sidney Stafford
Smythe, the Honourable Henry Bathurst, and Sir Richard Aston,
were now Commissioners for the custody of the Great Seal. Lord
Mansfield was, for a time, Speaker of the House of Lords, with a
salary of five thousand pounds a year.

Or, is he only the punch of the puppet shew ? &c.] This ridicule of Mr. Leigh, is eminently happy.

* This paragraph gagged poor *Leigh*. I am really concerned
for the man, and wish it were possible to open his mouth....He is a
very pretty orator.

In public affairs, my Lord, cunning, let it be ever so well wrought, will not conduct a man honourably through life. Like bad money, it may be current for a time, but it will soon be cried down. It cannot consist with a liberal spirit, though it be sometimes united with extraordinary qualifications. When I acknowledge your abilities, you may believe I am sincere. I feel for human nature, when I see a man, so gifted as you are, descend to such vile practices.....Yet do not suffer your vanity to console you too soon. Believe me, my good Lord, you are not admired in the same degree in which you are detested. It is only the partiality of your friends, that balances the defects of your heart with the superiority of your understanding. No learned man, even among your own tribe, thinks you qualified to preside in a Court of Common Law. Yet it is confessed that, under Justinian, you might have made an incomparable Prætor.....It is remarkable enough, but I hope not ominous, that the laws you understand best, and the judges you affect to admire most, flourished in the decline of a great empire, and are supposed to have contributed to its fall.

Here, my Lord, it may be proper for us to pause together.....It is not for my own sake that I wish

When I acknowledge your abilities, &c.] This paragraph bestows just and discriminating praise. And, in the whole, the character of Lord Mansfield, in this Letter, is in substance very little remote from the truth, if we overlook only a few exaggerating expressions.

you to consider the delicacy of your situation. Beware how you indulge the first emotions of your resentment. This paper is delivered to the world, and cannot be recalled. The persecution of an innocent printer cannot alter facts, nor refute arguments.....Do not furnish me with farther materials against yourself....An honest man, like the true religion, appeals to the understanding, or modestly confides in the internal evidence of his conscience. The impostor employs force instead of argument, imposes silence where he cannot convince, and propagates his character by the sword.

JUNIUS.

The prosecution of an innocent printer, &c.] This is sound sense, and plain argument, not wild menace. The peroration is not the weakest part of the Letter. And, of *it*, the whole appears to have been written with singular gravity and care.

LETTER XLII.

TO THE PRINTER OF THE PUBLIC ADVERTISER.

———

FALKLAND's Islands, adjacent to the Continent of South America, were discovered by the early navigators, more than two centuries since. The Spaniards considered them as included in the grant to their *Sovereigns from the Roman Pontiff.* The English claimed them by that right which was supposed to be conferred by priority of discovery. They remained desolate and neglected, till late in the eighteenth century. It was at last judged by the English, that, as a station from which the Spaniards of South America might be annoyed in war, or visited in gainful commerce during peace, those isles might be with great advantage seized, fortified, and colonized. The isles were occupied by an English force; and some slight fortifications were erected. Aware of the danger to their empire in South America, if a flourishing English Colony should be established so near; the Spaniards sent an armament from an American port, which dispossessed the English, and sent them ignominiously home. An act of such hostility was to be resented. Complaints were made to the Spanish Ambassador, and at the Court of Madrid; and preparations were at the same time commenced, for going to war if the Spaniards should refuse to restore the isle without a contest. The negociations were protracted: for the Spaniards saw, that the matter in contest, might ultimately prove to be of the greatest importance; and, amid the contests of parties, in England, they judged that they should find the English government irresolute and weak. At length, however, they agreed to restore the island; which, it was, at the same time, secretly understood, that the English would soon evacuate. Yet, in agreeing to restore it, they would not concede, that it was not theirs by original right. Hence the opponents of the ministry clamoured loudly, that the national honour was vilified. They desired, if they might not plunge the ministry *into an unsuccessful war, to render them odious by the means which were taken to avoid it.*

On the 22d of January 1771, the King was enabled to inform his parliament of the settlement of the dispute with Spain. Opposition arraigned the dishonour of the implied conditions. JUNIUS *undertook to rouse public opinion on their side. This Letter is much more ably written, than those on the subject of the London petitions........ Johnson wrote his pamphlet, on the Falkland Islands, at the request of ministry, in answer to it.*

———

SIR,   30. *January*, 1771.

IF we recollect in what manner the *King's Friends* have been constantly employed, we shall have no reason to be surprised at any condition of disgrace, to which the once respected name of Englishmen may be degraded.   His Majesty has no cares, but such as concern the laws and constitution of his country.   In his Royal breast there is no room left for resentment, no place for hostile sentiments against the natural enemies of his crown. The system of government is uniform....Violence and oppression at home can only be supported by treachery and submission abroad.   When the civil rights of the people are daringly invaded on one side, what have we to expect, but that their poli-

The King's Friends, &c.] It was said, that this negociation had been conducted much rather by those who were invidiously *nicknamed* the King's Friends, than by the official ministers.

Treachery and submission abroad.] JUNIUS was aware, that the Juries were ready to support him ; otherwise he would not have ventured to write this.

tical rights should be deserted and betrayed, in the same proportion, on the other ? The plan of domestic policy, which has been invariably pursued, from the moment of his present Majesty's accession, engrosses all the attention of his servants...... They know that the security of their places depends upon their maintaining, at any hazard, the secret system of the closet. A foreign war might embarrass, an unfavourable event might ruin the minister, and defeat the deep-laid scheme of policy, to which he and his associates owe their employments. Rather than suffer the execution of that scheme to be delayed or interrupted, the King has been advised to make a public surrender, a solemn sacrifice, in the face of all Europe, not only of the interests of his subjects, but of his own personal reputation, and of the dignity of that crown which his predecessors have worn with honour...... these are strong terms, Sir, but they are supported by fact and argument.

The King of Great Britain had been for some years in possession of an island, to which, as the ministry themselves have repeatedly asserted, the Spaniards had no claim of right. The importance of the place is not in question. If it were, a better judgment might be formed of it from the opinion * of Lord Anson and Lord Egmont, and from the

---

These are strong terms, Sir, &c.] They are. There is uncommon energy and pertinency, in this whole exordium.

. *Lord Egmont, &c.*] This nobleman, originally an Irish Peer, was eminent in the House of Commons, first under the title of

anxiety of the Spaniards, than from any fallacious insinuations thrown out by men whose interest it is to undervalue that property which they are determined to relinquish. The pretensions of Spain were a subject of negociation between the two courts. They had been discussed, but not admitted. The King of Spain, in these circumstances, bids adieu to amicable negociation, and appeals directly to the sword. The expedition against Port-Egmont does not appear to have been a sudden, ill-concerted enterprise. It seems to have been conducted not only with the usual military precautions, but in all the forms and ceremonies of war. A frigate was first employed to examine the strength of the place. A message was then sent, demanding immediate possession, in the Catholic King's name, and ordering our people to depart. At last a military force appears, and compels the garrison to surrender. A formal capitulation ensues; and his Majesty's ship, which might at least have been permitted to bring home his troops immediately, is

Lord Percival, and afterwards under that of Earl of Egmont, as one of the ablest speakers among the Tory opponents to the administration of the Pelhams. He had a place in the household of Frederick, Prince of Wales. He contended with Doddington for that Prince's favour; and seems to have prevailed. After the Prince's death, he was himself obliged to yield the ascendency to the Earl of Bute. He was, at first, refused an English peerage, upon the accession of the present King. But, in the year 1762, he was created Lord Lovel and Holland, of Emmore, in Somersetshire. He was in administration under George Grenville, as first Lord of the Admiralty, and was then the immediate author of the design of occupying Falkland's Islands. He died on the 4th of December 1770.

detained in port twenty days, and her rudder forcibly taken away. This train of facts carries no appearance of the rashness or violence of a Spanish
governor. On the contrary, the whole plan seems
to have been formed and executed, in consequence
of deliberate orders and a regular instruction from
the Spanish court. Mr. Bucarelli is not a pirate,
nor has he been treated as such by those who employed him. I feel for the honour of a gentleman, when I affirm that our King owes him a
signal reparation......Where will the humiliation
of this country end! A King of Great Britain, not
contented with placing himself upon a level with
a Spanish governor, descends so low as to do a
notorious injustice to that governor. As a salvo
for his own reputation, he has been advised to
traduce the character of a brave officer, and to
treat him as a common robber, when he knew
with certainty that Mr. Bucarelli had acted in obedience to his orders, and had done no more than
his duty. Thus it happens in private life, with
a man who has no spirit nor sense of honour....
One of his equals orders a servant to strike him....
Instead of returning the blow to the master; his
courage is contented with throwing an aspersion,
equally false and public, upon the character of the
servant.

I feel for the honour of a gentleman, &c.] This is well and forcibly put.

This short recapitulation was necessary to introduce the consideration of his majesty's speech of
the 13th November 1770, and the subsequent measures of government. The excessive caution with
which the speech was drawn up, had impressed
upon me an early conviction, that no serious resentment was thought of, and that the conclusion
of the business, whenever it happened, must, in
some degree, be dishonourable to England. There
appears, through the whole speech, a guard and
reserve in the choice of expression, which shews
how careful the ministry were, not to embarrass
their future projects by any firm or spirited declaration from the throne. When all hopes of peace are
lost, his majesty tells his parliament, that he is
preparing....not for barbarous war, but (with all his
mother's softness) *for a different Situation.....*An
open hostility, authorised by the Catholic King, is
called *an act of a Governor.* This act, to avoid the
mention of a regular siege and surrender, passes
under the piratical description of *seizing by force ;*
and the thing taken is described, not as a part of
the King's territory or proper dominion, but merely
as a *possession....*a word expressly chosen in contradistinction to, and exclusion of, the idea of *right,*

There appears....shews, &c.] In these two instances, JUNIUS
has plainly used the singular number instead of the plural, with a
negligence which cannot be easily pardoned.

With all his mother's softness, &c.] It was foolishly alledged, that
the Princess Dowager of Wales had made herself busy in this negociation.

and to prepare us for a future surrender both of the right and of the possession. Yet, this speech, Sir, cautious and equivocal as it is, cannot by any sophistry be accommodated to the measures which have since been adopted. It seemed to promise, that, whatever might be given up by secret stipulation, some care would be taken to save appearances to the public. The event shews us, that to depart in the minutest article from ·the nicety and strictness of punctilio, is as dangerous to national honour as to female virtue. The woman who admits of one familiarity, seldom knows where to stop, or what to refuse: and when the counsels of a great country give way in a single instance, when they once are inclined to submission; every step accelerates the rapidity of the descent. The ministry themselves, when they framed the speech, did not foresee, that they should ever accede to such an accommodation as they have since advised their master to accept of.

The King says, *The honour of my crown and the rights of my people are deeply affected.* The Spaniard, in his reply, says, *I give you back possession;*

Cautious and equivocal, &c.] The speech *was* cautious: but the preparations for war had been sufficiently vigorous. Johnson skilfully vindicates the moderation of the language of the speech.

Given up by secret stipulation, &c.] It was, no doubt, secretly stipulated that Falkland's Isles should soon be evacuated. Perhaps, if all had been quiet in North America; and had not the Opposition and the City of London, blustered so much at home; better

but I adhere to my claim of prior right; reserving the assertion of it for a more favourable opportunity.

The speech says, *I made an immediate demand of satisfaction; and, if that fails, I am prepared to do myself justice.* This immediate demand must have been sent to Madrid on the 12th of September, or in a few days after. It was certainly refused, or evaded; and the King *has not* done himself justice....When the first magistrate speaks to the nation, some care should be taken of his apparent veracity.

The speech proceeds to say, *I shall not discontinue my preparations, until I have received proper reparation for the injury.* If this assurance may be relied on; what an enormous expence is entailed, *sine die*, upon this unhappy country! Restitution of a possession, and reparation of an injury, are as different in substance, as they are in language. The very act of restitution may contain, as in this instance it palpably does, a shameful aggravation of

---

terms might have been obtained. As it was; there would have been extreme folly and atrocious guilt in going to war with Spain, for the sake of what was denied.

Must have been sent to Madrid, &c.] France took part in the negotiation, which was finally settled under the auspices of the French Court. Johnson details the particulars.

Is entailed, sine die, *&c.*] This might seem puerile, if it had not been intended for the small wits of the city coffee-houses.

the injury. A man of spirit does not measure the degree of an injury, by the mere positive damage he has sustained. He considers the principle on which it is founded; he resents the superiority asserted over him; and rejects, with indignation, the claim of right which his adversary endeavours to establish, and would force him to acknowledge.

The motives on which the Catholic King makes restitution, are, if possible, more insolent and disgraceful to our Sovereign, than even the declaratory condition annexed to it. After taking four months to consider, whether the expedition was undertaken by his own orders or not; he condescends to disavow the enterprize, and to restore the island; .....not from any regard to justice.....not from any regard he bears to his Britannic Majesty; but merely *from the persuasion in which he is, of the pacific sentiments of the King of Great Britain......* At this rate, if our King had discovered the spirit of a man......if he had made a peremptory demand of satisfaction; the King of Spain would have given him a peremptory refusal. But, why this unseason-

Pacific sentiments of the King of Great Britain........At this rate, &c.] These words are very unfairly interpreted by JUNIUS. The King of Spain's expressed persuasion of the pacific sentiments of the King of Britain could only mean; that he believed that this monarch had no wanton disposition to rush into unnecessary war; would make war for nothing but the just defence of the rights and possessions of his crown and subjects; and if his reasonable demands for these might be satisfied without war, would not take up arms.

able, this ridiculous mention of the King of Great
Britain's pacific intentions? Have they ever been
in question? Was *He* the aggressor? Does he
attack foreign powers without provocation? Does
he even resist, when he is insulted? No, Sir, if
any ideas of strife or hostility have entered his
Royal mind, they have a very different direction.
The enemies of England have nothing to fear from
them.

After all, Sir, to what kind of disavowal has the
King of Spain at last consented? Supposing it
made in proper time; it should have been accompanied with instant restitution : and if Mr. Bucarelli acted without orders; he deserved death. Now,
Sir, instead of immediate restitution, we have a
four months negociation; and the officer, whose act
is disavowed, returns to court, and is loaded with
honours.

If the actual situation of Europe be considered;
the treachery of the King's servants, particularly
of Lord North, who takes the whole upon himself,
will appear in the strongest colours of aggravation.
Our allies were masters of the Mediterranean.
The King of France's present aversion from war,

Was he the aggressor ? Does he attack, &c.] This is eloquent
exprobration : and the turn which the writer is about to give it, as
he goes on, is exceedingly artful.

The King of France's present aversion from war, &c.] What
JUNIUS relates of the temper and situation of the French court, is

and the distraction of his affairs, are notorious. He is now in a state of war with his people. In vain did the Catholic King solicit him to take part in the quarrel against us. His finances were in the last disorder; and it was probable, that his troops might find sufficient employment at home. In these circumstances, we might have dictated the law to Spain. There are no terms to which she might not have been compelled to submit. At the worst, a war with Spain alone carries the fairest promise of advantage. One good effect, at least, would have been immediately produced by it. The desertion of France would have irritated her ally: and, in all probability, have dissolved the family compact. The scene is now fatally changed. The advantage is thrown away. The most favourable opportunity is lost. Hereafter we shall know the value of it. When the French King is reconciled to his subjects; when Spain has compleated her preparations; when the collected strength of the House of Bourbon attacks us at once; the King himself will be able to determine upon the wisdom or imprudence of his present conduct. As far as the probability of argument extends, we may safely pronounce; that a conjuncture, which threatens the

---

true. Yet, Spain was so resolute for war, and considered its most important interests to be so immediately at stake; that its monarch would, in all probability, have rejected any plan of pacification, upon conditions more favourable to Britain. Had Spain taken up arms; France *must* have joined her. A general war would have inevitably ensued.

very being of this country, has been wilfully prepared and forwarded by our own ministry. How
far the people may be animated to resistance, under
the present administration, I know not: but this
I know with certainty, that under the present administration, or if any thing like it should continue,
it is of very little moment whether we are a conquered nation or not*.

Having travelled thus far in the high road of
matter of fact; I may now be permitted to wander
a little into the field of imagination. Let us banish
from our minds the persuasion, that these events
have really happened in the reign of the best of
Princes. Let us consider them as nothing more
than the materials of a fable, in which we may conceive the Sovereign of some other country to be

---

* The King's acceptance of the Spanish Ambassador's declaration, is drawn up in barbarous French, and signed by the Earl of
Rochford. This diplomatic Lord has spent his life in the study
and practice of *etiquettes*, and is supposed to be a profound master
of the ceremonies. I will not insult him by any reference to grammar or common sense. If he were even acquainted with the common forms of his office, I should think him as well qualified for
it as any man in his Majesty's service. The reader is requested
to observe Lord Rochford's method of authenticating a public instrument. " En foi de quoi, *moi* soussigne, un des principaux Se-
" cretaires d'Etat S. M. B. *ai* signe la presente de ma signature
" ordinaire, et icelle fait apposer le cachet de *nos* Armes.".......In
three lines, there are no less than seven false concords. But the
man does not even know the style of his office. If he had known
it ; he would have said, " *Nous* soussigne Secretaire d'Etat de S.
" M. B. *avons* signe, &c."

·concerned. I mean to violate all the laws of probability, when I suppose, that this imaginary King,
.after having voluntarily disgraced himself in the
eyes of his subjects, might return to a sense of his
dishonour......:that he might perceive the snare laid
for him by his ministers, and feel a spark of shame
kindling in his breast.....The part he must then be
obliged to act, would overwhelm him with confusion. To his parliament he must say, *I called
you together to receive your advice, and have never
asked your opinion......*To the merchant......*I have
distressed your commerce; I have dragged your seamen out of your ships; I have loaded you with a
grievous weight of insurances....*To the landholder...
*I told you war was too probable, when I was deter-
mined to submit to any terms of accommodation; I
extorted new taxes from you before it was possible
they could be wanted, and am now unable to account
for the application of them....*To the public creditor
....*I have delivered up your fortunes a prey to fo-
reigners, and to the vilest of your fellow-subjects.....*
Perhaps this repenting Prince might conclude with
one general acknowledgement to them all.....*I have
involved every rank of my subjects in anxiety and
distress; and have nothing to offer you in return, but*

I mean to violate, &c.] Let the reader think, what purpose
Junius had in view; then consider attentively the passage which
follows, to the end of this paragraph....is it excelled in the writings
of Demosthenes, or of Rousseau?....Nor does it end with this paragraph. The same strain of eloquence is continued through the next
following one.

the certainty of national dishonour, an armed truce, and peace without security.

If these accounts were settled, there would still remain an apology to be made to his navy and to his army. To the first he would say....*You were once the terror of the world. But go back to your harbours. A man dishonoured as I am, has no use for your service.* It is not probable that he would appear again before his soldiers, even in the pacific ceremony of a review*. But, wherever he appeared, the humiliating confession would be extorted from him. *I have received a blow....and had not spirit to resent it. I demanded satisfaction...... and have accepted a declaration, in which the right to strike me again is asserted and confirmed.* His countenance, at least, would speak this language, and even his guards would blush for him.

But, to return to our argument....The ministry, it seems, are labouring to draw a line of distinction between the honour of the Crown and the rights of the people. This new idea has yet been only started in discourse; for, in effect, both objects have been equally sacrificed. I neither understand

---

* A Mistake. He appears before them every day, with the mark of a blow upon his face.......*Proh pudor !*

The honour of the crown and the rights of the people.] Ministers alledged, that the honour of the crown was satisfied by the Spanish concession. JUNIUS would argue, that a national right had, however, been relinquished.

the distinction, nor what use the ministry propose to make of it. The King's honour is that of his people. *Their* real honour and real interest are the same......I am not contending for a vain punctilio. A clear, unblemished character, comprehends not only the integrity that will not offer, but the spirit that will not submit to, an injury; and, whether it belongs to an individual or to a community, it is the foundation of peace, of independence, and of safety. Private credit is wealth......public honour is security....The feather that adorns the royal bird supports his flight. Strip him of his plumage, and you fix him to the earth.

JUNIUS.

LETTER XLIII.

TO THE PRINTER OF THE PUBLIC ADVERTISER.

———

THE government found again advocates who were willing to defend their conduct in the Spanish negotiation, against the accusations of JUNIUS. *A writer, assuming the signature of* ANTI-JUNIUS, *endeavoured to point out inconsistencies and errors in* JUNIUS'S *last Letter ; and strove, by various reasonings, to invalidate this author's keenest and most forcible arguments on the subject of Falkland's Islands.*

PHILO-JUNIUS *advances, in this Letter, to the aid of his principal. With that genuine eloquence, to which even the most vigorous mind is best roused by the necessities of self-defence ; he successfully vindicates almost all those assertions and arguments, against which exception had been taken ; and by such a triumphant defence, establishes still more surely than at the first, the positions which had been disputed.*

This Letter is at once plain and elaborately eloquent. It may be studied as a model for the acute and artful eloquence of controversy.

———

SIR,   6. *February,* 1771.

I HOPE your correspondent JUNIUS is better employed than in answering or reading the criticisms of a newspaper. This is a task, from which, if he were inclined to submit to it, his friends ought

———

I hope your correspondent, JUNIUS, *&c.*] Here is high, though indirect, praise, of JUNIUS. He was evidently not without a good share of literary vanity ; yet, as it should seem, more arrogant than vain.

to relieve him. Upon this principle, I shall undertake to answer *Anti-Junius;* more, I believe, to his conviction than to his satisfaction. Not daring to attack the main body of J u n i u s's last Letter, he triumphs in having, as he thinks, surprized an outpost, and cut off a detatched argument, a mere straggling proposition. But even in this petty warfare, he shall find himself defeated. ,

J u n i u s does not speak of the Spanish *nation* as the *natural enemies* of England. He applies that description, with the strictest truth and justice, to the Spanish *Court.* From the moment when a Prince of the House of Bourbon ascended that throne, their whole system of government was inverted, and became hostile to this country. Unity of possession introduced a unity of politics ; and Lewis the Fourteenth had reason, when he said to

---

Surprized an out-post, &c.] A clear, impressive, and happily illustrative metaphor drawn from the art of war.

From the moment, &c.] This is not strictly true. While the Duke of Orleans, and the Duke of Bourbon, were masters of the power of the government of France, in the minority of Louis the Fifteenth.....especially at the time when the infanta was sent back to Spain ; Philip the Fifth was sufficiently willing to prefer an intimate alliance with Britain, to the friendship of France. By the injudicious policy of Walpole, a new and more confidential alliance was suffered to grow up between France and Spain. After the French were driven from North America : a new cause was necessarily created, of jealousy between Spain and Britain, of confidential friendship between France and Spain.

The Spaniards individually, and in their private capacities, still cherish a strong abhorrence of the French.

his grand son, " *The Pyrenees are removed.*" The History of the present century is one continued confirmation of the prophecy.

The assertion, " *That violence and oppression* " *at home, can only be supported by treachery and* " *submission abroad,*" is applied to a free people, whose rights are invaded, not to the government of a country where despotic or absolute power is confessedly vested in the Prince ; and with this application, the assertion is true. An absolute monarch having no points to carry at home, will naturally maintain the honour of his Crown in all his transactions with foreign powers. But, if we could suppose the Sovereign of a free nation possessed with a design to make himself absolute ; he would be inconsistent with himself, if he suffered his projects to be interrupted or embarrassed by a foreign war, unless that war tended, as in some cases it might, to promote his principal design. Of the three exceptions to this general rule of conduct, (quoted by *Anti-Junius,*) that of Oliver

---

That violence and oppression, &c.] JUNIUS's defence is not, here, quite satisfactory. His assertion would have been true ; if he had said, that *violence and oppression at home, are sometimes to be supported by treachery and submission abroad.* The reigns of Charles and James the Second, furnished examples of this. But, to render his assertion more forcible, he made the proposition *universal.* It became thus incorrect. He defends it ingeniously, and, eloquently, yet not altogether satisfactorily. But no man ever knew better than he how to get himself out of any *scrape* into which he had inadvertantly fallen.

Cromwell is the only one in point. Harry the Eighth, by the submission of his parliament, was as absolute a Prince as Lewis the Fourteenth. Queen Elizabeth's government was not oppressive to the people; and as to her foreign wars, it ought to be considered that they were *unavoidable*. The national honour was not in question. She was compelled to fight in defence of her own person, and of her title to the crown. In the common cause of selfish policy, Oliver Cromwell should have cultivated the friendship of foreign powers, or at least have avoided disputes with them, the better to establish his tyranny at home. Had he been only a bad man, he would have sacrificed the honour of the nation to the success of his domestic policy. But, with all his crimes, he had the spirit of an Englishman. The conduct of such a man must always be an exception to vulgar rules. He had abilities sufficient to reconcile contradictions, and to make a great nation at the same moment unhappy and formidable. If it were not for the respect I bear the minister, I could name a man, who, without one grain of understanding, can do half as much as Oliver Cromwell.

In the common cause, &c.] Junius here errs. Oliver Cromwell was much better supported in tyranny, by shewing the English, that he could still maintain the national glory, than if he had servilely courted the dishonest aid of Foreign powers. Though Charles and James the Second, sought to support themselves in violence and oppression at home, by treachery abroad; they were miserably successless in the attempt. They would have found it much more advantageous, to have acted like Elizabeth, or like Cromwell.

Whether or no there be a *secret system* in the closet, and what may be the object of it, are questions which can only be determined by appearances, and on which every man must decide for himself.

The whole plan of JUNIUS's Letter proves, that he himself makes no distinction between the real honour of the crown, and the real interests of the people. In the climax to which your correspondent objects, JUNIUS adopts the language of the court, and by that conformity, gives strength to his argument. He says, that " *the King has not only sacri-* " *ficed the interests of his people, but* (what was " likely to touch him more nearly) *his personal re-* " *putation and the dignity of his crown.*"

The queries put by *Anti-Junius* can only be answered by the ministry. Abandoned as they are, I fancy they will not confess that they have for so many years, maintained possession of another man's property. After admitting the assertion of the ministry, viz.....*that the Spaniards had no rightful claim*, and after justifying them for saying so....it is

---

Determined by appearances, &c. Public appearances without secret information, would not justify what JUNIUS had said of a secret system. JUNIUS has here made an inconsiderate concession highly unfavourable to his own purpose.

After admitting, &c. JUNIUS seems to have here the advantage over his adversary, only by that adversary's unskilfulness.

his business, not *mine* to give us some good reason for their *suffering the pretensions of Spain to be a subject of negociation.* He admits the facts....let him reconcile them if he can.

The last paragraph brings us back to the original question, whether the Spanish declaration contains such a satisfaction as the King of Great Britain ought to have accepted? This was the field upon which he ought to have encountered JUNIUS openly and fairly. But here he leaves the argument as no longer defensible. I shall therefore conclude with one general admonition to my fellow-subjects......that, when they hear these matters debated, they should not suffer themselves to be misled by general declamations upon the conveniencies of peace, or the miseries of war. Between peace and war, abstractedly, there is not, there cannot be a question, in the mind of a rational being. The real questions are, *Have we any security, that the peace we have so dearly purchased will last a twelvemonth?* and, if not....*have we, or have we not, sacrificed the fairest opportunity of making war with advantage?*

PHILO JUNIUS.

The real questions are, &c.] Possessing such extensive American dominions; Britain could expect to maintain steady peace with Spain, only by evincing a union of firmness and moderation, which might satisfy Spain, that Britain aimed not at the universal conquest of America, but would vigorously defend those unquestionable possessions which she had there acquired.

LETTER XLIV.

TO THE PRINTER OF THE PUBLIC ADVERTISER.

———

THE debates in parliament had never yet been regularly and avowedly made public, in the newspapers. But various artifices had been used, in order to make them known, under some slight and unconcealing disguise, by which the general curiosity might be gratified, without provoking parliamentary censure. Even this disguise began to be laid aside, under the licence of political publication which had been usurped by the patriots, since the commencement of the present reign. This licence was, however, frequently checked, by both Houses of Parliament. The Printers of any publication in which either House was mentioned, were liable to be summoned before that House, to be confined, reprimanded, severely fined, and at last dismissed, only after they had made the most humiliating submissions, and had paid large sums of money in fines and fees. The late Lord Marchmont especially, used to watch with suspicious vigilance, over the Newspapers, and to make motions against their printers in the House of Peers, whenever any of the proceedings of that House was, however slightly mentioned, in these Papers. The public endured this severe use of the privilege of parliament, with great impatience. The printers of the newspapers, were, from time to time, encouraged to set it at defiance. At length, in the beginning of March 1771, the matter was brought into trial between the people and the House of Commons.

Accounts of the proceedings in parliament had been printed in the different newspapers. Colonel Onslow made a motion in the House of Commons, against the printers, as guilty of a violation of the privileges of parliament. The printers were summoned to attend the House. Those who obeyed the summons, obtained, on easy terms, their pardon. Robert Thompson, and John Wheble, printers of the Gazetteer, and the Middlesex Journal, slighted the order : and a proclamation was therefore issued, offering a reward of fifty pounds, to whoever should apprehend them. On the 13th of March, the printers of the Morning Chronicle, the St. James's Chronicle, the London, the Whitehall, and the General Evening Posts, and the London Packet, were also ordered to attend the House of Commons. J. Miller, printer of the London Evening Post, slighting this order, a messenger from the Commons was, on the 14th, sent to take him into custody.

While these proceedings went on, in the House of Commons, against the printers; the City was in a commotion, at least of patriotic spirits, against their imputed tyranny. Wilkes, now Alderman of the Ward of Farringdon Without, concerted a plan to baffle all the wrath of the Commons. Wheble was apprehended, in consequence of the proclamation, on the 15th, and was brought before Mr. Wilkes, then the sitting Alderman at Guildhall. Wilkes, in contempt of the authority of the House of Commons, and the proclamation, discharged Wheble; bound him over to prosecute the person by whom he had been apprehended; obliged that person to give bail for his future appearance in trial; and sent notice of these proceedings to Lord Halifax, then one of the Secretaries of State. A messenger from the Serjeant at Arms, attending on the House of Commons, was sent to take into custody, Miller, the refractory printer of the London Evening Post. Miller, was instructed to charge that messenger, as guilty of an assault, if he should attempt to seize him, to call in a constable to take him into custody, and to carry him before the city magistrates. All this was done. Whittam, the messenger from the Serjeant at Arms, attempting to seize Miller; was, by him, carried before the Lord Mayor; who, with Aldermen Wilkes and Oliver, committed Whittam to Wood-street Compter, and afterwards held him to bail for his future appearance.

At the news of this invasion of their privileges, the Commons were highly enraged. They summoned Crosby, the Lord Mayor, to attend in his place, and give an account of his conduct in sending a messenger from the House of Commons into custody. Mr. Wilkes was also ordered to attend the House; but refused, unless he might attend in his place as Member for Middlesex. On the 19th, Crosby and Oliver, gave obedience to the order of the Commons. They justified, or attempted to justify, their conduct, by pleading their obli-

gation to maintain inviolate, the rights of the city. The ministers, and their friends, earnestly proposed, that the Lord Mayor, and Mr. Oliver, should be, at least, committed to the Tower, during the pleasure of the House. The minority contended, with every argument which zeal could suggest, in their favour. Oliver was sent to the Tower, immediately after the close of the debate. The recognizance of Whittam, the messenger, was erased out of the minute-book of recognizances, belonging to the Lord Mayor's Court. The determination in respect to Crosby, the Mayor, was delayed, only because illness made him unable to continue in the House, till the close of the proceedings of the day. On the 27th, the Lord Mayor again attended in his place, refused all concessions, and was also sent to the Tower. Wilkes had received a second order to attend the House, which he slighted equally as the first. He was, a third time, summoned, to attend on the 8th of April. But, the leaders of the majority, aware that he would still slight their summons, contrived to wave the contention which he courted, by adjourning over the day, on which he was last ordered to attend, and then ceasing from any farther repetition of their summons.

In the mean time, Crosby, Wilkes, and Oliver, were extolled as the firmest and most illustrious of patriots. The thanks of the Common Council were eagerly voted to them. A Committee of the Common Council were appointed to assist them in their defence. To defray the necessary expence, a sum of money was zealously granted. In their passage through the streets, between the Mansion-house, the House of Commons, and the Tower, they were followed by an immense crowd, consisting, not merely of rabble, but of the Livery, who were zealous in whatever could insult the House of Commons, or thwart the views of the administration. In the Tower, the Mayor and Alderman Oliver, were visited by the leaders of the minority in parliament ; and had a table kept for them, at the expence of the city. Application was made to the Chief Justices of the Courts of King's Bench and Common Pleas, to admit them to bail. Both these judges, however, acknowledged the authority of the House of Commons, and refused to interpose between that House and the prisoners. They remained, therefore, in confinement, till the prorogation of that session of parliament. They were, then, of course, set at liberty ; as

*the authority of the House of Commons had ceased. They were re-
ceived, when they left the Tower, with many expressions of congra-
tulation by their fellow-citizens. The printers were presented with a
gratification in money from the supporters of the Bill of Rights.
Whittam, the messenger, was saved by a* noli prosequi, *from the
prosecution, which was in the printers name urged against him.
The city, after Crosby and Oliver were at liberty, again petitioned
the King, against the House of Commons. It was accounted by the
people, that the city had triumphed....by the Commons, that they
had successfully vindicated their privileges. From that time, the
printers of newspapers have been tacitly suffered to publish such accounts, as they could procure, of the debates in the two Houses of
Parliament, without punishment, unless when those accounts have
misrepresented, or vilified, the proceedings of either House.*

On the 22d of April, while the Lord Mayor, and Alderman Oliver
were still in the Tower, JUNIUS wrote the following Letter. Its design is to prove, that the House of Commons had no right to imprison
for any contempt of their authority. I do not think it one of his best
productions. Yet, there is in it much of reason, and much of eloquence.

SIR,   22. *April*, 1771.

TO write for profit without taxing the press;
......to write for fame, and to be unknown......to
support the intrigues of faction, and to be disowned, as a dangerous auxiliary, by every party in

---

To be disowned as a dangerous auxiliary, &c.] Any party
would have rejoiced in the assistance of JUNIUS, if he would have
deigned to become the advocate of their cause, to echo their opinions, and implicitly to defend their party-measures. But, while
he so powerfully sustained the cause of the Opposition; he did so,
on principles which were, in some things, peculiar to himself. These
they would not own as theirs. His invectives, too, were severe beyond what any party could profess to throw out, even against their
bitterest adversaries. Hence another reason to make the Opposition fearfully disown him, even while he was their pride.

the kingdom.....are contradictions which the minister must reconcile, before I forfeit my credit with the public. I may quit the service; but it would be absurd to suspect me of desertion. The reputation of these papers is an honourable pledge for my attachment to the people. To sacrifice a respected character, and to renounce the esteem of society, requires more than Mr. Wedderburne's re-

Mr. Wedderburne's, &c.] Mr. Wedderburne, now Lord Loughborough, and Chancellor of Great Britain, had adhered, since the æra of the first Rockingham administration, to the party of George Grenville. He had taken a very active and zealous part against administration, in the case of the Middlesex election. But, George Grenville, died on the 13th of November, 1770. His death proved fortunate to administration; for, it produced a defection of his principal adherents from the party of the Opposition; and thus broke its strength. Among the deserters, upon this occasion, to the ministry, were, the Earl of Suffolk, who obtained the appointment of Lord Privy Seal.....and Mr. Wedderburne, who was now appointed Solicitor General, and Cofferer to the Queen. This is the defection to which JUNIUS alludes, in the Text.

The career of Lord Loughborough has been truly illustrious.

His descent is from an ancient Scottish family. He studied the Law of Scotland; was called to the bar at Edinburgh; and, had it not been for some discouragement which he received in his early pleadings before the Supreme Court in Scotland....might never perhaps have aspired to try his fortune, as an English barrister.

Forsaking that narrow field for ambition, on which he had at first entered; he was admitted of the Inner Temple, on the 8th of May, 1753. On the 25th of November, 1757, he was called to the English bar. In the intermediate space, he had prosecuted his studies with great diligence and success. His previous preparation for the Scottish bar, gave him, necessarily, considerable advantage for the study of the Laws of England. To free his eloquence from the infection of Scotticisms, and to attain to perfect propriety and ease in the enunciation of English speech, he received the lessons

solution; and though, in him, it was rather a profession than a desertion of his principles; [I speak
tenderly of this gentleman; for, when treachery is
in question, I think we should make allowances

of Sheridan, attended the performances of Garrick and other great
masters on the Theatre, listened to the elocution of the best speakers in parliament or at the bar, and eagerly pursued the writings
of those authors who were esteemed the classics of English literature.

Such were his native talents, and such the success of his studies;
that, he had no sooner been called to the English bar, than he began
to be distinguished as a Counsellor and Pleader. He was very soon
in full employment. The accession of our present Sovereign, favoured his advancement, by bringing his friend and patron, Lord
Bute, into power. He was appointed a King's Counsel, and obtained a seat in parliament. He was even understood to enjoy the
confidential friendship of Lord Bute. Amidst his business at the
bar, and his labours as a senator and politician, he still cultivated
elegant literature, and associated with the wits. His intimacy with
Murphy, has been commemorated in Churchill's Rosciad. Johnson
and Sheridan were indebted to his interposition with Lord Bute, for
their pensions. In Easter Term, 1763, he was admitted of Lincoln's Inn.

When a motion was made in the House of Commons, for the
impeachment of Lord Clive, the conqueror of the East; Mr. Wedderburne defended his Lordship, with a skill and eloquence which
were reckoned to exceed the abilities of almost all his contemporaries at the bar.

It was under the administration of George Grenville, that he
had been promoted. Grenville's opinions concerning the taxation
of America, were congenial with his: He disliked the doctrines of
Lord Chatham, and of the Rockingham party, in regard to the
measures which ought to be taken with the Americans: And he
therefore continued firm in his adherence to Grenville. Even the
coalition of Grenville with his brothers, and with the rest of the
Whigs, did not provoke Wedderburne to forsake him. His aid to
Opposition, in the contest respecting the Middlesex election, was

for a Scotchman;] yet we have seen him in the
House of Commons overwhelmed with confusion,
and almost bereft of his faculties. But, in truth,
Sir, I have left no room for an accommodation

vigorous and powerful. The death of Grenville seemed to set him
free from his engagements. The measures of government in regard
to America, were such as he approved. His appointment to the
office of Solicitor General, on the 23d of January, 1771, attached
him to Lord North. But, the Whigs, sensible how much they had
lost in him, long continued to accuse his apostacy.

From this period, to the year, 1780, he, with Thurlow, then Attorney General, were the co-adjutors and defenders of Lord North
in the House of Commons. He was the zealous advocate of all the
measures of the American war. Against Dr. Franklin, he pronounced, on a particular occasion, a memorable philippic before
the Privy Council, which has been celebrated as perhaps the greatest effort of his eloquence. With Lord North, he lived in habits of
confidential intimacy. He early distinguished the talents, and cultivated the friendship of Gibbon. It was by his advice, that Gibbon was employed to write the elaborate manifesto of the British
Court, against that of France, at the time when France began to
take part in the American war. The historian's appointment to the
office of a Lord of Trade, was at the solicitation of Mr. Wedderburne. Gibbon highly admired Wedderburne's talents, delighted
in his society, and was grateful for his patronage. After the abolition of the Board of Trade, he endeavoured, but without success,
to procure for his friend Gibbon, a seat at the Board of Customs.

In the year 1778, the promotion of Thurlow made way for the
advancement of Mr. Wedderburne, to the office of Attorney General. In 1780, he was raised to the office of Chief Justice of the
Common Pleas. That of Lord Chancellor, was supposed to be
still the object of his ambition.

He adhered steadily to the party of Lord North; while Thurlow became, for a time, the strength of the administration of Mr.
Pitt. After the famous coalition of the party of Lord North, with
the Whig followers of Fox; Lord Loughborough found himself once
more associated with those whom, since the year 1771, he had the

with the piety of St. James's. My offences are not to be redeemed by recantation or repentance. On one side, our warmest patriots would disclaim me as a burthen to their honest ambition. On the other, the vilest prostitution, if JUNIUS could descend to it, would lose its natural merit and influence in the cabinet, and treachery be no longer a recommendation to the royal favour.

The persons who, till within these few years, have been most distinguished by their zeal for high-church and prerogative, are now, it seems, the great assertors of the privileges of the House of

most strenuously opposed. He continued in opposition to the ministry of Mr. Pitt, till the nation was alarmed with fears of the overthrow of the constitution, by the invasion of the principles of French democracy. He was the negotiator, as is said, of the coalition between the party of the Duke of Portland, and that of Mr. Pitt. He succeeded Thurlow in the office of Lord Chancellor; and is the first Scotsman who has filled this high office for Great Britain. Even after Lord Thurlow, he has presided with great reputation in both the Court of Chancery, and the House of Peers.... His health is now said to be broken with the infirmities of age : and his intended retirement begins to be talked of. His personal aspect is noble and commanding. His conversation has been distinguished as rich, spirited, and pleasing. His elocution is graceful and flowing. His eloquence is strong, copious, and artful. His political conduct is at once manly, and of consummate prudence.

The great assertors of the privileges of the House of Commons.] The House of Commons, at first, remarkably a popular branch of the Sovereign authority, has, since, gradually become but a part of the aristocracy. It is natural, then, that its connexion with the Crown and with the Peers, should become continually greater; while its use, as the sole great organ of public opinion in political

Commons. This sudden alteration of their sentiments, or language, carries with it a suspicious appearance. When I hear the undefined privileges
of the popular branch of the legislature exalted
by Tories and Jacobites, at the expence of those
strict rights, which are known to the subject, and
limited by the laws; I cannot but suspect, that some
mischievous scheme is in agitation, to destroy both
law and privilege, by opposing them to each other.
They who have uniformly denied the power of the
whole legislature to alter the descent of the crown,
and whose ancestors, in rebellion against his Majesty's family, have defended that doctrine at the
hazard of their lives, now tell us, that privilege of
parliament is the only rule of right, and the chief
security of the public freedom....I fear, Sir, that
while forms remain, there has been some material
change in the substance of our constitution.   The
opinions of these men were too absurd to be so
easily renounced. Liberal minds are open to conviction....Liberal doctrines are capable of improvement.....There are proselytes from atheism; but
none from superstition....If their present professions were sincere, I think they could not but be
highly offended at seeing a question concerning

affairs, must be still more and more abridged. JUNIUS attributes
to an insulated and partial cause, that which was the effect of general and permanent ones.

  They who have uniformly, &c.] This was certainly a good argument against the Jacobites, who defended the ministerial decision in
the case of the Middlesex election.

parliamentary privilege unnecessarily started, at a season so unfavourable to the House of Commons, and by so very mean and insignificant a person as the minor *Onslow*. They knew, that the present House of Commons, having commenced hostilities with the people, and degraded the authority of the laws by their own example, were likely enough to be resisted, *per fas aut nefas*. If they were really friends to privilege, they would have thought the question of right too dangerous to be hazarded at this season; and without the formality of a convention, would have left it undecided'.

I have been silent hitherto; though not from that shameful indifference about the interests of society which too many of us profess, and call moderation.

Minor Onslow.] This gentleman had made himself odious to JUNIUS and his friends, by a prosecution against Mr. Horne....who had not then assumed the cognomen of Tooke, on account of defamation in a speech at a public meeting; in which Mr. Horne said, that, *though Mr. Onslow should promise his assistance, he would not believe him.* A verdict of four hundred pounds damages was at first, obtained by Mr. Onslow. It was afterwards set aside by a judgment of the Court of Common Pleas.

He had given new offence, as the author of the motion against the printers of the newspapers, in consequence of which the Lord-Mayor and Mr. Oliver were sent to the Tower. No wonder, then, that JUNIUS speaks of him with mingled indignation and contempt.

If they were really, &c.] There is much refinement in this argument. Its purport is, that the Jacobites and Tories wished to make the House of Commons contemptible in the eyes of the people, that they might, by its debasement, exalt the power of the crown.

I confess, Sir, that I felt the prejudices of my education, in favour of a House of Commons, still hanging about me. I thought that a question, between law and privilege, could never be brought to a formal decision, without inconvenience to the public service, or a manifest diminution of legal liberty....that it ought, therefore, to be carefully avoided : and when I saw that the violence of the House of Commons had carried them too far to retreat; I determined not to deliver a hasty opinion, upon a matter of so much delicacy and importance.

The state of things is much altered in this country, since it was necessary to protect our representatives against the direct power of the crown. We have nothing to apprehend from prerogative, but every thing from undue influence. Formerly, it was the interest of the people, that the privileges of parliament should be left unlimited and undefined. At present, it is not only their interest, but I hold it to be essentially necessary to the preservation of the constitution, that the privileges of parliament should be strictly ascertained, and confined within the narrowest bounds the nature of their institution will admit of. Upon the same principle, on which

---

I confess, Sir, &c.] Much of the orator's art is displayed in this paragraph. JUNIUS professes respect for the House of Commons, that he may be the more readily believed when he goes about to abuse it.

I would have resisted prerogative in the last century, I now resist privilege. It is indifferent to me, whether the crown, by its own immediate act, imposes new, and dispenses with old laws; or whether the same arbitrary power produces the same effects through the medium of the House of Commons. We trusted our representatives with privileges for their own defence and ours. We cannot hinder their desertion, but we can prevent their carrying over their arms to the service of the enemy....It will be said, that I begin with endeavouring to reduce the argument concerning privilege to a mere question of convenience; that I deny, at one moment, what I would allow at another; and that, to resist the power of a prostituted House of Commons, may establish a precedent injurious to all future parliaments.....To this I answer generally, that human affairs are in no instance governed by strict positive right. If change of circumstances were to have no weight in directing our conduct and opinions, the mutual intercourse of mankind would be nothing more than a contention between positive and equitable right. Society would be a state of war; and law itself would be injustice. On this general ground, it is highly rea-

---

Whether the crown.....imposes.....dispenses.....produces, &c.] JUNIUS, like many other classical English writers, commonly confounds the indicative with the subjunctive mood. This is not a heinous crime in composition, implying gross ignorance and weakness. But, it is an instance of incorrectness, which should not be imitated. He should have written....*impose....dispense....produce.*

sonable, that the degree of our submission to privileges which have never been defined by any positive law, should be considered as a question of convenience, and proportioned to the confidence we repose in the integrity of our representatives. As to the injury we may do to any future and more respectable House of Commons; I own, I am not now sanguine enough to expect a more plentiful harvest of parliamentary virtue in one year than another. Our political climate is severely altered:

Our political climate is severely altered, &c.] I should incline to maintain, even upon higher grounds, the same doctrine, which is here taught by JUNIUS, concerning the necessity of legally defining the privileges of parliament. It is true, as he alledges, that, while the House of Commons was, strictly speaking, a popular branch of the constitution, the people in asserting and yielding to its privileges, only created a power, which was to be their own defence against the authority of the crown. But, from the first, that House could never possess any other executive power, than was necessary to protect the freedom of their deliberations, and to give them every necessary advantage of information. In the earlier periods of the constitution, they carried on their deliberations so much under the authority of the King, that attendance in parliament was understood to be a service particularly paid to him. Their assembling was, as it were, in his very house. His servants were, therefore, to be ready in waiting upon them: and his Courts and Officers were, at hand, to carry their reasonable orders into execution. At that æra, then, their separate privileges of immediate executive authority could not be great. But, they gradually became more powerful against the crown, till at last a House of Commons usurped the whole Sovereign authority. The privileges of the Long Parliament were, for a while, unrestricted and undefined. Such privilege of parliament was subversive of the strength of the constitution. It was checked without being defined, under the reigns of Charles and James the Second. At the Revolution, it was again aggrandized. It continued in uncertainty from that æra downward, to the time of

and, without dwelling upon the depravity of modern times; I think no reasonable man will expect that, as human nature is constituted, the enormous influence of the crown should cease to prevail over the virtues of individuals. The mischief lies too deep to be cured by any remedy, less than some great convulsion, which may either carry back the constitution to its original principles, or utterly destroy it. I do not doubt that, in the first session after the next election, some popular measures may be adopted. The present House of Commons have injured themselves by a too early and public profession of their principles; and if a strain of prostitution which had no example, were within the reach of emulation; it might be imprudent to hazard the experiment too soon. But after all, Sir, it is very immaterial whether a House of Commons shall preserve their virtue for a week, a month, or a year. The influence, which makes a septennial parliament dependent upon the pleasure of the crown, has a permanent operation, and can-

these contentions. But all powers of the House of Commons, above what were necessary to its information, and freedom of debate, had been usurped. They had been occasionally not regularly exercised. When the powers of the constitution were more equally counterpoised; and when the laws, political and civil, became more clear and definite; it could not be, but that the privileges of that House should both be defined, and reduced nearly to what they had been in the first reign of feodism....Thus, its powers were not originally indefinite: they became such, amid darkness, usurpation, and confusion: they were to be defined and limited in the natural improvement of law, knowledge, and civil order: it was useful for all the branches of the constitution, that they should be thus defined.

not fail of success....My premises, I know, will be denied in argument, but every man's conscience tells him they are true.   It remains then to be considered, whether it be for the interest of the people, that privilege of parliament (which *, in respect to the purposes for which it has hitherto been acquiesced under, is merely nominal) should be contracted within some certain limits ; or whether the subject shall be left at the mercy of a power, arbitrary upon the face of it, and notoriously under the direction of the crown.

I do not mean to decline the question of *right*. On the contrary, Sir, I join issue with the advocates for privilege ; and affirm that, " excepting the " cases wherein the House of Commons are a " Court of Judicature, [to which, from the nature " of their office, a coercive power must belong ;] " and excepting such contempts as immediately " interrupt their proceedings ; they have no legal " authority to imprison any man, for any supposed " violation of privilege whatsoever."....It is not

* The necessity of securing the House of Commons against the King's power, so that no interruption might be given either to the attendance of the members in parliament, or to the freedom of debate, was the foundation of parliamentary privilege ; and we may observe, in all the addresses of new appointed Speakers to the Sovereign, the utmost privilege they demand is liberty of speech and freedom from arrests.   The very word *privilege*, means no more than immunity, or a safeguard to the party who possesses it, and can never be construed into an active power of invading the rights of others.

pretended that privilege, as now claimed, has ever been defined or confirmed by statute : neither can it be said, with any colour of truth, to be a part of the common law of England, which had grown into prescription long before we knew any thing of the existence of a House of Commons. As for the law of parliament, it is only another name for the privilege in question: and since the power of creating new privileges has been formally renounced by both houses; since there is no code in which we can study the law of parliament ; we have but one way left to make ourselves acquainted with it......that is, to compare the nature of the institution of a House of Commons with the facts upon record. To establish a claim of privilege in either house, and to distinguish original right from usurpation; it must appear, that it is indispensably necessary for the performance of the duty they are-employed in, and also that it has been uniformly allowed. From the first part of this description, it follows clearly that, whatever privilege does of right belong to the present House of Commons, did equally belong to the first assembly of their predecessors, was as compleatly vested in them, and might have been exercised in the same extent. From the second, we must infer that privileges, which for several centuries were not only never allowed, but never even claimed by the

To compare the nature of the institution, &c.] This is clearly discriminated, and well stated.

House of Commons, must be founded upon usurpation. The constitutional duties of a House of
Commons, are not very complicated nor mysterious. They are to propose or assent to wholesome
laws for the benefit of the nation; they are to grant
the necessary aids to the King; petition for the redress of grievances; and prosecute treason or high
crimes against the state. If unlimited privilege
be necessary to the performance of these duties;
we have reason to conclude that, for many centuries after the institution of the House of Commons,
they were never performed. I am not bound to
prove a negative; but I appeal to the English history, when I affirm that, with the exceptions already stated, (which yet I might safely relinquish)
there is no precedent, from the year 1265 to the
death of Queen Elizabeth, of the House of Commons having imprisoned any man (not a member
of their house) for contempt or breach of privilege. In the most flagrant cases, and when their
acknowledged privileges were most grossly violated, the poor *Commons*, as they then styled themselves, never took the power of punishment into
their own hands. They either sought redress by
petition to the King, or, what is more remarkable,
applied for justice to the House of Lords; and when
satisfaction was denied them, or delayed, their only
remedy was, to refuse proceeding upon the King's
business. So little conception had our ancestors of
the monstrous doctrines now maintained concerning privilege, that in the reign of Elizabeth, even

liberty of speech, the vital principle of a delibera-
tive assembly, was restrained by the Queen's authority to a simple *aye* or *no;* and this restriction,
though imposed upon three successive parliaments*,
was never once disputed by the House of Commons.

I know there are many precedents of arbitrary
commitments for contempt. But, besides that they
are of too modern a date to warrant a presumption
that such a power was originally vested in the
House of Commons....*Fact* alone does not constitute *Right*. If it does, general warrants were lawful; an ordinance of the two houses has a force equal
to law;. and the criminal jurisdiction assumed by
the Commons in 1621, in the case of Edward
Lloyd, is a good precedent, to warrant the like proceedings against any man, who shall unadvisedly
mention the folly of a King, or the ambition of a
Princess.....The truth is, Sir, that the greatest and
most exceptionable part of the privileges now contended for, were introduced and asserted by a

---

And this restriction, &c.] These are striking facts. But they
are instances of abuse and usurpation which do not clearly, truly,
exemplify the law of parliament.

* In the years 1593....1597....and 1601.

I know there are many precedents, &c.] It is absurd to deny
that the House of Commons has authority to imprison for contempt.
It could not otherwise assert its own dignity. A lawyer might reason against it : but no good lawyer would give a solemn opinion
against it. JUNIUS must surely have sacrificed his own judgment
to the wishes of his party, when he could thus far wrest the general
principle, from its proper use.

House of Commons which abolished both monarchy and peerage; and whose proceedings, although
they ended in one glorious act of substantial justice, could no way be reconciled to the forms of
the constitution. Their successors profited by
the example, and confirmed their power by a moderate or a popular use of it. Thus it grew by degrees, from a notorious innovation at one period,
to be tacitly admitted as the privilege of parliament
at another.

If, however, it could be proved, from consi-
derations or necessity of convenience, that an unlimited power of commitment ought to be entrusted to the House of Commons, and that *in fact* they
have exercised it without opposition; still, in con-
templation of law, the presumption is strongly
against them. It is a leading maxim of the laws
of England, (and, without it, all laws are nugatory)
that there is no right without a remedy, nor any
legal power without a legal course to carry it into
effect. Let the power now in question be tried by
this rule. The speaker issues his warrant of attachment. The party attached either resists force
with force, or appeals to a magistrate, who declares
the warrant illegal, and discharges the prisoner.
Does the law provide no legal means for enforcing
a legal warrant? Is there no regular proceeding
pointed out in our law books, to assert and vindicate the authority of so high a court as the House
of Commons? The question is answered directly by

the fact. Their unlawful commands are resisted, and they have no remedy. The imprisonment of their own members is revenge indeed, but it is no assertion of the privilege they contend for*. Their whole proceeding stops; and there they stand, ashamed to retreat, and unable to advance. Sir, these ignorant men should be informed, that the execution of the laws of England is not left in this uncertain, defenceless condition. If the process of the Courts of Westminster-Hall be resisted, they have a direct course, sufficient to enforce submission. The Court of King's Bench commands the Sheriff to raise the *posse comitatus*. The Courts of Chancery and Exchequer issue a *writ of rebellion*, which must also be supported, if necessary, by the power of the county......To whom will our honest

Their unlawful commands, &c.] It is clear, that none of their commands could be unlawful, which tended solely and expressly, to maintain the order and dignity of their proceedings. Did they command any thing which had not this object ; and was it contrary to law?....then, and only then, might their commands be resisted. However closely and forcibly JUNIUS may here reason ; he neither declares the law, nor even chooses with skill, the vantage ground.

* Upon their own principles, they should have committed Mr. Wilkes, who had been guilty of a greater offence than even the Lord Mayor or Alderman Oliver. But, after repeatedly ordering him to attend, they at last adjourned beyond the day appointed for his attendance ; and, by this mean, pitiful evasion, gave up the point....Such is the force of conscious guilt!

To whom will our honest representatives, &c.] In this case, the Commons must, of course, address the Crown ; requesting the interposition of its authority. Yet, so far as they can act for themselves, they certainly may, in the cases of extreme exigency, which are, above, supposed.

representatives direct *their* writ of rebellion? The guards, I doubt not, are willing enough to be employed; but they know nothing of the doctrine of writs, and may think it necessary to wait for a letter from Lord Barrington.

It may now be objected to me, that my arguments prove too much; for that, certainly, there may be instances of contempt and insult to the House of Commons, which do not fall within my own exceptions, yet, in regard to the dignity of the house, ought not to pass unpunished.   Be it so. ....The Courts of Criminal Jurisdiction are open to prosecutions, which the Attorney General may commence by information or indictment.   A libel, tending to asperse or vilify the House of Commons, or any of their members, may be as severely punished in the Court of King's Bench, as a libel upon the King.   Mr. De Grey thought so, when he drew up the information upon my letter to his Majesty, or he had no meaning in charging it to be a scandalous libel upon the House of Commons. In *my* opinion, they would consult their real dignity much better, by appealing to the laws, when they are offended, than by violating the first principle of natural justice, which forbids us to be judges when we are parties to the cause *.

* " If it be demanded, in case a subject should be committed
" by either House, for a matter manifestly out of their jurisdiction,
" what remedy can he have ? I answer, that it cannot well be ima-
" gined that the law, which favours nothing more than the liber-

I do not mean to pursue them through the remainder of their proceedings. In their first resolutions, it is possible they might have been deceived by ill-considered precedents. For the rest, there is no colour of palliation or excuse. They have advised the King to resume a power of dispensing with the laws by royal proclamation* ; and

" ty of the subject, should give us a remedy against commitments by
" the King himself appearing to be illegal, and yet give us no
" manner of redress against a commitment by our fellow-subjects,
" equally appearing to be unwarranted. But, as this is a case,
" which I am persuaded will never happen, it seems needless over-
" nicely to examine it."....*Hawkins* ii. 110........*N. B. He was a
good lawyer, but no prophet.*

They have advised the King to resume, &c.] JUNIUS alludes,
here, to the proclamation which, at the request of the Commons,
was issued, offering a reward for the apprehension of the printers,
by whom the order of the House had been slighted. That proclamation was certainly irregular. The Executive Power ought not to
have merely continued the Proceeding of the Commons. The proceedings should have been re-commenced, under its authority. The
printers should have been then brought to justice, in the common
course of law. And if it appeared in the whole, that the powers
of the House of Commons, thus limited, were unequal to maintain their dignity, as a branch of the legislature ; a new law ought
to have been made ; establishing a ready and effective mode of procedure, to be followed whenever such a case as that of those printers might again arise.

* That their practise might be every way conformable to their
principles, the House proceeded to advise the Crown to publish a
proclamation, universally acknowledged to be illegal. Mr. Moreton
publickly protested against it, before it was issued ; and Lord Mansfield, though not scrupulous to an extreme, speaks of it with horror.
It is remarkable enough, that the very men who advised the proclamation, and who hear it arraigned every day, both within doors
and without, are not daring enough to utter one word in its defence ;

Kings, we see, are ready enough to follow such advice.....By mere violence, and without the shadow of right, they have expunged the record of a judicial proceeding *. Nothing remained, but to attribute to their own vote a power of stopping the whole distribution of criminal and civil justice.

The public virtues of the chief magistrate have long since ceased to be in question. But it is said, that he has private good qualities; and I myself have been ready to acknowledge them. They are now brought to the test. If he loves his people, he will dissolve a parliament which they can never confide in or respect. If he has any regard for his .own honour, he will disdain to be any longer connected with such abandoned prostitution. But if it were conceivable, that a King of this country had lost all sense of personal honour, and all concern for the welfare of his subjects; I confess, Sir, I should be contented to˙renounce the forms of the

nor have they ventured to take the least notice of Mr. Wilkes, for discharging the persons apprehended under it.

Expunged the record of a judicial proceeding.] This was the recognizance of Whittam, expunged by the command of the House of Commons, from the minute-book of the Court at Guildhall. The legality of that act, was, likewise, exceedingly doubtful.

* Lord Chatham very properly called this the act of a mob, not of a senate.

Renounce the forms of the constitution, &c.] The tendency of this suggestion, was, to excite the people to dissolve the parliament by violence.

constitution once more, if there were no other way to obtain substantial justice for the people *.

JUNIUS.

* When Mr. Wilkes was to be punished, they made no scruple about the privileges of parliament; and although it was as well known as any matter of public record and uninterrupted custom could be, *that the members of either House are privileged, except in case of treason, felony, or breach of peace,* they declared, without hesitation, *that privilege of parliament did not extend to the case of a seditious libel*; and undoubtedly they would have done the same, if Mr. Wilkes had been prosecuted for any other misdemeanor whatsoever. The ministry are, of a sudden, grown wonderfully careful of privileges, which their predecessors were as ready to invade. The known laws of the land, the rights of the subjects, the sanctity of charters, and the reverence due to our magistrates, must all give way, without question or resistance, to a privilege of which no man knows either the origin or the extent. The House of Commons judge of their own privileges without appeal....they may take offence at the most innocent action, and imprison the person who offends them during their arbitrary will and pleasure..... The party has no remedy......he cannot appeal from their jurisdiction; and if he questions the privilege which he is supposed to have violated, it becomes an aggravation of his offence....... Surely this doctrine is not to be found in Magna Charta. If it be admitted without limitation, I affirm, that there is neither law nor liberty in this kingdom. We are the slaves of the House of Commons; and, through them, we are the slaves of the King and his minister.

Anonymous.

LETTER XLV.

TO THE PRINTER OF THE PUBLIC ADVERTISER.

———

IT was confidently urged, in opposition to the demands of JUNIUS *and his friends, for a dissolution of the parliament ; that such a dissolution would not effectually remove that* undue influence *of which they complained, nor thoroughly change the temper and principles of those of whom the House of Commons must still be composed ; and that, therefore, it was merely childish caprice, not a true discrimination of public good, by which those who clamoured against the present House of Commons, were actuated.*

PHILO JUNIUS, *in this short Letter, replies to that reasoning, and in a great measure refutes it.' Had the interposition of the virtuous and enlightened part of the constituents of the House of Commons been, in this instance, such as* JUNIUS *supposes ; it would have been wise to dissolve the parliament, in compliance with it. It is true, he alledges, that those may be reformed in part, who cannot be rendered perfect to our wishes. It is true, also, that the fear of an effectual interposition of their constituents, might render even a corrupt House of Commons, cautious of provoking it.*

This short Letter is a much more able and impressive one, than that which immediately precedes it. The author finds little difficulty in vindicating his own arguments and expressions.

SIR,   1. *May*, 1771.

THEY who object to detached parts of JUNIUS's last Letter, either do not mean him fairly, or have not considered the general scope and course of his argument....There are degrees in all the private vices....Why not in public prostitution ? .....The influence of the crown naturally makes a septennial parliament dependent....Does it follow, that every House of Commons will plunge at once into the *lowest depths* of prostitution!.....JUNIUS supposes, that the present House of Commons, in going such enormous lengths, have been *imprudent to themselves*, as well as wicked to the public..... that their example is *not within the reach of emulation*.....and that, in the first session after the next election, *some* popular measures may probably be adopted. He does not expect that a dissolution of parliament will destroy corruption; but that, at least, it will be a check and terror to their successors, who will have seen that, *in flagrant cases*, their constituents *can* and *will* interpose with effect...... After all, Sir, will you not endeavour to remove or alleviate the most dangerous symptoms, because you cannot eradicate the disease? Will you not punish *treason* or *parricide*, because the sight of a gibbet does not prevent highway robberies? When the main argument of JUNIUS is admitted to be unanswerable, I think it would become the minor critic, who hunts for blemishes, to be a little more distrustful of his own sagacity.....The other objection is hardly worth an answer. When JUNIUS observes, that Kings are ready enough to follow *such* advice, he does not mean to insinuate that, if the advice of parliament were good, the King would be so ready to follow it.

PHILO JUNIUS.

Will you not punish treason or parricide, &c.] This illustration is pertinent and forcible.

LETTER XLVI.

TO THE PRINTER OF THE PUBLIC ADVERTISER.

———

THIS Letter produces two great legal authorities, in support of the doctrine laid down by JUNIUS, *concerning the jurisdiction of the House of Commons, in the Letter immediately foregoing. The authorities of Noye and Coke are, certainly, high. But the house of Commons had not yet acquired, at the time when those great lawyers lived, the free enjoyment of those privileges, which, by the fundamental laws of the constitution, must necessarily belong to them. To ascertain the just extent of those privileges,* JUNIUS *ought to have set before him, the practice of the house of Commons, from the restoration of Charles the Second, to the accession of George the Third....to have distinguished those few cases in which it was clear that the Commons had usurped an irregular and unnecessary power, from those in which they had assumed only a privilege necessary to give due order to their proceedings, and to supply what information they wanted....then to have deduced from these, the Law of Parliament.*

But, the authorities which are in this Letter produced, would no doubt, have great weight with many : and it was worthy of JUNIUS'S *address in controversy, thus to bring them forward.*

———

SIR,   25. *May,* 1771.

     I CONFESS my partiality to JUNIUS, and feel a considerable pleasure in being able to communicate any thing to the public in support of his opinions. The doctrine laid down in his last Letter, concerning the power of the House of Commons to commit for contempt, is not so new as it appeared to many people; who, dazzled with the name of *privilege*, had never suffered themselves to examine the question fairly. *In the course of my reading this morning*, I met with the following passage in the Journals of the House of Commons. (Vol. I. page 603.) Upon occasion of a jurisdiction unlawfully assumed by the house in the year 1621, Mr. Attorney-General Noye gave his opinion as follows. " No doubt but, in some cases, this " house may give judgment....in matters of returns, " and concerning members of our house, or falling " out in our view in parliament; but, for foreign " matters, knoweth not how we can judge it...... " knoweth not that we have been used to give judg- " ment in any case, but those before-mentioned."

Sir Edward Coke, upon the same subject, says, (page 604) " No question but this is a house of re- " cord, and that it hath power of judicature in some " cases.........have power to judge of returns and " members of our house: one, no member, offend- " ing out of the parliament, *when he came hither* " *and justified it*, was censured for it."

Now, Sir, if you will compare the opinion of these great sages of the law with JUNIUS's doctrine, you will find they tally exactly......He allows the power of the house to commit their own members (which, however, they may grossly abuse). He allows their power in cases where they are acting as a court of judicature, viz. elections, returns, &c....

and he allows it in such contempts as immediately interrupt their proceedings; or, as Mr. Noye expresses it, *falling out in their view in parliament.*

They who would carry the privileges of parliament farther than JUNIUS, either do not mean well to the public, or know not what they are doing. The government of England is a government of law. We betray ourselves, we contradict the spi-

---

They who would carry the privileges of parliament, &c.] It appears to me, that, in the case of the printers, JUNIUS and his party did not choose the proper ground. In truth, by the essential nature of the British constitution, the deliberations, resolutions, and transactions in general of the House of Commons, ought to *pass as much in the presence of their constituents,* as is compatible with the objects for which that assembly exists....with the order, gravity, and occasional secrecy, which are necessary to its proceedings. The practice of the house had gradually come to comply fully with this fundamental principle. It was amidst the contempt that was thrown on the house, on account of Wilkes and the Middlesex election, that the idea of excluding the public from all knowledge of the proceedings in parliament, had been again eagerly taken up. JUNIUS ought therefore, to have argued; that, by the constitution, the proceedings in parliament were considered as passing in the presence of the people; that this publicity was to be restricted by nothing but the necessities of order, gravity, and secrecy; that the general practice of parliament, had sufficiently allowed this principle; and that printers were not lawfully to be punished by the house for publishing any accounts but what were false and libellous.

On this ground, they would have been invincible. As they argued; their most skilful efforts were only a labour to make the worst appear the better cause.

The House of Commons relinquished the authority of forbidding the publication of their proceedings; but not the power of punishing by imprisonment for contempts.

rit of our laws, and we shake the whole system of English jurisprudence, whenever we entrust a discretionary power over the life, liberty, or fortune of the subject, to any man or set of men whatsoever, upon a presumption that it will not be abused.

PHILO JUNIUS.

LETTER XLVII.

TO THE PRINTER OF THE PUBLIC ADVERTISER.

—

*JUNIUS, since his last Letter, had discovered, by more diligent
search in the Records of the House of Commons, an instance in
which that house carried its claim of privileges, considerably beyond what the present parliament regarded as just. The Parliament in which such extravagance of privileges was arrogated,
had by the violence of their proceedings, obliged queen Anne to
prorogue, and then dissolve them.*

*He hastened to lay before the public these facts, from which his own
inference was ; that the law of Parliament was altogether unsettled ;
but that it was usual for the Sovereign to dissolve his parliament
when their own refractory conduct, or the general wishes of the
people, strongly recommended such a measure.*

*In the first paragraph of this Letter, he skillfully discriminates and
exaggerates the differences between a resolution of the House of
Commons, and an act of the whole Legislature.*

*He, then, states from the Journals of that House, for the year 1704,
the great fact, for the purpose of holding which forth, this Letter
was written.*

*An application of this fact to the support of his own former doctrine
concerning the Law of Parliament, fills the next paragraph.*

*In the closing sentences, he employs, with triumph, the inference
which he had deduced, to expose to still stronger ridicule and more
abhorrent odium, that act of authority by which the House of Commons had sent Crosby and Oliver to the Tower.*

—

SIR,.   28. *May,* 1771.

ANY man who takes the trouble of perusing
the Journals of the House of Commons, will soon

be convinced, that very little, if any regard at all, ought to be paid to the resolutions of one branch of the legislature, declaratory of the law of the land, or even of what they call the law of parliament. It will appear that these resolutions have no one of the properties, by which, in this country particularly, *law* is distinguished from mere *will* and *pleasure;* but that, on the contrary, they bear every mark of a power arbitrarily assumed, and capriciously applied.....That they are usually made in times of contest, and to serve some unworthy purpose of passion or party......that the law is seldom

---

It will appear, &c.] This sentence includes all the arguments which could be mustered to prove, that the House of Commons, in enforcing their own resolutions as law, acted illegally.

1. They were made, as he would alledge, with partiality and in passion.

2. They were *ex post facto,*

3. They implied the union of legislation and jurisdiction in the same persons, and in the same act.

4. They shewed a court from which there was no appeal, assuming, in a criminal case, an original jurisdiction.

To all this, the obvious and decisive answer is, that the House, in the case against which the reasonings of Junius were directed, professed only to *judge* agreeably to law established, by the fundamental constitution of parliament, and explained by clear precedents : that even with the power which he would deny them, they could scarcely preserve the necessary order and dignity of their proceedings, much less, without it ; that a power of imprisonment which could not be enforced beyond the close of the session, and which did not supersede the Habeas Corpus Act, could never become formidable.

declared until *after* the fact by which it is supposed to be violated....that legislation and jurisdiction are united in the same persons, and exercised at the same moment.....and that a court from which there is no appeal, assumes an *original* jurisdiction in a criminal case.....in short, Sir, to collect a thousand absurdities into one mass, " we have a law which " cannot be known, because it is *ex post facto;* " the party is both legislator and judge; and the " jurisdiction is without appeal." Well might the judges say, *The law of parliament is above us.*

You will not wonder, Sir, that, with these qualifications, the declaratory resolutions of the House of Commons should appear to be in perpetual contradiction, not only to common sense, and to the laws we are acquainted with, (and which alone we can obey) but even to one another. I was led to trouble you with these observations by a passage, which, to speak in lutestring, *I met with this morning in the course of my reading,* and upon which I mean to put a question to the advocates for privilege.....On the 8th of March 1704, (*vide* Journals, Vol. XIV. p. 566.) the house thought proper to come to the following resolutions.....1. " That no " commoner of England, committed by the House " of Commons for breach of privilege, or contempt " of that house, ought to be, by any writ of *Ha-* " *beas Corpus,* made to appear in any other place, or " before any other judicature, during that session of " parliament wherein such person was so com- " mitted."

2. " That the Serjeant at Arms, attending this " house, do make no return of, or yield any obedi- " ence to, the said writs of *Habeas Corpus;* and for " such his refusal, that he have the protection of " the House of Commons*."

Welbore Ellis, What say you? Is this the law of parliament, or is it not? I am a plain man, Sir, and cannot follow you through the phlegmatic forms of an oration. Speak out, Grildrig.....say yes, or no......If you say *yes*, I shall then inquire by what authority Mr. De Grey, the honest Lord Mansfield,

---

* If there be, in reality, any such law in England, as the *law of parliament*, which, (under the exceptions stated in my letter on privilege) I confess, after long deliberation, I very much doubt; it certainly is not constituted by, nor can it be collected from, the resolutions of either House, whether *enacting* or *declaratory*. I desire the reader will compare the above resolution of the year, 1704, with the following of the 3d of April, 1628......." *Resolved*, That " the writ of *Habeas Corpus* cannot be denied, but ought to be " granted to *every* man that is committed or detained in prison, or " otherwise restrained, by the command of the King, the Privy " Council, or *any other*, he praying the same."

Speak out, Grildrig, &c.] This allusion to the appellation which Gulliver received among the Brobdignaggians, is exceedingly happy. Mr. Ellis, afterwards Lord Mendip, was but a little man in personal stature. His authority in regard to the forms of parliament was, at this time, in high estimation. He had taken an active part, in supporting the dignity of the House of Commons, against the city magistrates. Hence the eagerness of JUNIUS, to appeal to him, and to make him ridiculous.

By what authority Mr. De Grey, &c.] I think, that the positions and reasonings of JUNIUS in this place, may be easily turned against himself. He says, that the precedents in the practice of the House of Commons, are too irregular and capricious, to be referred

and the Barons of the Exchequer, dared to grant a
writ of *Habeas Corpus* for bringing the bodies of
the Lord Mayor and Mr. Oliver before them; and
why the Lieutenant of the Tower made any return
to a writ, which the House of Commons had, in a
similar instance, declared to be unlawful.....If you
say *no*, take care you do not at once give up the
cause in support of which you have so long and so
laboriously tortured your understanding. Take
care you do not confess that there is no test by
which we can distinguish.....no evidence by which
we can determine......what is, and what is not, the
law of parliament. The resolutions I have quoted
stand upon your Journals, uncontroverted and unre-
pealed......they contain a declaration of the law of
parliament, by a court competent to the question,
and whose decision, as you and Lord Mansfield say,
must be law, because there is no appeal from it;
and they were made, not hastily, but after long deliberation, upon a constitutional question.....What
farther sanction of solemnity will you annex to any

to, as authorities in law.   It was alledged, in favour of the conduct
of the House of Commons, that they acted by the precedents, of the
best times, and in their circumstances the most unexceptionable.
JUNIUS produces a precedent, the violence of which, the House
had not now imitated; nor had the judges allowed its authority. Is
not the plain inference then, that the House selected their precedents with due caution? and that the same Judges who had not refused a Habeas Corpus to Crosby and Oliver....though they might
have produced a specious precedent to justify the refusal....would
also have set those gentlemen at liberty, if this had been permitted by the law of parliament, interpreted consistently with the law
of the land?

resolution of the present House of Commons, beyond what appears upon the face of those two resolutions, the legality of which you now deny? If you
say that parliaments are not infallible, and that
Queen Anne, in consequence of the violent proceedings of that House of Commons, was obliged
to prorogue and dissolve them; I shall agree with
you very heartily, and think that the precedent
ought to be followed immediately. But you, Mr.
Ellis, who hold this language, are inconsistent with
your own principles. You have hitherto maintained, that the House of Commons are the sole
judges of their own privileges; and that their declaration does, *ipso facto*, constitute the law of parliament; yet now you confess that parliaments are
fallible, and that their resolutions may be illegal;
consequently, that their resolutions *do not* constitute
the law of parliament. When the King was urged
to dissolve the present parliament; you advised
him to tell his subjects, that *he was careful not to
assume any of those powers which the constitution had
placed in other hands, &c.* Yet Queen Anne, it
seems, was justified in exerting her prerogative to
stop a House of Commons, whose proceedings,
compared with those of the assembly of which you

You advised him to tell, &c.] The King did not, in that speech,
disclaim his authority to dissolve the parliament at his pleasure;
but only hinted to the Livery of London, that they were encroaching on the royal authority, on the authority of parliament, on the
rights of all their fellow subjects, when they so violently demanded
that the parliament should be, at the signification of their pleasure,
instantly dissolved.

are a most worthy member, were the perfection of justice and reason.

In what a labyrinth of nonsense does a man involve himself, who labours to maintain falsehood by argument! How much better would it become the House of Commons, to speak plainly to the people; and tell us, at once, *that their will must be obeyed, not because it is lawful and reasonable, but because it is their will?* Their constituents would have a better opinion of their candour; and, I promise you, not a worse opinion of their integrity.

PHILO JUNIUS.

LETTER XLVIII.

TO HIS GRACE THE DUKE OF GRAFTON.

———

THE death of George Grenville, the absurd violence of the Livery of London, with the mingled firmness and moderation of the King, his ministers, and their parliamentary friends, had, since the commencement of the Session of Parliament for 1770-71, *given new stability to the administration, and the plans of government which* JUNIUS *opposed. Persons who, a few months before, had shewn an inclination to abandon the ministry, as mariners forsake a ship that is going unavoidably to wreck, now returned to proffer their aid, and to court its alliance. Nor were their offers hastily slighted. The Opposition were still numerous, powerful, and active : and no means were to be neglected, which could confirm the government against their attacks.*

In this state of things, the Duke of Grafton, who had almost withdrawn from the administration, renewed his connexion with it, and obtained new proofs of his Sovereign's favour. He was appointed, on the 12th of June, 1771, *Lord Keeper of the Privy Seal, instead of Lord Suffolk, who succeeded the Earl of Halifax, as Secretary of State for the Northern department. On the 14th day of the same month, he was appointed, in succession to the Earl of Halifax, Ranger and Warden of Salcey Park, in Northamptonshire. Thus gratified with honours and emoluments, yet not urged into a situation of dangerous responsibility ; he was more closely than ever attached to the King and his present ministry.* JUNIUS *appeared to have menaced and inveighed, in vain. It seemed impossible, that the Duke of Grafton should ever again skulk back in shame, to take his place among the followers of the Earl of Chatham.*

JUNIUS *thought himself insulted by this new hardihood of the Duke. He was enraged equally ; that the Duke should dare to accept ministerial appointment ; and that the King should presume to employ and reward him. He determined to resume his strain of invective*

against the faithless friend of Wilkes, the apostate from the princi-
ples of Chatham ; and, not to spare even Majesty itself; since it
was probable, that however outrageous, he might still find protec-
tion for his printers, in the favour of a London Jury.

In this elaborate Letter, JUNIUS aims his invective, at first, more
against the King himself, than against his minister. He, then, very
. ingenuously hints, that the loudest outcry of some of the patriots,
had been but hollow pretence. He indignantly enumerates those acts
of imputed perfidy, by which alone, as he would insinuate, had the
Duke of Grafton gained his Sovereign's cordial favour. He in-
volves, in the current of his satire, various other names ; exhausts
his present stores of satyrical eloquence ; and menaces new terrors,
in a tone somewhat between the bullying of weakness, and the
haughty threat of conscious power.

Beside its outrageous violence; this eloquent Letter certainly betrays
an affected labour of composition. But, forget these faults ; and, in
almost all other respects, it cannot be too much admired.

———

MY LORD,   22. *June*, 1771.

THE profound respect I bear to the gracious
Prince who governs this country with no less honour to himself than satisfaction to his subjects,
and who restores you to your rank under his
standard, will save you from a multitude of reproaches. The attention I should have paid to
your failings, is involuntarily attracted to the hand
that rewards them ; and though I am not so partial
to the royal judgment, as to affirm that the favour
of a king can remove mountains of infamy, it
serves to lessen, at least, for undoubtedly it divides,
the burden. While I remember how much is due
to *his* sacred character, I cannot, with any decent

appearance of propriety, call you the meanest and the basest fellow in the kingdom. I protest, my Lord, I do not think you so. You will have a dangerous rival, in that kind of fame to which you have hitherto so happily directed your ambition, as long as there is one man living who thinks you worthy of his confidence, and fit to be trusted with any share in his government. I confess you have great intrinsic merit.....but take care you do not value it too highly. Consider how much of it would have been lost to the world, if the King had not graciously affixed his stamp, and given it currency among his subjects. If it be true that a virtuous man,

I protest, my Lord, I do not think you so.] None can approve the insinuation implied in these words. None can deny, that they exemplify at once the most exquisite refinement, and the bitterest severity, of invective.

Let it be remembered, that it was the Sovereign's steadiness which provoked an attack so malignant.

Even, in thus offering abuse against his King, JUNIUS does homage to the King's talents. Such would not have been the abuse that would have suggested itself, to be thrown out by such a mind as that of JUNIUS, against a weak prince.

If the King had not graciously affixed his stamp, &c.] The author's meaning is, that the rewards which the Duke of Grafton had lately obtained from his Sovereign....marked out his Grace to public infamy, much more certainly and conspicuously, than if, with the same demerits, he had received no testimonies of the Royal favour.

If it be true, &c.] The allusions in this period are, indeed, complex and laboured. But, how wonderfully they aggrandize and point the invective! The first part of the comparison is from a well-known expression of Seneca concerning Cato. The latter part is from the

struggling with adversity, be a scene worthy of the gods, the glorious contention between you and the best of Princes deserves a circle equally attentive and respectable. I think I already see other gods rising from the earth to behold it.

But this language is too mild for the occasion.... The King is determined, that our abilities shall not be lost to society. The perpetration and description of new crimes will find employment for us both. My Lord, if the persons who have been loudest in their professions of patriotism, had done their duty to the public with the same zeal and perseverance that I did, I will not assert that government would have recovered its dignity, but at

mouth of Saul, when he beheld the effect of the incantations of the witch of Endor.

But this language is too mild for the occasion.] This is skilful. JUNIUS seems to have been aware, that he made too much show of rhetorical labour, in the foregoing paragraph. He, therefore, breaks away at once in a natural tone of indignation. And the reader forgets that disgust, which the cold laboured artifices of what went before, were just beginning to excite in his mind.

If the persons who have been loudest in their professions of patriotism, &c.] The Whigs in general began to languish in their efforts ; as these, even where their hopes were the most sanguine, had been constantly disappointed. Divisions were arising among the city patriots. The Rockingham and the Pitt and Grenville Whigs were not in cordial union. The followers of George Grenville, were now among the pillars of administration. By all these mischances of the Opposition, the Duke of Grafton had hitherto escaped impeachment. Hence the complaint of JUNIUS against his party.

least our gracious Sovereign must have spared his subjects this last insult * ; which, if there be any feeling left among us, they will resent more than even the real injuries they received from every measure of your Grace's administration. In vain would he have looked round him for another character so consummate as yours. Lord Mansfield shrinks from his principles......his ideas of go-

---

* The Duke was lately appointed Lord Privy Seal.

Will resent more than even the real injuries, &c.] JUNIUS means, that the new rewards bestowed on the Duke of Grafton, ought to be regarded as a proof of insolent triumph, in the bestower, over the Opposition to those measures, on account of which, the Duke of Grafton had become the most obnoxious to popular odium.

Lord Mansfield shrinks from his principles, &c.] This alludes to a memorable contention which took place in the end of the year 1770, in the House of Lords, between the Earls of Mansfield and Camden.

Lord Mansfield, probably *ignorant of the origin and primary character of Juries in the English constitution*, had, ever since he was at the bar, maintained ; that it was the proper duty of Juries, *to find only the fact, without presuming to judge of its criminality or innocence.* This opinion he had lately endeavoured to enforce judicially, in the trials of the printers who were prosecuted on account of JUNIUS's Letter to the King. The Juries not being permitted to judge of the *intention*, would not find the *fact* : and the defendants in the trials were, therefore, in general, acquitted.

But, in consequence of the restrictions which Lord Mansfield had, as a judge, endeavoured to impose on the rights of Juries ; a motion was, on the 6th of December 1770, made in parliament, for the appointment of *a Committee to enquire into the proceedings of the Judges in Westminster-Hall, particularly in cases relating to the liberty of the press, and the constitutional power and duty of Juries.*

vernment perhaps go farther than your own, but his heart disgraces the theory of his understanding.....

The restriction of Juries to judge of the fact only....and the holding of a master as criminal in consequence of an official act of his servant to which he was not privy....were the capital facts in the conduct of the Judges, upon which this motion was founded. After a long debate, in which the doctrine of Lord Mansfield, and the other obnoxious conduct of the Judges, was partly defended upon high Whig authorities, and in part excused: the motion was rejected by no fewer than one hundred and eighty-four of a majority, in opposition to a minority of only seventy-six, whose voices went to support it.

Earl Mansfield was, however, considerably alarmed by this attack, and by the force with which it had been urged. Believing that he was in the right concerning the proper functions of Juries; conscious of talents to maintain his opinion, and to vindicate his conduct; and aware that he should have the support of a ministerial majority; his Lordship resolved to bring the matter under discussion in the House of Peers. He, therefore, gave notice for a call of the House. Much expectation was excited. It was generally supposed that, unless certain to triumph, his Lordship would never have been induced to bring the matter thus to issue. Earl Camden, and the Peers in opposition, prepared to encounter him with all their strength of eloquence and juridical argumentation.... The important day arived. But, in the mean time, Lord Mansfield *shrunk*, as JUNIUS, in the text observes, from the more solemn avowal and defence of his principles. Instead of opening any argument upon the rights of Juries, and founding upon it a motion; he only acquainted the House: that *he had left with their clerk, a paper containing the unanimous judgment of the Court of King's Bench, in the case of the King against Woodfall; and their lordships might, if they chose, read it, and take copies of it.* This act, accompanied with no motion, exceedingly disappointed the expectation of the public, and seemed to give the triumph to Opposition. They strove, in vain, to provoke a debate in which the point in contest should be fully discussed. Whether satisfied from enquiry, that his doctrine was not tenable; or willing to prevent the clamours and the new activity of Opposition, which a discus-

Charles Fox is yet in blossom; and as for Mr.
Wedderburne, there is something about him which
even treachery cannot trust. For the present,
therefore, the best of princes must have contented
himself with Lord Sandwich......You would long
since have received your final dismission and re-

sion might excite : his Lordship steadily resisted every endeavour
to draw him to a declaration of his sentiments, beyond that which
was expressed in the paper he had given in. Perhaps, he might
choose rather to suffer his opponents to commence an attack, and
then to stand upon his defence : perhaps, it might be thought to be
for the interest of government, that the question should remain still
undetermined.

Lord Camden, presuming on the apparent timidity of Lord
Mansfield, founded upon the tenets in the paper, certain interrogatories, tending to draw forth a more explicit declaration of that
Judge's doctrine. These interrogatories were, however, proposed
in vain to Lord Mansfield in the House of Peers. He refused any
immediate answer, but promised to give full satisfaction at some
future time. Lord Camden threatened to bring the matter to a
legal contest.

But, it was here suffered to rest. Lord Mansfield sought no new
occasion of vindicating himself. Lord Camden did not renew his
attack. It was alledged, in regard to the conduct of the latter ;
that, if he persisted in urging Mansfield farther ; the necessary
effect would be, to produce an authoritative confirmation of the doctrine which he wished to explode.

Charles Fox is yet in blossom, &c.] He was so. JUNIUS means
here, to mark the son of Lord Holland, as able and unprincipled ;
wanting nothing but years and experience, to be able to lead in
such an administration as that which JUNIUS opposed. Fox was at
this time one of the Lords of the Admiralty.

I shall seize this occasion, to introduce an account of this celebrated man, and of his father.

ward; and I, my Lord, who do not esteem you the more for the high office you possess, would willingly have followed you to your retirement. There is surely something singularly benevolent in the cha-

HENRY, the father of CHARLES FOX, was the youngest son of Sir Stephen Fox, born after his father had attained the age of eighty. He was introduced into Parliament, and to subordinate ministerial employment, under the auspices of Sir Robert Walpole. He is celebrated in one of the poems of Sir Charles Hanbury Williams, as having paid his court with no unsuccessful assiduity, to the Duchess Dowager of Manchester, grand-daughter to the Duchess of Marlborough, when she was admired as a charming widow, and before she became the wife of Edward Hussey, Lord Beaulieu. His other successes, too, in gallantry, were said to have essentially contributed both to the advancement of his political interest, and even to the immediate pecuniary improvement of his fortunes. Under the administration of the Pelhams, he became, by his skill in the detail of the public accompts, by his readiness and ability as a speaker in Parliament, by the unscrupulous pliancy of his political principles, one of the most useful of all the secondary members of the ministry.

He obtained, in marriage, Lady Georgina Carolina Lennox, sister to the present Duke of Richmond; rather by captivating the lady's affections, than by gaining the favour of her family.

While the two brothers, the Pelhams, became old and inactive; and Mr. Pitt and the Grenvilles, continually more formidable in Parliament; Mr. Henry Fox, the most powerful opponent of Pitt, attained still to greater weight in the administration. He had never affected the praise of patriotism: nor did he aim at more, than to do the business of government, the most successfully. He was a Whig of the School of Sir Robert Walpole, whose Whiggism consisted much rather in his connexions, than in his principles. The death of Mr. Pelham, leaving the Duke of Newcastle in an official situation, of which he could not discharge the duties, made way, of course, for the farther advancement of Mr. Fox. In the year 1754, he became Secretary at War. To the duties of that office, he was sufficiently equal. He paid his court, with assiduity, to William

racter of our Sovereign. From the moment he ascended the throne, there is no crime of which human nature is capable, (and I call upon the Recorder to witness it) that has not appeared venial

Duke of Cumberland; and was powerfully supported by that Prince's favour. In one of the changes which were made in the arrangements of the ministry, not long after the death of Mr. Pelham, Mr. Fox had accepted the office of Secretary of State, with the more important, secret and confidential one of.....*Manager of the House of Commons*. The duty of the *Manager of the House of Commons* was, secretly to solicit the voices of all the members in favour of government, upon the approach of every important discussion, and by all those means which government could put into his hands, to win a decisive majority to the support of its measures. This power, the Duke of Newcastle would not, at that time, intrust into other hands than his own: and the ambition of Mr. Fox was, hence, for a short time, disappointed. He was, at different times, named of the Regency, when the King went abroad. At last, in 1756, he was left by the imbecility of the Duke of Newcastle, to arrange a new administration, in which he was Secretary of State, and principal efficient minister. But, the plan of measures which he was, in this situation, obliged to adopt, could not command success. A powerful Opposition of intrigue and parliamentary interest, was soon formed against him. The nation called for Mr. Pitt: and Mr. Fox was obliged to retire to the subordinate, though exceedingly lucrative office, of Paymaster-General of the Forces.

All this while, Fox was one of the most amiable of men, in private life. He was an affectionate husband: as a father, tender, and attentive to educate his children upon that plan which his notions of virtue, ability, and accomplishments, made him believe to be the best: as a master and patron, he was generous, kind, affable, and not unsatisfiably severe in exaction. His morality was that of honour: his political principles had been learned in the School of Walpole. But, wherever these did not warp the native rectitude of his mind, he was a man of the best affections and the most virtuous conduct.

During the busiest period of his political life, Mr. John Calcraft was his confidential clerk and humble friend. He lived much in the

in his sight. With any other Prince, the shameful desertion of him in the midst of that distress which you alone had created....in the very crisis of danger, when he fancied he saw the throne already sur-

house of Calcraft, in Parliament street, while Mrs. G. A. Bellamy presided at that gentleman's table. She introduced to him, Dr. Philip Francis, the translator of Horace; who became his chaplain; was otherwise promoted under his patronage; was made the familiar companion of his convivial hours, at the house of Calcraft; and was probably excited by him, to undertake his translation of Demosthenes. Calcraft was enriched under Mr. Fox's protection, till he aspired to an equality with his master. When he could not rise to the height of his ambition on the same side in politics with Fox; he deserted to Lord Chatham and the Grenvilles, was received into their confidence, and became an outrageous patriot.

During the splendid administration of Mr. Pitt, the office of Paymaster-General of the Forces continued to be filled by Mr. Henry Fox. After the accession of George the Third, the Earl of Bute courted Fox's confidential friendship. It was, most probably, by his advice, that Mr. Pitt was gratified, upon his sudden resignation of the office of Secretary of State, with a pension for himself, and a peerage for his lady. The pecuniary generosity of that measure, and the art with which it was aimed to destroy the popularity of his rival, bespeak the contrivance and the liberality of, Fox. When the Earl of Bute negotiated the peace of 1763, he committed the *management of the House of Commons* to Mr. Fox. Fox was admirably qualified for this employment. In spite of all the dissatisfaction of the Newcastle, and of the Pitt and Grenville Whigs, he procured the peace to be approved by the votes of a great majority of the Commons. Five and twenty thousand pounds are said to have been issued to his order, in secret service money, on the first day of the session in which Parliament was to sanction or reject it. Mr. Fox, on account of the part which he was, on this occasion, called to act, became obnoxious to the attacks of Wilkes in the North Briton, as well as to the general odium of the party which Wilkes wrote to serve. He retired, with the Earl of Bute, from the administration; and was, upon that occasion, raised to

rounded by men of virtue and abilities, would have outweighed the memory of your former services.... But his Majesty is full of justice, and understands the doctrine of compensations......He remembers

the dignity of Lord Holland. In the new arrangements of ministry, which took place between the years 1763 and 1770, Lord Holland was believed to have been much consulted by the King and by the Earl of Bute. The Grenvilles and the Earl of Chatham, continued so much the more to cherish against him all the hatred of their ancient rivalship.

He had become Paymaster of the Forces in the year 1757. From that time, till he resigned his office, the disbursements upon account of the army, had been, necessarily, very great; and the Paymas-ter's income, was great in proportion. Without embezzling any of the money of government; as without neglecting, through scrupulous integrity or ostentatious patriotism, to avail himself of any fair advantage of his situation; he had, amidst a style of living magnificently expensive, accumulated a vast fortune. But, the accompts of the Paymaster of the Forces, in a war extending its operations over more than half the globe, were necessarily so complex, that they could not, till a considerable time after its termination, be finally settled. The accompts of Mr. Winnington, who was Paymaster-General, from December 1743, to June 1746, were not closed with the Treasury, till May 1760. The Earl of Chatham's accompts for the nine years and a half, betweeen June 1746, and December 1755, during which he held the office of Paymaster, were not declared to be finally settled, even in July 1769. The accompts of the Earls of Darlington and Kinnoul, for 1756, and those of the Earl of Kinnoul and Mr. Potter, for six months, ending on the 24th of June 1757, were only before the auditors in the Exchequer, in the year 1769. After these examples, it cannot appear surprising, that Lord Holland's accompts as Paymaster, from 1757 to 1764, should not have been closed with the Treasury in the year 1767.

In that year, however, while his old adversary, Lord Chatham, was, for a time, at the head of the administration, Lord Holland

with gratitude how soon you had accommodated
your morals to the necessity of his service.....how
chearfully you had abandoned the engagements of
private friendship, and renounced the most solemn

was pressed to give in his last accompts, without delay, to the Exchequer, with an earnestness which betrayed a strong disposition to
defame and embarrass him. He presented a memorial to the Lords
of the Treasury in which the impossibility was forcibly stated, of
his closing, in so short a time, accompts so complex and difficult.
The force of his reasons was allowed : and a warrant from the
King was granted, to stay those compulsory proceedings at law,
which had been oppressively begun against him. The proceedings
were stayed ; but, the popular obloquy which the friends of Chatham industriously excited, became for this, just so much the more
outrageous. Lord Holland was odious, as being supposed the confidential friend of the Earl of Bute ; and as such the secret inspirer
of those councils of the Sovereign, which were the most obnoxious
to the Whig party, and to the patriots of the city. They strove to
wreak their revenge by clamours against his malversation in office.
Mr. Beckford, in particular, accused him in the House of Commons, as a defaulter in his accompts, to the sum of forty millions.
Lord Holland, supposing Mr. Beckford sufficiently candid, not to
resist the force of evidence in his Lordship's favour, procured a
paper to be put into his hands, in which unanswerable reasons for
the delay in the final settlement of his Lordship's accompts, were
simply and clearly explained. But Beckford was not to be thus satisfied. He still encouraged the clamour : and strove to confirm, in
contradiction to his private knowledge, the credit of that which he
had, in parliament, so rashly affirmed. When in consequence of
this, the charge was more solemnly repeated in an address from
the City of London to the King ; Lord Holland thought it again requisite to make an attempt to undeceive those by whom he was
accused. The address characterized him, as a *Paymaster, the public defaulter of unaccounted millions.* He wrote politely to Turner
the Mayor, by whom that paper was presented ; complaining of
the imputation, expressing his hope that Beckford had not encouraged it, and requesting an explanation of the grounds on which
it was founded, that he might effectually vindicate himself. Turner

professions to the public. The sacrifice of Lord Chatham was not lost upon him. Even the cowardice and perfidy of deserting him may have done you no diservice in his esteem. The instance was painful, but the principle might please.

professed his ignorance of the grounds of the charge. Beckford, a master of negroes, was too flagitiously bold and insolent, not to own that, though the paper communicated to him, had in part altered his own conviction, yet he had concealed it so studiously, as not to have made it known to more than a single person. Lord Holland, then published in the newspaper called the Gazetteer, the statement which had been put into Beckford's hands, his own memorial to the Lords of the Treasury in the year 1767, and the King's warrant, by the authority of which, the proceedings begun against him, had been stayed. The publication of these satisfied all, whose minds were not blindly prepossessed against conviction, that his Lordship did not shun, with the fears of guilt, the due responsibility of his late office. He lived a few years longer. At the time of his death, his accompts with the Treasury were not yet finally settled: but, he left, with his executors a sufficient sum of money, particularly appropriated for the discharge of whatever he should in the end appear to owe to the Exchequer.

He must be owned, to have been a master in party and parliamentary intrigue; to have been expert in the business of the ministerial offices; to have had a deep and extensive knowledge of human character; to have been an able and argumentative speaker; and to have been in all respects, as virtuous, as was possible for a man of pleasure and a practical politician. He became, at first, a politician, both from ambition and for the sake of bread. These principles continued, to the last, to regulate his political life. He was ever careless of popularity; but not half so bad a man as the public often thought him. He appears to have been a classical scholar, and to have had a taste for the fine arts. His official papers were written with clearness, closeness, and simple propriety of composition. His character resembled that of Sir Robert Walpole; and that of Mr. Dundas is perhaps not unlike to it. His fortune is said to have amounted, at least, to several hundred thousand pounds.

You did not neglect the magistrate, while you flattered the *man*. The expulsion of Mr. Wilkes, predetermined in the cabinet....the power of depriving the subject of his birth-right, attributed

CHARLES JAMES FOX, was the second son of Henry Fox, Lord Holland. He was born in January 1749. His elder brother, Stephen, being, when very young, affected with a nervous disorder, which impaired equally the powers of his mind, and his bodily health, and which was liable to return, whenever his passions were, by any means, strongly agitated ; Charles was from that time, regarded as the principal hope of the family : and was, accordingly, treated with that indulgence, and that care for his education, which it was natural for such a consideration to suggest.

Nature had given him, simply *sanam mentem in sano corpore*, but not, as I should conceive, any other innate superiority over the rest of mankind. The tenderness and care with which he was brought up, in his first years ; preserving his health, and by consequence, that activity of his senses and perceptions, which is ever natural to healthy childhood ; in comparison with his elder brother, he might seem to himself and his parents, a genius. This notion of his powers made him so much the more brisk and forward, and perhaps, also, more apt in attending to the first lessons which were given him. His father's partiality was confirmed. And he resolved to form him to be a *leader in fashionable dissipation*, and a *politician*....such as he himself had been and even then was.

With these views, and this parental fondness, HENRY FOX employed toward his son, those winning manners by which he was accustomed to steal upon the confidence, and to unlock the bosoms, of the rest of mankind. He easily kindled in the mind of Charles, that passion for superiority, which is indispensably requisite to produce excellence of any sort. While this superiority was spiritedly asserted by the boy ; no indulgence which he could request, was denied him. At Westminster school, at which he began his classical studies, the discipline and order of the school, so restrained his forward irregularity, and so encouraged his emulation, that he soon greatly distinguished himself among his fellows. For whatever

to a resolution of one branch of the legislature......
the constitution impudently invaded by the House
of Commons......the right of defending it treacherously renounced by the House of Lords.....These

reason, he was removed from Westminster to Eton, before he had
passed through the usual course of scholastic instruction. At Eton,
he joined associates who were less advanced, than himself, in classical literature....and not having been brought up in London, nor
with such unrestrained indulgence.....were less acquainted with the
vices of premature manhood. He became, of consequence, a leader among them, both in their studies and in their amusements.
His literary proficiency was the pride of the governors of that se-
minary; while he gave them often great vexation by leading his
associates into a thousand irregularities. From Eton, he went to
Oxford, when he was equally distinguished by eminence in literature, and by spirited dissipation. His temper was, at the same
time, amiable; and he had all his father's power, to master the affections of his associates. Lord Holland still supplied his expences
with boundless liberality: and his splendid profusion, no doubt,
contributed greatly to give him the ascendency among other young
men of his own age. He went from Oxford, to make the fashionable journey for young men of fortune, through France and Italy....
His expences were very great, while he was abroad; nor is it certain, that he gained, during that time, any considerable improvement, except in the knowledge of the vices and follies fashionable
in the countries which he visited.

He had passed through this course of study, travel, and dissipation, before compleating the nineteenth year of his age. His father
was impatient to see him begin his political career. He himself and
his young companions, warmly anticipated, in imagination, the
splendid success of his parliamentary exertions. It is thus that youth
ever despises, in comparison with its own hopes, the efforts of age
in situations which itself has not yet tried. It is thus that parents
hope success for their children, when they are like to themselves.
In the year 1768, at his return from his travels, he took his seat,
for the first time, in the House of Commons, as representative for
the burgh of Midhurst in Sussex.

are the strokes, my Lord, which, in the present
reign, recommend to office, and constitute a minister. They would have determined your Sovereign's
judgment, if they had made an impression upon his

He entered parliament with a resolution to become a Speaker,
and to pursue that political career, which his father had marked out
for him. Lord Holland was attached to the government, whose general system of measures, since the commencement of the present
reign, had been considerably influenced by his own counsels......
Charles Fox's first speech in parliament was, therefore, on the subject of the Middlesex Election, and in opposition to the return of
Mr. Wilkes. It discovered a bold and manly elocution, a passion
for parliamentary business, and somewhat more of political knowledge than if the youth had not been brought up in the house of a
politician. For a short time, he continued to perform his parliamentary noviciate on the same side of the House, without obtaining any ministerial appointment. No member of parliament,
so young as he, was at this period so eminent as a speaker. He was
at the same time, a leader in every species of fashionable dissipation, among the young men of rank of his own age. His expences
were unbounded; and his debts, notwithstanding the liberality of
Lord Holland, already enormous. On the 13th of February 1770,
he was nominated one of the Lords of the Admiralty : a nomination sufficiently evincing both the high promise of his parliamentary talents, and the strength of Lord Holland's influence. In
1772, he was promoted to a place at the Treasury Board. His father still lived to see his son fulfil his fondest wishes ; and when
he beheld the display of his talents, was scarcely angry with his excesses.

But many of Charles's friends and relations were, by various
circumstances, engaged in the Opposition. The most splendid topics for oratory ; the fame of talents and of public virtue ; the
spirit of the fashionable philosophy ; and, for a young man, the
fairest hope of speedily attaining to a decisive ascendency ; were
upon the same side. Lord Holland became discontent with the
administration, in regard to the marriage-act, and some other measures. Charles began to press too boldly forward upon his seniors

heart. We need not look for any other species of merit, to account for his taking the earliest opportunity to recall you to his councils. Yet you have other merit in abundance.....Mr. Hine....the Duke

in office, and with the presumption of youth, to shew contempt of their abilities and their eloquence. A mutual dislike arose between him and the leading ministers. He dared to oppose some of the ministerial measures in parliament. He was remonstrated with, on account of this conduct. He persisted. While Lord Holland survived, however, he was not dismissed from office. In the year 1774, a new commision of the Treasury was made out, in which his name was omitted.

He was now, both angry and poor enough to become a patriot. The lucrative office of Clerk of the Pells in Ireland, a considerable land estate in Kent, and a large sum of money, were bequeathed to him by his father. But this property was entirely consumed almost as soon as obtained, by his previous debts, and by the new extravagance which the uncontrouled possession of such a fortune, provoked. Even his chance of succession to the estates of his elder brother, was sold, to obtain from Jewish money-dealers, a supply for his present necessities. His house was disfurnished by executions. For his last resource, he was reduced to depend on the fortune of the gaming-table at which his inheritance had been squandered.

I am inclined to think, that this dissipation of his patrimony, and his abrupt dismissal from ministerial employment, were the circumstances in the life of Charles Fox, which contributed the most essentially to the formation of whatever has been since the most excellent in his genius and character. He was now destitute of fortune; and, except those of politics and the gaming-table, no immediate means for subsistence remained to him. He had lost, if it might not yet be preserved by his parliamentary exertions, that ascendency over his fellows, with which he set out in early life. He saw himself humbled in the estimation of the world; and he had been dismissed by Lord North with as much indifference, as if he had been one of the most contemptible of the herd of placemen......
His talents; the fascination of his manners; connexions of friend-

of Portland....and Mr. Yorke.....Breach of trust, robbery, and murder. You would think it a compliment to your gallantry, if I added rape to the catalogue....but the stile of your amours secures

ship and consanguinity with some of the most powerful families in England; were still left to him. If he could not raise himself above the degradation of a ruined gambler; he must, in spite of these, sink into entire neglect. It would, on the other hand, be a proud gratification, to triumph over those who now presumed to look upon him with disdain, as having ceased by his own imprudence, to be worthy of their notice as a rival.

His mind had sensibility, fortitude, and rectitude of intelligence, to feel this misery and dishonour of his situation, to endure it, unbroken, to distinguish the fittest means of elevating himself above it. The study of the classics, the affectionate lessons of his father, his practice in the miniature world of Westminster, Eton, and Oxford, had given him a fund of the principles of common sense, which he might indeed abuse and neglect, but of which he could not divest himself. Besides, they were wild sallies of passion, not incurably debasing habits, which had so strikingly triumphed over the suggestions of his better genius.....A Duke of Wharton had, at years even more immature, displayed in the senate, eloquence much more splendidly persuasive than that of Fox; had, in mastering a party, and outwitting his opponents, shewn political sagacity, more profound and more actively inventive; had, in his papers of the *True Briton*, exhibited a masterliness of sophism and ironical wit, such as Swift did not excel, such as Charles Fox, was not destined ever to equal. But, with these talents, he wanted common sense; and ministers of talents more contemptible, than those of the adversaries of Fox, were easily able to ruin him......Young Lord Coke, whose eloquence was so conspicuously tried in the impeachments which succeeded the rebellion of 1745, was a youth of at least as promising parliamentary talents, as Fox. But, he became the slave of habitual drunkenness: and all the hopes of his family were frustrated....Fox, on the contrary, rose superior to his errors, and to the misfortunes with which they were punished; established his ascendency over his associates more surely than ever, at

you from resistance. I know how well these several charges have been defended. In the first instance, the breach of trust is supposed to have been
its own reward. Mr. Bradshaw affirms upon his

the moment when it seemed, that he must sink under the level of
their society ; and became an hundred times more formidable to
his opponents, from the very hour in which they probably supposed
that his power of opposition to them was crushed for ever.

He earnestly joined the Opposition to the ministry of Lord
North. The American war was in its commencement ; and was
with a great part of the nation, highly unpopular. In the debates which its prosecution excited, he made his first vigorous
attacks on the ministers who had driven him from amongst them.
Burke, Dunning, and Barre, were his eloquent co-adjutors. North,
Thurlow, and Wedderburne, were the parliamentary speakers,
against whom they had to contend. The first measures of unarmed
coercion and menace against the colonists ; the arguments by which
Briton's rights of sovereignty over the American provinces, were
maintained ; the levying of the necessary revenue ; the plans on
which the war was conducted ; the occasional attempts at concilia-
tion ; and the misfortunes which continually defeated the exertions
of the British arms ; were from the year 1774 to 1782, incessantly
attacked, opposed, deprecated, and condemned, by Fox and his
friends, with the utmost vehemence, artifice, and even pertinacious
loquacity, of opposition. At first, Fox was content to be but the
pupil of Burke, and of the other leaders among the Rockingham,
and the Pitt and Grenville Whigs. Reading, continued practice
in the business of parliament, meditation, and the quick apprehension of whatever lessons his older and more industrious associates
gave, with that ready command of his knowledge and faculties
for which he had been from infancy distinguished, gradually
raised him to an equality with the first men of his party. Burke
was more laborious, better informed, had more of formal eloquence,
had been more steady to his principles and party, enjoyed a
reputation more unspotted. But the family connexions of Fox,
his influence with the young men of rank and fashion, the superior

honour, (and so may the gift of smiling never depart from him!) that you reserved no part of Mr. Hine's purchase-money for your own use, but that every shilling of it was scrupulously paid to Governor

promptitude of his eloquence, and its more expressly practical character, gave him advantages over Burke and his other associates, by which he, within no long time, obtained an ascendency the most decisive, as the leader of the Rockingham Whigs. The best eloquence of the ministers, was confounded before him. In parliament, and without, it was fashionable to be upon his side. The wits were proud to enlist themselves under his banners: and he had the art to shew as if the splendour of genius, and of literature, graced his party alone. The sudden popularity of the first volume of Gibbon's History of the Roman Empire, took its rise from the praise bestowed by Fox, who then imagined that Gibbon was a convert to his politics. When Gibbon afterwards accepted a place under government, and devoted himself to the support of Lord North; Charles Fox was amongst the foremost to complain, that his genius was exhausted, and that the second and third volumes of his work were exceedingly inferior to the first. In the progress of the war, Fox acquired, every session, new importance with his own party, and with his opponents. The efforts of the Opposition; weakening the hands of the ministry; rendering them timid, uncertain, more anxious to avoid blame than by gigantic exertions to command success; thus contributed, signally, to produce that misconduct which they arraigned, and those misfortunes which they deplored. American freedom was vindicated, not more by the arms of Washington, than by the eloquence of Fox and Burke.

France, Spain, and Holland, interposed in a war in which the division of the British Empire against itself, gave them the hope of effectually breaking its strength, and of enriching themselves with its spoils. Opposition persevered in confounding the councils of the administration. The British arms, though every where else successful, met, in America, nought but disaster and disgrace. The ministers were at last reduced to a condition, in which they could neither prolong the war, nor negotiate a peace. Lord North retired from administration. And the Pitt and Grenville and the

Burgoyne.....Make haste my Lord.....another patent, applied in time, may keep the OAKS * in the
family....If not, Birnham Wood, I fear, must come
to the *Macaroni.*

Rockingham Whigs, were received into alliance with those who
called themselves the King's friends, and into the full enjoyment of
ministerial power.

It is chiefly from the year 1768 to the year 1782, that we are to
measure the period, during which, the permanent principles, political and moral, of Charles Fox, must have been formed. From
his father he had learned, to think, that every thing was pardon-
able to active and splendid political talents ; that by political exertion and intrigue, he ought to make his fortune ; that the fashionable excesses, if they could be reconciled with political industry,
were only commendable proofs of spirit and genius. From the
Rockingham Whigs, he learned to believe that the great Whig
families, whose ancestors were the Authors of the Revolution, and
of the settlement in favour of the House of Hanover, ought still to
hold the crown, as it were, in tutelage, and to leave to the Sovereign little more than the empty honours, and the merely nominal
power of the government. From JUNIUS, from Franklin, from
Dunning, from the remonstrances of the City of London, and of the
Americans, from Hume, Smith, Voltaire, and Price, he imbibed a
taste for that philosophy which prefers an ideal semblance of right
to tried order and expediency. Burke taught him to throw the veil
of fanciful ornament and of sophistical refinement, over that practical good sense which, in politics, it was almost natural for him,
even unconsciously to exercise. His practice at the gaming-table,
in the House of Commons, in the meetings of party-cabal, had
given him new confidence in his own powers, new controul over his
own passions, a deeper insight into the complexities of human character, and the frailties of human nature....not at all a greater delicacy of honour, or sanctity of moral principles....but certainly
more of that lofty magnanimity which the ingenuous mind delights
to cherish, when it feels itself capable of surmounting every difficulty of fortune, and of triumphing over the most skilful artifices of
its opponents.

* A superb villa of Colonel Burgoyne about this time advertised
for sale.

The Duke of Portland was in life your earliest
friend.   In defence of his property he had nothing
to plead but equity against Sir James Lowther, and
prescription against the crown.   You felt for your

Many persons incline to think, that the parliamentary exertions
of Fox, Burke, Pitt, and the other chiefs of the administration
and the opposition in our day, are of transcendent, gigantic, incomparable talents, such as scarce another age since the beginning
of the world has seen....such as hardly another individual among
all their contemporaries on the earth could display.   I own, I am
very far from being of this opinion.   The great topics of discussion
which occur in the course of the proceedings in parliament, are
not above ten or twelve in number.   Upon these the changes are
continually rung.   They are topics exceedingly general in their
nature, scarcely admitting any thing that is not trite and very much
of a common-place character, to be said upon them.   The known
forms of parliament, and the proposals from government, regulate
the course of the proceedings.   The ordinary deliberations and
acts of the legislature never rise greatly above the level even of the
vulgar knowledge of the age.   No man attains to eminence as a
Speaker, who is not greatly countenanced by the whole party,
either of the ministry or of the opposition.   The speeches have
wonderfully little influence upon the course of affairs.   But a few
in comparison attempt to speak ; still fewer speak in consequence
of careful enquiry and preparation ; still fewer, with incessant attention to the business of parliament, and free from those restraints
of influence and connexion, by which all reason and eloquence are
cramped and palsied.   Compare the parliamentary debates of the
last twenty years, with those of the twenty years immediately preceding....what a wonderful sameness and paucity of topics and
arguments, do we not find in the two periods ?   Will the Goddess of
Eloquence, think you, ever own those for her sons, whose chief
praise is, that they can speak for three, four, five, or six hours,
while their hearers come and go, eat, drink, and sleep ?   What
hall for academical declamation, what spouting club, what disputing society of young students, does not display as much of the
power and the grace of eloquence, as does the House of Com-

friend; *but the law must take its course.* Posterity will scarce believe that Lord Bute's son-in-law had barely interest enough at the treasury to get his grant compleated before the general election.*

mons, even on its days of keenest debate? No :....To be the orator of a party, does indeed require some share of talents : But, they who have praised either Mr. Fox or any of his parliamentary rivals for transcendent abilities, have undoubtedly mistaken splendour of situation for grandeur of exertions.

When the Whigs succeeded to the power of their rivals, in 1782; Mr. Fox, as Secretary of State, became the principal efficient minister. In the administration were joined....the King's friends or the genuine *modern Tories*....the *Rockingham* or Newcastle *Whigs*, among whom Fox now held precisely the same station which had been possessed in the same party, by his father, in the years 1755 and 1756....and the *Pitt and Grenville Whigs* who, though they had co-operated with the Rockingham party in opposition, were not likely to be satisfied with such share as *they* should assign to them, in the ministerial power. In the Opposition were, now, that combination of moderate whigs with moderate Tories, whom the love of place and emolument, and indifference to all but the substantial and fundamental principles of the constitution, had gradually brought into political union, between the beginning of the present reign, and the last misfortunes of the American war. The remains of the Bedford party, the many friends whom the disinterestedness of Lord North had attached to him, with all those who still obstinately approved the principles on which the American war was undertaken, composed the party who thus took their turn for accusation and attack. But they who were distinguished as the *King's friends*, were not disposed cordially to act with a party, whose avowed aim was, to restore the reign of

* It will appear by a subsequent Letter, that the Duke's precipitation proved fatal to the grant. It looks like the hurry and confusion of a young highwayman, who takes a few shillings, but leaves the purse and watch behind him.......And yet the Duke was an old offender!

Enough has been said of that detestable transaction which ended in the death of Mr. Yorke.....
I cannot speak of it without horror and compassion. To excuse yourself, you publickly impeach

the Whig aristocracy, and to conciliate to the great Whig families,
the favour of the people, by concessions which were judged to be
little compatible with the order of good government. Fox and
his friends rescinded the decision in the case of the Middlesex
Election ; condemned the principles upon which the American
war had been pursued ; attempted to open a negociation with the
Dutch ; and were proceeding to carry into execution all their
schemes for domestic government, and for the arrangement of the
foreign affairs of the empire; when the death of the Marquis of
Rockingham, the nominal head of the whole party, broke its
combination, and enabled the Sovereign once more to emancipate
himself from its controul. But for this event, the whole scheme
of government which had been pursued since the year 1757, must
have been destroyed, under the direction of Fox; and an aristocratical reign similar to that of the party of the Pelhams, would
have been restored.

Upon the death of the Marquis of Rockingham, Lord Shelburne....since, Marquis of Lansdowne....at that time, the leader
of the Pitt and Grenville Whigs ; deceived the confidence of his
allies of the party of Fox; entered into confidential engagements with those who were called the *King's Friends* ; agreed
to deliver his Sovereign from the usurpation of the Whig aristocracy ; and shewed a willingness to maintain those plans of government which had hitherto been acted upon, since the beginning of
the present reign. Lord Shelburne, from being Secretary of State,
was advanced to the vacant office of First Lord of the Treasury....
Mr. Fox and all his friends who were now denominated the *Portland*, instead of the *Newcastle*, or the *Rockingham* party, immediately retired in disgust from their offices....The *Pitt and Grenville*
Whigs, the *King's Friends*, and the remains of the *Bedford party*
who had not gone into opposition with Lord North, composed the
parliamentary support of Lord Shelburne's administration....While
the *Portland Whigs*, and the adherents of *Lord North*, though in

your accomplice; and to *his* mind, perhaps the ac‑
cusation may be flattery.   But in murder you are
both principals.   It was once a question of emulation; and, if the event had not disappointed the

oposition to Shelbure's ministry, were no less in oppposition to
one another; a general peace was successfully negociated ; and by
the whole train of the ministerial measures, the despondency of
the nation was cheared, and its confidence in the government, and
its dignity in the estimation of foreign powers, were, in a great
measure, restored.

Charles Fox, and his late adversary *Lord North*, when they
marked the growing strength of those by whom they and their ad‑
herents had been supplanted; and saw how utterly unable they
were, in this divided state of their party, to make any effectual
opposition ; resolved to forget their former hostility, and to unite,
for the overthrow of the administration.   Their coalition reduced
Lord Shelburne and his friends to resign.   A new administration
was formed upon the principles of the Rockingham party, tempered
with those of the Tories and the fluctuating Whigs who composed
the body of the followers of North.   The efficient authority of the
ministers, was divided between North and Fox, who became,
jointly, Secretaries of State.   Their measures of government, and the
manner in which they had forced themselves back into administration, were, as they well knew, far from being acceptable to the
Sovereign.   Their coalition was, in a considerable degree, odious
to the mob of the nation.   For these reasons, they warmly adopted
the principle of the Pelhams ; and endeavoured to establish them-
·selves so surely in the strong holds of administration, that neither
the King himself, nor any parliamentary opposition, should be
able to displace them.....America was lost.   Ireland was aspiring,
after the example of America, to at least a certain degree of independence.   Fortunately, the territorial acquisitions of the East-
India Company in Hindostan ; and the embarrassments in which
war and conquests had involved their commercial affairs ; created
a necessity for the interposition of government, to support their
credit, to regulate their future powers of administration, and their
relations to the other parts of the British empire.   Fox, North,

immediate schemes of the closet, it might still have been a hopeful subject of jest and merriment between you.

and their friends, saw, and seized the occasion. They resolved to fix the whole controul of India affairs, and the whole patronage of the East-India Company's service, as an inalienable inheritance, in the hands of the great Whig aristocracy....This measure, if accomplished, would have established Fox and his friends in office, and would have thoroughly overthrown whatever had been done : since the beginning of the present reign, to break the combination of the great Whig families, and to give to the Crown, some degree of independent influence in the government....A *bill* was, with this view, brought into parliament, by Mr. Fox. It was supported by all the strength of that which was called the *Coalition.* But those who derived their wealth and power from the present state of India affairs, were alarmed for their own fall, if the Company's possessions should immediately come under a direction so widely different. The Pitt and Grenville Whigs, the adherents of Shelburne, looked upon this as no common scheme of Opposition, but one that, if successfully carried into effect, must for ever exclude them from the hopes of ministerial emolument and power. Those who were distinguished as the King's Friends saw, that if the measure should take place, *their* political existence must be utterly annihilated. And, even the King himself was alarmed for the honour of his Crown, and for the independent strength of the royal authority. By this means, an exceedingly strong Opposition was excited against Fox's India Bill, and the party that supported it.... Even while they formed a majority in parliament, they were dismissed from their ministerial offices. The Pitt and Grenville Whigs with the new Tory party which had been formed under the auspices of Lord Bute, were again introduced to conduct the government. Appeals were, on both sides, made to the people, and to that independent part of the higher classes who stood unconnected with political party. The King dissolved his parliament, with spirit and with good reason, but somewhat in contradiction to the principle on which he had been supposed to refuse the prayers of the famous remonstrating petitions relative to the Middlesex election. The odium of the coalition, the unpopularity of the name

This Letter, my Lord, is only a preface to my future correspondence. The remainder of the summer shall be dedicated to your amusement. I mean now and then to relieve the severity of your morn-

of Fox among the distant and inferior part of the people, the complaints from the Sovereign of the threatened annihilation of the regal power, the clamour of a violated charter, the influence of the Treasury of the East-India Company and of its wealthy servants, the name of Pitt, the partiality which we naturally conceive in favour of weakness when it appears in contest with seemingly superior strength....prevailed in the election. The great aristocratical confederacy was defeated. A majority was returned to the new parliament, of members who were disposed to support that administration which the King had chosen, in opposition to those whom the Coalition strove to force upon him. After a contest of more than fifty years, the whole Whig party was, at last, subdued by the combination of the *newer* Whig families and Tories. That structure of administration which Earl Chatham had endeavoured in vain to form, in 1766 and 1767, was thus to be, at last solidly compleated under his son.

The *India Bill* of Fox, proposed with those views which were surely entertained by its authors, was undeniably a daring measure. Was it his measure? Or did it not rather originate with some one or other of his associates? The plan of circumscribing and fettering the power of the Crown, was that which the Newcastle, the Rockingham, and the Portland party, had long avowedly entertained: and, so far, therefore, as it was the object of the India Bill to increase the strength of that aristocratical body ; the Bill might possibly originate with its older members....since Fox was, but by accident, their associate and leader. But, again, the boldness, the grandeur, the temerity of this measure, the vast ability with which it was conceived and prosecuted, the egregious errors by which it was rendered fatal to the hopes of the party, are all, without doubt, to be attributed chiefly to Charles Fox. They bespeak the peculiar character of his mind, too unequivocally, to be mistaken.

Thus finally worsted in a struggle with the crown, and with the Pitt and Grenville division of the Whigs ; Fox was to return to his

ing studies, and to prepare you for the business of the day. Without pretending to more than Mr. Bradshaw's sincerity, you may rely upon my attachment as long as you are in office.

former station as a leader of Opposition. After a memorable contest, he succeeded, at a prodigious expence to his party, in procuring himself to be returned to parliament, as one of the representatives for Westminster. His service in the House of Commons, continued to be as vigilant, able and active as before. He became, now, even more than ever, the idol of his own party. *Though not in administration, he acted, in fact, the part perhaps of* FIRST, *undoubtedly of* SECOND MINISTER, *by suggesting, in contest, and in opposition, most of those measures which were, with some variation in non-essentials, actually carried into effect by the government.* The disappointment he had again experienced, was such as to enliven his ambition, and to rouse all the energies of his mind. He was scarcely yet five-and-thirty-years of age ; and therefore, in the very vigour of his faculties. During the American war, Burke was more popular, active and useful, for a time....more truly the first leader of his party, than Fox. But, Fox was now caressed, pitied, admired, and applauded, so as greatly to eclipse the lustre of the talents of all his co-adjutors. Without absolutely slighting Burke, he contrived to treat him less confidentially than before, to act more independently of him, to exclude him from some of the most secret consultations of those who were the chief supporters of the party. It was no longer the Marquis of Rockingham, the patron of Burke, who was named its head ; but, ever since the death of that nobleman, the Duke of Portland and Earl Fitzwilliam, the friends of Fox. Even the people, over whose affections, no object has, in certain circumstances, stronger power, than a great man in a state of humiliation, became, now, more partial to Fox than before. At the gaming-table, he began to become knowing and fortunate ; so that, if he could have ceased from again provoking the chances of the cards and dice....he was once in possession of a sufficient fortune, gained where he had spent his patrimony.

Although defeated, Fox and his party therefore, were yet formidable. Fox himself had still extraordinary influence among tne

Will your Grace forgive me, if I venture to express some anxiety for a man whom I know you
do not love? My Lord Weymouth has cowardice
to plead, and a desertion of a later date than your

young men of fashion. Lord North, a man of very amiable temper
and manners, and of great integrity, retained the kindness of most
of those who had once acted with him in the ministry, and was even
very little hated by his opponents. An administration, at the head
of which was a young man so inexperienced as Mr. Pitt, might be
expected to fall into many errors, of which adversaries' like Fox,
would easily take advantage. The young Prince of Wales was just
issuing out into public life. Fox and his friends contrived to attach
him to themselves: and, from his revenue, his passions, and the
chances of his accession, they derived, for the present, additional
reputation and means of support; while, for the future, a new field
for hope, opened before them. To avenge themselves of the East-
India interest; and, if possible, to embroil Mr. Pitt with his late
protectors: they instituted an impeachment of Mr. Hastings;
which, at one time, promised to fulfil their hopes; but, by the arts
of their political opponents, and still more, by the innocence and
extraordinary merits of the man whom they had impeached, in the
end turned out unsuccessfully. For several of the first years after
Mr. Pitt was established in administration, the exertions of the minority were keen, vigilant and impressive, as if they had been just
fresh from their memorable defeat, or, each moment, about to
grasp the prize of certain victory.

Their hopes and their resentments began, in time, to languish.
Mr. Fox, in 1788, wandered to the Continent, for the recovery of
his health, which had been injured, both by his political toils, and
by his excesses in fashionable dissipation. At Lausanne, he visited
Gibbon; and spent a day with him; in which his bewitching conversation, and warm, yet delicate flattery, highly captivated the
affections of the historian, who had been injured by his political
enmity. He continued his journey to Italy; and, no doubt, travelled, in this maturity of his mind and character, with the greatest
improvement and delight.

own. You know the privy-seal was intended for him; and if you consider the dignity of the post he deserted, you will hardly think it decent to quarter him on Mr. Rigby. Yet he must have bread, my

Upon the occasion of the memorable illness of the King, he was recalled from Italy by a messenger dispatched from his political friends in England. *Whether the Prince of Wales should succeed, of course, to the regency...or a regency should be appointed by parliament ?*....was the grand question which came, then, into discussion, between the contending parties......Those who consider the whole course of the British History, the fundamental principles of the British Constitution, and the essential nature of monarchy, will readily allow, that due regard to these, requires that the throne should never be, for a moment, vacant of a person, competent to perform the regal functions. It will appear, agreeably to this principle, that the Houses of Parliament have no constitutional power, in such a case, but to ascertain and declare the change. And this order must, also, be perceived to be, greatly, the most favourable to civil tranquillity, and to the rights of the inferior people....On the other hand, the laws in the case of private inheritance, the circumstances of different revolutions, and the high claims of the popular branch of such a government as that of Britain, might suggest much specious reasoning in favour of the position, that the two Houses of Parliament become, in such a case as then occurred, both guardians of the unfortunate monarch, and representatives of the crown and the nation for the choice of a regency....The former of these doctrines was that of Mr. Fox and his friends. The latter was, in England though not in Ireland, successfully maintained against them. Yet, they might have prevailed, in the end ; if the King's recovery had not, happily interrupted the contention.

We shall be the more entirely convinced, that, in this case, Fox and his friends reasoned justly ; if we reflect ; that the cessation of the exercise of the royal authority produces, except as to the declaration of a successor, a virtual dissolution of all the powers of legislature and government; that nothing less than the newly delegated representation of the whole people, for the express purpose, can, in this case, again fill the throne, and restore the energies of the

Lord;....or, rather, he must have wine. If you deny him the cup, there will be no keeping him within the pale of the ministry.

JUNIUS.

constitution ; that the danger of parliamentary usurpation is much greater, where the activity of the Monarch's power can be supposed to be at any time suspended in favour of the two Houses, than where the proper heir is allowed to succeed to the royal functions, as soon as the present possessor becomes incapable of them ; that for parliament to be guardians of the Prince, whose distempered health places him in a temporary incapacity, must be sufficient, in the common state of humanity, to prevent his being unfairly dealt with by his successor ; that the case of royalty differs widely from that of a private estate, inasmuch as the former respects *official duty*, the latter, only the *enjoyment of property.*

In maintaining a doctrine favourable rather to the power of the crown, than to that of the aristocracy, Fox might seem to have abandoned his former principles. But, it was in this instance, the interest of the aristocracy, to maintain that the energies of the sceptre, could not be interrupted. If the Prince of Wales had succeeded, of course, to the Regency ; the great Whig families would then have shared its power among them, and would have fixed themselves in office, too securely to be afterwards dismissed.

On the occasion of this great trial, as formerly, Fox found the want of character with the people to be highly injurious to his own interests, and those of his political associates. He himself, and the other leaders of his party, were thought to be but needy and desperate, political adventurers, who sought office only for the sake of its emoluments, who would shamelessly squander the public money upon vice....if it were intrusted to their hands, who would venture upon any measure, however unconstitutional and flagitious, that would but acquire and secure to them, the powers of the government.

Fox's parliamentary exertions were vigorously renewed and prosecuted, even after those hopes were frustrated, to which the illness of the King had given rise. He was often superior, as an orator, to every rival; never very much inferior tb any. He still ex- ercised, in opposition, the powers of *second minister* of the British government. Pitt's measures were often suggested, always cor- rected, sometimes disappointed, by him. When war was menaced against Russia, on account of the fortress of Oczakow; Mr. Fox, not only opposed the design in parliament, but even sent an Am- bassador from himself and his party, to the court of the late Rus- sian Empress, to concert with her, the best means for defeating the English minister's intention. When a contention arose with Spain respecting the settlement at Nootka Sound; Fox's opposition was, again, exercised, to avert the mischiefs of war.

Mr. Pitt, in administration, of necessity abandoned the almost democratical Whiggism, which had marked the last party and parliamentary exertions of his father. This began to make him less acceptable, than he had at the first been, to the people, who reverenced the name of Chatham. Mr. Fox had, on the other hand, learned, during the American war, to associate the prin- ciples of *democratical*, with those of *aristocratical* Whiggism. He had not, since, rigorously adhered to the former. Yet, they were deep-rooted in his heart. He, now, saw reason to return to them; and began to court popularity and the praise of sincere patriotism, with an assiduity and a zeal which he had not before affected. All his party followed the same example; courting the people, exasperating their political prejudices, making an ostenta- tion of ardent zeal for revolution principles, and professing earnest resolutions to labour till they should accomplish a salutary reform in the state of the constitution.

This plan of conduct was not unsuccessful. The nation began in general to become, more than ever, partial to Fox. It was thought, that there were in his character, an artless sincerity and candour which rendered him incapable of those mischievous de- signs of which he had been once suspected. All agreed, that, though he might be reconciled to his enemies, he was incapable of deceiv- ing the confidence of his friends. Though a gambler, he was said to be in the highest degree disinterested, and utterly incapable of fraud, avarice, or basely intriguing ambition. A mixed character, having follies and errors blended with great qualities continually rising above them, was much more acceptable to the feelings of men in general, and especially of Englishmen, than that sober cha- racter of discretion which pretended to be faultless, and in which

there was not spirit enough for the splendid vices. When to qualities such as these, Charles added the profession of principles of
democratical patriotism ; he became, indeed, the *man of the people*. It was not doubted, but he would, at a seasonable time,
prove his professions sincere. He had procured the famous decision on the Middlesex election to be rescinded from the Journals of the House of Commons. His honour was still sacred.
From this time, he seems to have joined to the power of his father
over the affections of his associates and his party, that which
Chatham had obtained over the people by the fame of his disinterestedness, by esteem for his democratical patriotism, and by
reverence of his talents, which judged their force and extent to be
unbounded.

The first events of the FRENCH REVOLUTION, now arose upon
the attention of mankind. In Britain, they were generally hailed
as auspicious to the improvement of the state of all social life.
Englishmen had pitied and despised the French as slaves : and
they rejoiced, with liberal philanthropy, to see those who had been
hitherto in servitude, at last emancipated into a freedom like
their own. They were proud to see France adopt the maxims,
and follow the example of Britain. Nor did they suppose, that the
French would aspire to any other state of liberty, than that which
was believed to be the true perfection of the British Constitution.
Among both the friends of ministry, and the followers of Opposition, the French Revolution was, in its first years, highly popular.
Yet, ministers whose business was to maintain the present order of
things in Britain, under all its imperfections, could not praise that
Revolution, as did Fox and his friends in the Opposition. These
seized the moment, in order to embarrass and overthrow their adversaries, by urging a parliamentary Reform, with an ardour, and
a general consent of the people, which the ministers might not be
able to withstand.

Fox's own mind seems to have been transported by the first
wildly beautiful and magnificent, but delusive, prospects, which
the French Revolution presented. He saw, that, in this instance,
his sentiments were happily in unison with those, not only of his
own party, but of the great body of the British nation. Pleased
to find himself thus becoming the idol of the people ; and aware
that the want of a due regard to *their* notions of character, had,
on former occasions, proved the greatest obstacle to his political

success; he heeded not that change of circumstances which began, every day more and more, to represent the French Revolution, as not a perfection, but an utter dissolution, of social order.....threatening to arrest the progress of moral, scientific, and political improvement throughout the world. For a while, the ministers, his adversaries, were considerably diffident in their disapprobation of those changes in France, in which Fox, and his party, and the people rejoiced. By degrees, as the French Reformers appeared to lose sight of all sober principles of expediency and virtue, the British government ventured with less hesitation to disapprove their conduct, and were filled with alarm for the consequences to which it was fast leading. Fox exulted so much the more : not as being unfriendly to the true interests of his country, not as desiring to see general disorder overspread the face of the political world; but as hoping, that the progress of the French Revolution, the great changes which it would effect in the politics of Europe, the influence it would exercise over public opinion in Britain, and the embarrassments in which it must, of necessity, involve administration, would at length reduce Mr. Pitt and his associates in office, to difficulties in which they would be forced to abandon the helm of government.

In cherishing these hopes and sentiments, Fox had begun to relinquish the ancient principles of the Whig aristocracy, of which he was the leader.

In the mean time, Edmund Burke; jealous of that ascendency in the party, which Fox had so decisively assumed; attached to the genuine old doctrines of the Whig aristocracy, which had been taught him in the beginning of his political career; cherishing many not unamiable prejudices of veneration for ancient things; and with views more perspicacious, and more truly philosophical, than those of Fox or the French Reformers, foreseeing, what mischiefs must necessarily be produced out of that Medea's cauldron in which those Reformers were pretending to renovate the youth of Civil Society; took occasion to sound the alarm of danger in the House of Commons, in a discussion concerning the government of the province of Canada; privately warned the Duke of Portland and the other subordinate chiefs of that which had once been the Rockingham party, that the French Revolution was leading to the ruin of political society in Europe, and that the plans which Fox was founding upon it, would end in the destruction of the

English aristocracy and constitution; and in a production the most eloquent and philosophical which proceeded from his pen, exposed the errors of that Revolution, and called on all Europe, by any means, however violent, to quench the spreading conflagration.

Such exertions by Burke, were seasonably useful to the ministers, his former foes, and to the constitution...fatally ruinous to the views and the party-superiority of Fox. Even the combination of foreign powers, which then prepared to go in arms, to restore the oppressed dignity of the monarchy in France, were animated in their preparations, by the eloquence of Burke. The ministers of Britain were encouraged to speak more decisively in favour of their design. Almost all who were likely to find their advantage, rather in the maintenance of order, than in revolution and anarchy, became inexpressibly anxious to prevent the farther propagation of French principles in this country. The leaders of the Whig aristocracy in particular, converted by the arguments of Burke, and by their own fears, began to think it high time for them, to unite cordially with the crown, and its ministerial and parliamentary supporters, in order to save Britain from that ruin, in which they saw France fatally overwhelmed.

Yet, before dividing from Fox, they performed in his favour, an act of noble generosity and substantial justice. After recovering his fortune at the gaming table, he was once more stripped of all his winnings, and left without a shilling. His political friends saw his distress; and resolved effectually to relieve him. By a general subscription, they provided among them, a sum sufficient to purchase to him for his life, an annuity of not less than three thousand pounds a year. This annuity they so settled, that it should not be possible for him to squander it by gaming....All his ministerial adversaries exulted over him, on this occasion, as a wretch undone by gaming, and subsisting on the dole of charity. I think the reproach extremely unjust and injudicious. Whatever the demerits of Charles Fox, certainly the services he had performed to Britain, in the course of nearly twenty years of parliamentary activity, during which, as the leader of Opposition, he exercised the duty of SECOND MINISTER....these services well entitled him to a provision much more ample, from the gratitude of the nation. It was to the honour of his party, that they voluntarily paid, to his merits, a part of the debt due from their country. It was a tribute to his talents and to the splendid virtues which, however allayed with imperfections, he undeniably possessed. Shall men whose services in parliament or in council, have been insignificant or pernicious, boast of the pensions, the honours, and the lucrative offices which they wrest from a government to which they are a burthen? and shall a nation's munificence be reckoned dishonouring to him for the compensation of whose public services, it has been spontaneously bestowed? in what other field of honourable exertion, could Fox have laboured so long, and with exertions so splendidly useful, without obtaining a princely fortune? No: to have received such a present from the grateful approbation of his party, did not dishonour the politician, and parliamentary orator, but stamp a new sanction upon the integrity of his fame!

A coalition was, soon after, negociated between the Portland party and that combination of the King's friends, with the Pitts and Grenvilles, of whom the administration had been for some time composed. Fox was earnestly solicited to take a part in the treaty, and unite with Pitt. But it should seem, that he entertained a horror of coalitions, in consequence of the misluck which had attended his coalition with Lord North. He was now at last in possession of the favour of the great body of the inferior people; and he resolved to preserve it. He perhaps expected necessities of revolution to arise, in which, if they should find him out of office, he could be much more useful to his country, than if they were to come while he was a minister: Perhaps, an equality of power with Mr. Pitt in the cabinet-council, was not offered to him: Or, it may be, that his assent was demanded to a declaration of war, which his principles, his hopes of popularity, and his insight into the probabilities of futurity, forbade him to sanction. He refused all coalition with Mr. Pitt. The Whig aristocracy forsook his banners. And he soon saw himself a leader almost without a party, left at the head of a small body of DEMOCRATICAL WHIGS, who had gradually arisen, amid the contentions respecting Wilkes, in the course of the American war, and especially since the commencement of the French revolution.

It was now resolved to go to war with France, for the sake of restoring the monarchy. Fox still true to his former principles, proposed in parliament, that, instead of declaring war against the

French, the British Court should send an ambassador to treat with them. But, those Republicans were, at that time, laying waste their country by the most atrocious crimes, outrageously professing revolutionary principles subversive of all order in Europe, abolishing religion, murthering their late Sovereign and his family, exterminating their nobility and priests. It was exclaimed, that, if Fox could propose to negociate with such men, he must be willing to share their crimes. A general outcry among the enemies of revolution, was excited against him. He was, himself, alarmed; and began to fear, that he might even have lost that favour of the people, which he had preferred to every other possession.

In this crisis of his fame, he thought it necessary to shew himself before the public, in the character of an author. By a letter addressed from the Press to the Electors of Westminster, he endeavoured to vindicate the wisdom, the integrity, and the constitutional propriety of those proposals for negotiation, on account of which he was the most abusively calumniated. Unity of design; an attention fixed, through every period, exclusively, on the object of persuasion for which he wrote; extreme simplicity of style and manner; an air of the most artless ingenuousness and candour; an absence of all impassionate sentiments, or decorative imagery, but such as seem to arise by a natural necessity in the train of thought passing through a mind unambitious of eloquence; a tone of sagacity which seems undesignedly to bespeak a penetration more than human into the future; an easy structure of sentences, with an infinitely delicate purity and propriety of phrase; an art, in short, concealing all art; strikingly appear in this short composition.

It is a more satisfactory evidence of his talents than all his parliamentary exertions together. It effectually accomplished the purpose for which it was written. The friends of peace were convinced by it, that there was no true political wisdom for Britain, but in remaining at peace with France: The authors of the war could, henceforth, only lament, that Fox's sincere, though erring conviction, made him adverse to it. No artifices of calumny have, since, been able to injure his reputation with the people. His Letter was seasonable. It said what it was necessary for him to say. It said nothing more. I do not affirm, that it was aught but a filmy web of sophistry.

For a while, he watched the progress of the war, with his wonted assiduity in parliamentary duty. At length, he became weary of merely lending his assistance to enlighten the ignorance of ministers, and to correct their errors in a manner that served to prolong their power by withholding them from extreme misconduct. He retired from ordinary service in parliament; and resolved to come forward only upon great occasions, when the nation might desire to listen to his voice, as to an oracle of wisdom. On every such occasion, when he believes that Pitt may be shaken, or that great and acceptable service to the nation, may be done by his attendance in the House of Commons......he does attend. At other times, he continues to live in seemingly contented retirement.

By those who have carefully marked the progress of the war, and who are unbiassed friends to their country, it is exceedingly lamented, that Mr. Fox did not agree to the war, and enter into administration with Lord Fitzwilliam and the Duke of Portland. The error of the present ministry has been....not that they entered into the war....but that they have not known to seize the most favourable moments for making peace with authority and advantage. It is probable, that Fox, if he had agreed to the war, and become a minister of it, would, however, have procured peace to be made on several occasions when Britain might have dictated the terms.... occasions which have been unhappily lost. France would, in this case, have been, *in the end*, not the less surely ruined as a republic : and much of bloodshed, want, and misery, would have been spared to all Europe....Besides, was it impossible for the efforts of Britain to command success, elswhere than by sea ?....Had Fox been the war minister....would the war have been as uniformly unfortunate as we have seen it, in all attempts by land?

It is impossible for honest political curiosity, not to wish to see Fox yet prime minister, if it were but for as short a period as the famous war-administration of the late Earl of Chatham. His understanding is now matured by years and experience. His turbulent passions are mellowed. His vicious habits have been subdued by experience and misfortune. It is probable, that he would now enter into no extravagantly bold projects; and that he would prefer the true welfare of his country, to every consideration, whether of party entanglement, or of mobbish applause. The British empire undoubtedly affords thousands whose talents are not inferior to his. Yet, he is, perhaps, at this time, the wisest of all our regularly-bred politicians.

His friends speak in terms of very high applause, of the elegance of his mode of life, and the charms of his conversation. Moderation is now his law of enjoyment. Reading, conversation, and manly exercises in the open air, fill up that time which he does not spend in political business. His residence is on St. Anne's Hill, near Egham. He visits London, but occasionally, to attend his duty in parliament, or the meetings of the Whig Club.

Had it not been....for the unpopularity of his father, and of his own first years....for the bold, impracticable magnificence of his leading views in politics....for a fidelity to his party, to which his own interest has been generally sacrificed.....for a timidity which, after the failure of every one of his projects, has continually driven him into error on the side directly opposite to that on which he erred before;....he might undoubtedly have been, at this time, the first minister of the British government.

It is not to be forgotten, that the sincerity of his Whiggism has been proved....by the *rescinding of the famous vote relative to the Middlesex election*....and by the *amendment of the law of libels*, in which the rights of Juries were sufficiently vindicated against the doctrine of Lord Mánsfield.

Mr. Hine....P. 239.] It was he who, by a bargain with Colonel Burgoyne, obtained the office of Comptroller of the Customs of Chester.

The Duke of Portland....P. 240.] Under the Duke of Grafton's administration, an attempt was made to deprive the Duke of Portland of Inglewood Forest, which his family had possessed for more than half a century, in virtue of a grant from the crown. That which was taken from the Duke of Portland, was destined to enlarge the estate, and to strengthen the election interest of Sir James Lowther, the son-in-law of Lord Bute. But, it was, afterwards, established by law; that the grant to Sir James Lowther, was illegal in its conditions; and that the Duke of Portland had a prescriptive right to the property, which was to have been wrested from him.

Style of your amours, &c....P. 240.] An allusion to the Duke's affair with Mrs. Parsons.

Your accomplice...P. 247.] It was said, that, in accepting of the office of Chancellor, Mr. Yorke, contrary to his own judgment and wishes, yielded only to the earnest intreaties of the King.

The severity of your morning studies, &c...P. 429.] The Duke had affected to talk of his morning studies, in the House of Peers.

My Lord Weymouth, &c...P. 251.] Lord Weymouth, dissatisfied with the negotiation with Spain, or expecting the speedy dissolution of the ministry to which he belonged, had, in December 1770, resigned the office of Secretary of State for the Southern Department. He was succeeded by the Earl of Rochford. He was not now in opposition to the government. And, it was therefore insinuated, that he also must, like the Duke of Grafton, be gratified with the emoluments of some sinecure office...unless the Paymaster of the Forces should be made to pay, for his use, a part of the income of that appointment.

If you deny him the cup, &c.....P. 253.] Lord Weymouth was said to be, then, addicted to excesses in wine. JUNIUS makes a profane allusion to the sacrament of the Eucharist, as it is administered among the Roman Catholics.

LETTER XLIX.

———

TO HIS GRACE THE DUKE OF GRAFTON.

———

CITY BUSINESS is the burthen of this Letter. Junius *connects it with the Duke of Grafton's name, solely for the sake of holding out his Grace, as much as possible, to public odium and obloquy.*

It relates, that the Secretary to the Treasury under Lord North, was as busy in dishonourable extra-official transactions, as Mr. Bradshaw, the Secretary under the Duke of Grafton, had been. It insults over the death of Mr. Dingley ; and brings into quaint comparison with his fate and his relations to the Duke, the name and character of the Sovereign, whom Junius *shews, on every occasion, a disposition to harass with more than the hostility of personal injury and resentment.*

In the second paragraph, the writer exults in the perseverance with which he continued to do what he supposed painful to his Sovereign : and boasts of the curiosity with which his invectives were read in foreign languages, while the lyrical panegyrics of Whitehead, were scarcely heard or known beyond the immediate sphere of the royal presence.

The Earl of Bute had, not very long before, returned from the continent to England : and, to excite new odium against the Duke of Grafton, Junius *represents the Duke's restoration to the Cabinet Council, as a consequence of the favourite's return.*

A great division had lately taken place in the Society for the support of the Bill of Rights. Oliver, proud of having resisted the authority of the House of Commons, of having braved the house in his place, as one of its members, of being committed to the Tower ; of being honoured, with Crosby, as one of the confessors of liberty....had refused to serve with John Wilkes in the office of Sheriff, and had haughtily recommended to Wilkes, not to stand candidate for the Shrievalty on the same year with him. Wilkes would not desist from his pretensions, at the bidding of one who had, hitherto, been but a mere puppet in his hands. Wilkes and Mr. Bull, therefore, in concert, stood candidates for the Shrievalty ; and were opposed by Messrs. Kirkman, Plumbe, and Oliver. Mr. Horne Tooke, who had not, then, thrown off the parson's gown, nor assumed the agnomen of Tooke, with a few others, envious of the success of Wilkes's patriotism, and of his ascendency in the party, supported with warmth, the pretensions of Oliver. No pains were spared by these former friends of Wilkes, to make him odious and contemptible. He triumphed over their opposition : and Oliver was even the lowest on the poll ; while Wilkes and Bull were, by a great majority, chosen Sheriffs. This dissension among the patriots, and the disgrace which it reflected on their whole party, was fatal to their hopes in the subsequent election of a Mayor for 1771-2. On the 28th of September 1771, Mr. Nash, a candidate acceptable to government, was chosen to the mayoralty, in preference to Alderman Bankes, Halifax, Sawbridge, Townshend, and Crosby, who stood candidates in competition with him. The Society for the Support of the Bill of Rights, was, in the progress of these dissentions, irreconcileably divided : and Mr. Horne and his friends deserted it.

JUNIUS, *in the four last paragraphs of this Letter, derides the ill success with which government had interposed in opposition to the patriot candidates for the Shrievalty ; and with indignation still greater than he could feel against the friends of government, attacks Mr. Horne, on account of the divisions which he had fomented among the patriots. Knowing, that Horne's conduct had been more hurtful to their cause, than if he had even been an avowed agent for government ;* JUNIUS *scruples not to accuse him, as such ; and to stir up against him, the enmity of the people, as if he had actually betrayed the patriots to administration. Then, from Horne and Oliver,* JUNIUS *turns again to the Duke of Grafton and the King, with a fury of attack in which eloquence seems lost in virulence.*

This is not one of JUNIUS's *best Letters. Yet, it is not without some admirable strokes of genius and indignation.*

MY LORD,   9. *July*, 1771.

THE influence of your Grace's fortune still seems to preside over the treasury.....The genius of Mr. Bradshaw inspires Mr. Robinson*. How remarkable it is, (and I speak of it not as a matter of reproach, but as something peculiar to your character) that you have never yet formed a friendship which has not been fatal to the object of it; nor adopted a cause, to which, one way or other, you have not done mischief. Your attachment is infamy while it lasts; and, which ever way it turns, leaves ruin and disgrace behind it. The deluded girl, who yields to such a profligate, even while he is constant, forfeits her reputation as well as her innocence, and finds herself abandoned at last to misery and shame.....Thus it happened with the best of Princes. Poor Dingley too!.....I protest I hardly know which of them we ought most to lament......the unhappy man who sinks under the sense of his dishonour, or him who survives it. Characters, so finished, are placed beyond the reach

Robinson.] Robinson was now Secretary to the Treasury, and the confidential agent of Lord North.

* By an intercepted letter from the Secretary of the Treasury, it appeared, *that the friends of government were to be very active* in supporting the ministerial nomination of sheriffs.

Thus it happened, &c.] He would represent the King, as unfortunate, equally in employing the Duke of Grafton, and in having suffered him to resign.

of panegyric. Death has fixed his seal upon Dingley; and you, my Lord, have set your mark upon
the other.

The only Letter I ever addressed to the King
was so unkindly received, that I believe I shall
never presume to trouble his Majesty, in that way,
again. But my zeal for his service, is superior to
neglect; and, like Mr. Wilkes's patriotism, thrives
by persecution. Yet his Majesty is much addicted
to useful reading; and, if I am not ill-informed, has
honoured the *Public Advertiser* with particular attention. I have endeavoured, therefore, and not without success, (as perhaps you may remember) to
furnish it with such interesting and edifying intelligence, as probably would not reach him through
any other channel. The services you have done the
nation....your integrity in office, and signal fidelity
to your approved good master....have been faithfully recorded. Nor have his own virtues been entirely neglected. These Letters, my Lord, are read
in other countries, and in other languages : and I
think I may affirm, without vanity, that the gracious

Yet his Majesty is much addicted to useful reading.] The King
is, in truth, well known to be an eager and diligent reader. No pe-
riodical publication of merit escapes his notice. And he is said to
be well acquainted with all the best productions of modern literature.

These Letters, &c.] This is but one of several occasions on which
the vanity of the author of these Letters, breaks out into exultation.

character of the best of Princes, is by this time not only perfectly known to his subjects, but tolerably well understood by the rest of Europe. In this respect alone, I have the advantage of Mr. Whitehead.

I have the advantage of Mr. Whitehead.] Mr. Whitehead was then, Poet-Laureat. His Birth-day Odes were not very commendable effusions of poesy. Nor are the Birth-day Odes of other Poets-Laureat, among the best poetical compositions of the age. Hence ; and because it has been, in prejudice, believed, that poetry must begin from inspiration or capricious choice, and cannot be, like a piece of prose, produced at command ; some of the best judges and most liberal thinkers on these matters, have earnestly suggested, that it would be honourable to our Sovereign, to discontinue the exaction of Birth-day Odes from the Poet-Laureat.

I cannot, however, embrace this opinion. We know, that the composition of poetry depends not, any more than that of prose, on mysterious, sudden, involuntary, and unmanageable inspiration ; but upon the voluntary and vigorous exercise of talents originally not mean, and carefully cultivated with a view to excellence in this particular branch of the literary arts. A poem may, therefore, be made, just as well as a piece of prose, for any particular occasion, whether that be chosen by yourself, or prescribed by another....provided only that you enter heartily upon the task, and ardently exert all your faculties in its performance. Is your subject a barren one? enrich, adorn, exalt it, by those wonders of association and transition, which the true poet well knows how to display. Is it a noble and fertile one ? with so much the less difficulty, may you compose an excellent poem upon it. Whatever be the case ; he who cannot produce good poetry, on a subject prescribed to him, will scarcely be able to do greatly better on one that he is left to choose for himself.

But, if a good poet may make good verses on any subject, whether chosen by himself, or prescribed by another ; why should not those topics of thought, which are suggested by the returning birthdays of a British King, be celebrated in verse ? An ode, or poem, on such an occasion, is of course devoted, not more to the praise of the monarch, than to that of the nation over which he reigns. The

His plan, I think, is too narrow. He seems to ma-
nufacture his verses for the sole use of the hero who
is supposed to be the subject of them; and, that his
meaning may not be exported in foreign bottoms,
sets all translation at defiance.

Your Grace's re-appointment to a seat in the
cabinet, was announced to the public by the ominous return of Lord Bute to this country. When
that noxious planet approaches England, he never

transactions, either in whole or in part, of the year which has just
passed, may become the topics of the Ode. Its imagery may be
selected from all the scenes of nature and society, which the empire embraces. National hopes, wishes, exultation, and resolution,
may afford sentiments. The poet's art must work all up into a
skilful and happy structure. If more be wanting; he can look back
upon the past, and forward on the future; he can conjure up all the
fairy forms of fancy's peculiar creation; he can introduce the dictates of moral wisdom; and he may dignify or deplore the common fate of human things. What themes, if not these, are worthy of poetic decoration? Could Pindar compose his immortal Odes
at the request of successful jockies, to celebrate the glories of
horse-races? And shall there be never a British bard, able to write
a series of Odes in honour of the great events in the contemporary
history of his country? If Cibber, if Whitehead, if Warton, if
even the worthy and ingenious Pye, have failed to dignify the honour of Poet-Laureat, by the composition of Birth-day Odes, the
pride of English poesy; we must blame the inability of some, the
indolence of others, and in them all, perhaps a want of a knowledge duly comprehensive and discriminating, of the duties of their
office, and of the advantages it affords for the performance of
them.

Noxious planet....to bring plague and pestilence, &c.] This is
imitated from Milton.
        " .... On the other side,
    " Incensed with indignation, *Satan stood*

fails to bring plague and pestilence along with him. The King already feels the malignant effects of your influence over his councils. Your former administration made Mr. Wilkes an alderman of London, and Representative of Middlesex. Your next appearance in office is marked with his election to the Shrievalty. In whatever measure you are concerned, you are not only disappointed of success, but always contrive to make the government of the best of Princes contemptible in his own eyes, and ridiculous to the whole world. Making all due allowance for the effect of the minister's declared interposition, Mr. Robinson's activity, and Mr. Horne's new zeal in support of administration, we still want the genius of the Duke of Grafton to account for committing the whole interest of government in the city to the conduct of Mr. Harley. I will not bear

> " Unterrified ; and, *like a comet, burn'd,*
> " That fires the length of Ophiuchus huge,
> " In the Arctic sky, and *from his horrid hair,*
> " *Shakes pestilence and war.*".............

Your former administration made Mr. Wilkes, &c.] This is literally the truth. It was in spite to the ministry, and especially to the Duke of Grafton, that the city friends of Mr. Wilkes, procured him to be chosen Alderman of the Ward of Farringdon Without. His election to the office of Sheriff was....partly in reward of the spirit with which he excited the opposition in favour of the printers, against the authority of the House of Commons....partly in pursuance of a general plan of his city friends, to exalt him as high as possible....since the court seemed to have illegally striven to debase him.

Mr. Harley.] The Right Honourable Thomas Harley....The Harleys were originally dissenters. Harley, Lord Treasurer to Queen Anne, had a brother, Mr. Auditor Harley : and these two

hard upon your faithful friend and emissary Mr. Touchet; for I know the difficulties of his situation, and that a few lottery tickets are of use to his œconomy. There is a proverb concerning persons in the predicament of this gentleman; which, however, cannot be strictly applied to him: *They commence dupes, and finish knaves.* Now Mr. Touchet's character is uniform. I am convinced that his sentiments never depended upon his circumstances; and that, in the most prosperous state of his fortune, he was always the very man he is at present.....But was there no other person of rank and consequence in the city, whom government could confide in, but a notorious Jacobite? Did you imagine that the whole body of the Dissenters, that the whole Whig interest of London, would attend at the levee, and submit to the direc-

---

were, then, the principal representatives of the family....The only son of the Treasurer, obtained in marriage, the only daughter and heiress of the Duke of Newcastle; and became, upon his father's death, the second Earl of Oxford. His only child was Lady Margaret, who became duchess of Portland, and was eminent for her taste in antiquities, in the elegant sciences, and in the fine arts. Her sons, the present Duke of Portland and Lord Edward Bentinck, with their families, are now, therefore, the representatives of the Lord Treasurer Harley......Upon the death of the second Earl of Oxford, the Earldom fell to the family of Mr. Auditor Harley. The father of the Right Honourable Thomas Harley was, I believe, the first Earl of Oxford of the younger branch. Mr. Harley is one of the few modern instances of a nobleman's son engaging in trade. His noble birth and his Tory connexion, were probably among his chief recommendations to the favour of the court. He was, also, a worthy man, of abilities not at all despicable.

tions of a notorious Jacobite? Was there no Whig magistrate in the city, to whom the servants of George the Third could entrust the management of a business so very interesting to their master, as the election of Sheriffs? Is there no room at St. James's, but for Scotchmen and Jacobites? My Lord, I do not mean to question the sincerity of Mr. Harley's attachment to his Majesty's government. Since the commencement of the present reign, I have seen still greater contradictions reconciled. The principles of these worthy Jacobites are not so absurd as they have been represented. Their ideas of divine right are not so much annexed to the person or family, as to the political character of the Sovereign. Had there ever been an honest man among the *Stuarts*, his Majesty's present friends would have been Whigs upon principle. But the conversion of the best of Princes has removed their scruples. They have forgiven him the sins of his Hanoverian ancestors, and acknowledge the hand of Providence in the descent of the crown upon the head of a true *Stuart*. In you, my Lord, they also behold, with a kind of predilection, which borders upon loyalty, the natural

---

A notorious Jacobite?] JUNIUS, evidently, repeats the epithet of *Jacobite*, with so much vulgar bitterness, merely because he knew it to be fitted to work upon the prejudices, the ignorance and the gross feelings of his city admirers.

Had there ever been an honest man among the Stuarts, &c.] The author speaks here to the prejudices of ignorance, a language which he had before too often disgustingly repeated.

representative of that illustrious family. The mode of your descent from Charles the Second, is only a bar to your pretensions to the crown, and no way interrupts the regularity of your succession to all the virtues of the *Stuarts.* .

The unfortunate success of the Reverend Mr. Horne's endeavours, in support of the ministerial nomination of Sheriffs, will, I fear, obstruct his preferment. Permit me to recommend him to your Grace's protection. You will find him copiously gifted with those qualities of the heart, which usually direct you in the choice of your friendships. He too was Mr. Wilkes's friend, and as incapable as you are of the liberal resentment of a gentleman. No my Lord.....it was the solitary, vindictive malice of a monk, brooding over the infirmities of his friend, until he thought they quickened into public life, and feasting with a rancorous rapture upon the sordid catalogue of his distresses. Now, let him go back to his cloister. The church is a proper retreat for him. In his principles he is already a Bishop.

The Reverend Mr. Horne.] The reader will find, in a subsequent note a detail of the most interesting particulars in the life of this gentleman.

No, my Lord,&c.] The worst features in the character of Horne, are admirably caricatured in this, and the following period. He gained the friendship of Mr. Wilkes; then, quarrelled with him, and abused him.

The mention of this man has moved me from my natural moderation. Let me return to your Grace. You are the pillow upon which I am determined to rest all my resentments. What idea can the best of Sovereigns form to himself of his own government ?....In what repute can he conceive that he stands with his people, when he sees, beyond the possibility of a doubt, that, whatever be the office, the suspicion of his favour is fatal to the candidate ; and that, when the party he wishes well to has the fairest prospect of success, if his royal inclination should unfortunately be discovered, it drops like an acid, and turns the election ? This event, among others, may perhaps contribute to open his Majesty's eyes to his real honour and interest. In spite of all your Graces ingenuity, he may at last perceive the inconvenience

The mention of this man, &c.] Junius here suggests, that there was, in Horne's opposition to Wilkes, an atrocity of faithlessness in friendship and treachery to patriotism, which he could not contemplate, without indignation, such as the crimes of ministers and courtiers could not provoke in his mind. Junius, evidently, wished to frighten Horne by what he threw out against him in this Letter.

When the party he wishes well to, &c.] Oliver, but for his disagreement with Wilkes, and for the suspicion which was excited against him, as if he acted in concert with the court, might, undoubtedly, have been chosen Sheriff for the City of London, and the County of Middlesex, in the year 1771-2.

It drops like an acid, and turns the election ?] This is a chemical metaphor. The infusion of an acid into a liquid mixture, will alter the *elective* attractions of its component principles, and form products very different from those which before existed in the mix-

of selecting, with such a curious felicity, every
villain in the nation to fill the various departments
of his government.   Yet I should be sorry to confine him in the choice either of his footmen or his
friends.

JUNIUS.

ture. There is somewhat of pun in JUNIUS's use of the word *elec-*
tion in this period.

Every villain in the nation,&c.] This is ribaldry, not eloquence.

LETTER L.

FROM THE REVEREND MR. HORNE TO JUNIUS.

---

*In this Letter Mr. Horne endeavours to vindicate himself against
the reproaches of* JUNIUS, *thrown out in the Letter immediately
preceding. It is the charge of having sold himself to government,
which he is chiefly solicitous to refute. He denies it with the confidence of a man, who well knew that it could never be proved
against him. He adds praises of himself, abuse of Wilkes, compliments and rebuffs to* JUNIUS. *The whole epistle bespeaks boldness,
firmness, address, and yet sincerity.
The composition is harsh, but clear, pure, unaffected, yet endowed
with spirit, and even rising into eloquence.*

SIR,

13. *July*, 1771.

FARCE, *Comedy*, and *Tragedy*.....*Wilkes,
Foote*, and JUNIUS, united at the same time against
one poor Parson, are fearful odds. The two former are only labouring in their vocation, and may

---

Farce.] By using this term in reference to Wilkes, Mr. Horne
means to insinuate, I suppose, that the patriotism of Wilkes was all
a farce.

Labouring in their vocation, &c.] Mr. Horne, however, certainly did not labour in his vocation, when he deserted his duties as

equally plead in excuse, that their aim is a liveli-
hood. I admit the plea for the *second* : his is an
honest calling, and my clothes were lawful game ;

a clergyman, in order to harangue election-mobs, to canvas for
votes in favour of patriots, and to fill the newspapers with violent,
political Letters. He ought to have known that the political condition of men in society, is not to be effectually improved, without
the previous improvement of their knowledge, industry, and virtue, as individuals. As a clergyman, therefore, he might have
gratified his political passion much more successfully by the best ·
exercise of his talents in delivering from the pulpits, sermons of
careful composition....in studying the principles and diversities of
human character, with a view to discourage vice and recommend
virtue with skill and success....in performing acts of charity....in
exciting to honest industry....in consoling with the promises of religion, the gloom and despondency of the death-bed....and in discharging with sacred fidelity, the other duties of the clerical office.
Never shall you see a perfect political constitution among a nation of
bad men. There is no sure way to true political reform, but by that
reformation of private manners which effectually anticipates it.....
You might as well build a man of war of decayed timber....or form
a palace having its walls infected with the *dry-rot*....as think of
amending the British Constitution, otherwise than by the amelio-
ration of the intelligence, and virtue of all the individuals living
under it.

My clothes were lawful game.] Samuel Foote, though he wrote
much more in the style of Aristophanes, than in that of Menander,
possessed perhaps more of the true *vis comica*, than any other English Dramatic writer, since the days of Shakspeare. Circumstances, however, confined him to write only broad, powerful satiri-
cal farce, to secure the success of which, he had recourse to all the
grosser arts of vulgar mimicry, and of personal allusion to conspicuous characters. None of his friends were safe from his satire. He
would entertain you at his table, he would eagerly visit you in
your own house, of purpose to study your peculiarities, that he
might take you off. He was accustomed to exhibit his personages
on the stage, in the very dress of the known characters which they

but I cannot so readily approve Mr. Wilkes, or commend him for making patriotism a 'trade, and a fraudulent trade. But what shall I say to JUNIUS? the grave, the solemn, the didactic! Ridicule, indeed, has been ridiculously called the test of truth; but

---

were satirically intended to represent. He had proposed to serve Dr. S. Johnson so; but was deterred from his purpose, by the threats of Johnson to chastise him with a cudgel, on the very stage, if he should make the attempt. He did actually make the trial with Mr. Horne, at the time, when, in consequence of the parson's disagreement with Mr. Wilkes, his popularity had, for a season, forsaken him. Horne could not successfully punish the affront; and, therefore, made as if he despised it.

Ridicule, indeed, has been ridiculously called the test of truth.] This doctrine of Shaftesbury, was furiously attacked by persons who did not understand it; and is now universally considered as a position of which the falsity has been indisputably proved.

It is, nevertheless, a certain, incontrovertible truth.

Ridicule, in its strict definition, is precisely.....: *That emotion of the will, which, in the first instance, arises upon every perception by the understanding, of an incongruity or disagreement between means and their end.* It is often but an inward feeling, unaccompanied with any exterior expression. It is often almost suppressed by other emotions, following the perception on which it depends. Though every perception of incongruity excite it more or less strongly; yet, while the incongruity is concealed, the emotion of ridicule cannot be excited. Nothing can be ridiculous, that is not, as it appears to the mind at the moment of the ridicule....false. No truth can ever, *independently and solely as such*, move the mind to ridicule. But truth may become the *remote*, though not the *proximate* cause of ridicule, by exposing to perception, the incongruity of falsehood. Falsehood is a *disagreement or incongruity* between knowledge *or* existence *and* assertion. *Falsehoods* are, therefore, one class of the incongruities or disagreements by which ridicule is necessarily excited. The exterior expressions of ridicule, are at-

surely, to confess that you lose your *natural modera-tion* when mention is made of the man, does not promise much truth or justice when you speak of him yourself.

You charge me with " a new zeal in support of " administration," and with " endeavours in sup-" port of the ministerial nomination of Sheriffs." The reputation which your talents have deservedly gained to the signature of JUNIUS, draws from

titudes, gestures, certain contortions of the muscles of the counte-nance, laughter, and contemptuous words.

A good man, a worthy action, a beautiful woman, a true doc-trine, may have been made ridiculous. But, then, they must have been first misrepresented, as to that point on which the ridicule turned.

Out of all the books which have been written, and from the whole history of the familiar converse of mankind, not a single in-stance can be produced, of any affirmation exciting ridicule, that was not in the light in which it at that moment appeared to the mind, absolutely false : nor an instance of ridicule at all moved, otherwise than by the perception of incongruity.

In truth, Shaftesbury may have used an unphilosophical loose-ness of expression, intimating, that nothing but what was funda-mentally false, could become a subject of ridicule ; and that ridicule was excited in the mind, independently of any previous act of the understanding : and so far, his position was incorrect.

But his opponents did not attack him on this score. They were alarmed for revelation, if ridicule were to be made the test of truth. They made an outcry, that it could not be so. And the world took them at their word.

It is remarkable, that Shaftesbury himself never succeeds so ill as when he attempts ridicule.

me a reply, which I disdained to give to the anonymous lies of Mr. Wilkes. You make frequent use
of the word *Gentleman;* I only call myself a *Man,*
and desire no other distinction : if you are either,
you are bound to make good your charges, or to
confess that you have done me a hasty injustice
upon no authority.

You make frequent use of the word gentleman ; *I only call myself*
a man, *&c.*] JUNIUS used the title of *gentleman* with affectation :
and it is affectedly, that Mr. Horne here arrogates the emphatic
appellation of a *man.* The word *gentleman....*or rather a phrase
precisely equivalent to it....was, in primary use, employed, among
the subjects of the Roman Empire, to signify a person of the same
descent and manners with themselves, in contradistinction to a bar-
barian and a slave. In the changes of European language and
manners, it was appropriated to denote a *free man who bore arms.*
It was introduced into England, only after the accession of William
of Normandy. By its next change of signification, it came to im-
ply a description of the courteous address, the elegance of personal
appearance, and the more luxurious style of living, peculiar to those
who were freemen, and devoted themselves to the military profession, exclusively. As the state of society varied; this word
came to signify, a person who, in consequence of his descent or personal atchievements, was entitled to the distinction of an armorial
bearing, and who had not dishonoured himself by the professional
practice of any of the sordid arts. In the farther advancement of
knowledge, refinement, and moral discrimination, it was used to
distinguish a person of manly virtues, polished manners, and fortune
setting him above the necessity of mean personal labour. JUNIUS
had applied it to himself in this sense.

The word *man,* as here used by Horne, means precisely the
same thing as *gentleman* in the sense in which *it* was employed by
JUNIUS. Horne meant by it, a person possessing the common sense,
the common honesty, and the kind affections expressing themselves
in gentleness and benignity, which are esteemed the only worthy
characteristics of human nature, neither excessively debased, nor
exceedingly exalted above its middle rate of excellence.

...I put the matter fairly to issue....I say, that so far from any new "zeal in support of administration," I am possessed with the utmost abhorrence of their measures : and that I have ever shewn myself, and am still ready, in any rational manner, to lay down all I have........my life, in opposition to those measures. I say, that I have not, and never have had, any communication or connection of any kind, directly or indirectly, with any courtier or ministerial man, or any of their adherents : that I never have received, or solicited, or expected, or desired, or do now hope for, any reward of any sort, from any party or set of men in administration or opposition. I say, that I never used any " endeavours in support of the ministerial nomination of Sheriffs:" that I did not solicit any one liveryman for his vote for any one of the candidates, nor employ any other person to solicit; and that I did not write one single line or word in favour

---

What Horne here says of *man* and *gentleman*, is, therefore, merely idle and impertinent cavil.

I am possessed with the utmost abhorrence of their measures.] It was, in truth, a fantastic misanthropy, a political wrong-headedness, a quarrelsomeness of spirit, a disposition to require that others should not do from avarice, such mischiefs as he himself did out of forward ill nature....not at all, any direct treachery....which set Horne in opposition to Wilkes. But, its effects on the interests and views of the party, were even more pernicious than if it had been treachery. JUNIUS judged of it by its effects; and called it, treachery, that, by destroying Horne's credit with the people, he might destroy his power to do mischief.

of Messrs. Plumbe and Kirkman, whom I understand have been supported by the ministry.

You are bound to refute what I here advance, or
to lose your credit for veracity. You must produce
facts; surmise and general abuse, in however elegant language, ought not to pass for proofs. You
have every advantage, and I have every disadvantage: you are unknown, I give my name; all parties, both in and out of administration, have their
reasons (which I shall relate hereafter) for uniting
in their wishes against me; and the popular prejudice is as strongly in your favour, as it is violent
against the Parson.

Singular as my present situation is, it is neither painful, nor was it unforeseen. He is not fit
for public business, who does not, even at his en-

Messrs. Plumbe and Kirkman, &c.] These candidates for the
Shrievalty, were actually supported by government. The same
support had been by the friends of Wilkes, attributed to Oliver, in
order to ruin his interest with the Livery.

All parties....have their reasons, &c.] All parties had indeed
their reasons for being hostile to Horne. He was then, and has been
ever since, merely a political Momus, ready to find fault with whatever is established, mistaking his misanthropy and self-conceit for
patriotism, inattentive in his speculations to the necessities of nature and political society, and fancying himself virtuous merely
because he has learned to call other men bad.

Singular as my present situation is, &c.] Horne had, at this
time, in consequence of his defection from Wilkes, fallen from the
highest popularity, into sudden odium with the people.

trance, prepare his mind for such an event. Health, fortune, tranquillity, and private connexions, I have sacrificed upon the altar of the public; and the only return I receive, because I will not concur to dupe and mislead a senseless multitude, is barely, that they have not yet torn me in pieces. That this has been the only return is my pride; and a source of more real satisfaction than honours or prosperity. I can practise, before I am old, the lessons I learned in my youth: nor shall I ever forget the words of my ancient Monitor:

" 'Tis the last key-stone
" That makes the arch: the rest that there were put
" Are nothing till that comes to bind and shut.
" Then stands it a triumphal mark! then men
" Observe the strength, the height, the why and when
" It was erected; and still, walking under,
" Meet some new matter to look up and wonder!"

I am, Sir,
Your humble servant,
JOHN HORNE.

That this has been, &c.] How the consciences of men deceive them, and act as panders to their vices! Horne, for the sake of political bustling, was unavoidably deserting all his clerical duties. And yet, he dared to talk thus!

LETTER LI.

TO THE REVEREND MR. HORNE.

HORNE readily sacrificed the general interests of his party, to his resentment against Wilkes, and to his conceit of his own political integrity and wisdom. JUNIUS *had scarcely attacked him in his last Letter, when he perceived, that farther contention with such a man, however easy a literary triumph it might afford, would materially hurt the cause of the Opposition, by increasing the divisions among the City-patriots, and by exposing the vices and follies of the whole patriot-party, to the ridicule and obloquy of their opponents. But, Horne, certain that he could not be convicted of direct treachery, was not to be easily persuaded to forego the honour of a public dispute, with the redoubtable* JUNIUS.

The following Letter, expostulating with Horne on his exciting divisions in the party, and in some sort apologizing for the charge offered against him, of treachery, was privately transmitted from JUNIUS *to Horne. Horne, with ostentation and pride, made it public; that he might, in a long exculpatory answer, produce a vindication of those parts of his conduct, which had rendered him suddenly unpopular.*

In the first paragraph of this Letter, JUNIUS *decisively shews, that the late conduct of Horne, actuated, if not by perfidy bought with the bribes of the court, at least by private resentments inconsistent with true patriotism, had proved highly injurious to the cause of which the parson boasted himself, a zealous partizan.*

He, next, maintains, that the vices and follies, of which Mr. Wilkes was accused, were not such as to render him, in any degree, unfit for an advocate of the rights of the people, or to make his general success not a matter of galling mortification to the supporters of the present system of government: and he insinuates, as a natural inference, that all who were not treacherous to the cause of patriotism, would still give Wilkes their steady support.

Horne's loss of popularity, the dishonesty of his clamorous pretences,
the shame and weakness of the other leading seceders from the so-
ciety of the supporters of the Bill of Rights, the unmanly illiberality
with which the name of Miss Wilkes had been exposed in a news-
paper, and the very impudence of Horne's supposing that by pro-
fessions alone he might preserve the character of a patriot, are the
subjects of the latter part of the Letter.

The Letter is well written, and entirely satisfactory against Horne.
Yet, it betrays, somewhat of a careless contempt of Horne's abilities,
from which I should infer, that the real character of his understand-
ing was not then known.

———

SIR,   30. *July,* 1771.

I CANNOT descend to an altercation with
you in the newspapers. But since I have attacked
your character, and you complain of injustice, I
think you have some right to an explanation. You
defy me to prove, that you ever solicited a vote, or
wrote a word in support of the ministerial Aldermen; Sir, I did never suspect you of such gross
folly. It would have been impossible for Mr.
Horne to have solicited votes, and very difficult to

It would have been impossible for Mr. Horne, &c.] The object
of JUNIUS is, here, to convict Horne of having done as much as he
durst, in order to promote the election of the ministerial candidates for the office of Sheriff. Had Horne used direct and open
personal solicitation, in favour of those candidates; the insincerity
of his patriotism would have been exposed at once to infamy......
His style, his leading sentiments, and the wonted expression of
his character in his writings, were so well known, that it would
even have been difficult for him to insert an anonymous Letter
in the Newspapers, that should not have been easily known to be
his. JUNIUS, therefore, artfully alledges, that those conspicuous

have written for the newspapers in defence of that
cause, without being detected and brought to shame.
Neither do I pretend to any intelligence concerning you, or to know more of your conduct than you
yourself have thought proper to communicate to
the public. It is from your own letters I conclude
that you have sold yourself to the ministry: or, if
that charge be too severe, and supposing it possible
to be deceived by appearances so very strongly
against you, what are your friends to say in your
defence? Must they not confess that, to gratify
your personal hatred of Mr. Wilkes, you sacrificed, as far as depended on *your* interest and abilities, the cause of the country? I can make allowance
for the violence of the passions; and if ever I
should be convinced that you had no motive but
to destroy Wilkes, I shall then be ready to do justice to your character, and to declare to the world,
that I despise you somewhat less than I do at present....But as a public man, I must for ever con-

exertions which Horne boasted that he had not used in favour of
the ministerial candidates, were exertions which it was impossible
for him to employ, however willing. He, then, infers, that, whatever Horne could do for the ministry, he had done with zeal......
He had already shewn, and he shews again, that no conduct could
have had a more direct and effectual tendency, than that of Mr.
Horne, to favour the ministry's views. And, to confound the parson so much the more, he maintains, that the evidence of his treachery was to be found in his own Letters. But, he was unwilling to
exasperate the friends of Horne too much ; and he, therefore, allows it to be not impossible, but Mr. Horne, after all, might be only
indiscreet and resentful, not treacherous.

demn you. You cannot but know....nay, you dare not pretend to be ignorant, that the highest gratification of which the most detestable ****** in this nation is capable, would have been the defeat of Wilkes. I know *that man* much better than any of you. Nature intended him only for a good-humoured fool. A systematical education, with long practice, has made him a consummate hypocrite. Yet this man, to say nothing of his worthy ministers, you have most assiduously laboured to gratify. To exclude Wilkes, it was not necessary you should solicit votes for his opponents. We incline the balance as effectually by lessening the weight in one scale, as by increasing it in the other.

The mode of your attack upon Wilkes, (though I am far from thinking meanly of your abilities) convinces me, that you either want judgment extremely, or that you are blinded by your resentment. You ought to have foreseen, that the charges you

---

I know that man, &c.] The allusion of JUNIUS, in this place, is infamously unjust.

You ought to have foreseen, &c.] It was known from the first, that Wilkes was, dissipated, needy from dissipation, and in consequence of all this, as willing as any courtier could be, to make money by his political exertions. His intrepidity, his skill to outwit his enemies, the illegalities of oppression which had been employed against him, and the desperate boldness of his spirit, were, what the public valued him for. Horne, however, unwisely imagined, that he might ruin Wilkes's popularity, by exposing the well known faults in his character. He erred. Wilkes had never pretended to be

urged against Wilkes could never do him any mischief. After all, when we expected discoveries
highly interesting to the community, what a pitiful
detail did it end in!....Some old cloaths....a Welsh
poney.....a French footman, and a hamper of claret. Indeed, Mr. Horne, the public should, and
will forgive him his claret and his footmen, and even
the ambition of making his brother chamberlain of
London, as long as he stands forth against a ministry and parliament, who are doing every thing they
can to enslave the country, and as long as he is a
thorn in the King's side. You will not suspect me
of setting up *Wilkes* for a perfect character. The
question to the public is, where shall we find a
man, who with purer principles, will go the lengths,
and run the hazards that he has done? The season
calls for such a man, and he ought to be supported.
What would have been the triumph of that odious
hypocrite and his minions, if *Wilkes* had been defeated! It was not *your* fault, reverend Sir, that he

perfect. He had been viewed as JUNIUS represents him. And the
clamours of Horne, were, therefore, ineffectual.

Ambitious of making his brother, &c.] John Wilkes's brother
Israel, did obtain, in one of these years, a consulship abroad.

The season calls for such a man, &c.] JUNIUS is here right....
The final success of Wilkes, in the capital points of his contest;
and the general approbation and usefulness of that success;
have evinced, that Wilkes was, assuredly, not in the wrong,
and that his services, on whatever principle given, were of use
to his country.

did not enjoy it compleatly.....But now, I promise you, you have so little power to do mischief, that I much question whether the ministry will adhere to the promises they have made you. It will be in vain to say, that I am a partizan of Mr. Wilkes, or personally your enemy. You will convince no man, for you do not believe it yourself. Yet, I confess, I am a little offended at the low rate at which you seem to value my understanding. I beg, Mr. Horne, you will hereafter believe, that I measure the integrity of men by their conduct, not by their professions. Such tales may entertain Mr. Oliver, or your grandmother; but, trust me, they are thrown away upon JUNIUS.   ·

You say you are a *man*. Was it generous, was it manly, repeatedly to introduce into a newspaper the name of a young lady, with whom you must heretofore have lived on terms of politeness and good-humour ?....But I have done with you. In *my* opinion, your credit is irrecoverably ruined. Mr. *Townshend*, I think, is nearly in the same predicament....Poor *Oliver* has been shamefully duped by you. You have made him sacrifice all the honour he got by his imprisonment....As for Mr. *Sawbridge*, whose character I really respect, I am asto-

---

But now, I promise you, &c.] This phraseology shews, that JUNIUS was accustomed to study the old writers.

Townshend....Oliver....Sawbridge.] These men did very well, as creatures of Wilkes ; but very ill, when Horne persuaded them to set up for themselves.

nished he does not see through your duplicity. Never was so base a design so poorly conducted.... This Letter you see, is not intended for the public; but, if you think it will do you any service, you are at liberty to publish it.

JUNIUS.

☞ This Letter was transmitted privately by the Printer to Mr. Horne, by JUNIUS's request. Mr. Horne returned it to the Printer, with directions to publish it.

This Letter, &c.] It is easy to see that JUNIUS perceived what was the proper conduct for the seceding City-patriots; but that they saw it not for themselves. Dr. Johnson took advantage, *artfully and successfully*, of JUNIUS's quarrel against these men. And I doubt not, but Johnson's suggestions had influence with JUNIUS, to make him at last cease from doing the drudgery of his party.

LETTER LII.

FROM THE REVEREND MR. HORNE TO JUNIUS.

As to fact and logic, the former Letter of JUNIUS *was unanswerable. Horne could defend himself with success, only by shewing,* 1st. *that he was himself a politician of infallible wisdom and blameless virtue ;* 2ndly, *that it was possible to find in Britain, many other politicians, as perfect in morals and intellect as himself ; and* 3dly, *that he had always believed Wilkes to be such, till at length the discovery that it was not so, made them quarrel. This, however, was a sort of defence, which Horne could not use. But, as madmen have been remarked, often to join extraordinary cunning with their frenzy ; so, Horne, with extreme absurdity of conduct, as to some things, could exercise in respect to others, consummate art. In the following Letter, he has contrived to parry the thrusts of* JUNIUS, *with no mean skill.*

To the capital charge he makes no direct reply. It could not be denied that his conduct had tended to break the strength of his party. Nor does he attempt to deny it.

But, he had not sold himself to the ministry : and on this head, he is loud and earnestly loquacious.

Mr. Wilkes had many faults : and these, though they were before well known, Horne again publishes with triumph.

JUNIUS *was not hostile to the leaders of the opposition. And Horne, therefore, insinuates, that he was, for dishonest ends, the drudge of the Marquis of Rockingham and the Earl of Chatham.*

There was room for something of mere logomachy in what JUNIUS *had written to Horne. And Horne seized the occasion with high delight. Horne might have concealed the Letter of* JUNIUS, *and waved the contest. But there was an air of boldness and honesty in choosing*

rather to publish it. There was credit to be found in a public con-
tention with JUNIUS. *And Horne, too, knew himself to be a master*
in the arts of disingenuous self defence.
The style is pure and vigorous; but without grace or delicacy.

———

31. *July*, 1771.

SIR,

YOU have disappointed me. When I told you, that surmise and general abuse, in however elegant language, ought not to pass for proofs, I evidently hinted at the reply which I expected : but you have dropped your usual elegance, and seem willing to try what will be the effect of surmise and general abuse in very coarse language. Your answer to my Letter, (which I hope was cool and temperate and modest) has convinced me, that my idea of a *man*, is much superior to yours of a *gentleman*. Of your former Letters, I

But you have dropped your usual elegance, &c.] Here Horne egregiously errs. JUNIUS's last Letter is written with as much correctness and elegance of style, as any of the former. Perhaps Horne might hope to provoke against himself a torrent of violent invective. In this, indeed, he was disappointed. JUNIUS would not honour such a person as Horne with indignant eloquence, such as he had lavished on the Duke of Grafton and Sir William Draper.

Temperate and modest.] So modest as to praise himself for wisdom and virtue which he did not possess ! So temperate as to throw out abuse the boldest and most inelegant, against Wilkes and JUNIUS !

Of your former Letters I have always said, &c.] He had not

have always said, *Materiem superabat opus :* I do not
think so of the present; the principles are more
detestable than the expressions are mean and illi-
beral. I am contented, that all those who adopt
the one, should for ever load me with the other.

I appeal to the common-sense of the public,
to which I have ever directed myself : I believe
they have it, though I am sometimes half-inclined
to suspect, that Mr. Wilkes has formed a truer
judgment of mankind than I have. However, of
this I am sure, that there is nothing else upon
which to place a steady reliance. Trick, and low
cunning, and addressing their prejudices and passions, may be the fittest means to carry a particular
point; but if they have not common-sense, there is
no prospect of gaining for them any real permanent
good. The same passions which have been art-

taste to judge aright : and he had envy and malignity to mislead his
judgment, even if he could have been otherwise correct.

I appeal to the common sense of the public, &c.] Common sense
had surely little to do with those political transactions in which
Horne had been, hitherto, chiefly engaged.

I am sometimes half inclined to suspect, &c.] Yet, Horne was
destined to make his fortune, in the end by politics, as well as Mr.
Wilkes.

*The same passions which have been artfully used by an honest
man, &c.*] Base perversion of language ! Daring audacity of vice !
Those men are strangers to honesty, who can descend to make an
artful use of the passions of others. The very stating of such a position hypothetically, implies a want of delicate rectitude, of moral
sentiment in the man by whom it is proposed.

fully used by an honest man for their advantage, may be more artfully employed by a dishonest man for their destruction. I desire them to apply their common-sense to this letter of JUNIUS; not for my sake, but their own: it concerns them most nearly; for the principles it contains, lead to disgrace and ruin, and are inconsistent with every notion of civil society.

The charges which JUNIUS has brought against me, are made ridiculous by his own inconsistency and self-contradiction. He charges me positively with " a new zeal in support of administration;" and with " endeavours in support of the ministerial " nomination of Sheriffs." And he assigns two inconsistent motives for my conduct: either that I have " *sold* myself to the ministry;" or am insti-

---

The principles it contains, &c.] This is wild rant, which might perhaps have its effect with Horne's own followers, but must have been scorned by all who wished to accomplish the original purpose of the patriots.

And he assigns two inconsistent motives, &c.] To bear a man through, in making such an assertion as this, required the most consummate impudence. JUNIUS proved, that Mr. Horne's late conduct was highly favourable to the ministry. He had proved, that this conduct could be prompted by no laudable motives of public spirit. There remained but *corruption* or *malignity*, to which it could be referred. JUNIUS insinuated, that both might have had a share in producing it. He knew the colour of Horne's mind: and he therefore believed that unprovoked gratuitous malice, might have had greater influence than any other principle, in exciting him to injure his party, that he might ruin Wilkes.

gated " by the solitary, vindictive *malice* of a
" monk : either that I am influenced by a sordid
" desire of *gain ;* or am hurried on by personal *ha-*
" *tred,* and blinded by *resentment.*" In his Letter
to the Duke of Grafton, he supposes me actuated
by both : in his Letter to me, he at first doubts
which of the two, whether interest or revenge, is
my motive. However, at last he determines for the
former ; and again positively asserts, " that the mi-
" nistry have made me promises:" yet he produces
no instance of corruption, nor pretends to have any
intelligence of a ministerial connexion. He mentions no *cause* of personal hatred to Mr. Wilkes,
nor any *reason* for my resentment or revenge; nor
has Mr. Wilkes himself ever hinted any, though
repeatedly pressed. When JUNIUS is called upon
to justify his accusation, he answers, " he cannot
" descend to an altercation with me in the news-
" papers." JUNIUS, who *exists* only in the newspapers, who acknowledges " he has attacked my
" character" *there,* and " thinks I have some right

No defence could, here, be useful to Horne, save the shewing,
that his conduct had not been hurtful to the views of the patriots,
or that the ministry were in the right.

When JUNIUS *is called upon, &c.*] Horne saw that JUNIUS was
afraid of hurting the patriot cause by pressing too earnestly upon
him : and for this very reason, as it should seem, he was the louder
in his outcries.

He sends me a Letter of abuse, &c.] The reader has seen the
arguments in that Letter. They were irresistibly convincing, as to
the *effect* of Horne's conduct. JUNIUS wished not to load Horne with

" to an *explanation ;*" yet this J un ius " cannot de-
" scend to an altercation in the newspapers!" And
because he cannot descend to an altercation with
me in the newspapers, he sends a Letter of abuse
by the Printer, which he finishes with telling me....
" I am at liberty to *publish* it." This, to be sure, is
a most excellent method to avoid an altercation in
the newspapers !

The *proofs* of his positive charges are as extraordinary. " He does not pretend to any intelligence
" concerning me, or to know more of my conduct
" than I myself have thought proper to communi-
" cate to the public." He does not suspect me of
such gross folly as to have solicited votes, or to
have written anonymously in the newspapers ; because it is impossible to do either of these, without
being detected and brought to shame. J un ius says
this !....who yet imagines that he has himself written two years under that signature, (and more under *others)* without being detected !....his warmest
admirers will not hereafter add, without being
brought to shame. But, though he did never suspect me of such gross folly as to run the *hazard* of
being detected and brought to shame by *anonymous* writing, he insists that I have been guilty of

---

too much of public infamy ; if private conviction might suffice.
Horne foolishly supposed it to be fear that disposed his adversary to
treat him with tenderness.

a much grosser folly, of incurring the certainty of shame and detection by writings *signed* with my name ! But this is a small flight for the towering JUNIUS : " He is FAR from thinking meanly of " my abilities," though he is " convinced that I " want judgment extremely ;" and can " really " respect Mr. Sawbridge's character," though he declares him * to be so poor a creature, as not to " see through the basest design conducted in the " poorest manner !" And this most base design is conducted in the poorest manner, by a man whom he does not suspect of gross folly, and of whose abilities he is FAR from thinking meanly !

Should we ask JUNIUS to reconcile these con-tradictions, and explain this nonsense ; the answer

This is a small flight, &c.] The reader will observe, that, ex-cept in unequalled impudence of affirmation, Horne's defence is, in all respects, greatly inferior to any of the other Letters to JUNIUS, which are included in this collection.

Mr. Sawbridge's character.] There is art in this endeavour of Horne, to connect the character of Sawbridge with his own.

* I beg leave to introduce Mr. Horne to the character of the *Double Dealer.* I thought they had been better acquainted.... " Another very wrong objection has been made by some, who have " not taken leisure to distinguish the characters. The hero of the " play (meaning *Mellefont)* is a gull, and made a fool, and cheated. " ....Is every man a gull and a fool that is deceived ?....At that rate " I am afraid, the two classes of men will be reduced to one, and " the knaves themselves be at a loss to justify their title. But if an " open, honest-hearted man, who has an entire confidence in one " whom he takes to be his friend, and who (to confirm him in his

is ready......" He cannot descend to an altercation " in the newspapers." He feels no reluctance to attack the character of any man : the throne is not too high, nor the cottage too low : his mighty malice can grasp both extremes : he hints not his accusations as *opinion*, *conjecture*, or *inference*, but delivers them as *positive assertions*. Do the accused complain of injustice ? He acknowledges they have some sort of right to an *explanation ;* but if they ask for *proofs* and *facts*, he begs to be excused : and though he is no where else to be encountered.... " he cannot descend to an altercation in the news- " papers."

And this, perhaps, JUNIUS may think " the " *liberal resentment of a gentleman :*" This skulking assassination he may call courage. In all things, as in this, I hope we differ.

> " I thought that fortitude had been a mean .
> " 'Twixt fear and rashness ; not a lust obscene,
> " Or appetite of offending ; but a skill
> " And nice discernment between good and ill.
> " Her ends are honesty and public good,
> " And without these she is not understood." ·

" opinion) in all appearance, and upon several trials, has been " so ; if this man be deceived by the treachery of the others, must " he of necessity commence fool immediately, only because the " other has proved a villain?"..,.YES, says Parson *Horne*. No, says *Congreve ;* and he, I think is allowed to have known something of human nature.

But if they ask for proofs and facts, &c.] It is scarcely necessary to remind the reader, that JUNIUS argued from facts which

Of two things, however, he has condescended
to give proof. He very properly produces a *young
lady*, to prove that I am not a man ; and a good *old
woman*, my grandmother, to prove Mr. Oliver a
fool. Poor old soul ! she read her Bible far otherwise than J u n i u s ! She often found there, that the
sins of the fathers had been visited on the children ;
and therefore, was cautious that herself, and her
immediate descendents, should leave no reproach on
her posterity : and they left none. How little could
she foresee this reverse of J u n i u s, who visits my
political sins upon my *grandmother!* I do not
charge this to the score of malice in him, it proceeded entirely from his propensity to blunder ; that
whilst he was reproaching me for introducing, in
the most harmless manner, the name of *one* female,
he might himself, at the same instant, introduce
two.

I am represented alternately as it suits J u n i u s's
purpose, under the opposite characters of a *gloomy
monk*, and a man of *politeness* and *good humour.* I
am called " *a solitary monk,*" in order to confirm
the notion given of me in Mr. Wilkes's anonymous
paragraphs, that I *never laugh:* and the terms of
politeness and *good-humour*, on which I am said to

---

were public, and which Horne himself did not deny. He never
pretended to have other evidence of Horne's corruption, than the
effects of his conduct.

Poor old soul! &c.] What a paragraph of buffoonery !

have lived heretofore with the *young lady*, are intended to confirm other paragraphs of Mr. Wilkes, in which he is supposed to have offended me by *refusing his daughter*. Ridiculous! Yet I cannot deny but that JUNIUS has proved me *unmanly* and *ungenerous*, as clearly as he has shewn me *corrupt* and *vindictive:* and I will tell him more; I have paid the present Ministry as many *visits* and *compliments* as ever I paid to the *young lady*, and shall all my life treat them with the *same politeness and good humour*.

But JUNIUS " begs me to believe, that he mea-
" sures the integrity of men by their *conduct*, not by
" their *professions:*" Sure this JUNIUS, must imagine his readers as void of understanding as he is of modesty! Where shall we find the standard of HIS integrity? By what are we to measure the *conduct* of this lurking assassin?...And he says this to me, whose conduct, wherever I could personally appear, has been as direct and open and public as my words. I have not, like him, concealed myself in my chamber, to shoot my arrows out of the window; nor contented myself to view the battle from afar; but publickly mixed in the engagement, and shared the danger. To whom have I, like him, refused my name, upon complaint of injury? What

---

Yet I cannot deny, &c.] All this is little to the purpose. The business of Horne was merely to shew, that he had not, by his late behaviour, *effectively* counteracted the purposes of the patriots for which he himself had professed such flaming zeal. ·

printer have I desired to conceal me? In the infinite variety of business in which I have been concerned, where it is not so easy to be faultless, which of my actions can he arraign? To what danger has any man been exposed, which I have not faced? ......*information, action, imprisonment, or death?* What labour have I refused? What expence have I declined? What pleasure have I not renounced? ....But, JUNIUS, *to whom no conduct belongs,* " mea-" sures the integrity of men by their *conduct*, not by " their *professions:*" himself, all the while, being nothing but *professions*, and those too *anonymous.* The political ignorance or wilful falsehood of this *declaimer* is extreme. His own *former* Letters justify both my conduct and those whom his *last* Letter abuses : for the public measures which JUNIUS has been all along defending, were ours, whom he attacks, and the uniform opposer of those measures has been Mr. Wilkes, whose bad actions and intentions he endeavours to screen.

Let JUNIUS now, if he pleases, change his abuse; and, quitting his loose hold of *interest* and *revenge,*

What labour have I refused, &c.] Here is considerable art. Horne waves the defence of that part of his conduct which had been accused ; and recounts, with ostentation, the circumstances of that indecent political bustle, for which he had deserted his proper duties, and by which he had made himself of account with the friends of Wilkes, before he divided from them.

And the uniform opposer, &c.] This is merely foolish assertion. But, the reader may observe, not without amusement and ridicule,

accuse me of *vanity*, and call this defence *boasting*. I own I have a pride to see statues decreed, and the highest honours conferred, for measures and actions which all men have approved; whilst those who counselled and caused them are execrated and insulted. The darkness in which Junius thinks himself shrouded, has not concealed him; nor the artifice of only *attacking under that signature* those he would pull down, (whilst he *recommends by other ways* those he would have promoted) disguised from me whose partizan he. is. When Lord Chatham can forgive the awkward situation, in which, for the

that these accusations by Horne, and his desertion of his former friends notably exposed the hollowness of all the pretensions of the patriots.

When Lord Chatham, &c.] Horne well knew it to be, at present, the general persuasion of the patriots, that the constitutional objects which they sought, were not to be obtained otherwise than by bringing into unlimited ministerial power, the united parties of the Earl of Chatham, and the Marquis of Rockingham. He knew, too, that there was a mixture of selfishness, even in the patriotism of these noblemen and their followers. He had, therefore, proposed that they should stipulate in a bargain with the City-patriots, to bring into effect, certain specified popular measures, whenever they should come into power. But this would have been, to raise *democratical* Whiggism from being the tool, to be the master, of the *aristocratical*. They would not consent. Horne claims the praise of merit for having been among the authors of that rejected proposition. He is willing to expose the patriotic pretences of those who rejected it, as insincere. But, he forgot, that, by exposing the hollowness of those men's pretences, he merely gratified his own spleen, and contributed to break up the popular cabal. Nothing could be better adapted than this conduct of Horne, to expose the weakness and selfishness of the patriots, or to prevent the accomplishment of the laudable objects which they had in view. Even in

sake of the public, he was designedly placed by the thanks to him from the city; and when *Wilkes's name* ceases to be necessary to Lord Rockingham to keep up a clamour against the *persons* of the ministry, without obliging the different factions now in opposition to bind themselves beforehand to some certain points, and to stipulate some precise advantages to the public; then, and not till then, may those whom he now abuses expect the approbation of JUNIUS. The approbation of the public for our faithful attention to their interest, by endeavours for those stipulations, which have made us as obnoxious to the factions in opposition as to those in administration, is not perhaps to be expected till some years hence; when the public will look back, and see how shamefully they have been deluded, and by what arts they were made to lose the golden opportunity of preventing what they will surely experience.....a change of ministers, without a *material* change of measures, and without any security for a tottering constitution.

But, what cares JUNIUS for the security of the constitution? He has now unfolded to us his diabolical principles. *As a public man,* he *must ever condemn* any measure, which may tend accidentally to *gratify* the Sovereign; and Mr. Wilkes is to be

writing this Letter, Horne was effectually serving the ministry. He was nearly right in fact. But he required unattainable perfection, which he himself knew not to exemplify.

Mr. Wilkes is to be supported....as long as he continues to be a thorn in the King's side!] If Horne had nothing in view, but to

supported and assisted in all his attempts, (no matter how ridiculous and mischievous his projects) *as long as he continues to be a thorn in the King's side !...* The *cause of the country*, it seems, in the opinion of JUNIUS, is merely to vex the King; and any rascal is to be supported in any roguery, provided he can only thereby plant *a thorn in the King's side...* This is the very extremity of faction, and the last degree of political wickedness. Because Lord Chatham has been ill treated by the King, and treacherously betrayed by the Duke of Grafton, the latter is to be " the pillow on which JUNIUS will rest his " resentment!" and the public are to oppose the measures of government, from mere motives of personal enmity to the Sovereign! These are the avowed principles of the man who in the same Letter says, " if ever he should be convinced that " I had no motive but to destroy Wilkes, he shall " then be ready to do justice to my character, and " to declare to the world that he despises me " somewhat less than he does at present!" Had I ever acted from personal affection or enmity to Mr. Wilkes, I should justly be despised. But what does he deserve, whose avowed motive is personal enmity to the Sovereign ? The contempt which I should otherwise feel for the absurdity

destroy the influence of JUNIUS with the public ; this too strong expression was very skilfully seized. But, nothing could be more frowardly injurious to the patriot-party, than this sort of attack on his former friends. JUNIUS sufficiently replies to this charge, in the Letter next following.

and glaring inconsistency of Junius, is here swallowed up in my abhorrence of his principle. The *right divine* and *sacredness* of Kings, is to me a senseless jargon. It was thought a daring expression of Oliver Cromwell, in the time of Charles the First, that if he found himself placed opposite to the King in battle, he would discharge his piece into his bosom as soon as into any other man's. I go farther: had I lived in those days, I would not have waited for chance to give me an opportunity of doing my duty; I would have sought him through the ranks, and without the least personal enmity have discharged my piece into his bosom *rather* than into any other man's. The King whose actions justify rebellion to his government, deserves death from the hand of every subject. And should such a time arrive, I shall be as free to act as to say. But, till then, my attachment to the person and family of the Sovereign shall ever be found more zealous and sincere than that of his flatterers. I would offend the Sovereign with as much reluctance as the parent; but, if the happiness and security of the whole family made it necessary, so far, and no farther, I would offend him without remorse.

Had I lived in those days, &c.] This is a highly laughable bravado. Junius, in the following Letter, brings Horne into a strange dilemma, by means of it.

And should such a time, &c.] Here was a compliment to Majesty, almost sufficient to justify the first insinuation of Junius.

But let us consider a little whither these principles of JUNIUS would lead us. Should Mr. Wilkes
once more commission Mr. Thomas Walpole to
procure for him a pension of *one thousand pounds*
upon the Irish establishment for thirty years; he
must be supported in the demand by the public....
because it would mortify the King!

. Should he wish to see Lord Rockingham and
his friends, once more in administration, *unclogged
by any stipulations for the people*, that he might
again enjoy a *pension of one thousand and forty
pounds* a year, viz. from the *first Lord of the Treasury, five hundred pounds;* from the *Lords of the
Treasury sixty pounds each;* from the *Lords of
Trade, forty pounds each, &c.* the public must give
up their attention to points of national benefit, and
assist Mr. Wilkes in his attempt....because it would
mortify the King!

Should he demand the government of *Canada,*
or of *Jamaica,* or the embassy to *Constantinople;*
and in case of refusal threaten to write them down,
as he had before served another administration, in
a year and a half; he must be supported in his pre-

Should Mr. *Wilkes once more, &c.*] This and the five following
paragraphs, relate to facts in the history of the life of Mr. Wilkes,
which certainly do shew, that he was endeavouring to make a trade
of his patriotism. But they do not shew him to have been unfit for
the purposes for which he was supported by the patriots. The ex-
posure of those facts must have been useful to the ministry, by discrediting the patriot-cause.

tensions, and upheld in his insolence....because it would mortify the King!

JUNIUS may chuse to suppose that these things cannot happen! But, that they have happened, notwithstanding Mr. Wilkes's denial, I do aver. I maintain that Mr. Wilkes did commission Mr. Thomas Walpole, to solicit for him a pension of *one thousand pounds* on the *Irish* establishment for *thirty years*; with which, and a pardon, he declared he would be satisfied: and that notwithstanding his letter to Mr. Onslow, he did accept a *clandestine, precarious,* and *eleemosynary* pension from the Rockingham administration; which they paid in proportion to, and out of, their salaries; and so entirely was it ministerial, that as any of them went out of the ministry, their names were scratched out of the list, and they contributed no longer. I say, he did solicit the governments, and the embassy, and threatened their refusal nearly in these words....
" It cost me a year and a half to write down the
" last administration; should I employ as much
" time upon you, very few of you would be in at
" the death." When these threats did not prevail, he came over to England, to embarrass them by his presence; and when he found that Lord Rockingham was something firmer and more manly than he expected, and refused to be bullied....into what he could not perform, Mr. Wilkes declared that he could not leave England without money; and the Duke of Portland and Lord Rockingham purchased

his absence with *one hundred pounds a-piece*, with which he returned to Paris. And for the truth of what I here advance, I appeal to the Duke of Portland, to Lord Rockingham, to Lord John Cavendish, to Mr. Walpole, &c. I appeal to the hand-writing of Mr. Wilkes, which is still extant.

Should Mr. Wilkes afterwards (failing in this wholesale trade) chuse to dole out his popularity by the pound, and expose the city offices to sale to his brother, his attorney, &c. JUNIUS will tell us, it is only an *ambition* that he has to make them *chamberlain*, *town-clerk*, *&c.* and he must not be opposed in thus robbing the ancient citizens of their birth-right....because any defeat of Mr. Wilkes would gratify the King !

Should he, after consuming the whole of his own fortune, and that of his wife, and incurring a debt of *twenty thousand pounds*, merely by his own private extravagance, without a single service or exertion all this time for the public, whilst his estate remained; should he, at length, being undone, commence patriot, have the good fortune to be illegally persecuted, and in consideration of that illegality be espoused by a few gentlemen of the purest public principles; should his debts, (though none of them were contracted for the public) and all his other incumbrances be discharged; should he be offered six hundred-pounds, or one thousand pounds a year, to make him independent for the future; and should he, after all, instead of gratitude for these services, insolently forbid his benefactors to bestow their own money upon any other object but himself, and revile them for setting any bound to their supplies ; JUNIUS (who, any more than Lord Chatham, never contributed one farthing to these enormous expences) will tell them, that if they think of converting the supplies of Mr. Wilkes's private extravagance to the support of public measures....they

Converting the supplies of Mr. Wilkes's private extravagance, &c.] It may be of consequence, here, to review, somewhat in detail, the particulars of Wilkes's life.

JOHN WILKES was born in St. John's, Clerkenwell, on the 28th of October, 1727. His father was a distiller in extensive trade. He had two other sons, whose names were Israel and Eaton, and a daughter who became the wife of Mr. Alderman Hayley ; beside other children of whom less is known. Their mother was a dissenter. And the whole family and their friends were of warmly Whiggish sentiments in politics.

John received his early education, first in the town of Hertford, afterwards in Buckinghamshire under a private tutor. He was sent to finish his studies at the university of Leyden, then in greater reputation among the Whigs, than either Oxford or Cambridge, and distinguished also the scene of the education of Aikenside, the Honourable Charles Townshend, and Jeremiah Dyson. Mr. Andrew Baxter, a Scottish travelling tutor of great learning, was one of the gentlemen whose friendship he cultivated while abroad. His intimacy, when he was but a youth of about eighteen years of age, with such a man, is a proof, that he was then an eager student, and not at all abandoned to dissipation and folly.

After his return to England he married a Miss Mead, who possessed a considerable fortune ; fixed his residence at Aylesbury, in Buckinghamshire ; and led, for a while, the life of an idle young man of talents, fortune, and fashion. He became, about this time, an associate in dissipation with his neighbour Sir Francis Dash-

are as great fools as my *grandmother ;* and that Mr.
Wilkes ought to hold the strings of their purses....
as long as he continues to be a thorn in the King's
side !

wood, afterwards Lord Le Despencer, and a few other men of wit
and pleasure. And the orgies which this party were wont to celebrate, at a seat which they jointly hired for that purpose, are famous
as exceeding in the varieties of Bacchanalian and obscene excess,
even those of the Regent Duke of Orleans, or those of the Court
of Louis the Fifteenth of France, when he was but a youth newly
initiated in debauchery.

In the year 1754, he, at the age of seven and twenty, stood candidate for the parliamentary representation of the town of Berwick-
upon-Tweed; but was disappointed in his canvas. He was, however, chosen into that parliament, as one of the burgesses for Aylesbury. When the militia was formed, during the glorious administration of Mr. Pitt, he became, under his friend, Sir Francis Dash-
wood, Lieutenant Colonel of the Regiment for Buckinghamshire.
Sir Francis resigning, after some time, the Colonelcy, Mr. Wilkes
was appointed to the chief command of the regiment. The
Grenvilles were his friends. Lord Temple, his neighbour in the
country : and during the ministry of Pitt and Temple, Wilkes was
an adherent, and even a favourite of the ministers. When, upon
the accession of our present Sovereign, power passed into other
hands ; Mr. Wilkes, for a time, hesitated, whether he should not
attach himself to Lord Bute. But, when Pitt and Lord Temple retired from official employment : Wilkes was led to adopt, with
warmth, the resentments of his friend Temple. Much of his fortune was, by this time, squandered : and it became necessary for
him to try, whether he might not re-establish it, as a patriot, if not
as a pensioner of administration. It was supposed, that, against
such odds, Lord Bute's administration could not stand long ; so
that Wilkes might naturally expect, soon to see that party in power,
whose cause he now espoused.

Wilkes was, at this time, a person of no small consideration as a
political associate. He was eminent for fluency, liveliness, elegance, and happy unstudied wit in conversation. No man alive

Upon these principles I never have acted, and I
never will act. In my opinion, it is less dishonourable to be the creature of a court, than the-tool of a
faction. I will not be either. I understand the

had more of fearless personal bravery, or less of peevish blustering
irritability : he possessed taste in the fine arts, was a master in
classical literature, especially in the airy and smutty parts of it ;
and could write his native language with admirable sprightliness
and purity : into the grossness of sensual and convivial pleasures,
he could introduce a charm which might seem almost to convert the
Caliban into an Ariel. His fortune was not yet wholly gone;
though the last remains of it were, now, in waste. His power, as a
gay associate, over the minds of the young men of fortune, rank,
and fashion, was absolutely unbounded. When once seated with
him round the convivial table, neither young nor old, could either
think of rising, or suffer him to rise. Gibbon describes his conversation to have been, at an accidental dinner at which he met
with him, in the highest degree fascinating ; and relates that, after
Wilkes had, at a late hour, retired to rest, Sir Thomas Worsely,
and, as it should seem, the elder Mr. Gibbon, broke into his chamber, and would not leave him till they had, in their fondness for
his gay conversation, made him drink a bottle of claret in bed.

He was re-elected in 1761, to represent the burgh of Aylesbury,
in the House of Commons. But, from whatever disadvantage, he
was less successful as a parliamentary speaker, than in most other
trials of his powers. To aid the Pitt and Grenville opposition, he
had, therefore, recourse to the use of his pen. His first production
with this view, was intitled....." *Observations on the Papers relative to a rupture with Spain.*"....On the 5th of June 1762, he began
the publication of the famous " *North Briton.*" In its composition,
he was assisted by Churchill, Lloyd, and perhaps others of the wits
of the day. He now associated familiarly with the wits : and his
conversation was not less acceptable to them, than it had always
been to the dissipated young men of rank and fashion. The papers
of the North Briton were written with purity and liveliness of style,
with great violence of satire, with a knowledge of the more secret
political anecdotes of the time, with a perfect adaptation of their

two great leaders of opposition to be Lord Rockingham and Lord Chatham; under one of whose
banners, all the opposing members of both houses,
who desire to get places, enlist. I can place no

spirit to the tone of vulgar prejudice, often with exquisite wit and
humour, sometimes with genuine strokes of serious eloquence, never
with considerable depth or force of argument. Their success, both
in irritating the ministry, and gratifying the Opposition, was truly
astonishing. In the course of their publication, Lord Talbot, stew-
ard of the King's household, was provoked to demand of Wilkes,
whether he were the author of the North Briton for the 21st of
August, 1762. Wilkes refused an answer to this question, in terms
which provoked Lord Talbot to send him a challenge. Wilkes
with alacrity, agreed to fight his Lordship. They met: and Lord
Talbot, with a sort of blustering anger that seemed to have its
origin in fear, strove to frighten Wilkes to a concession that should
prevent the combat. Wilkes declined all concession; and with
sportive gaiety turned into ridicule, that confusion of passion
which appeared in his Lordship's words and manner. They took
their ground, and fired. Neither of them was wounded. Wilkes,
then, advancing to Lord Talbot, owned himself the author of the
paper to which his Lordship's enquiry related. His Lordship, upon
this, exclaimed....such was the impression of Wilkes's frank and
fearless gallantry, on his mind..." *That he was the noblest fellow*
" *God ever made !*" They drank a bottle of claret together at the
next inn; and parted, in friendship. The publication of the papers
of the North Briton was continued, till the *forty-fifth* appeared.
That paper contained observations which, seeming to attack the
King himself, were viewed as treasonable and seditious. A GENE-
RAL WARRANT was then issued from the office of the Secretary
of State, for the seizure of its *authors, printers*, and *publishers*.

Before having recourse to this measure, the ministry had used
pains to procure the North Briton to be written down by authors
who were attached to them. *Smollet* wrote the *Briton;* and *Murphy* the *Auditor*. John Home and others were also industriously
at work with the same purpose. *Smollet* was a man, in every accomplishment of eloquence, wit, and political knowledge, exceedingly

confidence in either of them, or in any others, unless they will now engage, whilst they are o u t, to grant certain essential advantages for the security of the public, when they shall be i n administration.....

superior to Wilkes. But the Briton was perhaps directed not so much by his judgment as by that of his employers: and in this case, the energy of his genius could not be put forth. There was, besides, a tide of popular sentiment in favour of the side on which Wilkes wrote, which would have preferred even much poorer writing than the North Briton, if only in the same tone of politics, to the best eloquence of administration. Where Smollet failed, it was scarcely to be supposed, that the others should succeed. It was when in despair....as to the power of their writers, that the ministers had recourse to a state-prosecution.

On the 29th of April, 1763, Mr. Wilkes was seized, in his house, under the authority of the General Warrant. He refused obedience to the Warrant: and its execution was deferred till the day following. He was then compelled to submit to be conducted to the Secretary of State's Office. From that office he was sent to the Tower. His papers, including even letters of love and gallantry, were seized. And he was detained, for about a week, in close and rigorous custody.

But now began his triumph. The Court of Common Pleas, upon application from his friends, issued, in his favour, a writ of Habeas Corpus, directed to the Lieutenant of the Tower. Mr. Wilkes, was, accordingly brought before that Court: and the cause of his imprisonment was solemnly argued. It was decided, that the warrant by which he had been apprehended, was illegal; and that the privilege of parliament had been violated in his person. He was, therefore, by the authority of the Court, set at liberty. In writing the North Britons, he had proceeded to indecent outrage, the moderate and legal punishment of which would not, probably, have roused any very powerful sympathy of the public in his favour. But, the illegality of the measures which were taken against him, seemed to identify his cause with that of the laws and the constitution, and left him no longer to the fate of a puny, solitary individual. From

These points they refuse to stipulate, because they are fearful lest they should prevent any future over- tures from the court. To force them to these stipu- lations has been the uniform endeavour of Mr. Saw-

---

this time, his vices and follies were forgotten; and he became, emi- nently, *the Man of the People.*

Disappointed in their first rash measure of punishment, the ministry, next deprived him of his commission as Colonel of the Buckinghamshire militia: and commenced a prosecution against him in the Court of King's Bench. Parliament, in the mean while, assembled: And while Mr. Wilkes was preparing to complain of that breach of privilege by which he had suffered; Mr. Grenville, the minister, accused him as the author of the North Britons: pro- cured the forty-fifth number of that work to be declared a seditious libel, and to be burnt, as such, by the hands of the common hang- man; and even prevailed with the House to surrender one of their unquestioned rights, and to resolve, that *privilege of Parliament did not extend to the case of libels.*

Hitherto, Wilkes was safe against all the power and artifices of ministerial persecution. But, with a wantonness of indiscretion not easily to be accounted for, he chose to reprint the North Britons, at a private press in his own house;....and thus to confide the secret, that he was their author, to a new set of men, whose faith was un- tried, and who might be more easily tempted to betray it, than those with whom it had been before intrusted. Beside the North Britons, he printed, at his private press, an obscene parody on Pope's Essay on Man, which he called *an Essay on Woman.* One of his working printers betrayed him. The Bishop of Gloucester and Lord Sandwich accused his guilt in the House of Peers. The Peers, with indignation, voted an address for another prosecution against him.

But, while these events were advancing; he, in prospect of them, retired out of the kingdom.....A Mr. Martin, one of the sub- jects of his invective in the North Britons, had in the House of Commons, branded their author, as a lurking coward. Personal bravery, however, comprehended, in Wilkes's estimation almost

bridge, Mr. Townshend, Mr. Oliver, &c. and, THEREFORE, they are abused by JUNIUS. I know no reason but my zeal and industry in the same cause, that should entitle me to the honour of

all the virtues. He avowed himself the author of the abuse of which Martin complained. A duel at the ring in Hyde-Park ensued. Wilkes was wounded in the groin. In meeting his antagonist, under the agony of his wound, and while Mr. Martin's personal safety might seem endangered by the consequences....he behaved with a cool fearlessness, and with a gallant generosity, which won the esteem and subsequent kindness of his antagonist. While he remained ill of his wound; the proceedings in parliament on account of his blasphemy, and in the Court of King's Bench for his seditious libels, were earnestly urged against him. The last remains of his own fortune, too, were entirely consumed; and he was reduced even to the miserable necessity of soliciting the loan of so small a sum as five guineas from Dr. Brockelsby. His great friends, seeing him in these circumstances of poverty and prosecution, *prudently* abandoned him. To avoid the last consequences of the prosecution, he judged it proper to retire to Paris, as soon as his convalescence from his wound would permit.

He continued at Paris, though summoned home. The House of Commons voted him guilty of a contempt of their authority; and, then, on account of his writings, expelled him from his seat in the House. In the Court of King's Bench, he was prosecuted to outlawry. His first triumph over the ministry in their attack on him, by a General Warrant, was reversed. His adversaries had, now, the forms of law in their favour. By these, they prevailed; and he had fled, in ignominy, from the consequences. Even those who had been his friends, were now much more earnest to exculpate themselves from the suspicion of having encouraged his satire, and immorality, than to offer him support under persecution, or to defend him against its most outrageous severity. Wilkes recovering, abroad, from the effects of his wound, endeavoured to forget, in gay conviviality, his late misadventures. He made an excursion to Italy: and, while he could procure supplies of money for his suf-

being ranked by his abuse with persons of their fortune and station. ' It is a duty I owe to the memory of the late Mr. Beckford to say, that he had no other aim than this, when he provided that

ficient subsistence : he was not of a temper to lose his relish for the gay enjoyments of life,'on account of such annoyances as would have brought most others to despondency.

And, he had still a class of friends in England, who would not abandon him. Those were....persons, who, though distant from the sphere of interested political intrigue, delighted in the bustle for English liberty....persons who zealously cherished the ancient un-associating prejudices of the English against the Scots....others who admired, above all things else, that intrepidity of licentious-ness which could insult Majesty and bid defiance to all the legal authorities....some who could not but esteem that union of wit, bravery, and profligacy, which the character of Wilkes displayed ....and some who, though they disliked all else in him, thought they saw him likely to fall the victim of mean oppression from a mighty hand, and were, on this account alone, moved to espouse his cause. These persons composed a powerful and active body, to gratify whose clamours, even his less faithful political friends were forced to make as if they had not finally deserted him. The outcry on account of his persecution, contributed not a little to unsettle the authority of that administration in which George Gren-ville was connected with the Duke of Bedford. The promise of a reversal of the proceedings against him, if they should come into office, was a lure for popularity which the leaders of the opposition held out to the nation. Perhaps, indeed, Earl Temple....and if so, he alone....was sincere. But, they were, all, taken at their word : and, the strength of the opposition was greatly increased by the wishes and the efforts of the friends of Wilkes.

Earl Temple and Mr. Pitt would not come into responsible of-ficial employment, without the stipulation of terms which the King could not grant. The Marquis of Rockingham and the Duke of Grafton, were less scrupulous. They engaged in the business of

sumptuous entertainment at the Mansion-house for
the members of both houses in' opposition. At that
time he drew up the heads of an engagement, which
he gave to me, with a request that I would couch

administration, without fixing those conditions which, as they
meant to proceed, were without doubt, requisite for their security.
That the proceedings against Wilkes, should not be reversed, nor
he himself received into any sort of ministerial favour.....was probably a restrictive stipulation to which they were themselves obliged
to give their express consent. The nation, however, and the friends
of Wilkes himself expected, that, when these men were in office, he
would not be long left to languish in exile. General surprize and
offence were created by the delay to recall and vindicate him. He
himself more impatient, and impatient from the necessities of his
situation, sent to demand of the new ministers, the fulfilment of
their former promises. To procure a reversal of the proceedings
against him, might be difficult. He was willing, therefore, to set
aside for a time, the consideration of public principles ; and accept,
on humbler terms, the restoration of his private fortunes. A pardon, a pension of a thousand pounds a year on the Irish establishment, a colonial government, or a distant embassy, were the grati-
fications which he desired. But the King would not permit him to
be thus gratified ; the Rockingham administration hoped, that
Wilkes's name and injuries might be quickly forgotten, amid the
wisdom and virtue of their government : and they thought, too,
that it would be unsafe and dishonourable, publickly to ally themselves to his infamy. Wilkes would not endure a denial. When
the applications of his friends were slighted or invaded ; he, in great
indignation, hastened home. Though the Rockingham administration could not gratify his wishes : yet they dared not to provoke
him to open hostility against them. They bought his silence and
return to the continent with immediate supplies of money, a pension contributed by themselves in common, out of their ministerial salaries, and the promise of a pardon from the King, and
honourable restitution to his country, as soon as their firm establishment in power should enable them to venture on such a measure....
Had he remained in England ; they must either....by openly es-

it in terms so cautious and precise, as to leave no room for future quibble and evasion; but to oblige them either to fulfil the intent of the obligation, or to sign their own infamy, and leave it on record;

pousing his cause, have ruined their interest with their Sovereign, ...or by treating him as an outlaw, have exposed themselves to the hatred and execrations of the people. He did not see, that he could find his interest in embarrassing them too much : and he, therefore, accepted their money, their excuses, and their new engagements....and returned to Paris.

They fell....though not by his hostilities: and a new administration succeeded, from whom, it might seem, that he had still more to hope. The Duke of Grafton, its ostensible chief, had been his private and convivial friend : even Lord Chatham, who had personally stood aloof from him, had been benefited by his injuries and sufferings. A message to him from the Duke of Grafton, anticipated his applications, and promised every redress that he could ask. He returned, upon this, to England. He had dreaded, lest the Duke's professions might be insincere : and, he determined to reduce his Grace at once to the necessity of either gratifying *him* to his wishes, or breaking with the people. The Duke could not *fulfil* his promises : for, he might not propose to the King to pardon and reward a man so obnoxious as Wilkes. Wilkes, then, in defiance of the power of Government, appeared in public, though an outlaw; canvassed for the parliamentary representation of the city of London....and afterwards more successfully for that of Middlesex ; and, with his accustomed boldness, proceeded to force the minister into decisive hostility against him. The Duke of Grafton and his friends, uncertain, at first, how to act, dared not to urge his sentence of outlawry into execution. But, after the electors of Middlesex, indignant to see Wilkes deserted by the ministers, had chosen him to represent them in the parliament which was about to open ; he offered himself to justice; procured the sentence of outlawry which had been pronounced against him, to be annulled : and was condemned to suffer by fine and imprisonment, agreeably to the former sentences, for the libellous sedition of his North Britons, and for the obscenity and blasphemy of his Essay on Woman. Even in these

and this engagement he was determined to propose to them at the Mansion-house, that either by their refusal they might forfeit the confidence of the pub-

sentences, however, they were alledged to be illegalities which bespoke a malignity against Wilkes, that was still furiously bent to wreak itself even in violation of the forms of law and the principles of the constitution. His success and the continued but impotent rage of his enemies, rendered Wilkes, therefore now more popular than ever. Since the minister, his quondam friend, could abandon him so far as self-interest would permit ; Wilkes, therefore scorned all moderation and compromise ; and by engaging to his constituents of Middlesex to demand from Parliament, the redress of his wrongs, shewed the Duke of Grafton, that he must not hope to maintain a medium between warm friendship with Wilkes, and the most desperate hostility against him. Ere hostilities had yet commenced between them in parliament, the Duke of Grafton made it to be signified to Mr. Wilkes, that he should be expelled from his seat, if he dared to provoke a parliamentary discussion of the circumstances of his case. This menace only irritated Wilkes, and made him so much the more resolute to proceed. He knew that the people were on his side : he might gain much : he had little to lose.

The circumstances of his case were, by a petition from himself, and by the motions of his friends, forcibly urged upon the attention of the House of Commons. He demanded the redress of his wrongs. The friends of the ministry talked of his crimes ; and, as had been threatened by the Duke of Grafton, insisted, that he should be expelled, as unworthy of a seat in that House. A new attack for breach of privilege was at the same time menaced against him from the House of Lords. He *was* accordingly, expelled, under new accusations of libel, from among the representatives of the Commons. His expulsion only inflamed his pride, and enhanced his popularity. A new writ was issued to the electors of Middlesex ; and they again returned Mr. Wilkes. The election was by the House of Commons declared void ; but, even the third time, the freeholders of Middlesex still adhered to their first choice. At a fourth election, Mr. Luttrel stood candidate in opposition to Mr. Wilkes. Only a very few of the electors gave their votes for Luttrel : and Wilkes

lic, or by the engagement lay a foundation for confidence.

When they were informed of the intention, Lord
Rockingham and his friends flatly refused any en-

was accordingly returned by the Sheriffs, as duly chosen by a vast
majority. But, the House of Commons hastily decided, that the
votes for Mr. Wilkes, were null, as having been illegally given ;
and declared the election to be, therefore, in favour of his opponent. Now began that dispute concerning the Middlesex election
in which JUNIUS so successfully took part. The freeholders of
Middlesex and the citizens of London, from this time, espoused
the cause of Wilkes as if it had been their own. He was destined
to make his fortune by their favour, and finally to triumph as to the
disputed principle by their support. In spite of every labour to the
contrary, the whole public were soon convinced, that the constitution had been violated by the preference of Luttrel.

From the time of the contest respecting the Middlesex election,
Mr. Wilkes's fortune went on mending. His great friends could
no longer make him their dupe. He saw, that the people were
much rather to be trusted ; fixed himself upon popular favour ; and
took care to preserve it, till he had regained more than his first independence. In January 1769, his friends resolving to make him
a city magistrate, since they could not seat him in the House of
Commons, as representative for Middlesex.....procured him to be
elected Alderman of the Ward of Faringdon Without. A society
formed for the support of the Bill of Rights raised large contribu-
tions for his support in his opposition to Government, and even for
the payment of his debts and the re-establishment of his fortune.
By a composition with his creditors, his debts, amounting to above
seventeen thousand pounds, were actually discharged by that society. While the society was preparing to do still more for him,
it was divided and set at variance with itself by Horne and some
others who envied Wilkes the gains of his patriotism. After he
himself had suffered the effects of his sentences, he found likewise,
some compensation for his sufferings, in a verdict of four thousand
pounds damages from Lord Halifax, and one thousand pounds from

gagement; and Mr. Beckford as flatly swore, they should then......" eat none, of his broth;" and he was determined to put off the entertainment: But Mr. Beckford was prevailed upon by******to in-

Mr. Wood, on account of their illegal use of a General Warrant against him. In the contention with the House of Commons relative to the seizure of the printers, the circumstances of which, have been already related....he distinguished himself as the leader of the powers of the city...and gave the highest satisfaction to those by whom he had been, hitherto, the most zealously supported.

It was now, that his success among the city-patriots provoked the jealousy of Mr. Horne and others, who, from his assistants, aspired to become his rivals. They represented his patriotism as insincere; exclaimed against his dishonest compromises with the Rockingham administration: accused him as the creature of Lord Rockingham and Lord Chatham; accused the gaieties and errors of his private life; and boasted the superior purity of their own public virtue. The quarrel essentially injured the general cause of the patriots, by breaking their strength, and exposing their selfishness to abhorrence and ridicule. But, Wilkes it could not very essentially injure; because his imperfections were known, before the public adopted him as their champion: and nothing but a proof that his zeal against Government had become less ardent, could now have alienated the people from him. Assisted by JUNIUS, he contrived effectually to ruin for the time, the popularity of Mr. Horne.

He offered himself in concert with Mr. Bull, a candidate for the shrievalty: and was elected to it. He discharged the duties of that office with honour, and without any forfeiture of popularity. In October 1774, he was chosen Lord-Mayor; an office in which also his conduct gave entire satisfaction to the city. On the same year, after the dissolution of the Parliament out of which he had been expelled, he was again elected as one of the representatives for the county of Middlesex. During the progress of the American war, he continued to oppose it in the House of Commons, with many violent sallies of Democratical whiggism. In the year 1779, he was elected to the lucrative office of chamberlain to the city of London.

dulge them in the ridiculous parade of a popular procession through the city, and to give them the foolish pleasure of an imaginary consequence, for the real benefit only of the cooks and purveyors.

During all this while he continued to enjoy life like a disciple of Epicurus ; tempering voluptuousness with wit, elegance, and still as he grew older, with more and more of moderation. He had separated from his wife, within a few years after their marriage : and a mistress occupied *her* place in his bed. His daughter, the only child of that marriage, enjoyed an independent fortune from her mother, which remained untouched by her father's extravagances : and *her* filial tenderness never deserted him in his greatest difficulties. His residence was sometimes in the house of his daughter; occasionally at Kensington or in its vicinity ; and often in summer, at a favourite cottage in the Isle of Wight. He had a natural son on whose education he took much successless pains. Classical literature, and especially the *smutty* parts of it, often entertained his leisure hours. He delighted in social converse : and in conversation, still retained all his early power to captivate.

In his official duty, as Chamberlain, Mr. Wilkes acquitted himself with great fidelity and honour. He was diligent in his attendance at Guildhall, and accurate in his accompts. As a magistrate, he was wont, in disputes especially between masters and their apprentices, to incline...at times perhaps with a blameable lenity... to favour the apprentice. He might remember on such occasions, the follies of his own youth : or he might still be desirous to retain the partiality of the mob. In the year 1780, however, when the *no popery* riots were excited by Lord George Gordon ; Wilkes who had been himself the hero of the last great riots in London, was of all the magistrates, the most effectually active against the rioters. The Bank, but for his efforts, had not, perhaps, have been saved from pillage. He exerted himself, on this occasion with a degree of spirit and vigilance, and spoke against the causes of the riots with a hearty indignation, which were highly pleasing even to the King himself, who had long been considered as entertaining a fixed aversion for Wilkes. Wilkes was given to understand, that his appearance at the royal *levee* would not be unpleasing to his Sovereign.

It was the same motive which dictated the thanks of the city to Lord Chatham; which were expressed to be given for his declaration in favour of *short parliaments:* in order thereby to fix Lord

He went to court; and was graciously received. He was likewise honoured with the thanks of the privy council for his services amid the riots. The entire completion of his triumph was at hand. When the Rockingham whigs came into administration, in the year 1782, they found it necessary to gratify the people by vindicating Wilkes and his adherents from the abuses of a former House of Commons. In that House, therefore it was, on the 3d of May 1780, *resolved*, on the motion....I think.... of Charles Fox, *that all the declarations, orders, and resolutions respecting the election of John Wilkes, Esq. should be expunged from the Journals of the House, as subversive of the rights of the whole body of electors in the kingdom.*

He followed the Pitt and Grenville whigs, when these, under the present Marquis of Lansdowne divided themselves from the counsels of the followers of the Duke of Portland and Charles Fox. He applauded the piqce of which Lord Lansdowne was the author. And, when Fox and Lord North, by their coalition, appeared likely to regain the powers of the government; Wilkes in a sort of moody despair, or that he might not give offence to his old friends, resolved to retire from parliamentary life. The electors of Middlesex, partial to the merits of Charles Fox, had begun already to withdraw from him, a part of their ancient favour. He would not hang upon them till he should become utterly their aversion. He was disposed to defend the merits of Mr. Hastings from the first proposal of the impeachment against him : and this, also, was to his constituents a cause of offence. But, he had the good sense to withdraw himself from political life, precisely at the proper season.

His subsequent years were spent nearly in the same tenor with those which had passed since his election to a city-magistracy. Next after his recovery of the King's good graces....one of the most remarkable incidents in his life, was his captivating, in an in-

Chatham at least to that one constitutional remedy, without which all others can afford no security.... The embarrassment, no doubt, was cruel. He had his choice either to offend the Rockingham party,

terview at the house of Mr. Dilly the bookseller, the favour of Dr. Samuel Johnson. He used to talk, from time to time, of giving a *new* edition of these Letters of Junius*, to which he intended to add notes illustrating the text by all those facts of contemporary history to which it perpetually alludes.

With his daughter, he continued to live in exemplary friendship ; expressing the highest gratitude for her filial attentions to him, amid his misfortunes ; and evincing himself, on every occasion, to be highly proud of her accomplishments and virtues. He amused himself with the publication of elegant editions of the *Characters* of Theophrastus, and the *Poems* of Catullus, each in its original language. He had made some progress in a poetical translation of the *Odes* of Anacreon, which, however, he left unfinished. For his speeches in parliament, he retained a partial regard, perhaps above their desert: and he was therefore, careful to give a genuine edition of them in the year 1787, which, in the year 1788, he augmented with the supplement of a single speech he had made in defence of Mr. Hastings. To the last, he delighted to associate chiefly with persons of taste and literature, with democratical whigs, with men of wit and fashion. His habits of life were now regular ; and his plan of expense was considerably within his income.

He died, on the 26th of December, 1797, at the age of seventy years.

A review of the incidents of his life, will discover the character of his mind to have been bold, shrewd, unfettered by any restraints but the laws of honour, the pride of wit, the ambition of the praise of taste and genius in dissipation, and a native tincture of democratical whiggism. His education had made him only a classical scholar and an admirer of wit. His converse with whigs and republicans in England and Holland, gave him a bias to bustle in politics, rather as a troubler of government, than as one of its crea-

* He superintended the printing of Woodfall's Edition, after which the text is, in the present one, printed.

who declared *formally* against short **parliaments,**
and with the assistance of whose numbers in both
houses, he must expect again to be minister; or to
give up the confidence of the public, from whom

tures. His passions, his freedom from the restraints of principle,
his love of admiration, and the character of the fashionable society
into which he fell, naturally drove him into that wild profligacy in
which his fortune was consumed, and his fair character, lost......
When his fortune was nearly wasted ; want then produced a change
on his character ; and he began to add to dissipation, a desire to
make his fortune anew by politics. He dashed into politics in his
own way, and in a manner agreeable to his particular character.
It was perhaps, because he could not as a speaker, do justice to his
spirit and talents, that he tried his ability, as a writer. He trusted at this time, to the great party-leaders for his reward. The
success of his North Britons proved his skill to catch the prejudices of the day, and probably flushed him with hopes the most extravagant of success. In the course of his subsequent perils, he
learned to distrust his great friends, to be dissipated with discretion,
to fix himself on the favour of the people, and to miss no occasion
for making his fortune. Like all men who have abandoned their
youth to the sensual passions, he became selfish in his old age....
Indeed, he seems to have been so, in a great degree from the very
first trial of his talents in public life. Services such as those which
he rendered to the laws and liberties of his country, were certainly
wanted. For those services, he well deserved all the compensations
which he finally obtained. He was much indebted for his success,
to the Letters of JUNIUS. Massaniello, and Jack Cade, were not
half so fortunate. His personal figure was tall and meagre ; he
squinted ; and had an unpleasing voice.

I will not be either, &c.....P. 310.] Horne's character in politics has ever been, to be the marplot of the party to which he belongs.

To force them to these stipulations, &c....P. 313.] It is proper
to observe, that all combinations for purposes not expressly specified
in the constitutional laws of the empire, are illegal and unconstitutional....however patriotic their ostensible intention. The stipula-

finally all real consequence must proceed. Lord
Chatham chose the latter: and I will venture to say,
that, by his *answer* to those thanks, he has given up
the people without gaining the friendship or cordial
assistance of the Rockingham faction; whose little
politics are confined to the making of matches, and

---

tions which Horne here mentions, were proposed from a combination
of political busy-bodies, and were designed to extend and strengthen
that combination. They were, therefore, illegal, and unjust. They
proceeded, besides, from an ambition in those contemptible politicians whom Horne names, to controul the great powers of the legislature and government. And for this reason, also, they deserved to
be scornfully rejected. It may be, that the persons by whom they
were refused, refused them upon base and dishonest principles....
However that might be ; it was well that they were not adopted.
Sixteen or seventeen years afterwards, the great political leaders
were to act with less prudence, and to make engagements with the
populace, which it would have been ruin to the constitution to
fulfil.

Sumptuous entertainment at the Mansion-House, &c....P. 316.]
This was in the second mayoralty of Beckford. Horne was, I think,
his chaplain. The leaders of the parties in opposition, were invited
to dine with him. He proposed to entrap them into a foolish and unquestionably illegal engagement with which they were to purchase
his dinner. They refused. He blustered. They were firm. He
submitted to entertain them on their own terms. Horne, at that
time, thought himself the very Pythoness of his party. ——

To fix Lord Chatham, &c. P. 322.] It is greatly to the honour of
the memory of Lord Chatham; that though he had at this time, unhappily declined too far into democratical politics; yet he had ever
too magnanimous and firm a spirit to suffer himself to be constrained
by the popular tools of his ambition.

Whose little politics are confined to the making of matches, &c.]
It must be owned, that Horne has here not unskilfully marked the
character of the party of which he speaks. A Burke and a Fox
may have been associated with them, and have inspired some oc-

extending their family connexions, and who think they gain more by procuring one additional vote to their party in the House of Commons, than by adding their languid property and feeble character to the abilities of a *Chatham*, or the confidence of a public.

Whatever may be the event of the present wretched state of politics in this country, the principles of JUNIUS will suit no form of government. They are not to be tolerated under any constitution. Personal enmity is a motive fit only for the devil. Whoever, or whatever, is Sovereign, demands the respect and support of the people.... The union is formed for their happiness, which cannot be had without mutual respect; and he counsels maliciously who would persuade either to a wanton breach of it. When it is banished by either party, and when every method has been tried in vain to restore it, there is no remedy but a divorce: But, even then, he must have a hard and wicked heart indeed, who punishes the greatest criminal merely for the sake of the punishment; and

---

casional activity: but the bulk of the party has ever been a languid mass of property and connexion; deficient in energy and intelligence; and preferring party interests to public good.

The principles of JUNIUS *will suit, &c.*] It is, on the contrary, the chief excellence of JUNIUS, that his views and principles were practical, and actually produced strong and direct practical effects. *They* were founded on a knowledge of human nature: Horne's upon wild-goose imaginations.

who does not let fall a tear for every drop of blood
that is shed in a public struggle, however just the
quarrel.

JOHN HORNE.

LETTER LV.

TO THE PRINTER OF THE PUBLIC ADVERTISER.

THE following Letter is the answer of JUNIUS *to the foregoing accusations and self-defence of Horne. The force of reasoning with which* JUNIUS *exposes Horne's conduct, as in fact injurious to the patriot cause, is irresistible. His exculpation of his friends and himself, is satisfactory. His praises of the great chiefs of opposition are manly, candid, liberal. He still deals much more gently with Horne, than one should have expected. But, he was unwilling to exasperate those who might incline to think Horne an honest man, and to put a value on his former service. After the preceding Letters, and the illustrations with which they are accompanied, the facts and allusions in this Letter will be understood, without much explanation, by the reader.*

This Letter is written with perhaps as much address, as any of the preceding ones. And indeed no small address was required, to confound Horne himself, without offending his friends, to vindicate JUNIUS *without a dereliction of his principles, and especially to reconcile the city patriots to the conduct of the great leaders of the opposition, which Horne had arraigned.*

---

15. *August*, 1771.

SIR,

I OUGHT to make an apology to the Duke of Grafton, for suffering any part of my attention to be diverted from his Grace to Mr. Horne. I am not justified by the similarity of their dispositions. Private vices, however detestable, have not dignity sufficient to attract the censure of the press, unless they are united with the power of doing some signal mischief to the community..... Mr. Horne's situation does not correspond with his intentions....In my own opinion, (which, I know, will be attributed to my usual vanity and presumption) his Letter to me does not deserve an answer. But I understand that the public are not satisfied with my silence...that an answer is expected from me; and that, if I persist in refusing to plead, it will be taken for conviction. I should be inconsistent with the principles I profess, if I declined an appeal to the good sense of the people, or did not willingly submit myself to the judgment of my peers.

If any coarse expressions have escaped me, I am ready to agree that they are unfit for JUNIUS to make use of, but I see no reason to admit that they have been improperly applied.

Mr. Horne, it seems, is unable to comprehend how an extreme want of conduct and discretion can consist with the abilities I have allowed him; nor can he conceive that a very honest man, with a very good understanding, may be deceived by a knave. His knowledge of human nature must be

---

Comprehend, how an extreme want of conduct, &c.] This paragraph contains one of those masterly distinctions in the character of human nature, which frequently occur throughout these Letters, and are the best proofs of the maturity and the force of the genius of their author.

limited indeed.   Had he never mixed with the
world, one would think that even his books might
have taught him better.   Did he hear Lord Mansfield, when he defended his doctrine concerning
libels?.....Or when he stated the law in prosecutions
for criminal conversation?....Or when he delivered
his reasons for calling the House of Lords together
to receive a copy of his charge to the jury in
Woodfall's trial?....Had he been present upon any
of these occasions, he would have seen how possible it is for a man of the first talents, to confound
himself in absurdities which would disgrace the
lips of an ideot.   Perhaps the example might have
taught him not to value his own understanding so
highly.....Lord Lyttleton's integrity and judgment
are unquestionable...yet he is known to admire that
cunning Scotchman, and verily believes him an
honest man.   I speak to facts, with which all of us
are conversant....I speak to men and to their experience, and will not descend to answer the little

In prosecutions for criminal conversation ?] In the action brought
by Lord Grosvenor against the late Duke of Cumberland for criminal conversation with his wife, Lord Mansfield argued, in his
charge to the jury, that no higher damages were due to a peer than
to a cobler, for adultery with his wife. This is the doctrine to which
Junius here alludes. It was generally condemned among the
lawyers.

Lord Lyttleton's, &c.] George Lord Lyttleton.....the author
of the Essay on the Conversion of St. Paul....the orator, poet, and
statesman. He was a truly good man, and a man of talents. His
approbation was, therefore, a noble testimony in favour of Lord
Mansfield.

sneering sophistries of a collegian.....Distinguished talents are not necessarily connected with discretion. If there be any thing remarkable in the character of Mr. Horne, it is that extreme want of judgment should be united with his very moderate capacity. Yet I have not forgotten the acknowledgement I made him. He owes it to my bounty: and though his Letter has lowered him in my opinion, I scorn to retract the charitable donation.

I said it would be *very difficult* for Mr. Horne to write directly in defence of a ministerial measure, and not be detected; and even that difficulty I confined to *his* particular situation. He changes the terms of the proposition : and supposes me to assert, that it would be *impossible* for *any* man to write for the newspapers, and not be discovered.

He repeatedly affirms, or intimates at least, that he knows the Author of these Letters....With what colour of truth, then, can he pretend, *that I am no where to be encountered but in a newspaper?*....I shall leave him to his suspicions. It is not necessary that I should confide in the honour or discretion of a man who already seems to hate me with as much rancour as if I had formerly been his

---

I scorn to retract the charitable, &c.] A skilful method this of retracting praise !

With as much rancour as if I had formerly been his friend, &c.] An allusion to Mr. Horne's former friendship and present quarrel with Mr. Wilkes.

friend.....But he asserts, that he has traced me through a variety of signatures. To make the discovery of any importance to his purpose, he should have proved, either that the fictitious character of JUNIUS has not been consistently supported, or that the author has maintained different principles under different signatures......I cannot recal to my memory the numberless trifles I have written; but I rely upon the consciousness of my own integrity, and defy him to fix any colourable charge of inconsistency upon me.

I am not bound to assign the secret motives of his apparent hatred to Mr. Wilkes: nor does it follow that I may not judge fairly of his conduct, though it were true *that I had no conduct of my own.* .....Mr. Horne enlarges, with rapture, upon the importances of his services.......the dreadful battles which he might have been engaged in, and the dangers he has escaped.....In support of the formidable description, he quotes verses without mercy. The gentleman deals in fiction, and naturally appeals to the evidence of the poets.....Taking

---

Charge of inconsistency, &c.] I suspect the word *colourable* to belong to the list of those which are improperly coined in the carelessness of conversation. Its use might, indeed, be, with some labour defended. But, it were perhaps better not at all to use it.

The dreadful battles which he might have been engaged in, &c.] This ridicule, the reader, by comparing it with the passage to which it alludes in Horne's Letter, will perceive to be both just and eminently happy.

him at his word, he cannot but admit the superiority of Mr. Wilkes in this line of service. On
one side, we see nothing but imaginary distresses....
On the other, we see real prosecutions....real penalties.....real imprisonment.....life repeatedly hazarded....and, at one moment, almost the certainty
of death. Thanks are undoubtedly due to every
man who does his duty in the engagement ; but it
is the wounded soldier who deserves the reward.

I did not mean to deny, that Mr. Horne had
been an active partizan. It would defeat my own
purpose, not to allow him a degree of merit which
aggravates his guilt. The very charge *of contributing his utmost efforts to support a ministerial measure,* implies an acknowledgment of his former services. If he had not once been distinguished by
his apparent zeal in defence of the common cause,
he could not now be distinguished by deserting it.
....As for myself, it is no longer a question, *whether I shall mix with the throng, and take a single
share in the danger.* Whenever JUNIUS appears, he
must encounter a host of enemies. But is there
no honourable way to serve the public, without engaging in personal quarrels with insignificant in-

He cannot but admit the superiority of Mr. Wilkes, &c.] The
comparison between the services of Wilkes and those of Horne, in
this and the following period, seems to have been well adapted to
win the favour of the public to the former, and to make them view
the pretensions of the latter with derision.

Personal quarrels with insignificant individuals, &c.] The allusion here is to the abuse which Horne threw out against Mr. Ons-

dividuals, or submitting to the drudgery of canvass-
ing votes for an election? Is there no merit in dedi-
cating my life to the information of my fellow-subjects?.....What public question have I declined?
What villain have I spared?....Is there no labour in
the composition of these Letters? Mr. Horne, I
fear, is partial to me, and measures the facility of
my writings by the fluency of his own.

He talks to us, in high terms, of the gallant feats
he would have performed, if he had lived in the last
century. The unhappy Charles could hardly have
escaped him. But living Princes have a claim to
his attachment and respect. Upon these terms
there is no danger in being a patriot. If he means
any thing more than a pompous rhapsody, let us
try how well his argument holds together....I presume he is not yet so much a courtier as to affirm
that the constitution has not been grossly and daringly violated under the present reign. He will
not say, that the laws have not been shamefully
broken or perverted....that the rights of the subject have not been invaded, or that redress has not

---

low at a meeting of electors, and to the prosecution which Mr.
Onslow, in consequence of that, raised against him.

Is there no labour in the composition of these Letters?] The author was conscious of his eloquence, and proud of it.

So much a courtier as to affirm, &c.] This whole paragraph is
admirable. JUNIUS proves in it, that Mr. Horne, by his own principles ought, at present, to attempt high treason; and that, if he did
not attempt it, he must be either absurd or insincere.

been repeatedly solicited and refused....Grievances like these, were the foundation of the rebellion in the last century; and, if I understand Mr. Horne, they would, at that period, have justified him to his own mind, in deliberately attacking the life of his Sovereign. I shall not ask him, to what political constitution this doctrine can be reconciled; But, at least, it is incumbent upon him to shew, that the present King has better excuses than Charles the First, for the errors of his government. He ought to demonstrate to us, that the constitution was better understood a hundred years ago than it is at present.....that the legal rights of the subject, and the limits of the prerogative, were more accurately defined, and more clearly comprehended..... If propositions like these cannot be fairly maintained, I do not see how he can reconcile it to his conscience, not to act immediately with the same freedom with which he speaks. I reverence the character of Charles the First as little as Mr. Horne; but I will not insult his misfortunes, by a comparison that would degrade him.

It is worth observing, by what gentle degrees the furious, persecuting zeal of Mr. Horne, has

---

It is worth observing, &c.] Horne, deserting his former associates, was obliged to attempt the formation of a new system of principles for himself. In that attempt, he involved himself in contradictions which made all his pretences ridiculous. He accounted JUNIUS too vindictive. Attempting to shew himself less so, he wandered into a violation of all the principles which he pretended to respect the most.

softened into moderation. Men and measures were yesterday his object. What pains did he once take to bring that great state criminal *Macquirk* to execution!....To-day he confines himself to measures only....No penal example is to be left to the successors of the Duke of Grafton....To-morrow, I presume, both men and measures will be forgiven. The flaming patriot, who so lately scorched us in the meridian, sinks temperately to the west, and is hardly felt as he descends.

I comprehend the policy of endeavouring to communicate to Mr. Oliver and Mr. Sawbridge a share in the reproaches with which he supposes me to have loaded him. My memory fails me, if I have mentioned their names with disrespect....unless it be reproachful to acknowledge a sincere respect for the character of Mr. Sawbridge, and not to have questioned the innocence of Mr. Oliver's intentions.

It seems I am a partizan of the great leader of the opposition. If the charge had been a reproach, it should have been better supported. I did not

The flaming patriot, &c.] Here is a good metaphor, given in a tone, partly serious, in part burlesque.

My memory fails me, &c.] Horne endeavoured to make his own disgrace lighter, by pretending that it was shared with Oliver and Sawbridge. JUNIUS, therefore, found it necessary to vindicate himself from the imputation of having attacked them. He does it handsomely.

intend to make a public declaration of the respect
I bear Lord Chatham, I well knew what unworthy
conclusions would be drawn from it. But I am
called upon to deliver my opinion; and surely it is
not in the little censure of Mr. Horne to deter me
from doing signal justice to a man, who, I confess,
has grown upon my esteem. As for the common,
sordid views of avarice, or any purpose of vulgar
ambition, I question whether the applause of Junius would be of service to Lord Chatham. *My*
vote will hardly recommend him to an increase of
his pension, or to a seat in the cabinet. But, if his
ambition be upon a level with his understanding....
if he judges of what is truly honourable for himself, with the same superior genius which animates
and directs him to eloquence in debate, to wisdom
in decision, even the pen of Junius shall contribute to reward him. Recorded honours shall ga-
ther round his monument, and thicken over him.
It is a solid fabric, and will support the laurels that

As for the common, sordid views, &c.] This praise of Lord
Chatham, is manly and noble. It is, at the same time, artful.
Junius praises Lord Chatham's talents and exertions: avoids
speaking of his disinterestedness, or selfish ambition; shews, that
he himself was not that nobleman's creature.....A subsequent note
will present sketches of the Life of Lord Chatham, and of his
Son.

It is a solid fabric, and will support the laurels, &c.] Junius,
has here suffered himself to be betrayed into the burlesque. It is
certainly burlesque to talk of *laurels*, even in figure, as if there were
danger that the weight of them might crush an ordinary *funeral
monument.*

adorn it....I am not conversant in the language of panegyric....These praises are extorted from me; but they will wear well, for they have been dearly earned.

My detestation of the Duke of Grafton is not founded upon his treachery to any individual; though I am willing enough to suppose that, in public affairs, it would be impossible to desert or betray Lord Chatham, without doing an essential injury to this country. My abhorrence of the Duke arises from an intimate knowledge of his character; and from a thorough conviction, that his baseness has been the cause of greater mischief to England, than even the unfortunate ambition of Lord Bute.

The shortening the duration of parliaments is a subject on which Mr. Horne cannot enlarge too warmly; nor will I question his sincerity. If I did

His baseness has been the cause, &c.] It was understood, that, if the Duke of Grafton had remained faithful to Lord Chatham, had scorned all political association equally with the Bedford party, as with those who called themselves the King's friends; the combination of the Pitt and Grenville with the Newcastle and Rockingham Whigs, had been, ere this time, triumphant; and the King would have been obliged to resign the reigns of his government into their hands, upon their own conditions. The prevention of this, was the great crime of the Duke of Grafton, in the eyes of the Whigs. This was the cause of JUNIUS's abhorrence of him.

The shortening the duration, &c.] The shortening *of the* duration, &c. according to the rules of Lowth, and the true analogy of Grammar.

not profess the same sentiments, I should be shame-fully inconsistent with myself. It is unnecessary to bind Lord Chatham by the written formality of an engagement. He has publicly declared himself a convert to Triennial Parliaments; and though I have long been convinced that this is the only pos-sible resource we have left to preserve the substan-tial freedom of the constitution, I do not think we have a right to determine against the integrity of Lord Rockingham or his friends. Other measures may undoubtedly be supported in argument, as better adapted to the disorder, or more likely to be obtained.

Mr. Horne is well assured, that I never was the champion of Mr. Wilkes. But though I am not obliged to answer for the firmness of his future ad-

---

It is unnecessary, &c.] JUNIUS here evades any decision be-tween the principles of the two subdivisions of the Whig party. He was afraid to stir up any discussion which might tend to set them, unseasonably, at variance. The grand distinction between them, as to principle, respected the reform of parliament. The New-castle and Rockingham Whigs were disposed to preserve septennial parliaments; while the followers of Pitt and the Grenvilles were half inclined to gratify the popular cry for the restoration of trien-nial elections. One cannot enough admire the address with which JUNIUS praises and justifies both, and strives to confirm their mutual reconciliation; yet without making himself responsible for the principles and conduct of either.

His future adherence, &c.] Here is another striking instance of the admirable oratorical art of the Author of these Letters. He well knew, that Wilkes's negociations with the Rockingham admi-nistration, of 1766, could not well be justified, to the satisfaction

herence to the principles he professes, I have no reason to presume that he will hereafter disgrace them. As for all those imaginary cases, which Mr. Horne so petulantly urges against me, I have one plain, honest answer, to make to him....Whenever Mr. Wilkes shall be convicted of soliciting a pension, an embassy, or a government, he must depart from that situation, and renounce that character, which he assumes at present, and which, in *my* opinion, entitle him to the support of the public. By the same act, and at the same moment, he will forfeit his power of mortifying the King; and though he can never be a favourite at St. James's, his baseness may administer a solid satisfaction to the royal mind. The man I speak of, has not a heart to feel for the frailties of his fellow-creatures. It is their virtues that afflict, it is their vices that console him.

I give every possible advantage to Mr. Horne, when I take the facts he refers to for granted. That they are the produce of his invention, seems

of all the patriots. He therefore, calls their jealous attention to the future ! insinuates great things of Wilkes's future integrity; and bespeaks for him the protection of the people, only till he should accomplish his reconciliation with the Court.

The succeeding paragraph is filled also with the defence of Wilkes. By conceding a little, JUNIUS contrives to gain every thing from his reader's generosity. He places Horne in a truly ludicrous predicament, by shewing, that he had contributed to the support of Wilkes, even at a time when he had the same reason, as now, to oppose him.

highly probable; that they are exaggerated, I have
no doubt. At the worst, what do they amount to,
but that Mr. Wilkes, who never was thought of as a
perfect pattern of morality, has not been at all
times proof against the extremity of distress. How
shameful is it, in a man who has lived in friendship
with him, to reproach him with failings too naturally connected with despair! Is no allowance to
be made for banishment and ruin? Does a two
years imprisonment make no atonement for his
crimes?...The resentment of a priest is implacable.
No sufferings can soften, no penitence can appease
him.....Yet he himself, I think, upon his own system, has a multitude of political offences to atone
for. I will not insist upon the nauseous detail,
with which he so long disgusted the public. He
seems to be ashamed of it. But what excuse will
he make to the friends of the constitution for labouring to promote *this consummately bad man* to a
station of the highest national trust and importance?
Upon what honourable motives did he recommend
him to the livery of London for their representative;....to the ward of Farringdon for their Alderman; to the county of Middlesex for their knight?
Will he affirm that, at that time, he was ignorant
of Mr. Wilkes's solicitations to the ministry?....
That he should say so, is indeed very necessary for
his own justification; but where will he find credulity to believe him?

In what school this gentleman learned his ethics,
I know not. His *logic* seems to have been studied

under Mr. Dyson. That miserable pamphleteer, by dividing the only precedent in point, and taking as much of it as suited his purpose, had reduced his argument upon the Middlesex election to something like the shape of a syllogism. Mr. Horne has conducted himself with the same ingenuity and candour. I had affirmed, that Mr. Wilkes would preserve the public favour, " as long as he stood forth " against a ministry and parliament, who were do- " ing every thing they could to enslave the coun- " try, *and* as long as he was a thorn in the King's " side." Yet, from the exulting triumph of Mr. Horne's reply, one would think that I had rested my expectation, that Mr. Wilkes would be supported by the public upon the single condition of his mortifying the King. This may be logic at Cambridge, or at the Treasury ; but among men of sense and honour, it is folly or villany in the extreme.

I see the pitiful advantage he has taken of a single unguarded expression, in a Letter not intended for the public. Yet it is only the *expression* that is unguarded. I adhere to the true meaning

---

I had affirmed, &c.] This and the subsequent paragraph contain JUNIUS's defence of himself against the charge of mere diabolical malignity. His logic and his principles are, in these paragraphs, good against Horne, and to the Whigs....not, however, if absolutely considered. He sufficiently evinces, that he wished offence to be given to the King, only because he thought such offence necessary to give triumph to the interests and the principles of his party.

of that member of the sentence, taken separately
as *he* takes it; and now, upon the coolest deliberation, re-assert that, for the purposes I referred to, it
may be highly meritorious to the public, to wound
the personal feelings of the Sovereign. It is not a
general proposition, nor is it generally applied to
the chief magistrate of this or any other constitution. Mr. Horne knows as well as I do, that the
best of Princes is not displeased with the abuse
which he sees thrown upon his ostensible ministers.
It makes them, I presume, more properly the objects
of his royal compassion.....neither does it escape
his sagacity, that the lower they are degraded in the
public esteem, the more submissively they must
depend upon his favour for protection. This I
affirm upon the most solemn conviction, and the
most certain knowledge, is a leading maxim in the
policy of the closet. It is unnecessary to pursue the
argument any farther.

Mr. Horne is now a very loyal subject. He
laments the wretched state of politics in this country; and sees, in a new light, the weakness and
folly of the opposition. *Whoever, or whatever, is
Sovereign, demands the respect and support of the*

Mr. Horne is now a very loyal subject.] JUNIUS, in this paragraph, renews against Horne, the charge that he had become a
creature of the Ministry. He blends with the accusation of Horne,
hints of ridicule, and invective against his Sovereign. The paragraph is well written.

people;* it was not so, *when Nero fiddled while Rome was burning*. Our gracious Sovereign has had wonderful success in creating new attachments to *his person and family*. He owes it, I presume, to the regular system he has pursued in the mystery of conversion. He began with an experiment upon the Scotch; and concludes with converting Mr. Horne....What a pity it is, that the *Jews* should be condemned by Providence to wait for a Messiah of their own!

The priesthood are accused of misinterpreting the scriptures. Mr. Horne has improved upon his profession. He alters the text, and creates a refutable doctrine of his own. Such artifices cannot long delude the understanding of the people; and, without meaning an indecent comparison, I may venture to foretel, that the Bible and JUNIUS will be read, when the commentaries of the Jesuits are forgotten.

JUNIUS.

* The very soliloquy of Lord Suffolk, before he passed the Rubicon.

The Bible and JUNIUS, *&c.*] The comparison is extravagantly bold, and almost impious. The hint of the Jesuitism of Mr. Horne was admirably adapted to serve JUNIUS's purpose.

LETTER LIV.

TO THE PRINTER OF THE PUBLIC ADVERTISER.

—

JUNIUS had provoked against himself, as every exhibition of formidable talents always does, an host of enemies. The force of his arguments, the art of his persuasions, the fierce vehemence of his satire, were not to be denied nor resisted. But, envy, resentment, and malignity, however comparatively feeble, would still be nibbling. The loftiness of his pretensions, the extreme bitterness of his invectives, the boldness of his metaphors pushed at times to incorrect extravagance, some few negligences of phrase, and allusions rashly profane.....however strongly expressive, to sacred things, became the topics of their censure. At censure of this sort, Horne and his associates were sufficiently ready. It was, therefore, with eager activity, exercised upon the Letter immediately foregoing. Profanity was, in this case, the strong charge: and some former slips in this way were not now forgotten. The present Letter, with the signature of PHILO JUNIUS, *is intended to refute these charges. Against the censurers to whom it was addressed, it is sufficiently powerful. But, from the accusation of profanity in a few occasional allusions to religion,* JUNIUS *can never be effectually vindicated.*

—

26. *August,* 1771.

SIR,

THE enemies of the people, having now nothing better to object to my friend JUNIUS, are at last obliged to quit his politics, and to rail at him for crimes he is not guilty of. His vanity and impiety are now the perpetual topics of their abuse.

I do not mean to lessen the force of such charges, (supposing they were true) but to shew that they are not founded. If I admitted the premises, I should readily agree in all the consequences drawn from them. Vanity, indeed, is a venial error; for it usually carries its own punishment with it:...but, if I thought JUNIUS capable of uttering a disrespectful word of the religion of his country, I should be the first to renounce and give him up to the public contempt and indignation. As a man, I am satisfied that he is a Christian upon the most sincere conviction; as a writer, he would be grossly inconsistent with his political principles, if he dared to attack a religion established by those laws which it seems to be the purpose of his life to defend.....Now for the proofs....JUNIUS is accused of an impious allusion to the holy sacrament, where he says, that *if Lord Weymouth be denied the cup, there will be no keeping him within the pale of the ministry.* Now, Sir, I affirm, that this passage refers entirely to a ceremonial in the Roman catholic church, which denies the cup to the laity: it has no manner of relation to the Protestant creed: and is, in this country, as fair an object of ridicule as *transubstantiation,* or any other part of Lord *Peter's* history in the Tale of the Tub.

A ceremonial in the Roman Catholic Church, &c.] True, it does. But, yet, it introduces a solemn religious ordinance into the mind, in connexion with light ideas of satire and degrading vice. It *is*, therefore, profane. Yet, this defence of it, is wonderfully artful.

But JUNIUS is charged with equal vanity and impiety, in comparing his writings to the Holy Scripture.....The formal protest he makes against any such comparison avails him nothing. It becomes necessary, then, to shew that the charge destroys itself...If he be *vain*, he cannot be *impious*. A vain man does not usually compare himself to an object which it is his design to undervalue. On the other hand, if he be *impious*, he cannot be *vain*. For his impiety, if any, must consist in his endeavouring to degrade the Holy Scriptures by a comparison with his own contemptible writings. This would be folly indeed 'of the grossest nature, but where lies the vanity ?...I shall now be told..." Sir, " what you say is plausible enough, but still you " must allow that it is shamefully impudent in " JUNIUS, to tell us that his works will live as long " as the Bible." My answer is.....*Agreed: but first prove that he has said so.* Look at his words, and you will find, that the utmost he expects is, that the Bible and JUNIUS will survive the commentaries of the Jesuits, which may prove true in a fortnight. The most malignant sagacity cannot shew that his works are, *in his opinion*, to live as long as the Bible. .....Suppose I were to foretell, that *Jack* and *Tom* would survive *Harry*.....Does it follow that *Jack* must live as long as *Tom?* I would only illustrate my meaning, and protest against the least idea of profaneness.

A vain man, &c.] The logical dexterity displayed in this paragraph is not exceeded even by any other passage in these Letters.

Yet this is the way in which Junius is usually answered, arraigned, and convicted. These candid critics never remember any thing he says in honour of our holy religion; though it is true, that one of his leading arguments is made to rest *upon the internal evidence which the purest of all religions carries with it.* I quote his words; and conclude, from them, that he is a true and hearty Christian, in substance, not in ceremony; though possibly he may not agree with my Reverend Lords the Bishops, or with the Head of the Church, *that prayers are morality, or that kneeling is religion.*

PHILO JUNIUS.

Or with the Head of the Church, &c.] Even while busy in direct self-defence, Junius forgets not to aim a back-stroke against his Sovereign.

LETTER LV.

FROM THE REVEREND MR. HORNE TO JUNIUS.

———

HORNE was a man of invincible impudence. In the Letter immediately preceding, JUNIUS has sufficiently vindicated the justice of almost every one of the charges which he had formerly thrown out against Horne. But, he had not shewn, that Horne had actually taken money from the ministry, as a bribe to betray the patriots. Horne, therefore, as if he had not, out of absurd pertinacity, out of ambitious affectation of odd integrity, out of misanthropical perverseness of humour, done much greater mischief to the cause of the patriots, than even if he had betrayed it for money....ventures to reply to JUNIUS, *in this Letter, with the utmost briskness of effrontery. He denies, in it, that he had ever taken a bribe : pronounces his own panegyric : and throws out vulgar abuse against his adversary, such as sufficiently shews, that bitterness and malignity are not, always, of necessity, eloquent.*

———

17. August, 1771.

I CONGRATULATE you, Sir, on the recovery of your wonted style, though it has cost you a fortnight. I compassionate your labour in the composition of your Letters, and will communicate to you the secret of my fluency....Truth needs no or-

———

The recovery of your wonted style, &c.] The loss and recovery of style by JUNIUS, of which Horne speaks, in this and a former Letter, were absolutely imaginary. In the Letter which was transmitted to Horne unprinted, the wonted eloquence, and the peculiar style of JUNIUS were just as apparent, as in the other Letters in these volumes. The reader has only to make the comparison, that he may perceive the truth of what is here asserted.

nament; and, in my opinion, what she borrows of
the pencil is deformity.

You brought a positive charge against me of
corruption. I denied the charge, and called for
your proofs. You replied with abuse, and re-as-
serted your charge. I called again for proofs. You
reply again with abuse only, and drop your accusation. In your fortnight's Letter there is not one
word upon the subject of my corruption.

I have no more to say, but to return thanks to
you for your *condescension*, and to a *grateful* public
and *honest* ministry for all the favours they have
conferred upon me. The two latter, I am sure,
will never refuse me any grace I shall solicit; and
since you have been pleased to acknowledge that
you told a deliberate lye in my favour out of bounty,

What she borrows of the pencil is deformity.] All ornaments
cease to be such, when they do not suit the character of the object to which they are applied. Even truth rejoices in ornaments
which are grand and simple as herself. The maxim stated here
by Horne, is, therefore, not universally true. But, it is not easy
to understand his meaning when he talks of the ornaments she
borrows from the pencil. If he mean, that truth needs not gor-
geous embellishment; his meaning is right; but his expression
awkward and obscure.....since the appellation of *ornament* merely,
would have better served his purpose. If he mean, that the art of
painting cannot happily express truth; the meaning is equally absurd and unseasonable.

Drop your accusation, &c.] The substantial parts of the accusation had not been dropped.

Lye in my favour, &c.] JUNIUS was merely willing to think and
speak of the talents of Horne, as little unfavourably as possible. .

and as a charitable donation, why may I not expect that you will hereafter (if you do not forget you ever mentioned my name with disrespect) make the same acknowledgment for what you have said to my prejudice?....This second recantation will perhaps be more abhorrent from your disposition; but should you decline it, you will only afford one more instance how much easier it is to be generous than just, and that men are sometimes bountiful who are not honest.

At all events, I am as well satisfied with your panegyric as Lord Chatham can be. Monument I shall have none; but over my grave it will be said, in your own words, " *Horne's situation did not correspond with his intentions.**"

JOHN HORNE.

This second recantation, &c.] In this and the preceding period, the logical art of JUNIUS himself is not badly imitated.

* The epitaph would not be ill suited to the character....at the best, it is but equivocal.

Horne's situation did not correspond with his intentions, &c.] It will be proper to give, here, a short sketch of the life of so remarkable a man as MR. HORNE.

He was born about the year 1737. His father was a tradesman in London. After passing through that which is the usual course of classical school education in England, he was sent to the university of Cambridge. His course of life, during his residence at that university, was sober, studious, and inoffensive, free from every moral stain, but marked by a pragmatic disposition to bustle in politics, and by a passionate tendency in his opinions to the extreme of democratical whiggism.

About the year 1750, when he might, probably imbibe his first notions of politics, the Opposition of the school of Bolingbroke, and the Ministry who were chiefly from that of Walpole, were zealously contending....who should, in the eyes of the people, bear away the palm of the purest whiggism? In the contention, they both avowed impracticable principles. Hoadly, Squire, the speeches of the whig managers of the trial of Sacheverel, the boldest papers of the Craftsman, with the orations of Pitt, Lyttleton, and a few others, and the most eloquent remains of the literature of the authors of the grand rebellion, and of the revolution, formed the favourite political library of those who were the votaries of whiggism. These books were read with so much the more earnestness, because they were accounted to breathe much of the spirit of the classical authors of Greece and Rome. To them, therefore, the attention of the ingenuous youth who aspired to skill in eloquence, was naturally directed. They were, of course, put, at an early period into the hands of Mr. Horne. In adopting the notion of the necessity of a reform of the constitution such as should bring it back to the principles on which it was established at the revolution, he but re-echoed the perpetual clamours of the tories against the corruption of the revolution principles by those whigs who had so long held the reins of government.

Having studied, for a sufficient number of years, and with exemplary diligence, at the university of Cambridge ; he became a candidate for the wonted academical honours. But, before he could obtain that of master of arts, he had begun to publish in the newspapers, political letters to Mr. Wilkes. The university of Cambridge, though ever partial to Whiggism, preserved, nevertheless, moderation and decency in its whiggism. On this account, the wild democracy and the outrageous boldness of Horne's political writings gave great offence to its governors. They wished to deny him the degree which he now solicited......of master of arts. They sought about for every pretence by which they might withhold the honour, without violating the constitutional statutes. But, on all sides, save that of politics, Horne was *totus in se teres atque rotundus*. He obtained his degree in spite of the reluctance of those by whom it was conferred.

His professional destination was for the church. He became curate of Brentford. In this situation he mingled zealously in the political bustle respecting the elections of Wilkes to represent the county of Middlesex. He was one of those who were the most outrageous in asserting the rights of the electors against the decision of the House of Commons, which seated it in Colonel Luttrell as representative for that county. The violence with which he distinguished himself in the political bustle of the men at that time, exposed him to a prosecution for calumny by 'Mr. Onslow, which he fancied to endow him with merits in the eyes of the public, scarce less important than those of Wilkes. He began to compare his own purity with Wilkes's looseness and corruption.....to regard himself as the clearest sighted and the most disinterested of patriots, ...to despise, in comparison of his own whiggism, that of all the leaders in the opposition.....and to traverse the views of his own party, by requiring of them, a disinterestedness, and a political wisdom, of which he and they were alike incapable. His views of the perfection of political society had no respect to the capacities, passions, and prejudices of human nature ; but were, like those of the French Philosophers, framed, as if he could have contrived a scheme of government.....and could then have made a race of men, of express purpose, to live under it. In his discontent with his associates, he strove to divide and disperse the society for the support of the Bill of Rights. He was, in the attempt, considerably successful : and it proved, contrary to his intentions, an essential service to government. He opposed the election of Wilkes to the office of sheriff. The indignation of JUNIUS was, hence, excited against him. He rather sought than declined a literary contest with JUNIUS. The Letters in that contest were written, as we have seen, with great want of judgment, great and pertinacious impudence, and in some particulars, even with very artful cunning. But, Horne was not a match for JUNIUS. The hollowness of his pretences, was sufficiently exposed ; and his conduct was demonstrated to be, on the whole, as hurtful to the purposes of the patriots, as if he had been bought by government to act against them.

From this time, Horne could no longer confine his exertions within the sphere of a clergyman's duty. He threw off the clerical gown; and betook himself to the study of law. But, after he had passed the usual time, as a student in one of the inns of court, he could not procure himself to be called to the bar, because he was in orders as a clergyman. He was therefore left to the pursuits of a politician and a man of letters.

Though he accused the selfishness and corruption of the patriotism of Wilkes; he was himself nevertheless destined to make his
fortune by his patriotism. From political motives, he took part,
upon an important occasion, in the interests of a Mr. Tooke. His
services were so seasonable, and were so gratefully received, that
this gentleman determined to reward him with a share of his fortune. At his request, Horne assumed the additional name of
Tooke: and it is understood, that the immediate gift of a considerable annuity, and an eventual settlement by which more was to be
bestowed, were the rewards of his attachment to his generous patron. The man who could make his fortune in this way, must certainly be capable of many soothing compliances which persons of a
manly independent spirit, could not well endure.

Those who are wrong-headed in one way, are often not without
great wisdom in other directions of the exercise of their talents....
Horne Tooke, accordingly, pursued grammatical and philosophical
studies more judiciously and successfully than either law or politics.
The works of Harris and Monboddo, rendering the science of UNI-
VERSAL GRAMMAR, an object of regard among the learned, contributed to fix Mr. Horne Tooke's attention upon this subject.....
His study of the subtleties of legal deeds, in cases in which he was
personally concerned, led him to a glimpse of what seemed to promise a discovery of infinite importance in grammatical science......
He pursued it farther; read every useful or noted grammatical
treatise; inspected the elementary structure of a great diversity of
languages; with the writers on logic and metaphysics, considered
the origin of human thought, and the relation between the notions
in the mind and the various signs by which they are denoted........
These researches were at last crowned with one of the most important philosophical discoveries of the present age. He has demonstrated in a work made public under the appellation of DIVER-
SIONS OF PURLEY; that *those which are commonly called in
grammar, the Indeclinable parts of speech....Adverbs, Conjunc-
tions, Prepositions, Interjections....have, all, been originally, in
every language, Nouns or Verbs....and have been reduced into
their present state, only by a gradual and unperceived abbreviation,
accommodating the whole structure of the language, more perfectly, to the uses of reasoning and refined thought.* The former doctrine of grammarians, was, that these indeclinable parts of speech,
were *words incapable of independent signification, and invented to*

*connect together those other words which were independently sig-
nificant.* The new discovery was complete and indisputable. The
benefits it has conferred upon grammatical, upon logical, and upon
rhetorical science, are more than can be easily enumerated or imagined. It has ranked Mr. Horne Tooke among the chief authors of
learned discovery in the present age.

But, his unquiet spirit could not confine itself to study in the
closet. He offered himself a candidate for the parliamentary representation of Westminster, in opposition to Mr. Fox. He was
unsuccessful in the competition. He petitioned the House of Commons against Fox's election. He was again unsuccessful. Mr.
Fox prosecuted him for damages ; and obtained a verdict against
him. His object in this competition was, to maintain the cause of
democratical whiggism. A surprising number of the electors had espoused his interest.

When the æra of the French revolution arrived ; none rejoiced
more than Horne Tooke, in the prospect which it presented ; none
was more zealous to apply its principles to the reform of the British
constitution. Experience had now made him not less cunning than
turbulent. In most of the associations for political reform, he was
accustomed to appear : and in their meetings, he set himself to
harass and ensnare Fox, Sheridan, and those others whom he suspected of insincerity in the profession of democratical whiggism.
While the revolution in France went on ; he still watched its progress ; and, though cautious, failed not to use every means which
was not directly illegal, in order to procure a similar revolution for
the improvement of political society in Britain. He was among
those who the most earnestly disapproved the war against France.
Even after all but the ignorant, the mean, and those who inclined
to sedition, had retired from the dangerous bustle of the political
associations ; Horne Tooke continued to assist occasionally at
their meetings. It, at last, appeared, that they were rushing into
treason against the government and laws of their country. A number of those who seemed to be the busiest in intrigue and the most
guilty, were selected for trial by law. Among these, was Horne
Tooke. To perish for treason, on the scaffold, might seem the natural consummation of a life so politically turbulent as his.

But, when the trials of Horne Tooke and his supposed accomplices came on, it appeared, that, however wickedly inclined at

heart, they had partly from caution, partly from inability of talents, abstained from any regular concert of actual treason. Mr. Horne Tooke wonderfully distinguished himself throughout the course of his trial, by the firmness and presence of mind which he discovered, and by the address with which he parried the arguments of the counsel who were employed to establish the certainty of his guilt. In the examination of the witnesses particularly....... he shewed incomparable address and comprehension of mind. While the counsel, the court, and the witnesses saw not the drift of his questions; he was eliciting testimony the most useful whether to vindicate himself, or to destroy the credibility of witnesses whose depositions were against him.....The English lawyers are remarkable for address in examining witnesses. Yet, no English lawyer is remembered to have ever shewn skill in this difficult piece of the business of the bar, equal to that of Horne Tooke. He was acquitted of the charge. His supposed accomplices were also acquitted. Great was the triumph of their party upon an occasion so important.

Since that time, he has continued to live in retirement from all public bustle. He prosecutes his grammatical and philosophical studies; and is frequently visited by the chiefs of the party of the democratical whigs. Though his domestic establishment be such as cannot, one should think, be maintained for less than at least three hundred, or four hundred pounds a year; yet, he contrived to satisfy the commissioners for the income tax, that his revenue did not exceed sixty pounds a year. He usually entertains, at his table, on Sunday, a weekly party of his political friends.

He is undeniably a man of talents, learning, and....as one should candidly hope....genuine integrity. But, he has been unfortunate in receiving an early impression on his mind; that to bustle for political liberty was the first of duties; and that the perfection of this liberty was not to be accomplished without changes, which are evidently irreconcileable with the present good of society.

LETTER LVI.

TO HIS GRACE THE DUKE OF GRAFTON.

———

JUNIUS'S rage against the quondam friend of Lord Chatham and Mr. Wilkes, was not to be appeased. He had been unwillingly entangled in the controversy with Horne : and he, therefore, made his escape from it with as much haste as was possible. But, he delighted to hurl all his invectives against the Duke of Grafton : and on this subject he was, therefore, earnestly disposed to dwell, as long as the public were not unwilling to listen.

In the present Letter he begins with general invectives against the Duke and his Sovereign. From these, he turns to a recent dispute between his Grace and the officers of the Crown, relative to the timber in Whittlebury-Forest, of which the Duke was hereditary ranger. He represents the Duke's conduct in that dispute in a light the most odious and offensive. He then contrasts it with the case of the invasion of the grant to the Duke of Portland, when the Duke of Grafton was at the head of the Treasury. The whole Letter is adapted to point out, or to create, an odious feature in the character of the Duke of Grafton, which JUNIUS might think, that he had not, before, brought sufficiently into notice.

Nothing is more remarkable in this Letter, than the wonderful power to diversify invective, which the author displays in it.

———

28. *September,* 1771.

MY LORD,

THE people of England are not apprised of the full extent of their obligations to you. They have yet no adequate idea of the endless variety of your character. They have seen you distinguished

and successful in the continued violation of those
moral and political duties, by which the little, as
well as the great societies of life, are collected and
held together. Every colour, every character became you. With a rate of abilities, which Lord
Weymouth very justly looks down upon with contempt, you have done, as much mischief to the
community as *Cromwell* would have done, if *Crom-*
well had been a coward, and as much as *Machia-*
vel, if *Machiavel* had not known, that an appearance of morals and religion are useful in society....
To a thinking man, the influence of the Crown
will, in no view, appear so formidable, as when he
observes to what enormous excesses it has safely
conducted your Grace, without a ray of real understanding, without even the pretensions to common
decency or principle of any kind, or a single spark
of personal resolution. What must be the operation of that pernicious influence, (for which our
Kings have wisely exchanged the nugatory name
of prerogative) that, in the highest stations, can so
abundantly supply the absence of virtue, courage,
and abilities, and qualify a man to be the minister
of a great nation, whom a private gentleman would
be ashamed and afraid to admit into his family!

Cromwell....Machiavel....] With what address, JUNIUS contrives to represent the object of his invective, as inferior to every
villain, in every thing but villany.

Pernicious influence, &c.] Never was the influence of the crown
inveighed against, with eloquence more admirable than that of this
paragraph.

Like the universal passport of an ambassador, it supercedes the prohibitions of the laws, banishes the staple virtues of the country, and introduces vice and folly triumphantly into all the departments of the state. Other princes, besides his Majesty, have had the means of corruption within their reach, but they have used it with moderation. In former times, corruption was considered as a foreign auxiliary to government, and only called in upon extraordinary emergencies. The unfeigned piety, the sanctified religion of *George the Third*, have taught him to new model the civil forces of the state. The natural resources of the Crown are no longer confided in. Corruption glitters in the van....collects and maintains a standing army of mercenaries; and, at the same moment, impoverishes and enslaves the country....His Majesty's predecessors, (excepting that unworthy family, from which you, my Lord, are unquestionably descended) had some generous qualities in their composition, with vices, I confess, or frailties in abundance. They were kings or gentlemen, not hypocrites or priests. They were at the head of the church, but did not know the value of their office. They said their prayers without ceremony, and had too little priestcraft in their understanding, to reconcile the

---

Unfeigned piety, &c.] JUNIUS here speaks in irony. But the whole tenor of our Sovereign's life and reign, has sufficiently evinced his piety to be genuine and sincere.

Corruption glitters in the van, &c.] This poetical image is evidently borrowed from Gray.

sanctimonious forms of religion with the utter destruction of the morality of their people.....My
Lord, this is fact, not declamation....With all your
partiality to the house of *Stuart*, you must confess,
that even *Charles the Second* would have blushed at
that open encouragement, at those eager, meretri-
cious caresses, with which every species of private
vice and public prostitution is received at *St.
James's*....The unfortunate house of *Stuart* has been
treated with an asperity, which, if comparison be a
defence, seems to border upon injustice. Neither
Charles nor his brother were qualified to support
such a system of measures, as would be necessary,
to change the government, and subvert the constitution of England. One of them was too much
in earnest in his pleasures....the other in his religion. But the danger to this country would cease
to be problematical, if the crown should ever descend to a Prince, whose apparent simplicity might
throw his subjects off their guard....who might be
no libertine in behaviour, who should have no sense
of honour to restrain him, and who, with just religion enough to impose upon the multitude, might
have no scruples of conscience to interfere with his
morality. With these honourable qualifications,
and the decisive advantage of situation, low craft

Neither Charles nor his brother were qualified, &c.] Here is
praise extorted from the mouth of invective....*Were*, in the words
quoted, ought in propriety to have been written *was*.——

Situation, &c.] The following train of this paragraph is one
of the noblest specimens which English literature affords, of vigo-

and falsehood are all the abilities that are wanting to destroy the wisdom of ages, and to deface the noblest monument that human policy has erected .....I know *such* a man.....My Lord, I know you both; and, with the blessing of God, (for I too am religious) the people of England shall know you as well as I do. I am not very sure that greater abilities would not in effect be an impediment to a design, which seems at first sight to require a superior capacity. A better understanding might make him sensible of the wonderful beauty of that system he was endeavouring to corrupt. The danger of the attempt might alarm him. The meanness, and intrinsic worthlessness of the object, (supposing he could attain it) would fill him with shame, repentance and disgust. But these are sensations, which find no entrance into a barbarous, contracted heart. In some men, there is a malignant passion to destroy the works of genius, literature, and freedom. The *Vandal* and the *Monk* find equal gratification in it.

Reflections like these, my Lord, have a general relation to your Grace, and inseparably attend you, in whatever company or situation your character occurs to us. They have no immediate connexion with the following recent fact, which I lay before the public, for the honour of the best of Sovereigns, and for the edification of his people.

rous thinking, and of splendid, energetic eloquence. But, nothing more can be said in its praise.

A Prince (whose piety and self-denial, one would think, might secure him from such a multitude of worldly necessities) with an annual revenue of near a million sterling, unfortunately *wants money*. ....The navy of England, by an equally strange concurrence of unforeseen circumstances, (though not quite so unfortunately for his Majesty) is in equal want of timber. The world knows, in what a hopeful condition you delivered your navy to your successor, and in what a condition we found it in the moment of distress. You were determined it should continue in the situation in which you left it. It happened, however, very luckily for the privy purse, that one of the above wants promised fair to supply the other. Our religious, benevolent, generous Sovereign, has no objection to selling *his own* timber to *his own* admiralty, to repair *his own* ships, nor to putting the money into *his own* pocket..... People of a religious turn naturally adhere to the principles of the church. Whatever they acquire falls into *mortmain*....Upon a representation from the admiralty of the extraordinary want of timber, for the indispensable repairs of the navy, the surveyor-general was directed to make a survey of the timber in all the royal chases and forests in Eng-

With an annual revenue, &c.] The sum which the King had accepted for the civil list was not always adequate to its expense. There were, consequently, debts upon it to be discharged, from time to time, by parliament.

Luckily for the privy purse, &c.] The timber from the royal forests was, as it should seem, to be paid for, out of the grants of parliament for the expense of the navy.

land. Having obeyed his orders with accuracy and attention, he reported, that the finest timber he had any where met with, and the properest in every respect for the purposes of the navy, was in *Whittlebury Forest*, of which your Grace, I think, is hereditary ranger. In consequence of this report, the usual warrant was prepared at the treasury, and delivered to the surveyor, by which he or his deputy were authorised to cut down any trees in *Whittlebury Forest*, which should appear to be proper for the purposes above-mentioned. The deputy being informed that the warrant was signed and delivered to his principal in London, crosses the country to Northamptonshire, and with an officious zeal for the public service, begins to do his duty in the forest. Unfortunately for him, he had not the warrant in his pocket. The oversight was enormous, and you have punished him for it accordingly. You have insisted that an active, useful officer, should be dissmissed from his place. You have ruined an innocent man, and his family.....In what language shall I address so black, so cowardly a tyrant.....thou worse than *one* of the *Brunswicks*, and all the *Stuarts!*.....To them who know Lord

---

You have ruined, &c.] When equipments were made in the prospect of a war with Spain, this timber was wanted. The Duke of Grafton claimed the *underwood* of the forest; argued, that, if the oaks were then felled, the underwood would be destroyed; acted with irritation to the officers; and finally prevailed to procure the cutting to be delayed, though not without giving offence and exposing himself to obloquy.

North, it is unnecessary to say, that he was mean
and base enough to submit to you....This however
is but a small part of the fact.　After ruining the
surveyor's deputy, for acting without the warrant,
you attacked the warrant itself.　You declared it
was illegal, and swore, in a fit of foaming, frantic
passion, that it never should be executed.　You asserted upon your honour, that in the grant of the
rangership of *Whittlebury Forest*, made by *Charles
the Second*, (whom, with a modesty that would do
honour to Mr. Rigby, you are pleased to call your
ancestor) to one of his bastards, (from whom I make
no doubt of your descent) the property of the timber is vested in the ranger....I have examined the
original grant, and now, in the face of the public,
contradict you directly upon the fact.　The very
reverse of what you have asserted upon your honour
is the truth.　The grant *expressly and by a particular clause*, reserves the property of the timber for
the use of the crown...In spite of this evidence....in
defiance of the representations of the admiralty.....
in perfect mockery of the notorious distresses of the
English navy, and those equally pressing, and
almost equally notorious necessities of your pious
Sovereign....here the matter rests....The Lords of
the Treasury recal their warrant; the deputy-sur-
veyor is ruined for doing his duty....Mr. John Pitt,
(whose name I suppose is offensive to you) submits
to be brow-beaten and insulted....the oaks keep
their ground....the King is defrauded, and the navy
of England may perish for want of the best and

finest timber in the island. And all this is submitted
to....to appease the Duke of Grafton!.....to gratify
the man, who has involved the King and his kingdom in confusion and distress, and who, like a treacherous coward, deserted his Sovereign in the midst
of it!

There has been a strange alteration in your doctrines, since you thought it adviseable to rob the
Duke of Portland of his property, in order to

Rob the Duke of Portland, &c.] The circumstances of the attempt to transfer, for the sake of election influence, the property
of the Duke of Portland to the present Lord Lonsdale, have been
already mentioned in these Notes. That attempt was finally defeated; because the grant to Sir James Lowther was not made
under those conditions which the law required; and because the
Duke of Portland had acquired, against all but the crown, a pro-
scriptive right to the property in question....and the perpetuity of
the claim of the crown, founded on the *nullum tempus* act, was too
invidious to be, in such a case, steadily insisted upon.

The DUKE of PORTLAND, the representative of the family of
BENTINCK, the favourite of King William, and of HARLEY Earl
of Oxford, the minister of Queen Anne, has, almost since the very
commencement of the present reign, acted a conspicuous part on
the theatre of public affairs. He inherited the whig sentiments of
his paternal ancestors. He became, at his first entrance upon public life, an associate of the old aristocratical whigs, the party of the
Duke of Newcastle and the Marquis of Rockingham. His attachments to that party rendered him obnoxious to the King's friends
and the followers of the Duke of Bedford. It was, on this account,
that the attempt was made, to deprive him of Inglewood Forest.
That attack on his family inheritance, and the success with which
he resisted it, encouraged him in opposition to the associated tories
and recreant whigs who composed the strength of the administration, till the close of the American war.

strengthen the interest of Lord *Bute's* son-in-law, before the last general election. *Nullum tempus occurrit regi*, was then your boasted motto, and the cry of all your hungry partizans. Now it seems a

---

Upon the death of the Duke of Newcastle, he became, next after the Marquis of Rockingham, the ostensible, if not the effective, leader of the Whig interest. During the American war, his fortune was not a little impaired by the sacrifices which he made for the support of his party. His parliamentary interest, his pecuniary generosity, the candour and uprightness distinguishing his personal character, were, much more than his actual exertions of either eloquence or intrigue, the causes of his importance both with his own party, and in the eyes of his opponents. Burke, Fox, and the other efficient leaders of the opposition, were, in some sort but agents upon the great fund of the property and interest of the Marquis of Rockingham, the Duke of Portland, and a few other opulent noblemen and commoners in the opposition.

With Mr. Fox and the Marquis of Rockingham, the Duke of Portland was brought also into administration, when the combination of the whigs reduced Lord North to resign. His partizans had destined him to succeed to the office of first lord of the treasury at a time when their intentions were anticipated and disappointed by the defection of the Marquis of Lansdowne, then Earl of Shelburne. He participated in all the subsequent measures of the Rockingham and Portland Whigs, their abrupt resignation, their coalition with the friends of Lord North, their return into office, those bold plans of aristocracy in the accomplishment of which they were thwarted and defeated.

He was dismissed with his party from ministerial power. He, then, became, with the Duke of Devonshire, Earl Derby, Earl Fitzwilliam, and others, the support, as before, of an opposition. Its expense fell again heavily upon those of its members who had fortune to lavish in maintaining it. One session of parliament after another still renewed to them the hope of a return to power, and the disappointment of their hopes. Still the Duke of Portland remained faithful to his political friends. His pecuniary affairs were even tending to a state of distressing embarrassment;

grant of *Charles the Second* to one of his bastards
is to be held sacred and inviolable !. It must not be
questioned by the King's servants, nor submitted
to any interpretation but your own......My Lord,

when the death of his mother whose jointure settlement had been
very ample, afforded a seasonable enlargement of his income.
Even after the æra of the French revolution had commenced, he
continued in opposition to the measures of government, till the
representations of Mr. Burke satisfied him, that the interests of
the crown and the aristocratical whigs, had become the same.

At last, the progress of the revolution and the representations
of Burke chiefly convinced those who still cherished the old principles of the Pelham whigs, that it was urgently their duty to cease
from party opposition, and immediately to strengthen the hands
of the Monarch. The Duke of Portland, Earl Fitzwilliam, Lord
Spencer, and all those of their party whose principles agreed with
theirs, with little delay, joined the King's friends, the Pitt and
Grenville whigs, and the remains of the old Bedford party in the
duties and the responsibility of the administration. The Duke of
Portland became secretary of state for the home department.
His principal friends accepted other appointments. The business
of his office has been administered since that time, with a diligence and an intelligent activity sufficiently honourable to him.
He has steadily supported the wishes of his Sovereign, in the continued prosecution of the war. The talents and the upright exertions of his friends Lord Spencer and Mr. Windham have been
eminently beneficial in the conduct of the whole affairs of the
government. The worth of their private characters combines
with their ability in administration, to preserve to them, a great
share of the public esteem. Since the æra of the accession of the
House of Hanover, the aristocratical whigs never enjoyed, in a
higher degree than at present, the confidence of all the independent part of the nation. They owe it, in a great degree, to
the public and private virtue of the Duke of Portland. He has
never attempted to distinguish himself as a public speaker in the
House of Peers. Nor does even his eldest son, the Marquis of
Titchfield, attempt to act the part of an efficient political leader.

this was not the language you held, when it suited you to insult the memory of the glorious deliverer of England from that detested family, to which you are still more nearly allied in principle than in blood........In the name of decency and common-sense, what are your Grace's merits, either with King or ministry, that should entitle you to assume this domineering authority over both?......Is it the fortunate consanguinity you claim with the house of *Stuart ?*....Is it the secret correspondence you have for so many years carried on with Lord Bute, by the assiduous assistance of your *cream-coloured parasite ?* Could not your gallantry find sufficient employment for him, in those *gentle* offices by which he first acquired the tender friendship of *Lord Barrington ?*....Or is it only that wonderful sympathy of manners, which subsists between your Grace and one of your superiors, and does so much honour to you both ?....Is the union of *Blifil* and *Black George* no longer a *romance ?*....From what-ever origin your influence in this country arises, it is a phænomenon in the history of human virtue and understanding....Good men can hardly believe

---

His younger sons have lately been in diplomatic employments, abroad.

Cream coloured parasite.... gentle offices....] Accusations the most infamous are here insinuated. The accusations were undoubt-edly false. To hint them, bespeaks extraordinary malignity, and wonderful art in abuse.

A Phænomenon.] *Phænomenon* is here improperly used for ex-traordinary *Phænomenon.*

the fact. Wise men are unable to account for it. Religious men find exercise for their faith, and make it the last effort of their piety, not to repine against Providence.

JUNIUS.

LETTER LVII.

ADDRESSED TO THE LIVERY OF LONDON.

THE period was arrived for the election of a LordMayor for the city of London for the year 1771-2. That election was regulated principally, though not exclusively, by the rule of seniority among the Aldermen. If the senior Alderman should be, on this occasion advanced to the Mayoralty ; Mr. Nash, a gentleman unentangled in the schemes of the patriots, would be the Lord Mayor of the ensuing year. During his authority, the powers of the city would not be, as on former years, at the command of Wilkes and the opposition. For these reasons, the patriots exercised all their activity and influence to disappoint the hopes of Mr. Nash. But, their divisions had greatly diminished that influence : the honesty of their patriotism was no longer unsuspected : the better part of the citizens were sick of that turbulence which they had so long kept up : the case was not thought of sufficient magnitude to justify the violation of the wonted rule : and Mr. Nash was elected.

JUNIUS wrote the following Letter, to persuade the Livery to pass by Mr. Nash. Its purpose is, to shew, that the election of Nash would be an utter dereliction of the patriot cause ; that Crosby or Sawbridge, if in the Mayoralty would be much more likely to oppose the House of Commons with fierce zeal, as well as to call the freemen of London, to frequent deliberations in their common hall. The excellence of this Letter consists in the pertinency of its application to the design of the writer, in the brevity and plainness with which the arguments are stated, and in the skill with which the eloquence of bold metaphor and vehement interrogation is associated with simple language, and the greatest closeness of reasoning.

———

30. September, 1771.

GENTLEMEN,

IF *you* alone were concerned in the event of the present election of a chief magistrate of the metropolis, it would be the highest presumption in a stranger, to attempt to influence your choice, or even to offer you his opinion. But the situation of public affairs has annexed an extra-ordinary importance to your resolutions. You cannot, in the choice of your magistrate, deter-mine for *yourselves only*. You are going to deter-mine upon a point, in which every member of the community is interested. I will not scruple to say, that the very being of that law, of that right, of that constitution, for which we have been so long contending, is now at stake. They, who would ensnare your judgment, tell you, it is a *common*, *ordinary* case, and to be decided by ordinary pre-cedent and practice. They artfully conclude, from moderate peaceable times, to times which *are not* moderate, and which *ought not* to be peaceable..... While they solicit your favour, they insist upon a rule of rotation, which excludes all idea of elec-tion.

Let me be honoured with a few minutes of your attention....The question, to those who mean fairly to the liberty of the people, (which we all profess to have in view) lies within a very narrow com-pass....Do you mean to desert that just and ho-nourable system of measures which you have hi-therto pursued, in hopes of obtaining from par-liament, or from the Crown, a full redress of past grievances, and a security for the future?...Do you think the cause desperate, and will you declare that you think so to the whole people of England?

......If this be your meaning and opinion, you will act consistently with it in chusing Mr. Nash....I profess to be unacquainted with his private character. But he has acted as a magistrate....as a public man....As such, I speak of him....I see his name in a protest against one of your remonstrances to the crown....He has done every thing in his power to destroy the freedom of popular elections in the city, by publishing the poll upon a former occasion; and I know, in general, that he has distinguished himself, by slighting and thwarting all those public measures, which *you* have engaged in with the greatest warmth, and hitherto thought most worthy of your approbation....From his past conduct what conclusion will you draw, but that he will act the same part as *Lord Mayor*, which he has invariably acted as *Alderman* and *Sheriff?* He cannot alter his conduct, without confessing that he never acted upon principle of any kind....I should be sorry to injure the character of a man, who perhaps may be honest in his intention, by supposing it *possible*, that he can ever concur with you in any political measure, or opinion.

I should be sorry to injure, &c.] This conclusion of the paragraph is admirably artful. It reduces the question concerning Mr. Nash to a dilemma. If an honest man ; he would remain faithful to his former engagements; and therefore could not deserve to become the object of choice to the patriots. If a rascal ; he must be still less fit for their choice. In either case, then, they must reject him.

If, on the other hand, you mean to persevere in those resolutions for the public good, which though not always successful, are always honourable, your choice will naturally incline to those men, who, (whatever they be in other respects) are most likely to co-operate with you in the great purposes which you are determined not to relinquish:.... The question is not, of what metal your instruments are made, but *whether they are adapted to the work you have in hand?* The honours of the city, *in these times*, are improperly, because exclusively, called a *reward.* You mean not merely to *pay*, but to *employ*....Are Mr. Crosby and Mr. Sawbridge likely to execute the extraordinary, as well as the ordinary duties of Lord Mayor?....Will they grant you common halls when it shall be necessary?....Will they go up with remonstrances to the

Of what metal your instruments are made, &c.] This is an apology for recommending Sawbridge and Crosby. Sawbridge was popularly said to be a weak man : Crosby was but a mean and vulgar man. The scandal of the day had hinted, that the hands of the latter were not of the utmost possible purity.

Common Halls, &c.] Upon any occasion that may seem of importance to the Livery of London, a respectable member may request the Lord Mayor to summon a general meeting of the Livery. The Lord Mayor is to consider of the importance of the occasion, and the weight of the request. He can often, though not always, find means to avoid summoning a meeting which he dislikes. When he complies ; the Livery are summoned. Their meeting is familiarly called a *Common Hall.* The subject for discussion is proposed by those at whose request, the Livery were summoned. The Livery deliberate and determine according to the powers which the city's charter has bestowed.

King?......Have they firmness enough to meet the fury of a venal House of Commons?....Have they fortitude enough not to shrink at imprisonment?.... Have they spirit enough to hazard their lives and fortunes in a contest, if it should be necessary, with a prostituted legislature?.....If these questions can fairly be answered in the affirmative, your choice is made. Forgive this passionate language.......I am unable to correct it....The subject comes home to us all....It is the language of my heart.

JUNIUS.

LETTER LVIII.

TO THE PRINTER OF THE PUBLIC ADVERTISER.

———

THE dissensions among the patriots, were discrediting their cause, and defeating all their purposes. The Rockingham whigs and the followers of Lord Chatham had each a particular creed respecting the government of America. The Society for the support of the Bill of Rights had been divided, and in some sort broken up, by the contentions and mutual recriminations between Wilkes and Horne. Amid these divisions, the city patriots especially forgot their complaints and efforts against those whom they had accounted the common enemy. The aversion which Horne excited against Wilkes, and the still greater aversion which was raised against Horne, hindered their respective friends from due co-operation to defeat Nash's election. The ministry and their friends grew daily stronger in the weakness of the patriots. The former Letter of JUNIUS had not been successful to his wishes. He was not yet without hopes, that as in the affair of the Shrievalty, the friends of Wilkes had succeeded, so they might now, by a struggle succeed. The purport of this Letter, is, to persuade the subdivided patriots, that, notwithstanding their differences among themselves, they ought to act in union for a purpose so important as that of the election of a Lord Mayor who would favour their patriot purposes. He produces a number of specious arguments. As if ashamed of the meanness of city politics, he endeavours to dignify his theme, by deriving his illustrations from subjects of the highest grandeur and importance. He contrives to escape to the examination of the parliamentary conduct of the opposition: and, shewing that its leaders refused no aid, and sacrificed, each to union with his confederates, some of his own private sentiments; strives to recommend, by this example, the same conduct, to heal the divisions among the city patriots. He pleads, again, the apology of Wilkes. He hints, anew, at the mischievously divisive spirit of Horne. He pronounces the encomium of Sawbridge; and soothes the grumblings of Town-

send. He artfully endeavours to rouse, anew, among the citizens, an indignation against the leaders in the government that should draw their minds away from brooding over their own mutual discontents. To Lord Mansfield he turns, as to a favourite subject of invective; and strives to represent him as the worst, because he was the ablest and the most artful of all the associates of the ministry. He kindles into added wrath, as he proceeds: and endeavours to animate against the House of Commons, and against septennial elections, that indignation which began to flag. The reader cannot but remark, with pleasure and surprize, how artfully the latter part of this Letter, is addressed to rouse a public spirit that should stifle those private dissensions which it's first part strives to soothe!

———

SIR, 5. *October*, 1771.

NO man laments, more sincerely than I do, the unhappy differences, which have arisen among the friends of the people, and divided them from each other. The cause undoubtedly suffers, as well by the diminution of that strength, which union carries with it, as by the separate loss of personal reputation, which every man sustains, when his character and conduct are frequently held forth in odious or contemptible colours.........These differences are only advantageous to the common enemy of the country......The hearty friends of the cause are provoked and disgusted....The lukewarm advocate avails himself of any pretence to relapse

---

These differences, &c.] This and the three following periods exhibit a picture equally just and striking, of the effects of dissension among persons confederated for any common purpose. They might be applied to the alliances which have been successively undertaken to destroy the French Republic.

into that indolent indifference about every thing
that ought to interest an Englishman, so unjustly
dignified with the title of moderation..........The
false, insidious partizan, who creates or foments
the disorder, sees the fruit of his dishonest industry ripen beyond his hopes, and rejoices in the promise of a banquet, only delicious to such an appetite as his own....It is time for those, who really
mean the *Cause* and the *People*, who have no view
to private advantage, and who have virtue enough
to prefer the general good of the community to
the gratification of personal animosities......it is
time for such men to interpose.....Let us try whether these fatal dissensions may not yet be reconciled; or, if that be impracticable, let us guard at
least against the worst effects of division, and endeavour to persuade these furious partizans, if they
will not consent to draw together, to be separately
useful to that cause which they all pretend to be
attached to.....Honour and honesty must not be renounced, although a thousand modes of right and
wrong were to occupy the degrees of morality between Zeno and Epicurus. The fundamental prin-

It is time for those, &c.] An address, the most skilfully directed to make every man who called himself a patriot, to yield to
the persuasions of JUNIUS.

Honour and honesty, &c.] JUNIUS seems to have had in his
eye, when he wrote this period, the following lines of Pope:
" For *modes* of faith, let graceless zealots fight;
" His can't be wrong, whose life is in the *right.*"

Between Zeno and Epicurus, &c.] *Zeno* taught that the good
of the whole universe was the only principle from which the laws

ciples of Christianity may still be preserved, though
every zealous sectary adheres to his own exclusive
doctrine, and pious ecclesiastics make it part of
their religion to persecute one another.....The civil
constitution too, that legal liberty, that general
creed, which every Englishman professes, may still
be supported, though Wilkes, and Horne, and
Townshend, and Sawbridge, should obstinately refuse to communicate; and even if the fathers of
the church, if Saville, Richmond, Camden, Rockingham, and Chatham, should disagree in the ceremonies of their political worship, and even in the
interpretation of twenty texts in Magna Charta....
I speak to the people, as one-of the people......Let
us employ these men in whatever departments their
various abilities are best suited to, and as much
to the advantage of the common cause as their different inclinations will permit. They cannot serve
us, without essentially serving themselves.

If *Mr. Nash* be elected, he will hardly venture,
after so recent a mark of the personal esteem of his
fellow-citizens, to declare himself immediately a
courtier. The spirit and activity of the Sheriffs

of moral conduct were to be deduced, *Epicurus* taught that private
and sensual pleasure, was the proper object of virtuous conduct.
Yet, though differing thus widely as to the first principles of their
respective systems, both *Zeno* and *Epicurus* were teachers of virtue.

If Mr. Nash be elected, &c.] JUNIUS was now doubtful of the
success of the endeavours against Mr. Nash. He, therefore,
drops a conciliating expression meant to win him, if possible, to the
patriot cause.

will, I hope, be sufficient to counteract any sinister intentions of the Lord Mayor. In collision with *their* virtue, perhaps he may take fire.

It is not necessary to exact from Mr. Wilkes the virtues of a Stoic. They were inconsistent with themselves, who, almost at the same moment, represented him as the basest of mankind, yet seemed to expect from him such instances of fortitude and self-denial, as would do honour to an apostle. It is not however flattery to say, that he is obstinate, intrepid, and fertile in expedients....That he has no possible resource, but in the public favour, is, in my judgment, a considerable recommendation of him. I wish that every man, who pretended to popularity, were in the same predicament. I wish that a retreat to St. James's were not so easy and open, as Patriots have found it. To Mr. Wilkes there is no access. However he may be misled by passion or imprudence, I think he cannot be guilty of a deliberate treachery to the public. The favour of his country constitutes the shield, which defends him against a thousand daggers. Desertion would disarm him.

I can more readily admire the liberal spirit and integrity, than the sound judgment, of any man

To exact from Mr. Wilkes, &c.] Junius is never happier in his eloquence, than when pleading the apology, and marking the leading features in the character of Mr. Wilkes.

I can more readily, &c.] The reader who shall attentively peruse this paragraph, will perceive, that Junius was not, *in princi-*

who prefers a republican form of government, in this or any other empire of equal extent, to a monarchy so qualified and limited as ours. I am convinced, that neither is it in theory the wisest system of government, nor practicable in this country. Yet, though I hope the English constitution will for ever preserve its original monarchical form, I would have the manners of the people purely and strictly republican.....I do not mean the licentious spirit of anarchy and riot....I mean a general attachment to the common weal, distinct from any partial attachment to persons or families....an implicit submission to the laws only, and an affection to the magistrate, proportioned to the integrity and wisdom, with which he distributes justice to his people, and administers their affairs. The present habit of our political body appears to me the very reverse of what it ought to be. The form of the constitution leans rather more than enough to the popular branch; while in effect, the manners of the people (of those at least who are likely to take a lead in the country) incline too generally to a dependance upon the crown. The real friends of arbitrary power combine the facts, and are not inconsistent with their principles, when they stre-

---

ple, of the party of the democratical whigs. His recommendation of Sawbridge to represent the city in Parliament, is accommodated with great skill to his own principles. No paragraph in these Letters evinces more clearly, than this one, how well the nature of the British constitution and government was understood by their author.

nuously support the unwarrantable privileges assumed by the House of Commons....In these circumstances, it were much to be desired, that we had many such men as Mr. Sawbridge to represent us in parliament.....I speak from common report and opinion only, when I impute to him a speculative predilection in favour of a republic..... In the personal conduct and manners of the man, I cannot be mistaken. He has shewn himself possessed of that republican firmness, which the times require, and by which an English gentleman may be as usefully and as honourably distinguished, as any citizen of ancient Rome, of Athens, or Lacedæmon.

Mr. Townshend complains, that the public gratitude has not been answerable to his deserts.....It is not difficult to trace the artifices, which have suggested to him a language so unworthy of his understanding. A great man commands the affections of the people. A prudent man does not complain when he has lost them. Yet they are far from being lost to Mr. Townshend. He has treated our opinion a little too cavalierly. A young man is apt to rely too confidently upon himself, to be as attentive to his mistress, as a polite and passionate lover ought to be. Perhaps he found her

Mr. Townshend, &c.] Townshend's political conscience was, at this time, under the direction of Mr. Horne. JUNIUS strives to soothe his resentments against the party of Wilkes, in order to promote a general reconciliation of the divided patriots.

at first too easy a conquest....Yet, I fancy, she will be ready to receive him, whenever he thinks proper to renew his addresses. With all his youth, his spirit, and his appearance, it would be indecent in the lady to solicit his return.

I have too much respect for the abilities of Mr. Horne, to flatter myself that these Gentlemen will ever be cordially reunited. It is not, however, unreasonable to expect, that each of them should act his separate part, with honour and integrity to the public.....As for differences of opinion upon speculative questions, if we wait until *they* are reconciled, the action of human affairs must be suspended for ever. But neither are we to look for perfection in any one man, nor for agreement among many........When *Lord Chatham* affirms, that the authority of the British legislature is not supreme over the colonies, in the same sense in which it is supreme over Great Britain........when

---

That the authority of the British Legislature, &c.] Lord Chatham, who was no profound lawyer, nor deeply skilled in the metaphysical distinctions and principles of political science....was led by his passions....to conceive ; that, as the colonies had been established under charters, as the colonists could not in America assist in the choice of British Members of Parliament, as their local distance from Britain was so great.....The American colonies could not be justly subjected to the exercise in detail of the legislative supremacy of the British Parliament. The followers of the Marquis of Rockingham, and even of the people in general who had true English hearts, could not adopt such a principle; yet, did not, for this, refuse all political association with the Earl of Chatham.

Lord Camden supposes a necessity, (which the King is to judge of) and, founded upon that necessity, attributes to the crown a legal power (not given by the act itself) to suspend the operation of an act of the legislature....I listen to them both with diffidence and respect, but without the smallest degree of conviction or assent. Yet, I doubt not, they delivered their real sentiments, nor ought they to be hastily condemned.....I *too* have a claim to the candid interpretation of my country, when I acknowledge an involuntary, compulsive assent, to one very unpopular opinion. I lament the unhappy necessity, whenever it arises, of providing for the safety of the state, by a temporary invasion of the personal liberty of the subject. Would to God it were practicable to reconcile these important objects, in every possible situation of public affairs !.....I regard the legal liberty of the meanest man in Britain, as much as my own, and would

---

Lord Camden supposes a necessity, &c.] A power in the crown to suspend, till the meeting of Parliament, the action of a law, that was confessedly mischievous....had been asserted, in the Privy Council, by Lord Camden, in consistency with the opinions of Lord Chatham. The doctrine was not a good one. But, the principles of the school of Chatham, owned the utmost arbitrariness as to the exercise of the executive authority, if that exercise were by themselves, and for an undubitably good purpose.

I too have a claim, &c.] At once to vindicate himself; and to procure to the less reasonable opinions of others, that indulgence which he claimed to his own ; JUNIUS here enters on the discussion of the right to press seamen into the Royal Navy. His arguments have satisfied his country.

defend it with the same zeal. I know we must stand or fall together. But I never can doubt, that the community has a right to command, as well as to purchase, the service of its members. I see that right founded originally upon a necessity, which supercedes all argument. I see it established by usage immemorial, and admitted by more than a tacit assent of the legislature. I conclude there is no remedy, in the nature of things, for the grievance complained of; for, if there were, it must long since have been redressed. Though numberless opportunities have presented themselves, highly favourable to public liberty, no successful attempt has ever been made for the relief of the subject in this article. Yet it has been felt and complained of, ever since England had a navy......
The conditions, which constitute this right, must be taken together. Separately, they have little weight. It is not fair to argue, from any abuse in the execution, to the illegality of the power; much less is a conclusion to be drawn from the navy to the land service. A seaman can never be employed but against the enemies of his country. The only case in which the King can have a right to arm his subjects in general, is that of a foreign force being actually landed upon our coast. Whenever that case happens, no true Englishman will enquire, whether the King's right to compel him to defend his country be the custom of England, or a grant of the legislature. With regard to the press for seamen, it does not follow that the symptoms may

not be softened, although the distemper cannot be cured. Let bounties be increased as far as the public purse can support them. Still they have a limit; and when every reasonable expence is incurred, it will be found, in fact, that the spur of the press is wanted to give operation to the bounty.

Upon the whole, I never had a doubt about the strict right of pressing, until I heard that Lord Mansfield had applauded Lord Chatham for delivering something like this doctrine in the House of Lords. That consideration staggered me not a little. But, upon reflection, his conduct accounts naturally for itself. He knew the doctrine was unpopular, and was eager to fix it upon the man who is the first object of his fear and detestation. The cunning Scotchman never speaks truth without a fraudulent design. In council, he generally affects to take a moderate part. Besides his natural timidity, it makes part of his political plan, never to be known to recommend violent measures. When the guards are called forth to murder their fellow-subjects, it is not by the ostensible advice of Lord Mansfield. That odious office, his prudence tells him, is better left to such men as Gower and Weymouth, as Barrington and Grafton. Lord Hillsborough wisely confines *his* firmness to the distant

---

He knew the doctrine was unpopular, &c.] JUNIUS certainly wrongs, on many occasions, the exalted character of Lord Mansfield. Yet, I should incline to think, that, in this instance, he, at least conjectured shrewdly.

Americans....The designs of Mansfield are more subtle, more effectual, and secure......Who attacks the liberty of the press?....Lord Mansfield....Who invades the constitutional power of juries?....Lord Mansfield.....What judge ever challenged a juryman but Lord Mansfield?.....Who was that judge, who, to save the King's brother, affirmed that a man, of the first rank and quality, who obtains a verdict in a suit for criminal conversation, is entitled to no greater damages than the meanest mechanic?....Lord Mansfield....Who is it makes commissioners of the Great Seal?....Lord Mansfield.... Who is it forms a decree for those commissioners, deciding against Lord Chatham, and afterwards (finding himself opposed by the judges) declares in parliament, that he never had a doubt that the law was in direct opposition to that decree?.....Lord Mansfield....Who is he, that has made it the study and practice of his life, to undermine and alter the whole system of jurisprudence in the Court of King's Bench?....Lord Mansfield. There never existed a man but himself, who answered exactly to so complicated a description. Compared to these enormities, his original attachment to the Pretender, (to whom his dearest brother was confi-

What judge ever challenged a juryman, &c.] The reader will find an explanation of this allusion, in a subsequent Letter.

There never existed a man, &c.] The preceding series of interrogations is admirably eloquent. But, here, JUNIUS's rage against Lord Mansfield, seems to betray him into the burlesque.

dential secretary) is a virtue of the first magnitude. But the hour of impeachment *will* come, and neither he nor Grafton shall escape me. Now let them make common cause against England and the house of Hanover. A Stuart and a Murray should sympathise with each other.

When I refer to single instances of unpopular opinions delivered and maintained by men, who may well be supposed to have no view but the public good, I do not mean to renew the discussion of such opinions. I should be sorry to revive the dormant questions of *Stamp-act, Corn-bill,* or *Press-warrant.* I mean only to illustrate one useful proposition, which it is the intention of this paper to inculcate....*That we should not generally reject the friendship or services of any man, because he differs from us in a particular opinion.* This will not appear a superfluous caution, if we observe the ordinary conduct of mankind. In public affairs, there is the least chance of a perfect concurrence of sentiment or inclination. Yet every man is able to contribute something to the common stock, and no man's contribution should be rejected. If individuals have no virtues, their vices may be of use to us. I care not with what principle the new-born patriot is animated, if the measures he supports

---

When I refer, &c.] In this paragraph, the writer applies the particular instances which he had specified, to the general purpose, for the sake chiefly of which they were introduced. He, then vigorously resumes the leading thread of his reasonings.

are beneficial to the community. The nation is interested in his conduct. His motives are his own. The properties of a patriot are perishable in the individual, but there is a quick succession of subjects, and the breed is worth preserving....The spirit of the Americans may be an useful example to us. Our dogs and horses are only English upon English ground; but patriotism, it seems, may be improved by transplanting.....I will not reject a bill, which tends to confine parliamentary privilege within reasonable bounds, though it should be stolen from the house of Cavendish, and introduced by Mr. Onslow. The features of the infant are a proof of the descent, and vindicate the noble birth from the baseness of the adoption. I willingly accept of a sarcasm from *Colonel Barre*, or a simile from *Mr. Burke*. Even the silent vote of *Mr. Calcraft* is worth reckoning in a division....What

---

I will not reject a bill, &c.] It was thought skilful in the ministry to become authors of popular bills which could not well be rejected : and of which the opposition were eager to obtain the credit. Lord John Cavendish had originally suggested that definition of the privileges of Parliament which was accomplished in the bill of Mr. Onslow the son of the famous Speaker.

A sarcasm from Colonel Barre, or a simile from Mr. Burke, &c.] How powerfully, in two phrases, JUNIUS marks the character of the eloquence of these two orators !

Even the silent vote of Mr. Calcraft, &c.] It has been already explained in these notes ; that Mr. Calcraft was originally the clerk of Mr. Fox, the first Lord Holland ; that, by means of Mr. Fox, he was introduced into much lucrative employment as an army-agent, and otherwise gratified with great emoluments; that

though he riots in the plunder of the army, and has only determined to be a patriot, when he could not be a peer! Let us profit by the assistance of such men, while they are with us, and place them, if it be possible, in the post of danger, to prevent desertion. The wary *Wedderburne*, the pompous *Suffolk*, never threw away the scabbard, nor ever went upon a forlorn hope. They always treated the King's servants as men, with whom some time or other, they might possibly be in friendship.....
When a man who stands forth for the public, has gone that length, from which there is no practicable retreat.....when he has given that kind of personal offence, which a pious monarch never pardons, I then begin to think him in earnest, and that he never will have occasion to solicit the forgiveness of his country....But instances of a determination so entire and unreserved are rarely met with. Let us take mankind *as they are*. Let us distribute the virtues and abilities of individuals, according to the offices they affect, and when they quit the service, let us endeavour to supply their places with better men than we have lost. In this country, there are

he lived a dissolute life, accumulated immense wealth, and at last turned his back on his patron; that he was received, in the end, with open arms by the Pitt and Grenville party ; but died without attaining to the height of his ambition in a peerage.

The pompous Suffolk, &c.] Lord Suffolk was at the head of those friends of Mr. George Grenville who, upon *his* death, deserted the opposition, were reconciled to the court, and by adding their strength to that of the administration, rendered the success of the opposition much more hopeless than it had, just before, been.

always candidates enough for popular favour. The temple of *fame* is the shortest passage to riches and preferment.

Above all things, let me guard my countrymen against the meanness and folly of accepting of a trifling or moderate compensation for extraordinary and essential injuries. Our enemies treat us, as the cunning trader does the unskilful Indian. They magnify their generosity, when they give us baubles, of little proportionate value, for ivory and gold. The same House of Commons, who robbed the constituent body of their right of free-election, who presumed to *make* a law under pretence of *declaring* it, who paid our good King's debts, without once enquiring how they were incurred; who gave thanks for repeated murders committed at home, and for national infamy incurred abroad; who screened *Lord Mansfield;* who imprisoned the magistrates of the metropolis, for asserting the subjects' right to the protection of the laws; who erased a judicial record, and ordered all proceed-

The temple of fame, &c.] JUNIUS shews himself skilled in practical politics....and in his principles, differing exceedingly from the wild theories of Mr. Horne. But, perhaps while he advised not to reject the bad, he might encourage that wickedness which he wished to be used, only as a tool.

Above all things, &c.] This is a noble paragraph. How eloquently the wrongs supposed to have been committed by the House of Commons, are contrasted with the single concession made in the passing of the bill brought in by Onslow, and the election bill of Grenville.

ings in a criminal suit to be suspended....this very House of Commons have graciously consented, that their own members may be compelled to pay their debts, and that contested elections shall, for the future, be determined with some decent regard to the merits of the case. The event of the suit is of no consequence to the Crown. While parliaments are septennial, the purchase of the sitting member, or of the petitioner, makes but the difference of a day......Concessions, such as these, are of little moment to the sum of things; unless it be to prove, that the worst of men are sensible of the injuries they have done us, and perhaps to demonstrate to us the imminent danger of our situation. In the shipwreck of the state, trifles float and are preserved; while every thing solid and valuable sinks to the bottom, and is lost for ever.

JUNIUS.

LETTER LIX.

TO THE PRINTER OF THE PUBLIC ADVERTISER.

THE friends of Lord Camden were dissatisfied, that JUNIUS *should have attributed to him, an illegal doctrine. A Letter with the subscription of* Scævola *was published to palliate the alledged illegality of the act which Lord Camden had advised. It asserted, that the act became law when approved by the two Houses of Parliament. The fair consequence was ; that ministers, when Parliament was not sitting, might, under the pretence of necessity, do any thing for which they could hope the future sanction of a venal vote ; that the Crown might thus entirely usurp the initiative power in legislation ; and, that a corrupt parliament might thus quickly surrender all the liberties of the people, and annihilate the constitution. This Letter successfully defends against* Scævola *and Lord Camden, the doctrine of* JUNIUS.

---

15. *October,* 1771.

SIR,

I AM convinced that JUNIUS is incapable of wilfully misrepresenting any man's opinion, and that his inclination leads him to treat *Lord Camden* with particular candour and respect. The doctrine attributed to him by JUNIUS, as far as it goes, corresponds with that stated by your correspondent *Scævola*, who seems to make a distinction without a difference, *Lord Camden*, it is agreed, did certainly maintain that, in the recess of parliament, the King (by which we all mean the *King in Council*, or the executive power) might suspend the operation of an act of the legislature ; and he founded his doctrine upon a supposed necessity, of which the King, *in the first instance*, must be judge. The Lords and Commons cannot be judges of it in the first instance, for they do not exist....Thus far JUNIUS.

But, says *Scævola*, *Lord Camden* made *parliament*, and not the *King*, judges of the necessity.... That parliament may review the acts of ministers is unquestionable; but there is a wide difference between saying that the crown has a *legal* power, and that ministers may act *at their peril*. When we say an act is *illegal*, we mean that it is forbidden by a joint resolution of the three estates. How a subsequent resolution of two of those branches can make it *legal ab initio*, will require explanation. If it could, the consequence would be truly dreadful, especially in these times. There is no act of arbitrary power, which the King might not attribute to *necessity*, and for which he would not be secure of obtaining the approbation of his prostituted Lords and Commons. If *Lord Camden* admits that the subsequent sanction of parliament

---

How a subsequent resolution, &c.] The original act is not, by such a resolution, made legal; though the illegality be pardoned. JUNIUS's reasoning is invincible. According to Lord Camden; the *proclamation* against exporting corn, was legal, because uttered in compliance with the necessity which parliament could not deny; and, therefore, needed no enactment of the legislature to give it validity. The more legitimate doctrine is; that its necessity might, indeed extort its forgiveness; but that a new law was requisite to indemnify its authors, and to give to its action, constitutional force.

was necessary to make the proclamation *legal*, why did he so obstinately oppose the bill, which was soon after brought in, for indemnifying all those persons who had acted under it ?....If that bill had not been passed, I am ready to maintain, in direct contradiction to *Lord Camden's* doctrine, (taken as *Scævola* states it) that a litigious exporter of corn, who had suffered in his property in consequence of the proclamation, might have laid his action against the custom-house officers, and would infallibly have recovered damages. No jury could refuse them; and if I, who am by no means litigious, had been so injured, I would assuredly have instituted a suit in Westminster Hall, on purpose to try the question of right. I would have done it upon a principle of defiance of the pretended power of either or both Houses to make declarations inconsistent with law, and I have no doubt that, with an act of parliament on my side, I should have been too strong for them all. This is the way in which an Englishman should speak and act, and not suffer dangerous precedents to be established, because the circumstances are favourable or palliating.

With regard to *Lord Camden*, the truth is, that he inadvertently over-shot himself, as appears plainly by that unguarded mention of *a tyranny of forty days*, which I myself heard. Instead of asserting that the proclamation was *legal*, he *should* have said, " My Lords, I know the proclamation " was *illegal;* but I advised it, because it was in-

" dispensably necessary to save the kingdom from
" famine, and I submit myself to the justice and
" mercy of my country. "

Such language as this would have been manly,
rational, and consistent....not unfit for a lawyer,
and every way worthy of a great man.

PHILO JUNIUS.

P. S. If *Scævola* should think proper to write
again upon this subject, I beg of him to give me a
direct answer, that is, a plain affirmative or negative, to the following questions :....In the interval
between the publishing such a proclamation (or order of council) as that in question, and its receiving the sanction of the two houses, of what nature
is it....is it *legal* or *illegal*; or is it neither one nor
the other?....I mean to be candid, and will point out
to him the consequence of his answer either way.
....If it be *legal*, it wants no farther sanction....If it
be *illegal*, the subject is not bound to obey it, consequently it is a useless, nugatory act, even as to its
declared purpose. Before the meeting of parliament, the whole mischief, which it means to prevent, will have been compleated.

If it be legal, &c.] The force of this dilemma is irresistable.
Junius, on every great occasion, when it could suit his purpose,
shews the discernment of an able and learned lawyer.

LETTER LX.

TO ZENO.

———

A PERSON, assuming the signature of Zeno, *attempting the defence of Lord Mansfield against the last attack of* JUNIUS. PHILO JUNIUS *again stood forth. In the following Letter, the accusations of* JUNIUS *are, one by one, compared with the defences of* Zeno, *and are confirmed with greater force and earnestness than had been given to them at the first. The Letter of* Zeno, *was written with considerable dexterity. It therefore called forth a masterpiece in controversial reasoning. There is a great resemblance between the tenor of the following Letter, and the manner of Chillingworth in his happiest moments of controversy.*

———

17. *October,* 1771.

SIR,

THE sophistry of your Letter in defence of *Lord Mansfield*, is adapted to the character you defend. But *Lord Mansfield* is a man of *form*, and seldom in his behaviour transgresses the rules of decorum. I shall imitate his Lordship's good manners, and leave *you* in the full possession of his principles. I will not call you *liar, jesuit,* or *villain*; but, with all the politeness imaginable, perhaps I may prove you so.

I will not call you, &c.] Vulgarity and shrewd eloquence seem to be in strife for this period.

Like other fair pleaders in *Lord Mansfield's* school of justice, you answer JUNIUS by misquoting his words, and mistaking his propositions. If I am candid enough to admit that this is the very logic taught at *St. Omer's*, you will readily allow, that it is the constant practice in the court of *King's Bench*....JUNIUS *does not say*, that he never had a doubt about the strict right of pressing, *till he knew Lord Mansfield was of the same opinion.* His words are, *until he heard that Lord Mansfield had applauded Lord Chatham for maintaining that doctrine in the House of Lords.* It was not the accidental concurrence of Lord Mansfield's opinion, but the suspicious applause given by a cunning Scotchman to the man he detests, that raised and justified a doubt in the mind of JUNIUS. The question is not, whether Lord Mansfield be a man of learning and abilities, (which JUNIUS has never disputed) but whether or no he abuses and misapplies his talents.

JUNIUS did *not* say that Lord Mansfield had advised the calling out of the guards. On the contrary, his plain meaning is, that he left that odious office to men less cunning than himself....Whether

---

The suspicious applause, &c.] JUNIUS thought Lord Mansfield pleased, that Lord Chatham should embrace a doctrine which he believed to be bad. He supposed Lord Mansfield too much the enemy of Lord Chatham's fame, to rejoice in his adopting any doctrine that was not bad.

Lord Mansfield's doctrine concerning libels be or be not an attack upon the liberty of the press, is a question which the public in general are very well able to determine. I shall not enter into it at present. Nor do I think it necessary to say much to a man, who had the daring confidence to say to a jury, "Gentlemen, you are to bring in a verdict "*guilty* or *not guilty*, but whether the defendant "be guilty or innocent, is not matter for *your* con- "sideration." Clothe it in what language you will, this is the sum total of Lord Mansfield's doctrine. If not, let *Zeno* shew us the difference.

But it seems, *the liberty of the press may be abused*, and *the abuse of a valuable privilege is the certain means to lose it.* The *first* I admit....but let the *abuse* be submitted to a jury, a sufficient and indeed the only legal and constitutional check upon the licence of the press. The *second*, I flatly deny. In direct contradiction to Lord *Mansfield*, I affirm that "the abuse of a valuable privilege *is not* the *certain* "means to lose it." If it were, the English nation would have few privileges left; for where is the privilege that has not, at one time or other, been abused by individuals. But it is false in reason

Concerning libels, &c.] It is needless to make, here, any addition to what has been, in these Notes already stated respecting this subject.

The liberty of the press may be abused, &c.] This paragraph most eloquently destroys the inference, that, because the liberty of the press may be abused, it ought, therefore, to be abolished.

and equity; that particular abuses should produce
a general forfeiture. Shall the community be deprived of the protection of the laws, because there
are robbers and murderers?...Shall the community
be punished, because individuals have offended?
Lord Mansfield says so, consistently enough with
his principles, but I wonder to find him so explicit.
Yet, for one concession, however extorted, I confess myself obliged to him....The liberty of the
press is after all a *valuable privilege*. I agree with
him most heartily, and will defend it against him.

You ask me, What *juryman* was challenged by
Lord Mansfield?.....I tell you his name was *Benson*.
When his name was called, Lord Mansfield ordered
the clerk to pass him by. As for his reasons, you
may ask himself, for he assigned none. But I can
tell you what all men thought of it. This *Benson*
had been refractory upon a former jury, and would
not accept of the law as delivered by Lord Mansfield;
but had the impudence to pretend to think for himself....But you it seems, honest *Zeno*, know nothing
of the matter! You never read JUNIUS's Letter to
your patron! You never heard of the intended instructions from the city to impeach Lord Mansfield!
....You never heard by what dexterity of *Mr. Pater-
son* that measure was prevented! How wonderfully
ill some people are informed!

Intended instructions, &c.] The leaders in the city, were, at one
time sufficiently mad and daring to attempt almost any thing.

JUNIUS did never affirm that the crime of seduc-
ing the wife of a mechanic or a peer, is not the same,
taken in a moral or religious view. What he
affirmed in contradiction to the levelling principle
so lately adopted by Lord Mansfield was, *that the
damages should be proportioned to the rank and fortune of the parties.;* and for this plain reason, (admitted by every other judge that ever sat in Westminster Hall) because, what is a compensation or
penalty to one man, is none to another. The sophistical distinction you attempt to draw between
the person, *injured,* and the person *injuring,* is
Mansfield all over. If you can once establish the
proposition, that the injured party is not entitled to
receive large damages; it follows pretty plainly, that
the party *injuring* should not be compelled to *pay*
them; consequently the King's brother is effectually
screened by *Lord Mansfield*'s doctrine. Your reference to *Nathan* and *David* come naturally in aid

*Because what is a compensation or penalty to one man, is none
to another, &c.*] These words clearly and decisively express the indisputable reason for JUNIUS's opinion.

Your reference to Nathan, &c.] The argument delivered by
Lord Mansfield in the prosecution by Lord Grosvenor against the
Duke of Cumberland, is the subject of this discussion. Zeno appealed to the parable addressed by Nathan to David, in order to shew,
that the crime of the Duke was less heinous than if he had seduced
from Lord Grosvenor's affection, a wife whom he truly loved......
This doctrine is allowed in the courts. Smaller damages are
granted to a husband who has not valued and caressed his wife,
than to one that has. JUNIUS so far as he reasons against this distinction, is in an error, and reasons vainly. He concludes this
paragraph with wit and humour.

of your patron's professed system of jurisprudence.
He is fond of introducing into the *court of King's
Bench* any law that contradicts or excludes the
common law of England; whether it be *canon,
civil, jus gentium,* or *levitical.* But, Sir, the Bible
is the code of our religious faith, not of our muni-
cipal jurisprudence; and though it was the pleasure
of God to inflict a particular punishment upon
David's crime (taken as a breach of his divine commands) and to send his prophet to denounce it, an
English jury have nothing to do either with David
or the prophet. They consider the crime, only as
it is a breach of order, an injury to an individual,
and an offence to society; and they judge of it by
certain positive rules of law, or by the practice of
their ancestors. Upon the whole, the man *after
God's own heart* is much indebted to you for comparing him to the Duke of Cumberland. That his
Royal Highness may be the man after *Lord Mansfield's* own heart, seems much more probable; and
you, I think, Mr. *Zeno,* might succeed tolerably
well in the character of *Nathan.* The evil deity,
the prophet, and the royal sinner, would be very
proper company for one another.

You say Lord Mansfield did not *make* the commissioners of the Great Seal, and that he only advised the King to appoint. I believe JUNIUS
meant no more, and the distinction is hardly worth
disputing....

You say he *did not* deliver an opinion upon Lord Chatham's appeal....I affirm that he *did*, directly in favour of the appeal. This is a point of fact, to be determined by evidence only. But you assign no reason for his supposed silence, nor for his desiring a conference with the judges the day before. Was not all Westminster Hall convinced that he did it with a view to puzzle them with some perplexing question, and in hopes of bringing some of them over to him ?....You say the commissioners were *very capable of framing a decree for themselves.* By the fact, it only appears, that they were capable of framing an *illegal* one ; which, I apprehend, is not much to the credit either of their learning or integrity.

We are both agreed that *Lord Mansfield* has incessantly laboured to introduce new modes of proceeding in the court where he presides ; but *you* attribute it to an honest zeal in behalf of innocence oppressed by quibble and chicane. I say that he

---

Lord Chatham's appeal, &c.] An estate was left to Lord Chatham by Sir William Pynsent. The heirs-at-law of Pynsent disputed the validity of the bequest. The cause was brought by appeal before the Commissioners who held the Great Seal between the Chancellorship of Mr. Charles Yorke, and that of Lord Bathurst. They decided against Lord Chatham. Their sentence was reversed by the House of Peers. Lord Chatham finally triumphed.

Introduce new modes, &c.] It is owned that Lord Mansfield introduced more of general reason into the law of England. It is not denied, that, if he had not been vigilantly watched, he might have subverted its proper character, and altered its genuine spirit.

has introduced *new law* too, and removed the land-marks established by former decisions. I say that his view is to change a court of common law into a court of equity, and to bring every thing within the *arbitrium* of a *prætorian* court. The public must determine between us. *But now for his merits.* *First* then, the establishment of the judges in their places for life, (which you tell us was advised by Lord Mansfield) was a concession merely to catch the people. It bore the appearance of a royal bounty, but had nothing real in it. The judges were already for life, excepting in the case of a *demise.* Your boasted bill only provides that it shall not be in the power of the King's successor to re-move them. At the best therefore, it is only a legacy, not a gift, on the part of his present Majesty; since, for himself, he gives up nothing......That he did oppose *Lord Camden* and *Lord Northington* upon the proclamation against the exportation of corn, is most true, and with great ability. With his talents, and taking the right side of so clear a question, it was impossible to speak ill....His mo-tives are not so easily penetrated. They, who are acquainted with the state of politics, at that period, will judge of them somewhat differently from *Zeno.* Of the popular bills, which you say he supported in the House of Lords, the most material is unques-tionably that of *Mr. Grenville,* for deciding con-

---

His motives, &c.] JUNIUS is too zealous to find out bad motives for Lord Mansfield's good actions; and, perhaps, but too successful.

tested elections....But I should be glad to know upon what possible pretence any member of the Upper House could oppose such a bill, after it had passed the *House of Commons?*....I do not pretend to know what share he had in promoting the other two bills, but I am ready to give him all the credit you desire. Still you will find, that a whole life of deliberate iniquity is ill atoned for by doing now and then a laudable action upon a mixed or doubtful principle......If it be unworthy of him, thus ungratefully treated, to labour any longer for the public, in God's name let him retire. His brother's patron, (whose health he once was anxious for) is dead, but the son of that unfortunate prince survives, and, I dare say, will be ready to receive him.

PHILO JUNIUS.

His brother's patron, &c.] The pretender James the Eighth.

LETTER LXI.

TO AN ADVOCATE IN THE CAUSE OF THE PEOPLE.

Junius might prove the honesty of his patriotism, by daring to espouse an unpopular principle when he thought it right. But, it was not easy to dispel by ingenuousness and reasoning, the prejudices of people who could not reason. The defender of the right of pressing seamen was attacked in the newspapers, relatively to that doctrine. He here defends himself....and with sufficient skill.

18. *October*, 1771.

SIR,

YOU do not treat JUNIUS fairly. You would not have condemned him so hastily, if you had ever read *Judge Foster*'s argument upon the legality of pressing seamen. A man who has not read that argument, is not qualified to speak accurately upon the subject. In answer to strong facts and fair reasoning, you produce nothing but a vague comparison between two things which have little or no resemblance to each other. *General Warrants*, it is true, had been often issued, but they

---

If you had ever read Judge Foster's argument, &c.] This mention of the name of Judge Foster, is a lawyer's artifice. Reason could not become more reasonable from the mouth of Foster. But, JUNIUS knew, how much was, on this occasion to be gained by a shew of juridical erudition, and of deference for a popular law-authority. The distinction between *General Warrants* and *Press Warrants*, which follows, in this paragraph, clears the doctrine of JUNIUS, from the objection which had been urged against it.

had never been regularly questioned or resisted, until the case of *Mr. Wilkes.* He brought them to trial; and the moment they were tried, they were declared *illegal.* This is not the case of *Press Warrants.* They have been complained of, questioned, and resisted, in a thousand instances; but still the legislature have never interposed, nor has there ever been a formal decision against them in any of the superior courts. On the contrary, they have been frequently recognized and admitted by parliament, and there are judicial opinions given in their favour by judges of the first character. Under the various circumstances, stated by JUNIUS, he has a right to conclude, *for himself,* that there is no remedy. If you have a good one to propose, you may depend upon the assistance and applause of JUNIUS. The magistrate who guards the liberty of the individual, deserves to be commended. But let him remember, that it is also his duty to provide for, or at least not to hazard, the safety of the community. If, in the case of a foreign war and the expectation of an invasion, you would rather keep your fleet in harbour, than man it by pressing seamen who refuse the bounty, I have done.

You talk of disbanding the army with wonderful ease and indifference. If a wiser man held such language, I should be apt to suspect his sincerity.

As for keeping up, &c.] This paragraph evidently issues from the mind of a man who was not incapable of entering deeply into the principles of commercial philosophy.

As for keeping up a *much greater* number of seamen in time of peace, it is not to be done. You will oppress the merchant, you will distress trade, and destroy the nursery of your seamen. He must be a miserable statesman, who voluntarily, by the same act, increases the public expence, and lessens the means of supporting it.

PHILO JUNIUS.

LETTER LXII.

———

THIS is another Letter to support what JUNIUS *had advanced in cri-mination of Lord Mansfield. It is in answer to one who had writ-ten against him, with the signature of* A Barrister at Law. *It repeats the accusations, and speciously supports them.*

———

22. *October*, 1771.

A FRIEND of JUNIUS desires it may be ob-served, (in answer to *A Barrister at Law,)*

1. That the fact of Lord Mansfield's having or-dered a juryman to be passed by, (which poor *Zeno* never heard of) is now formally admitted. When *Mr. Benson*'s name was called, *Lord Mansfield* was observed to flush in the face, (a signal of guilt not uncommon with him) and cried out, *Pass him by*. This I take to be something more than a pe-remptory challenge. It is an *unlawful command*, without any reason assigned. That the counsel did not resist, is true; but this might happen either from inadvertence, or a criminal complaisance to Lord Mansfield.....You *Barristers* are too apt to be civil to my Lord Chief Justice, at the expence of your clients.

That the counsel did not resist, &c.] No: the negligence of the counsel cannot excuse the judge. The judge should not do wrong in such a case. If wrong be attempted; the counsel ought vigilantly to resist it for the interest of his client.

2. JUNIUS never did say that Lord Mansfield had *destroyed* the liberty of the press. " That his " lordship has *laboured to destroy*.....that his doc- " trine is an *attack* upon the liberty of the press.... " that it is an *invasion* of the right of juries, " are the propositions maintained by JUNIUS. His opponents never answer him in point, for they never meet him fairly upon his own ground.

3. Lord *Mansfield's* policy, in endeavouring to screen his unconstitutional doctrines behind an act of the legislature, is easily 'understood....Let every Englishman stand upon his guard....the right of juries to return a general verdict, in all cases whatsoever, is a part of our constitution. It stands in need of a bill, either *enacting* or *declaratory*, to confirm it.

4. With regard to the *Grosvenor cause*, it is pleasant to observe that the doctrine attributed by JUNIUS to Lord Mansfield, is admitted by *Zeno*, and directly defended. The *Barrister* has not the assurance to deny it flatly, but he evades the charge, and softens the doctrine, by such poor, contemptible, quibbles, as cannot impose upon the meanest understanding.

5. The quantity of business in the *Court of King's Bench* proves nothing but the litigious spirit

The quantity of business, &c.] The reasoning of JUNIUS is not here, quite fair. The increased population and wealth of the

of the people, arising from the great increase of wealth and commerce. These, however, are now upon the decline, and will soon leave nothing but *law suits* behind them. When J u n i u s affirms, that Lord Mansfield has laboured to alter the system of jurisprudence, in the court where his lordship presides, he speaks to those who are able to look a little farther than the vulgar. Besides that the multitude are easily deceived by the imposing names of *equity* and *substantial justice*, it does not follow that a judge, who introduces into his court new modes of proceeding, and new principles of law, intends, *in every instance*, to decide unjustly. Why should he, where he has no interest?....We say that Lord Mansfield is a bad *man*, and a worse *judge*.... but we do not say that he is a *mere devil*. Our adversaries would fain reduce us to the difficulty of proving too much....This artifice, however, shall not avail him. The truth of the matter is plainly this. When *Lord Mansfield* has succeeded in his scheme of changing a court of *common law* to a court of *equity*, he will have it in his power to do injustice, *whenever he thinks proper*. This, though a wicked purpose, is neither absurd nor unattainable.

6. The last paragraph, relative to *Lord Chatham's* cause, cannot be answered. It partly refers to facts

country concurred with the abilities of Lord Mansfield, to bring so much business into the Court of King's Bench. But, if the public confidence in Lord Mansfield had not been high; that court would have been, as much as possible, avoided. The rest of the paragraph is artful and malignant.

of too secret a nature to be ascertained, and partly is unintelligible. " Upon *one* point, the cause is " decided against Lord Chatham....Upon *another* " point, it is decided for him. "....Both the *law* and the *language* are well suited to a *Barrister* !....If I have any guess at this honest gentleman's meaning, it is, that, " whereas the commissioners of the Great " Seal saw the question in a point of view unfavour- " able to *Lord Chatham*, and decreed accordingly, " ....Lord Mansfield, out of sheer love and kindness " to Lord Chatham, took the pains to place it in a " point of view more favourable to the *appellant*. " ....*Credat Judæus Apella*....So curious an assertion would stagger the faith of *Mr. Sylva*.

LETTER LXIII.

———

Junius was still attacked by patriots of the party of Horne, or by friends to the ministry, whom he had so harassed. This Letter consists of explanations which had been demanded from him, respecting ....the right of taxation, over the Americans....the impressing of Seamen....and the Game Laws.

———

2. November, 1771.

WE are desired to make the following declaration, in behalf of JUNIUS, upon three material points, on which his opinion had been mistaken, or misrepresented.

1. JUNIUS considers the right of taxing the colonies by an act of the British legislature, as a *speculative* right merely, never to be *exerted*, nor ever to be *renounced*. To *his* judgment it appears plain, " That the general reasonings which were " employed against that power, went directly to " our whole legislative right; and that one part of " it could not be yielded to such arguments, without a virtual surrender of all the rest. "

A speculative right, &c.] This doctrine of JUNIUS is utterly absurd. A right never to be exerted, is no right. Undoubtedly, Britain had a clear right to exact taxes from the Americans for the general defence of the empire. That expired by the change of political utility, and by voluntary dereliction.

2. That with regard to press-warrants, his argument should be taken in his own words, and answered strictly.....that comparisons may sometimes illustrate, but prove nothing; and that, in this case, an appeal to the passions is unfair and unnecessary. JUNIUS feels and acknowledges the evil in the most express terms, and will shew himself ready to concur in any rational plan, that may provide for the liberty of the individual, without hazarding the safety of the community. At the same time, he expects that the evil, such as it is, be not exaggerated or misrepresented. In general, it is *not* unjust that, when the rich man contributes his wealth, the *poor* man should serve the state in person....otherwise the latter contributes nothing to the defence of that law and constitution, from which he demands safety and protection. But the question does not lie between *rich* and *poor*. The laws of England make no such distinction. Neither is it true, that the poor man is torn from the care and support of a wife and family, helpless without him. The single question is, whether the *seamen* *, in times of public danger, shall serve the merchant or the state, in that profession to which he was bred, and by the exercise of which alone he

---

With regard to press-warrants, &c.] Nothing can be usefully added to what JUNIUS has, here, and on some previous occasions, said respecting this matter. His reasonings have fully satisfied the public.

* I confine myself strictly to *seamen*; if any others are pressed, it is a gross abuse, which the magistrate can and should correct.

can honestly support himself and his family.....Ge-
neral arguments against the doctrine of *necessity*,
and the dangerous use that may be made of it, are
of no weight in this particular case. *Necessity* includes the idea of *inevitable*. Whenever it is so, it
creates a law, to which all *positive* laws, and all
positive rights, must give way. In this sense the
levy of *ship-money* by the King's warrant was not
necessary, because the business might have been as
well or better done by parliament. If the doctrine,
maintained by Junius, be confined within this
limitation, it will go but very little way in support
of arbitrary power. That the King is to judge of
the occasion, is no objection, unless we are told
how it can possibly be otherwise. There are other
instances, not less important in the exercise, nor
less dangerous in the abuse, in which the constitution relies entirely upon the King's judgment. The
executive power proclaims war and peace, binds
the nation by treaties, orders general embargoes,
and imposes quarantines, not to mention a multitude of prerogative writs, which, though liable to
the greatest abuses, were never disputed.

3. It has been urged, as a reproach to Junius,
that he has not delivered an opinion upon the Game
Laws, and particularly the late Dog-Act. But
Junius thinks he has much greater reason to complain, that he is never assisted by those who are
able to assist him, and that almost the whole labour
of the press is thrown upon a single hand, from

which a discussion of *every* public question whatsoever is unreasonably expected.　He is not paid
for his labour, and certainly has a right to choose
his employment.....As to the *Game Laws*, he never
scrupled to declare his opinion, that they are a
species of the *Forest Laws*, that they are oppressive to the subject, and that the spirit of them is
incompatible with legal liberty....that the penalties,
imposed by these laws, bear no proportion to the
nature of the offence; that the mode of trial, and
the degree and kind of evidence necessary to convict, not only deprive the subject of all the benefits
of a trial by jury, but are in themselves too summary, and to the last degree arbitrary and oppressive.　That, in particular, the late acts to prevent
dog-stealing, or killing game between sun and sun,
are distinguished by their absurdity, extravagance,
and pernicious tendency.　If these terms are weak,
or ambiguous, in what language can J u n i u s express
himself?...It is no excuse for *Lord Mansfield* to say
that he *happened* to be absent when these bills passed
the House of Lords.　It was his duty to be present.
Such bills could never have passed the House of
Commons without his knowledge.　But we very

If these terms are weak or ambiguous, &c.] No ; they are not
weak, nor ambiguous.　Yet the Game Laws are still, considerably
severe.

Lord Mansfield....happened to be absent, &c.] The artifice of
neglecting attendance in parliament, in order to avoid a declaration
of his sentiments on occasions of delicacy and importance, was
often charged against Lord Mansfield. J u n i u s fairly exposes it.

well know by what rule he regulates his attendance. When that order was made in the House of Lords, in the case of *Lord Pomfret*, at which every Englishman shudders, my honest *Lord Mansfield* found himself, *by mere accident*, in the Court of King's Bench....Otherwise, he would have done wonders in defence of law and property! The pitiful evasion is adapted to the character. But JUNIUS will never justify himself, by the example of this bad man. The distinction between *doing wrong*, and *avoiding to do right*, belongs to Lord Mansfield. JUNIUS disclaims it.

Case of Lord Pomfret.] This case respected a dispute concerning a common...I think...in Yorkshire.

The distinction, &c.] This distinction is, here, very strongly put.

JUNIUS *disclaims it.*] He might. He had given, in this Letter, the explanations which were demanded from him.

LETTER LXIV.

TO LORD CHIEF JUSTICE MANSFIELD.

———

A NEW occasion offered to enable Junius, *to gratify his resentment against Lord Mansfield. John Eyre, a man possessing a fortune of about thirty thousand pounds, was detected in the theft of paper in quires out of an office at Guildhall. The magistrates before whom he was brought, would not admit him to bail, because he had been found with the stolen goods about his person. He procured himself to be carried before Lord Mansfield, and was, by him admitted to bail. A question arose even among the lawyers, concerning the legality of what Lord Mansfield had done. Eyre afterwards surrendered himself to justice.*

———

2. *November,* 1771.

AT the intercession of three of your countrymen, you have bailed a man, who, I presume, is also a *Scotchman,* and whom the Lord Mayor of London had refused to bail. I do not mean to enter into an examination of the partial, sinister motives of your conduct; but, confining myself strictly to the fact, I affirm, that you have done that, which by law you were not warranted to do. The thief was taken in the theft....the stolen goods were found upon him, and he made no defence. In these circumstances, (the truth of which You dare not deny, because it is of public notoriety) it could not stand indifferent whether he was guilty or not, much less could there be any presumption of his innocence; and, in these circumstances, I affirm, in contradiction to YOU, LORD CHIEF JUSTICE MANSFIELD, that by the laws of England, he was *not bailable.* If ever *Mr. Eyre* should be brought to trial, we shall hear what You have to say for Yourself; and I pledge myself, before God and my country, in proper time and place to make good my charge against you.

JUNIUS.

LETTER LXV.

TO THE PRINTER OF THE PUBLIC ADVERTISER.

In this short Letter, JUNIUS merely fixes the time within which he was to make good his charge against Lord Mansfield.

---

9. *November,* 1771.

JUNIUS engages to make good his charge against *Lord Chief Justice Mansfield,* some time before the meeting of parliament, in order that the House of Commons may, if they think proper, make it one article in the impeachment of the said *Lord Chief Justice.*

LETTER LXVI.

TO HIS GRACE THE DUKE OF GRAFTON.

———

THE litigation which had arisen in consequence of the attempt to grant away the Duke of Portland's estate to Sir James Lowther, had ended in favour of the Duke. Inglewood Forest, was found to have been not legally granted to Sir James....and to be not legally resumable from the Duke of Portland. The Duke of Grafton was minister when the grant to Sir James Lowther passed from the Treasury. And, JUNIUS, *therefore, eagerly seizes this last opportunity to insult his feelings. This Letter only repeats the old themes of reproach. It is interspersed with digressions respecting the Luttrells, with exultations over Sir James Lowther, with hinted abuse of the King. It is eloquent ; but contains little or nothing to demand new illustration.*

———

27. *November*, 1771.

WHAT is the reason, my Lord, that, when almost every man in the kingdom, without distinction of principles or party, exults in the ridiculous defeat of Sir James Lowther, when good and bad men unite in one common opinion of that baronet, and triumph in his distress, as if the event (without any reference to vice or virtue) were interesting to human nature, your Grace alone should appear so miserably depressed and afflicted ? In such universal joy, I know not where you will look for a compliment of condolence, unless you appeal to the tender, sympathetic sorrows of Mr. Bradshaw. That cream-coloured gentleman's tears, affecting as they are, carry consolation along with them. He never weeps, but, like an April shower, with a lambent ray of sunshine upon his countenance. From the feelings of honest men, upon this joyful occasion, I do not mean to draw any conclusion to your Grace. *They* naturally rejoice, when they see a signal instance of tyranny resisted with success......of treachery exposed to the derision of the world....an infamous informer defeated, and an impudent robber dragged to the public gibbet....But, in the *other* class of mankind, I own I expected to meet the Duke of Grafton. Men, who have no regard for justice, nor any sense of honour, seem as heartily pleased with Sir James Lowther's well-deserved punishment, as if it did not constitute an example against themselves. The unhappy Baronet has no friends, even among those who resemble him. You, my Lord, are not reduced to so deplorable a state of dereliction, Every villain in the kingdom is your friend; and, in compliment to such amity, I think you should suffer your dismal countenance to clear up. Besides, my Lord, I am a little anxious for the consistency of your character. You violate your own rules of decorum, when you do not insult the man whom you have betrayed.

The divine justice of retribution seems now to have begun its progress. Deliberate treachery entails punishment upon the traitor. There is no

possibility of escaping it, even in the highest rank
to which the consent of society can exalt the
meanest and worst of men. The forced, unnatural
union, of Luttrell and Middlesex, was an omen of
another unnatural union, by which indefeasible
infamy is attached to the house of Brunswick. If
one of those acts was virtuous and honourable, the
best of Princes, I thank God, is happily rewarded
for it by the other.... Your Grace, *it has been said*,
had some share in recommending Colonel Luttrell
to the King....or was it only the gentle Bradshaw,
who made himself answerable for the good behaviour of his friend ? An intimate connexion has
long subsisted between him and the worthy Lord
Irnham. It arose from a fortunate similarity of
principles, cemented by the constant mediation of
their common friend Miss Davis *.

* There is a certain family in this country, on which nature
seems to have entailed an hereditary baseness of disposition. As
far as their history has been known, the son has regularly improved
upon the vices of his father, and has taken care to transmit them
pure and undiminished into the bosom of his successor. In the
senate, their abilities have confined them to those humble, sordid
services, in which the scavengers of the ministry are usually employed. But in the memoirs of private treachery, they stand first
and unrivalled. The following story will serve to illustrate the
character of the respectable family, and to convince the world
that the present possessor has as clear a title to the infamy of his
ancestors as he has to their estate. It deserves to be recorded for
the curiosity of the fact, and should be given to the public as a
warning to every honest member of society.

The present Lord Irnham, who is now in the decline of life,
lately cultivated the acquaintance of a younger brother of a family

Yet I confess I should be sorry that the oppro-
brious infamy of this match should reach beyond
the family......We have now a better reason than
ever to pray for the long life of the best of Princes,
and the welfare of his royal *issue*....I will not mix
any thing ominous with my prayers....but let parliament look to it.... A *Luttrell* shall never succeed
to the crown of England....If the hereditary virtues
of the family deserve a kingdom, Scotland will be
a proper retreat for them.

The next is a most remarkable instance of the
goodness of Providence. The just law of retalia-
tion has at last overtaken the little, contemptible
tyrant of the North. To this son-in-law of your
dearest friend the Earl of Bute, you meant to transfer the Duke of Portland's property; and you has-

---

with which he had lived in some degree of intimacy and friendship.
The young man had long been the dupe of a most unhappy attachment to a common prostitute. His friends and relations foresaw
the consequences of this connexion, and did every thing that depended upon them to save him from ruin. But he had a friend in
Lord Irnham, whose advice rendered all their endeavours ineffectual. This hoary letcher, not contented with the enjoyment of
his friend's mistress, was base enough to take advantage of the passions and folly of a young man, and persuaded him to marry her.
He descended even to perform the office of father to the prostitute.
He gave her to his friend, who was on the point of leaving the kingdom, and the next night lay with her himself.

Whether the depravity of the human heart can produce any
thing more base and detestable than this fact, must be left undetermined, until the son shall arrive at his father's age and experience.

tened the grant, with an expedition unknown to
the Treasury, that he might have it time enough to
give a decisive turn to the election for the county.
The immediate consequence of this flagitious robbery was, that he lost the election, which you meant
to insure to him, and with such signal cirumstances
of scorn, reproach, and insult, (to say nothing of
the general exultation of all parties) as, (excepting the King's brother-in-law, Colonel Luttrell, and
old *Simon* his father-in-law) hardly ever fell upon a
gentleman in this country....In the event, he loses
the very property of which he thought he had
gotten possession ; and after an expense, which
would have paid the value of the land in question
twenty times over....The forms of villany, you see,
are necessary to its success. Hereafter you will
act with greater circumspection, and not drive so
directly to your object. To *snatch a grace*, beyond
the reach of common treachery, is an exception,
not a rule.

And now, my good Lord, does not your conscious heart inform you, that the justice of retribution begins to operate, and that it may soon approach your person?...Do you think that Junius
has renounced the Middlesex election?....or that
the King's timber shall be refused to the Royal
Navy with impunity?.....or that you shall hear no
more of the sale of that patent to *Mr. Hine*, which
you endeavoured to screen, by suddenly dropping
your prosecution of *Samuel Vaughan*, when the

rule against him was made absolute? I believe, indeed, there never was such an instance in all the history of negative impudence....But it shall not save you. The very sunshine you live in, is a prelude to your dissolution. When you are ripe, you shall be plucked.

JUNIUS.

P. S. I beg you will convey to our gracious master my humble congratulations upon the glorious success of peerages and pensions, so lavishly distributed as the rewards of Irish virtue.

LETTER LXVII.

TO LORD CHIEF JUSTICE MANSFIELD.

———

THIS is the threatened proof of the charge of illegality in the admitting of Eyre to bail. It attempts to evince ; that the superior power of the Court of King's Bench to bail, rests not upon positive law ; that in a case so clear as that of Eyre, there was no room for the discretion of the judges to act ; that, in all the circumstances of that case, no juridical authority known to the law of England could legally bail the culprit. There are infinite ingenuity and erudition in the argument. Valeat quantum valere potest. *The invective connected with it degenerates occasionally into vulgar abuse.*

21. *January*, 1772.

I HAVE undertaken to prove, that when, at the intercession of three of your countrymen, you bailed *John Eyre*, you did that, *which by law you were not warranted to do ;* and that a felon, under the circumstances, *of being taken in the fact, with the stolen goods upon him, and making no defence, is not bailable* by the laws of England. Your learned advocates have interpreted this charge into a denial that the Court of King's Bench, or the judges of that court during the vacation, have any greater authority to bail for criminal offences, than a justice of peace. With the instance before me, I am supposed to question your power of doing wrong, and to deny the existence of a power at the same moment that I arraign the illegal exercise of it. But the opinions of such men, whether

wilful in their malignity, or sincere in their ignorance, are unworthy of my notice. You, Lord
Mansfield, did not understand me so; and, I promise
you, your cause requires an abler defence.....I am
now to make good my charge against you. However dull my argument, the subject of it is interesting. I shall be honoured with the attention of
the public, and have a right to demand the attention
of the legislature. Supported, as I am, by the whole
body of the criminal law of England, I have no
doubt of establishing my charge. If, on your part,
you shall have no plain substantial defence, but
should endeavour to shelter yourself under the
quirk and evasion of a practising lawyer, or under
the mere, insulting assertion of power without right,
the reputation you pretend to is gone for ever; you
stand degraded from the respect and authority of
your office, and are no longer *de jure*, Lord Chief
Justice of England. This Letter, my Lord, is addressed, not so much to *you*, as to the public....
Learned as you are, and quick in apprehension,
few arguments are necessary to satisfy you, that
you have done that, which by law you were not
warranted to do. Your conscience already tells
you, that you have sinned against knowledge, and
that whatever defence you make contradicts your
own internal conviction. But other men are willing enough to take the law upon trust. They rely
upon your authority, because they are too indolent
to search for information; or, conceiving that there
is some mystery in the laws of their country, which

lawyers are only qualified to explain, they distrust their judgment, and voluntarily renounce the right of thinking for themselves. With all the evidence of history before them, from *Tresillian* to *Jefferies*, from *Jefferies* to *Mansfield*, they will not believe it possible that a learned judge can act in direct contradiction to those laws, which he is supposed to have made the study of his life, and which he has sworn to administer faithfully. Superstition is certainly not the characteristic of this age. Yet some men are bigotted in politics who are infidels in religion....I do not despair of making them ashamed of their credulity.

The charge I brought against you is expressed in terms guarded and well considered. They do not deny the strict power of the judges of the Court of King's Bench to bail in cases not bailable by a justice of peace, not replevisable by the common writ, or *ex officio* by the Sheriff. I well knew the practice of the court, and by what legal rules it ought to be directed. But, far from meaning to soften or diminish the force of those terms I have made use of, I now go beyond them, and affirm,

I. That the superior power of bailing for felony, claimed by the Court of King's Bench, is founded upon the opinion of lawyers, and the practice of the court....that the assent of the legislature to this

power is merely negative, and that it is not supported by any positive provision in any statute
whatsoever....If it be, produce the statute.

II. Admitting that the judges of the Court of
King's Bench are vested with a discretionary power
to examine and judge of circumstances and allegations, which a justice of peace is not permitted to
consider, I affirm, that the judges, in the use and
application of that discretionary power, are as
strictly bound by the spirit, intent, and meaning,
as the justice of peace is by the words of the legislature. Favourable circumstances, alledged before
the judge, may justify a doubt whether the prisoner
be guilty or not; and where the guilt is doubtful,
a presumption of innocence should, in general, be
admitted. But, when any such probable circumstances are alledged, they alter the state and condition of the prisoner. *He* is no longer that *all-but-
convicted* felon, whom the law intends, and who by
law is *not bailable at all.* If no circumstances whatsoever are alledged in his favour....if no allega-
tion whatsoever be made to lessen the force of that
evidence, which the law annexes to a positive
charge of felony, and particularly to the fact of
being taken with the maner, I then say that the
Lord Chief Justice of England has no more right
to bail him than a justice of peace. The discretion of an English judge is not of mere will and
pleasure; it is not arbitrary....it is not capricious;
but, as that great lawyer, (whose authority I wish

you respected half as much as I do) truly says,* " Discretion, taken as it ought to be, is, *discernere* " *per legem quid sit justum.* If it be not directed " by the right line of the law, it is a crooked cord, " and appeareth to be unlawful.".......If discretion were arbitrary in the judge, he might introduce whatever novelties, he thought proper ; but, says Lord Coke, " Novelties, without warrant of pre- " cedents, are not to be allowed; some certain " rules are to be followed....*Quidquid judicis autho-* " *ritati subjicitur, novitati non subjicitur ;*" and this sound doctrine is applied to the Star-chamber, a court confessedly arbitrary. If you will abide by the authority of this great man, you shall have all the advantage of his opinion, wherever it appears to favour you. Excepting the plain, express meaning of the legislature, to which all private opinions must give way, I desire no better judge between us than Lord Coke.

III. I affirm that, according to the obvious, indisputable meaning of the legislature, repeatedly expressed, a person positively charged with *feloniously stealing*, and taken *in flagrante delicto*, with the stolen goods upon him, is *not bailable*. The law considers him as differing in nothing from *a convict*, but in the form of conviction, and (whatever a corrupt judge may do) will accept of no security, but the confinement of his body within

---

* 4 Inst. 41. 66.

four walls. I know it has been alledged in your
favour, that you have often bailed for murders,
rapes, and other manifest crimes. Without ques-
tioning the fact, I shall not admit that you are to be
justified by your own example. If that were a
protection to you, where is the crime that, as a judge,
you might not now securely commit? But neither
shall I suffer myself to be drawn aside from my
present argument, nor *you* to profit by your own
wrong....To prove the meaning and intent of the
legislature will require a minute and tedious de-
duction. To investigate a question of law demands some labour and attention, though very little
genius ' · sagacity. As a practical profession, the
study of the law requires but a moderate portion
of abilities. The learning of a pleader is usually
upon a level with his integrity. The indiscriminate
defence of right and wrong contracts the understanding, while it corrupts the heart. Subtlety is
soon mistaken for wisdom, and impunity for virtue.
If there be any instances upon record, as some there
are undoubtedly, of genius and morality united in
a lawyer, they are distinguished by their singularity, and operate as exceptions.

I must solicit the patience of my readers. This
is no light matter; nor is it any more susceptible
of ornament, than the conduct of Lord Mansfield is
capable of aggravation.

As the law of bail in charges of felony, has been
exactly ascertained by acts of the legislature, it is

at present of little consequence to enquire how it stood at common law before the statute of Westminster. And yet it is worth the reader's attention to observe, how nearly, in the ideas of our ancestors, the circumstance of being taken *with the maner* approached to the conviction of the felon*. It " fixed the authoritative stamp of verisimilitude " upon the accusation, and by the common law, " when a thief was taken *with the maner* (that is, " with the things stolen upon him, *in manu)* he " might, so detected *flagrante delicto*, be brought " into court, arraigned and tried, *without indict-* " *ment;* as by the Danish law, he might be taken " and hanged upon the spot, without accusation or " trial." It will soon appear that our statute law, in this behalf, though less summary in point of proceeding, is directed by the same spirit. In one instance, the very form is adhered to. In offences relating to the forest, if a man was taken with vert, or venison†, it was declared to be equivalent to indictment. To enable the reader to judge for himself, I shall state, in due order, the several statutes relative to bail in criminal cases, or as much of them as may be material to the point in question, omitting superfluous words. If I misrepresent, or do not quote with fidelity, it will not be difficult to detect me.

* Blackstone, 4. 303.

† 1 Ed. III. cap. 8. and 7 Rich. II. cap. 4.

* The statute of Westminster the first, in 1275, sets forth that, " Forasmuch as Sheriffs and others, " who have taken and kept in prison persons de- " tected of felony, and incontinent have let out by " replevin such as were *not replevisable*, because " they would gain of the one party and grieve the " other; and, forasmuch as, before this time, it " was not determined which persons were replevi- " sable and which not, it is provided and by the " King commanded that such prisoners, &c. as be " *taken with the maner*, &c. or for *manifest* offences, " shall be *in no wise* replevisable by the common " writ, nor without writ." †....Lord Coke, in his exposition of the last part of this quotation, accu- rately distinguishes between *replevy* by the common writ or *ex officio*, and *bail* by the King's Bench. The words of the statute certainly do not extend to the judges of that court. But, besides that the reader will soon find reason to think that the legis- lature in their intention, made no difference between *bailable* and *replevisable*, Lord Coke himself (if he be understood to mean nothing but an exposi-

---

* " *Videtur que le statute de mainprise nest que rehersall del* " *comen ley.*" Bro. Mainp. 61.

† " There are three points to be considered in the construction " of all remedial statutes......the old law, the mischief, and the " remedy.....that is, how the common law stood at the making of " the act, what the mischief was for which the common law did not " provide, and what remedy the parliament hath provided to cure " this mischief. It is the business of the judges so to construe the " act, as to suppress the mischief and advance the remedy." *Blackstone,* 1. 87.

tion of the statute of Westminster, and not to
state the law generally) does not adhere to his own
distinction. In expounding the other offences
which, by this statute, are declared not *replevisable*,
he constantly uses the words *not bailable*......" That
" outlaws, for instance, are *not bailable at all*......
" that persons, who have abjured the realm, are
" attainted upon their own confession, and there-
" fore *not bailable at all by law*.....that provers are
" not *bailable*....that notorious felons are not *bail-*
" *able*." The reason, why the superior courts were
not named in the statute of Westminster, was
plainly this, " because anciently most of the busi-
" ness, touching bailment of prisoners for felony
" or misdemeanors, was performed by the Sheriffs,
" or special bailiffs of liberties, either by writ, or
" *virtute officii**;" consequently the superior courts
had little or no opportunity to commit those abuses,
which the statute imputes to the Sheriffs.....With
submission to Dr. Blackstone, I think he has fallen
into a contradiction, which, in terms at least, appears irreconcileable. After enumerating several
offences not bailable, he asserts, without any condition or limitation whatsoever†, " all these are
" clearly not admissible to bail." Yet in a few
lines after he says, " *it is agreed* that the Court of
" King's Bench may bail for any crime whatsoever,
" *according to circumstances of* the case." To his

* Hale, P. C. 128, 136.

† Blackstone, 4, 296.

first proposition he should have added, *by Sheriffs or Justices;* otherwise the two propositions contradict each other; with this difference however, that the first is absolute, the second limited by *a consideration of circumstances.* I say this without the least intended disrespect to the learned author. His work is of public utility, and should not hastily be condemned.

The statute of 17 Richard II. cap. 10. 1393, sets forth, that " forasmuch as thieves notoriously de-
" famed, *and others taken with the maner,* by their
" long abiding in prison, were delivered by char-
" ters, and favourable inquests procured, to the
" great hindrance of the people, two men of law
" shall be assigned, in every commission of the
" peace, to proceed to the deliverance of such
" felons," &c. It seems by this act, that there was a constant struggle between the legislature and the officers of justice. Not daring to admit felons *taken with the maner* to bail or mainprize, they evaded the law by keeping the party in prison a long time, and then delivering him without due trial.

The statute of 1 Richard III. in 1483, sets forth, that, " forasmuch as divers persons have been daily
" arrested and imprisoned for *suspicion* of felony,
" sometime of malice, and sometime of *a light*
" *suspicion,* and so kept in prison without bail or
" mainprize, be it ordained, that every justice of
" peace shall have authority, by his discretion, to

" let such prisoners and persons so arrested to bail
" or mainprize."....By this act it appears, that there
had been abuses in matter of imprisonment, and
that the legislature meant to provide for the immediate enlargement of persons arrested on *light suspicion* of felony.

The statute of 3 Henry VII. in 1486, declares,
that " under colour of the preceding act of
" Richard the Third, persons, *such as were not
" mainpernable*, were oftentimes let to bail or main-
" prize, by justices of the peace, whereby many
" murderers and felons escaped, the King, &c.
" hath ordained, that the justices of the peace, or
" two of them at least (whereof one to be of the
" *quorum)* have authority to let any such prisoners
" or persons, mainpernable by the law, to bail or
" mainprize. "

The statute of 1st and 2d of Philip and Mary, in
1554, sets forth, that " notwithstanding the pre-
" ceding statute of Henry the Seventh, *one* justice
" of peace hath oftentimes, by sinister labour and
" means, set at large the greatest and notablest
" offenders, *such as be not replevisable by the laws of
" this realm.* and yet, the rather to hide their affec-
" tions in that behalf, have signed the cause of
" their apprehension to be but only for *suspicion* of
" felony, whereby the said offenders have escaped
" unpunished, and do daily, to the high displeasure
" of Almighty God, the great peril of the King

" and Queen's true subjects, and encouragement
" of all thieves and evil-doers.....for reformation
" whereof be it enacted, that no justices of peace
" shall let to bail or mainprize any such persons,
" which, for any offence by them committed, be
" declared *not* to be *replevised*, or *bailed*, or be for-
" bidden to be *replevised* or *bailed* by the statute of
" Westminster the first; and furthermore that any
" persons, arrested for manslaughter or felony, *be-*
" *ing bailable by the law*, shall not be let to bail
" or mainprize, by any justices of peace, but in the
" form therein after prescribed."....In the two preceding statutes, the words *bailable*, *replevisable*, and
mainpernable, are used synonymously*, or promis-
cuously, to express the same single intention of the
legislature, viz. *not to accept of any security but the
body of the offender ;* and when the latter statute
prescribes the form, in which persons arrested on
suspicion of felony *(being bailable by the law)* may
be let to bail, it evidently supposes that there are
some cases, *not* bailable by the law....It may be
thought perhaps, that I attribute to the legislature
an appearance of inaccuracy in the use of terms,
merely to serve my present purpose. But, in truth,
it would make more forcibly for my argument, to
presume that the legislature were constantly aware
of the strict legal distinction between *bail* and
replevy, and that they always meant to adhere to it†.

* 2 Hale, P. C. 2, 124.

† Vide 2d Inst. 150, 186...." The word *replevisable* never signi-
" fies *bailable*. *Bailable*, is in a court of record by the King's jus-
" tices; but *replevisable* is by the Sheriff." *Selden*, St. Tr. 7. 149.

For if it be true that *replevy* is by the Sheriffs, and *bail* by the higher courts at Westminster, (which I think no lawyer will deny) it follows that, when the legislature expressly say, that any particular offence is by law *not bailable*, the superior courts are comprehended in the prohibition, and bound by it..... Otherwise, unless there was a positive exception of the superior courts (which I affirm there never was in any statute relative to bail) the legislature would grossly contradict themselves, and the manifest intention of the law be evaded. It is an established rule that, when the law is *special*, and reason of it general, it is to be *generally* understood; and though, by custom, a latitude be allowed to the Court of King's Bench, (to consider circumstances inductive of a doubt whether the prisoner be guilty or innocent) if this latitude be taken as an arbitrary power to bail, when no circumstances whatsoever are alledged in favour of the prisoner, it is a power without right, and a daring violation of the whole English law of bail.

The act of the 31st of Charles the Second (commonly called the *Habeas Corpus Act)* particularly declares, that it is not meant to extend to treason or felony plainly and specially expressed in the warrant of commitment. The prisoner is therefore left to seek his *Habeas Corpus* at common law; and so far was the legislature from supposing that persons, (committed for treason or felony plainly and specially expressed in the warrant of commitment) could be let to bail by a single judge, or by the whole court, that this very act provides a remedy for such persons in case they are not indicted in the course of the term or session subsequent to their commitment. The law neither suffers them to be enlarged before trial, nor to be imprisoned after the time in which they ought regularly to be tried. In this case the law says, " It shall and may " be lawful to and for the judges of the Court of " King's Bench, and justices of oyer and terminer, " or general gaol delivery, and they are hereby re- " quired, upon motion to them made in open court, " the last day of the term, session, or gaol delivery, " either by the prisoner or any one in his behalf, " to set at liberty the prisoner upon bail; unless it " appear to the judges and justices, upon oath " made, that the witnesses for the King could not " be produced the same term, sessions, or gaol de- " livery. "....Upon the whole of this article I ob- serve, 1. That the provision, made in the first part of it, would be, in a great measure, useless and nugatory, if any single judge might have bailed the prisoner *ex arbitrio*, during the vacation; or if the court might have bailed him immediately after the commencement of the term or sessions....... 2. When the law says...:*It shall and may be lawful* to bail for felony under particular circumstances, we must presume that, before the passing of that act, it was *not* lawful to bail under those circum- stances. The terms used by the legislature are *enacting*, not *declaratory*.....3. Notwithstanding the party may have been imprisoned during the greatest part of the vacation, and during the whole session, the court are expressly forbidden to bail him from that session to the next, if oath be made that the witnesses for the King could not be produced that same term or sessions.

Having faithfully stated the several acts of par. liament relative to bail in criminal cases, it may be useful to the reader to take a short historical review of the law of bail, through its various gradations and improvements.

By the ancient common law, before and since the conquest, all felonies were bailable, till murder was excepted by statute; so that persons might be admitted to bail, before conviction, almost in every case. The statute of Westminster says that, before that time, it had not been determined, which offences were replevisable, and which were not, whether by the common writ *de homine replegiando*, or *ex officio* by the Sheriff. It is very remarkable that the abuses arising from this unlimited power of replevy, dreadful as they were, and destructive to the peace of society, were not corrected or taken notice of by the legislature, until the commons of the kingdom had obtained a share in it by their representatives; but the House of Commons had scarce begun to exist, when these formidable abuses were corrected by the statute of Westminster. It is highly pro- bable that the mischief had been severely felt by the people, although no remedy had been provided for it by the Norman Kings or Barons. * " The " iniquity of the times was so great, as it even " forced the subjects to forego that, which was in " account a great liberty, to stop the course of a " growing mischief." The preamble to the statutes, made by the first parliament of Edward the First, assigns the reason of calling it †, " because " the people had been otherwise entreated than " they ought to be, the peace less kept, the laws " less used, and *offenders less punished* than they " ought to be, by reason whereof the people feared " less to offend;" and the first attempt to reform these various abuses was by contracting the power of replevying felons.

For above two centuries following, it does not appear that any alteration was made in the law of bail, except that *being taken with vert or venison* was declared to be equivalent to indictment. The legislature adhered firmly to the spirit of the statute of Westminster. The statute of 27th of Edward the First, directs the justices of assize to enquire and punish officers bailing such as were *not bailable*. As for the judges of the superior courts it is probable that, in those days, they thought themselves bound by the obvious intent and meaning of the legislature. They considered not so

* *Selden*, by *N. Bacon*. 182.
† Parliamentary History. 1, 82.

much to what particular persons the prohibition
was addressed, as what the *thing* was, which the
legislature meant to prohibit, well knowing that
in law, *quando aliquid prohibetur, prohibetur et
omne, per quod devenitur ad illud.* " When any
" thing is forbidden, all the means, by which the
" same thing may be compassed or done, are
" equally forbidden."

By the statute of Richard the Third, the power
of bailing was a little enlarged. Every justice of
peace was authorised to bail for felony; but they
were expressly confined to persons arrested *on light
suspicion;* and even this power, so limited, was
found to produce such inconveniences that, in three
years after, the legislature found it necessary to repeal it. Instead of trusting any longer to a single
justice of peace, the act of 3d. Henry VIIth, re-
peals the preceding act, and directs, " that no
" prisoner, *(of those who are mainpernable by the
" law)* shall be let to bail or mainprise, by less than
" *two* justices, whereof one to be of the quorum."
And so indispensably necessary was this provision
thought, for the administration of justice, and for
the security and peace of society, that, at this
time, an oath was proposed by the King to be
taken by the knights and esquires of his household,
by the members of the House of Commons, and
by the peers spiritual and temporal, and accepted
and sworn to *quasi una voce* by them all, which,
among other engagements, binds them " not to let

" any man to bail or mainprise, knowing and
" deeming him to be a felon, upon your honour
" and worship. So help you God and all saints.*"

In about half a century, however, even these pro-
visions were found insufficient. The act of Henry
the Seventh was evaded, and the legislature once
more obliged to interpose. The act of 1st and 2d
of Philip and Mary takes away entirely from the
justices all power of bailing for offences declared
not bailable by the statute of Westminster.

The illegal imprisonment of several persons,
who had refused to contribute to a loan exacted by
Charles the First, and the delay of the *Habeas
Corpus*, and subsequent refusal to bail them, constituted one of the first and most important grievances of that reign. Yet when the House of Commons, which met in the year 1628, resolved upon
measures of the most firm and strenuous resistance
to the power of imprisonment assumed by the
King or privy-council, and to the refusal to bail the
party on the return of the *Habeas Corpus*, they did
expressly, in all their resolutions, make an exception of commitments, where the cause of the restraint was expressed, and did by law justify the
commitment. The reason of the distinction is,
that, whereas when the cause of commitment is
expressed, the crime is then known and the offender

* Parliamentary History. 2. 419.

must be brought to the ordinary trial; if, on the contrary, no cause of commitment be expressed, and the prisoner be thereupon remanded, it may operate to perpetual imprisonment. This contest with Charles the First produced the act of the 16th of that King, by which the Court of King's Bench are directed, within three days after the return to the *Habeas Corpus*, to examine and determine the legality of any commitment by the King or privy-council, and to do *what to justice shall appertain* in delivering, bailing, or *remanding* the prisoner..... *Now*, it seems, it is unnecessary for the judge to do what appertains to justice. The same scandalous traffic, in which we have seen the privilege of parliament exerted or relaxed, to gratify the present humour, or to serve the immediate purpose of the crown, is introduced into the administration of justice. The magistrate, it seems, has now no rule to follow, but the dictates of personal enmity, national partiality, or perhaps the most prostituted corruption.

To complete this historical inquiry, it only remains to be observed that, the *Habeas Corpus* act of 31st of Charles the Second, so justly considered as another Magna Charta of the Kingdom *, " ex-
" tends only to the case of commitments for such
" criminal charge, as can produce no inconveni-
" ence to public justice by a temporary enlarge-

---

* Blackstone. 4. 137.

" ment of the prisoner."....So careful were the legislature, at the very moment when they were providing for the liberty of the subject, not to furnish any colour or pretence for violating or evading the established law of bail in the higher criminal offences. But the exception, stated in the body of the act, puts the matter out of all doubt. After directing the judges how they are to proceed to the discharge of the prisoner upon recognizance and surety, having regard to the quality of the prisoner and nature of the offence, it is expressly added, " unless it shall appear to the said Lord " Chancellor, &c. that the party, so committed, is " detained for such matters, or offences, for the " which, BY THE LAW THE PRISONER IS NOT " BAILABLE."

When the laws, plain of themselves, are thus illustrated by facts, and their uniform meaning established by history, we do not want the authority of opinions however respectable, to inform our judgment or to confirm our belief. But I am determined that you shall have no escape. Authority of every sort shall be produced against you, from *Jacob* to *Lord Coke*, from the dictionary to the classic......In vain shall you appeal from those upright judges, whom you disdain to imitate, to those whom you have made your example. With one voice, they all condemn you.

" To be taken with the *maner*, is where a thief, " having stolen any thing, is taken with the same

" about him, as it were in his hands, which is
" called *flagrante delicto.* Such a criminal is *not*
" *bailable by law.*"....*Jacob under the word Maner.*

" Those who are taken with the *Maner*, are ex-
" cluded, by the statute of Westminster, from the
" benefit of a replevin....*Hawkins. P. C.* 2. 98.

" Of such heinous offences no one, who is no-
" toriously guilty, seems to be *bailable* by the in-
" tent of this statute."....*D°.* 2. 99.

" The common practice, and allowed general
" rule is, that bail is only then proper where it
" stands *indifferent* whether the party were guilty
" or innocent.".....*D°. D°.*

" There is no doubt but that the bailing of a
" person, *who is not bailable by law*, is punishable,
" either at common law, as a negligent escape, or
" as an offence against the several statutes relative
" to bail."...*D°.* 89.

" It cannot be doubted but that, neither the
" judges of this, nor of any other superior court of
" justice, are strictly within the purview of that
" statute, yet they will always, in their discretion,
" pay a due regard to it, and not admit a person to
" bail who is expressly declared by it irreplevi-
" sable, *without some particular circumstance in his*
" *favour ;* and therefore it seems difficult to find an

" instance, where persons, attainted of felony, or
" notoriously guilty of treason or manslaughter,
" &c. by their own confession, or *otherwise*, have
" been admitted to the benefit of bail, without
" some special motive to the court to grant it."....
D°. 114.

. " If it appears that any man hath injury or
" wrong by his imprisonment, we have power to
" deliver and discharge him.....if otherwise, *he is*
" *to be remanded* by us to prison again."....*Lord Ch.*
J. Hyde. State Trials, 7, 115.

" The statute of Westminster was especially
" for direction to the sheriffs and others, but to
" say courts of justice are excluded from this sta-
" tute, I conceive it cannot be. "....*Attorney Gene-*
ral Heath. D°. 132.

" The court, upon view of the return, judgeth
" of the sufficiency or insufficiency of it. If they
" think the prisoner *in law to be bailable*, he is
" committed to the Marshal and bailed; if not,
" he is remanded. "....Through the whole debate
the objection, on the part of the prisoners, was, that
no cause of commitment was expressed in the warrant; but it was uniformly admitted by their counsel that, if the cause of commitment had been
expressed for treason or felony, the court would
then have done right in remanding them.

The Attorney General having urged, before a committee of both houses, that, in Beckwith's case and others, the lords of the council sent a letter to the Court of King's Bench to bail; it was replied by the managers of the House of Commons, that this was of no moment, " for that either the pri-
" soner was *bailable by the law*, or *not bailable*....if
" bailable by the law, then he was to be bailed
" without any such letter....if not bailable by the
" law, then plainly the judges could not have
" bailed him upon the letter, without breach of
" their oath, which is, *that they are to do justice*
" *according to the law, &c.*"....*State Trials.* 7. 175.

" So that, in bailing upon such offences of the
" highest nature, a kind of discretion, rather than
" a constant law, hath been exercised, when it
" stands *wholly indifferent* in the eye of the court,
" whether the prisoner be guilty or not." *Selden.*
St. Tr. 7. 230. 1.

" I deny that a man is always bailable, when
" imprisonment is imposed upon him for custody."
" *Attorney General Heath. d°.* 238....By these quotations from the State Trials, though otherwise
not of authority, it appears plainly that, in regard
to bailable or *not bailable*, all parties agreed in admitting one proposition as incontrovertible.

" In relation to capital offences, there are espe-
" cially these acts of parliament that are the com-

" mon *landmarks** touching offences bailable or not
" bailable." *Hale.* 2 *P. C.* 127. The enumeration includes the several acts cited in this paper.

" Persons taken with the *Manouvre*, are not
" bailable, because it is *furtum manifestum.*" *Hale.*
2 *P. C.* 133.

" The writ of *Habeas Corpus* is of high nature;
" for if persons be wrongfully committed, they are
" to be discharged upon this writ returned; or, if
" bailable, they are to be bailed.....*if not bailable,*
" *they are to be committed.*" *Hale.* 2 *P. C.* 143. This
doctrine of Lord Chief Justice Hale refers immediately to the superior courts from whence the writ
issues......" After the return is filed, the court is
" either to discharge, or bail, or *commit* him, as the
" nature of the cause requires." *Hale.* 2 *P. C.* 146.

" If bail be granted, *otherwise than the law*
" *alloweth*, the party that alloweth the same, shall
" be fined, imprisoned, render damages, or forfeit
" his place, as the case shall require." *Selden by*
N. Bacon, 182.

" This induces an absolute necessity of express-
" ing, upon every commitment, the reason, for
" which it is made : that the court, upon a *Habeas*
" *Corpus*, may examine into its validity, and, *ac-*

---

* It has been the study of Lord Mansfield to remove landmarks.

" *cording to the circumstances of the case*, may dis-
" charge, admit to bail, or *remand* the prisoner."
Blackstone. 3, 133.

" Marriot was committed for forging indorse-
" ments upon bank bills, and upon a *Habeas Cor-*
" *pus*, was bailed, because the crime was only a
" great misdemeanor.....for though the forging the
" bills be felony, yet forging the indorsement is
" not." *Salkeld.* 1. 104.

" Appell de Mahem, &c. ideo ne fuit lesse a
" baille, nient plus que in appell de robbery ou
" murder; quod nota, et que in robry et murder
" le partie n'est baillable." *Bro. Mainprise*, 67.

" The intendment of the law in bails is, *quod*
" *stat indifferenter* whether he be guilty or no; but,
" when he is convict by verdict or confession, then
" he must be deemed in law to be guilty of the
" felony, and therefore *not bailable at all.*" *Coke.*
2 *Inst.* 188....4. 178.

" Bail is *quãdo stat indifferenter*, and *not* when
" the offence is open and manifest." 2 *Inst.* 189.

" In this case *non stat indifferenter* whether he
" be guilty or no, being taken with the *Maner*, that
" is, with the thing stolen, as it were in his hand."
D°. D°.

" If it appeareth that this imprisonment be just
" and lawful, he *shall be remanded* to the former
" gaoler; but, if it shall appear to the court that
" he was imprisoned against the law of the land,
" they ought, by force of this statute, to deliver
" him; if it be *doubtful,* and under consideration,
" he may be bailed. " 2 *Inst.* 55.

It is unnecessary to load the reader with any
farther quotations. If these authorities are not
deemed sufficient to establish the doctrine maintained in this paper, it will be in vain to appeal to
the evidence of law-books, or to the opinions of
judges. They are not the authorities by which
Lord Mansfield will abide. He assumes an arbitrary power of doing right; and if he does wrong,
it lies only between God and his conscience.

Now, my Lord, although I have great faith in
the preceding argument, I will not say that every
minute part of it is absolutely invulnerable. I am
too well acquainted with the practice of a certain
court, directed by your example, as it is governed
by your authority, to think there ever yet was an
argument, however conformable to law and reason,
in which a cunning, quibbling attorney, might not
discover a flaw. But, taking the whole of it together, I affirm, that it constitutes a mass of demonstration, than which nothing more compleat or
satisfactory can be offered to the human mind.....
How an evasive, indirect reply, will stand with your

reputation, or how far it will answer in point of defence at the bar of the House of Lords, is worth
your consideration. If, after all that has been said,
it should still be maintained, that the Court of
King's Bench, in bailing felons, are exempted from
all legal rules whatsoever, and that the judge has
no direction to pursue, but his private affections, or
more unquestionable will and pleasure, it will follow plainly, that the distinction between *bailable*
and *not bailable*, uniformly expressed by the legislature, current through all our law books, and
admitted by all our great lawyers without exception, is in one sense a nugatory, in another a pernicious distinction. It is nugatory, as it supposes a
difference in the bailable quality of offences, when,
in effect, the distinction refers only to the rank of
the magistrate. It is pernicious, as it implies a
rule of law, which yet the judge is not bound to
pay the least regard to, and impresses an idea upon
the minds of the people, that the judge is wiser
and greater than the law.

It remains only to apply the law, thus stated,
to the fact in question. By an authentic copy
of the *mittimus* it appears that John Eyre was
committed for felony, plainly and specially expressed in the warrant of commitment. He was
charged before Alderman Halifax by the oath
of Thomas Fielding, William Holder, William
Payne, and William Nash, for *feloniously stealing* eleven quires of writing paper, value six

shillings, the property of Thomas Beach, &c....
by the examinations, upon oath, of the four persons mentioned in the *mittimus*, it was proved,
that large quantities of paper had been missed,
and that eleven quires (previously marked from
a suspicion that Eyre was the thief) were found
upon him.· Many other quires of paper, marked
in the same manner, were found at his lodg-
ings; and after he had been some time in Wood-
Street Compter, a key was found in his room
there, which appeared to be a key to the closet at
Guildhall, from whence the paper was stolen......
When asked what he had to say in his defence, his
only answer was, *I hope you will bail me.* Mr.
Holder, the Clerk, replied, *That is impossible.....*
There never was an instance of it, when the stolen
Goods were found upon the thief. The Lord Mayor
was then applied to, and refused to bail him.....Of
all these circumstances it was your duty to have
informed yourself minutely. The fact was remarkable, and the chief magistrate of the city of London was known to have refused to bail the offender.
To justify your compliance with the solicitations of
your three countrymen, it should be proved that
such allegations were offered to you in behalf of
their associate, as honestly and *bona fide* reduced it
to a matter of doubt and indifference whether the
prisoner was innocent or guilty......Was any thing
offered by the Scotch triumvirate that tended to invalidate the positive charge made against him by
four credible witnesses upon oath ?....Was it even

insinuated to you, either by himself or his bail, that no felony was committed....or that *he* was not the felon....that the stolen goods were *not* found upon him....or that he was only the receiver, not knowing them to be stolen?....Or, in short, did they attempt to produce any evidence of his insanity?... To all these questions, I answer for you, without the least fear of contradiction, positively NO. From the moment he was arrested, he never entertained any hope of acquittal; therefore thought of nothing but obtaining bail, that he might have time to settle his affairs, convey his fortune into another country, and spend the remainder of his life in comfort and affluence abroad. In this prudential scheme of future happiness, the Lord Chief Justice of England most readily and heartily concurred. At sight of so much virtue in distress, your natural benevolence took the alarm. Such a man as Mr. Eyre, struggling with adversity, must always be an interesting scene to Lord Mansfield....Or was it that liberal anxiety, by which your whole life has been distinguished, to enlarge the liberty of the subject?....My Lord, we did not want this new instance of the liberality of your principles. We already knew what kind of subjects they were, for whose liberty you were anxious. At all events, the public are much indebted to you for fixing a price at which felony may be committed with impunity. You bound a felon, notoriously worth thirty thousand pounds, in the sum of three hundred. With your natural turn to equity, and knowing, as you are, in the doctrine of precedents, you undoubtedly meant to settle the proportion between the fortune of the felon and the fine by which he may compound for his felony. The ratio now upon record, and transmitted to posterity under the auspices of Lord Mansfield, is exactly one to a hundred. ....My Lord, without intending it, you have laid a cruel restraint upon the genius of your countrymen. In the warmest indulgence of their passions they have an eye to the expense, and if their other virtues fail us, we have a resource in their œconomy.

By taking so trifling a security from John Eyre, you invited and manifestly exhorted him to escape. Although in bailable cases, it be usual to take four securities, you left him in the custody of three Scotchmen, whom he might have easily satisfied for conniving at his retreat. That he did not make use of the opportunity you industriously gave him neither justifies your conduct, nor can it be any way accounted for, but by his excessive and monstrous avarice. Any other man, but this bosom-friend of three Scotchmen, would gladly have sacrificed a few hundred pounds, rather than to submit to the infamy of pleading guilty in open court. It is possible indeed that he might have flattered himself, and not unreasonably, with the hopes of a pardon. That he would have been pardoned seems more than probable, if I had not directed the public attention to the leading step you took in favour of him. In the present gentle reign, we well know what use has been made of the lenity of the court and of the mercy of the crown. The Lord Chief Justice of England accepts of the hundreth part of the property of a felon taken in the fact, as a recognizance for his appearance. Your brother *Smythe* brow-beats a jury, and forces them to alter their verdict, by which they had found a Scotch serjeant guilty of murder; and though the Kennedies were convicted of a most deliberate and atrocious murder, they still had a claim to the royal mercy.....They were saved by the chastity of their connexions.....They had a sister......yet it was not her beauty, but the pliancy of her virtue, that recommended her to the King....The holy author of our religion was seen in the company of sinners; but it was his gracious purpose to convert them from their sins. Another man, who in the ceremonies of our faith might give lessons to the great enemy of it, upon different principles keeps much the same company. He advertises for patients, collects all the diseases of the heart, and turns a royal palace into an hospital for incurables......A man of honour has no ticket of admission at St. James's. They receive him, like a virgin at the Magdalen's....*Go thou and do likewise.*

My charge against you is now made good. I shall however be ready to answer or to submit to fair objections. If, whenever this matter shall be agitated, you suffer the doors of the House of Lords to be shut, I now protest, that I shall consider you as having made no reply. From that moment, in the opinion of the world, you will stand self-convicted. Whether your reply be quibbling and evasive, or liberal and in point, will be matter for the judgment of your peers....but if, when every possible idea of disrespect to that noble house, (in whose honour and justice the nation implicitly confides) is here most solemnly disclaimed, you should endeavour to represent this charge as a contempt of their authority, and move their lordships to censure the publisher of this paper, I then affirm that you support injustice by violence, that you are guilty of a heinous aggravation of your offence, and that you contribute your utmost influence to promote, on the part of the highest court of judicature, a positive denial of justice to the nation.

JUNIUS.

LETTER LXVIII.

TO THE RIGHT HONOURABLE LORD CAMDEN.

———

LORD Camden stood in rivalship to the Earl of Mansfield. He had threatened him in the last session of Parliament. But Lord Mansfield dexterously eluded every attempt to draw him into any open and lengthened contention relative to his principles of decision. Hopes were entertained, that another session of Parliament might see the contest renewed, and Lord Mansfield. It was with a view to this, that JUNIUS so laboriously resumed his attack against the Chief Justice. In this Letter, he calls on Lord Camden almost with threats, and with reproach, to make the bailing of Eyre, the subject of a new motion against Lord Mansfield in the House of Peers. The call was fruitless.

This Letter ends the Series. The probable reasons of it's termination here, are explained in another place.

———

MY LORD,

I TURN with pleasure, from that barren waste, in which no salutary plant takes root, no verdure quickens, to a character fertile, as I willingly believe, in every great and good qualification. I call upon you, in the name of the English nation, to stand forth in defence of the laws of your country, and to exert, in the cause of truth and justice, those great abilities, with which you were entrusted for the benefit of mankind. To ascertain the facts set forth in the preceding paper, it may be necessary to call the persons, mentioned in the *mitti-*

mus, to the bar of the House of Lords. If a motion for that purpose should be rejected, we shall know what to think of Lord Mansfield's innocence. The legal argument is submitted to your lordship's judgment. After the noble stand you made against Lord Mansfield upon the question of libel, we did expect that you would not have suffered that matter to have remained undetermined. But it was said that Lord Chief Justice Wilmot had been *prevailed upon* to vouch for an opinion of the late Judge Yates, which was supposed to make against you; and we admit of the excuse. When such detestable arts are employed to prejudge a question of right, it might have been imprudent, at that time, to have brought it to a decision. In the present instance you will have no such opposition to contend with. If there be a judge, or a lawyer of any note in Westminster-hall, who shall be daring enough to affirm that, according to the true intendment of the laws of England, a felon, taken with the *Maner*, *in flagranti delicto*, is bailable; or that the discretion of an English judge is merely arbitrary, and not governed by rules of law.....I should be glad to be acquainted with him. Whoever he be, I will take care that he shall not give you much trouble. Your lordship's character assures me that you will assume that principal part, which belongs to you, in supporting the laws of England, against a wicked judge, who makes it the occupation of his life, to misinterpret and pervert them. If you decline this honourable office, I fear it will be said that, for some months past, you have kept too much company with the Duke of Grafton. When the contest turns upon the interpretation of the laws, you cannot, without a formal surrender of all your reputation, yield the post of honour even to Lord Chatham. Considering the situation and abilities of Lord Mansfield, I do not scruple to affirm, with the most solemn appeal to God for my sincerity, that, in *my* judgment, he is the very worst and most dangerous man in the kingdom. Thus far I have done my duty in endeavouring to bring him to punishment. But mine is an inferior, ministerial office, in the temple of justice. I have bound the victim, and dragged him to the altar.

JUNIUS.

SUPPLEMENT.

THE following Extract from a Letter, which JUNIUS *did not choose to preserve entire, contains his doct; ine concerning the Reform of Parliament. It is that of a Lawyer, and a true friend to the fundamental principles of the Constitution, not of a democratical* enrage'.

THE Reverend Mr. John Horne having, with his usual veracity and honest industry, circulated a report that JUNIUS, in a Letter to the Supporters of the Bill of Rights, had warmly declared himself in favour of long parliaments and rotten boroughs, it is thought necessary to submit to the public the following Extract from his Letter to John Wilkes, Esq. dated the 7th of Sept. 1771, and laid before the Society on the 24th of the same month.

" With regard to the several articles, taken se-
" parately, I own I am concerned to see that the
" great condition, which ought to be the *sine qua*
" *non* of parliamentary qualification.....which ought
" to be the basis (as it assuredly will be the only
" support) of every barrier raised in defence of the
" constitution, *I mean a declaration upon oath to*
" *shorten the duration of parliaments*, is reduced to
" the fourth rank in the esteem of the society;
" and, even in that place, far from being insisted

" on with firmness and vehemence, seems to have
" been particularly slighted in the expression....
" *You shall endeavour to restore annual parliaments!*
" ....Are these the terms, which men, who are in
" earnest, make use of, when the *salus reipublicæ* is
" at stake?....I expected other language from Mr.
" Wilkes....Besides my objection in point of form, ‗
" I dissapprove highly of the meaning of the fourth
" article as it stands. Whenever the question
" shall be seriously agitated, I will endeavour (and
" If I live will assuredly attempt it) to convince the
" English nation, by arguments to *my* understand-
" ing unanswerable, that they ought to insist upon
" a triennial, and banish the idea of an annual
" parliament. . . . . I am convinced that,
" if shortening the duration of parliaments (which
" in effect is keeping the representative under the
" rod of the constituent) be not made the basis of
" our new parliamentary jurisprudence, other
" checks or improvements signify nothing. On
" the contrary, if this be made the foundation,
" other measures may come in aid, and as auxili-
" aries, be of considerable advantage. Lord Chat-
" ham's project, for instance, of increasing the
" number of knights of shires, appears to me ad-
" mirable. . . . . . . As to cutting away the rotten
" boroughs, I am as much offended as any man at
" seeing so many of them under the direct influ-
" ence of the crown, or at the disposal of private
" persons. Yet, I own, I have both doubts and
" apprehensions, in regard to the remedy you pro-

" pose. I shall be charged, perhaps, with an usual
" want of political intrepidity, when I honestly
" confess to you, that I am startled at the idea of
" so extensive an amputation....In the first place,
" I question the power, *de jure*, of the legislature to
" disfranchise a number of boroughs, upon the ge-
" neral ground of improving the constitution.
" There cannot be a doctrine more fatal to the li-
" berty and property we are contending for, than
" that which confounds the idea of a *supreme* and
" an *arbitrary* legislature. I need not point out to
" you the fatal purposes, to which it has been, and
" may be applied. If we are sincere in the politi-
" cal creed we profess, there are many things,
" which we ought to affirm, cannot be done by
" King, Lords and Commons. Among these I
" reckon the disfranchising of boroughs with a ge-
" neral view of improvement. I consider it as
" equivalent to robbing the parties concerned of
" their freehold, of their birth-right. I say that,
" although this birth-right may be forfeited, or the
" exercise of it suspended in particular cases, it
" cannot be taken away, by a general law, for any
" real or pretended purpose of improving the con-
" stitution. Supposing the attempt made, I am
" persuaded you cannot mean that either King, or
" Lords, should take an active part in it. A bill,
" which only touches the representation of the
" people, must originate in the House of Commons.
" In the formation and mode of passing it, the ex-
" clusive right of the Commons must be asserted as

" scrupulously, as in the case of a money-bill.
" Now, Sir, I should be glad to know by what kind
" of reasoning it can be proved, that there is a
" power vested in the representative to destroy his
" immediate constituent. From whence could he
" possibly derive it? A courtier, I know, will be
" ready to maintain the affirmative. The doctrine
" suits him exactly, because it gives an unlimited
" operation to the influence of the crown. But
" we, Mr. Wilkes, ought to hold a different lan-
" guage. It is no answer to me to say, that the
" bill, when it passes the House of Commons, is
" the act of the majority, and not the representa-
" tives of the particular boroughs concerned. If
" the majority can disfranchise ten boroughs, why
" not twenty, why not the whole kingdom? Why
" should not they make their own seats in parlia-
" ment for life?....When the septennial act passed,
" the legislature did what, apparently and palpa-
" bly, they had no power to do; but they did more
" than people in general were aware of: they, in
" effect, disfranchised the whole kingdom for four
" years.

" For argument's sake, I will now suppose, that
" the expediency of the measure, and the power
" of parliament are unquestionable. Still you will
" find an insurmountable difficulty in the execu-
" tion. When all your instruments of amputation
" are prepared, when the unhappy patient lies
" bound at your feet, without the possibility of re-

" sistance, by what infallible rule will you direct
" the operation ?....When you propose to cut away
" the *rotten* parts, can you tell us what parts are
" perfectly *sound?*....Are there any certain limits,
" in fact or theory, to inform you at what point you
" must stop, at what point the mortification ends ?
" To a man so capable of observation and reflec-
" tion as you are, it is unnecessary to say all that
" might be said upon the subject. Besides that I
" approve highly of Lord Chatham's idea *of in-*
" *fusing a portion of new health into the constitution*
" *to enable it to bear it's infirmities*, (a brilliant ex-
" pression, and full of intrinsic wisdom) other rea-
" sons concur in persuading me to adopt it. I
" have no objection," &c.

The man, who fairly and completely answers
this argument, shall have my thanks and my applause. My heart is already with him....I am ready
to be converted....I admire his morality, and would
gladly subscribe to the articles of his faith....Grate-
ful, as I am, to the GOOD BEING, whose bounty has
imparted to me this reasoning intellect, whatever it
is, I hold myself proportionably indebted to him,
from whose inlightened understanding another ray
of knowledge communicates to mine. But neither
should I think the most exalted faculties of the human mind, a gift worthy of the divinity; nor any
assistance, in the improvement of them, a subject

of gratitude to my fellow creature ; if I were not satisfied, that really to inform the understanding corrects and enlarges the heart.

JUNIUS.

THE END.

INDEX

TO THE

SECOND VOLUME.

———

INDEX.

INDEX.

PRINTED BY ROBERT CARR,
NO. 10, CHURCH-STREET.

CPSIA information can be obtained at www.ICGtesting.com
Printed in the USA
BVOW08*1135120214

344699BV00005B/245/P